crime & criminology

crime & criminology

FIFTH EDITION

| Rob White
| Fiona Haines
| Nicole Asquith

OXFORD
UNIVERSITY PRESS
AUSTRALIA & NEW ZEALAND

OXFORD
UNIVERSITY PRESS

Oxford University Press is a department of the University of Oxford.

It furthers the University's objective of excellence in research, scholarship, and education by publishing worldwide. Oxford is a registered trademark of Oxford University Press in the UK and in certain other countries.

Published in Australia by
Oxford University Press
253 Normanby Road, South Melbourne, Victoria 3205, Australia
© Rob White, Fiona Haines, Nicole Asquith 2012

National Library of Australia Cataloguing-in-Publication entry

Author: White, R. D. (Robert Douglas), 1956–
Title: Crime and criminology / Rob White, Fiona Haines, Nicole Asquith.
Edition: 5th ed.
ISBN: 9780195518306 (pbk.)
Notes: Includes bibliographical references and index.
Subjects: Crime.
        Criminology.
Other Authors/Contributors: Haines, Fiona.
                Asquith, Nicole.

Dewey Number: 364

Reproduction and communication for educational purposes
The Australian *Copyright Act 1968* (the Act) allows a maximum of one chapter or 10% of the pages of this work, whichever is the greater, to be reproduced and/or communicated by any educational institution for its educational purposes provided that the educational institution (or the body that administers it) has given a remuneration notice to Copyright Agency Limited (CAL) under the Act.

For details of the CAL licence for educational institutions contact:

Copyright Agency Limited
Level 15, 233 Castlereagh Street
Sydney NSW 2000
Telephone: (02) 9394 7600
Facsimile: (02) 9394 7601
Email: info@copyright.com.au

Edited by Valina Rainer
Cover design by Canvas
Typeset by diacriTech, India
Proofread by Joy Window
Indexed by Russell Brooks
Printed by Sheck Wah Tong

Links to third party websites are provided by Oxford in good faith and for information only. Oxford disclaims any responsibility for the materials contained in any third party website referenced in this work.

{contents}

contents
p.vi.

{**preface**}

It is with great pleasure that we present the fifth edition of *Crime and Criminology*. As each year passes, it is clear that change is fundamental to what is happening in contemporary global society and that this needs to be reflected in the new edition of this book. We are aware that developments within and outside of academia will affect the relevance of any particular or perspective. Accordingly, we have tried to make new analytical connections, summarise present trends in criminological theory, and be of general interest to the reader. In this edition, a third author—Nicole Asquith—has joined the writing team. Nicole adds a new dimension to our theoretical analysis, including the development of a new recurring feature entitled, *From Theory to Practice*. This feature offers readers an opportunity to see theory in action, and evaluate the ways in which these theories are employed by criminologists in their analysis of contemporary criminological issues. We believe that we have provided a comprehensive, yet concise, introduction to the major theories and perspectives in criminology. We hope that you find the book of use and interest as you explore the wide variety of explanations for many different types of crime and social harm.

We are grateful to many people for their assistance in the development and further revision of this book. Our special thanks go to Steve James and Santina Perrone, who, as fellow lecturers in the introductory criminology subject at various points in time, helped to mould and shape the ways in which the material was actually developed for teaching purposes. We are also grateful to the many tutors and students over the years who have assisted us in refining and simplifying the core ideas of the field. Thanks also to the academic and general staff in the Department of Criminology at the University of Melbourne for their ongoing encouragement for projects of this nature, and to support staff at the University of Tasmania for their assistance. Finally, we are grateful once again to all the people at Oxford University Press—especially Katie Ridsdale and Michelle Head—for their constant enthusiasm and genuine interest in the book.

the
study of
crime

{introduction}
—

This book is about the causes of crime. More specifically, it describes the diverse and at times competing perspectives within criminology, and their attempts to explain why certain types of people engage in certain types of behaviour that have been identified as being criminal in nature.

The aim of this chapter is to introduce the reader to the study of crime, and in so doing to explore a series of issues relating to the definition and measurement of crime. A major part of the chapter describes the criteria that serve to differentiate the many perspectives on crime. In particular, the chapter explores the different levels of analysis used to explain crime, and the different political perspectives that impinge on a criminological analysis. Overall, this chapter aims to make sense of how we can distinguish between different theoretical perspectives by looking at similarities and differences in broad approach.

—

~~criminology~~ as a field of study

Before we discuss the nature of crime, it is useful first to say a few words about criminology as a field of study. As we shall see, criminology, like crime, is not a monolith; it encompasses varied and competing perspectives. The different levels of analysis apparent in criminology are partly a reflection of the diverse disciplines that have contributed to the study of crime over a number of years. Researchers, scholars and writers in areas such as biological science, psychology, philosophy, law, sociology, forensic medicine, political economy, education, history and cultural studies have all contributed to the multidisciplinary nature of criminology. Each discipline brings to bear its own concepts, debates and methods when examining a criminological issue or problem. This means that within criminology there is a natural diversity of viewpoints, as different writers and researchers 'see' the world through very different analytical spectacles. Such differences are also reflected in the adoption of a wide range of techniques and methodologies in the study of crime. These include historical records, use of surveys, participant observation, interviews, evaluation of official statistics, study of policy documents and discourse analysis. This variety of perspectives should be considered in light of the social context of the production of intellectual knowledge.

For instance, the production of knowledge is itself a social and material process. When any kind of knowledge is produced, we must ask who has control over this process—not only the production of knowledge itself, but also the ownership and use of the results of research and scholarship. In a similar vein, specific types of 'knowledge' or 'truth' are not always recognised or visible in the public domain. This can happen for a variety of reasons—because there is no market for them, because of publishing rivalries, or because the 'knowledge' is not deemed to conform to particular academic standards or mainstream political agendas.

Knowledge has distinctive international dimensions. For example, in the field of criminology each country may have its own unique social concerns, intellectual milieux, political traditions, historical development, and hence its own theoretical emphases and biases. In the UK, for instance, debates over policing and antisocial behaviour have been prominent in recent years, whereas in the USA major concerns have been expressed over ghetto neighbourhoods, unemployment and the social prospects of the huge numbers of offenders re-entering the community after serving time in prison. In Canada debates have centred on changes to drug law enforcement, while media treatment of criminal justice issues in Australia has featured extensive moral panics over so-called ethnic youth gangs and the use of the illicit drug 'ice'.

Cutting across all of these debates in each of the regions, however, have been a series of general issues relating to the nature of crime and the social control of crime. Invariably, analysis of specific issues has employed abstract concepts that are designed to explain why particular phenomena should be dealt with in any particular way. Major themes of this book are: to explore the nature of the more generalised statements regarding crime; to examine the broad social and historical context within which certain theories and concepts have emerged; and to demonstrate the application of these theoretical understandings to selected issues and criminal justice reform.

While 'theory' informs everything that criminologists do, not every criminologist is a theorist. To understand what criminologists actually do, and why theory is relevant to their practice, we need to appreciate the dual nature of much contemporary criminology. On the one hand, many people adopt what could be called an administrative or professional approach to criminology. In this view, the role of criminology is tied to improving the immediate practices of the criminal justice system and to solving crime problems in the community. This approach seeks to study, analyse and research alternative theories in order to institute reform of some kind. Generally, it is directed at making some aspect of the criminal justice system 'better' at some level—a program, an institution or a strategy. Often it is linked to attempts to solve a 'social problem' or an administrative difficulty within the existing system.

On the other hand, there is a strand of criminology in which the emphasis is on a critical or analytical approach. Unlike the previous approach, this tends not to be a nuts-and-bolts view of the criminal justice system, particularly with respect to making minor changes within the existing institutional frameworks of criminal justice. Rather, it is suggested that one must stand back from policy decisions and ask bigger questions, such as 'What if ... ?' This approach delves into the deeper philosophical issues of the day; for example, why do we continue to have and use institutions such as prisons when they demonstrably do not work to prevent offending or reoffending? The approach here is not to suggest improvements to the existing penal system, but to question whether it is valid or viable to begin with. Indeed, an informed opinion might simply advocate the abolition of such institutions in their present shape and form.

It is essential to note, however, that often there are strong links between these two approaches. The variability in criminological perspectives in general is due in part to the nature of the relationship between the practical administrative orientation (with a focus on what can be done here and how to improve the system) and its critical counterpart (with a focus on why things ought to be done in one way or another). In turn, the expected 'audience' of criminological research will also affect the level of theoretical analysis. A commissioned report on crime prevention for a government department will engage with theory in a different way to an independently funded project that seeks to test a theoretical perspective. We must also be aware of the uncertainties of knowledge. For instance, whatever area of criminology one may concentrate on, there are almost always unintended consequences that emerge from the knowledge we acquire and the reforms we put forward. Knowledge is a guide to the future—it does not fix the future on one single pathway.

Generally speaking, criminology focuses on three main areas:

1\ the sociology of law, which examines why and how societies define crime a particular way and the implications this understanding has for the lives of people within those societies
2\ theories of crime causation, sometimes referred to as criminogenesis
3\ the study of social responses to crime, which examines in more depth the formal institutions of criminal justice, such as the police, courts and corrections.

As pointed out earlier, the main theme of this book is the theories that relate to the causes of crime. As will be seen, however, the other domains of criminology often overlap, and are inseparable parts of any review of causal theories.

defining crime

There is no straightforward, universal definition of crime, as there are constantly changing ideas, perceptions and conceptions regarding what constitutes criminal behaviour. To a certain extent, both crime and criminology are uncertain, in the sense that one's definition of crime is dependent upon one's particular interests and particular worldview. This becomes clearer when we discuss the various definitions put forward for crime.

There are competing views of crime, yet crime is always socially defined. This, of course, can lead to debate: for example, should crime always be defined by law? Could or should it instead be based upon moral and social conceptions, such as social harm? To illustrate the difficulties surrounding different definitions of crime, we might consider the film *Schindler's List*. In the movie (and in real life) Schindler broke Nazi law in order to assist Jewish people. But was he then a criminal? Who defines the law? What about cases today where people may actively break the law in the name of social justice? There are unjust systems in the world, and it may well be the case that many legal definitions are built on highly contentious and unjust or unfair propositions.

¬ legal and sociological definitions of crime

There are many diverse conceptions of crime, each of which reflects a different scientific and ideological viewpoint. Hagan (1987), for example, identifies seven different approaches to the definition of crime, ranging from a 'legal-consensus' definition to a 'human rights' definition. For present purposes, we can summarise broad differences in definition in the following way:

- A *formal legal* definition says that a crime is whatever the state identifies as a crime; that is, if something is written into the criminal law, and is subject to state sanction in the form of a specific penalty, then that activity is a crime.

- A *social harm* conception of crime says that crime involves both criminal offences (such as assault) and civil offences (such as negligence), in that each type of action or inaction brings with it some type of harm. Each should therefore attract some sort of penalty.

- A *cross-cultural universal norm* argument states that crime, in essence, does not vary across different cultures. Thus, murder is murder regardless of the society, and we can postulate conduct norms that cut across diverse cultural backgrounds.

- A *labelling* approach to the definition of crime argues that crime only really exists when there has been a social response to a particular activity that labels that activity as criminal. If there is no label, there is in effect no crime.

- A *human rights* approach says that crime occurs whenever a human right has been violated, regardless of the legality or otherwise of the action. Such a conception also expands the definition of crime to include oppressive practices such as racism, sexism and class-based exploitation.

_ A *human diversity* approach defines crime in terms of the manner in which deviance represents a normal response to oppressive or unequal circumstances. A major focus here is on power relations, and the attempts by dominant groups to restrict human diversity of experience, language and culture.

Our intention here is neither to explain fully each type of definition of crime, nor to evaluate the explanatory or practical usefulness of each definition (instead, see Hagan 1987; Nettler 1984; Lacey 2007; Downes & Morgan 2007; Garwood et al. 2000; Laslett 2010). Rather, we wish to alert the reader to the fact that there are important differences in how people conceive of crime.

Further, the variation in definition often has real consequences upon how different types of behaviour are dealt with at a practical level. For example, we might consider the issue of violence (Alder 1991: 61):

> In the home, parents hit children; on the playing field, sportsmen assault each other; at work, industrial 'accidents' occur; in our community, dangerous chemicals are dumped; our governments turn a blind eye to the practices of some police officers; and our governments are responsible for the mass violence of war.

How violence is perceived and responded to by criminal justice institutions depends very much upon a range of political and social factors. Crime is not inherent in an activity: it is defined under particular material circumstances and in relation to specific social processes.

¬ historical constructions of crime

While criminologists may argue about the definition of crime, ultimately it is the legal definition of crime that determines how we as a society formally respond to certain acts deemed wrongful. But, we might ask, who actually makes the laws, and why are they made? Whose interests are reflected in those laws and how are they enforced? In line with the broad theme of the variability of definitions of crime, it is also useful to acknowledge that legal definitions of crime themselves change over time. The law itself is thus socially produced and is not static. As it changes, so too does the definition of crime. In this sense we can say that morality itself is variable, at least insofar as it is reflected in the laws of a country. What is legally defined as crime varies according to social and historical contexts. For example:

- As early as 1530, in England there existed the crime of being a vagabond, which, in effect, meant that a person was unemployed and idle. Any person so identified could be branded a criminal—figuratively and literally (through burning of the gristle of the right ear with a hot iron). Vagabonds over the age of eighteen could be hanged if they did not obtain suitable employment for two years. Revived in 1743, the Vagrancy Acts expanded the types of persons liable for prosecution to include a wide variety of homeless and poor people (see Chambliss 1975a). This crime no longer exists, although one could be tempted to draw similarities with the negative status accorded to the young unemployed or homeless people today, and the imposition of control mechanisms such as the UK's Anti-Social Behaviour Orders.

- In the seventeenth century, witchcraft was a common crime in Europe. Crime here was constructed in terms of religion, and referred to conduct allegedly against (the Christian) God. By and large, such laws pertaining to witchcraft targeted women, as a means of controlling them (see Holmes 1993; Noonan 2002), particularly those displaying eccentric and secretive tendencies. Such laws are not common in the criminal law today. However, in some jurisdictions crimes related to witchcraft are still on the statute books, such as reading of tarot cards. Similarly, some of the public concern about heavy metal or Gothic 'shock rock' music, and supernatural entities (such as vampires) in film/TV appears to have vestiges of the moral and religious panics over witchcraft that swept Europe several hundred years ago.

- Property and theft are historically and culturally specific concepts. In many traditional Australian Aboriginal and other Indigenous communal societies, everything is shared. There is no concept of theft (which is premised on the notion of ownership of personal property), because in these cultures property is communal. Concepts of land ownership likewise differ from mainstream legal conceptions. Some members of Indigenous communities hold the belief that they do not really own the land, so it cannot be taken away from them. To put it differently, land is not a possession; it is something that you have a relationship with. Crime in traditional Indigenous communities is associated with the abuse of sacred knowledge, custom, spirituality, witchcraft and ritual—it is not centred upon property, as is most Western law (see Bottomley et al. 1991).

Crime is thus an offence of the time. For a large part of recorded European history, crime was intimately linked to moral prescriptions as defined by religious bodies. One reason for this was that between the 1400s and 1600s, the Church was the body that had access to the tools of justice administration. This was because literacy tended to be the preserve of the clergy, who therefore were in a position to construct the laws. Later on, it was the preserve of the state to determine laws. Accordingly, crime became defined as a transgression against the state, not against God. Even today, however, there are vestiges of conflict between the secular and non-secular law, as indicated in legal action taken over the ordination of women in some Christian denominations.

¬ popular media images of crime

The media have a significant influence on the general portrayal of crime in society. The images that permeate popular consciousness of crime are mainly generated by, and reflected in, the electronic and print media. In this way the media have a tremendous impact in terms of how crime is generally defined in society (see Sarre 1994; Grabosky & Wilson 1989; Ericson et al. 1991; Mooney & Young 2006; Surette 2010).

According to the media, in both fictional and factual types of programs and reportage, crime tends to be defined primarily as 'street crime'. Such crime is thus associated with personal terror and fear, and violence is seen as central. Crime is sensationalised, with important implications for the fear of crime among certain sections of the population. This fear is heightened by the way in which crime is seen to be random in nature, with anyone and everyone a possible target for victimisation.

As well, there is often the idea that crime is related to morality, and specifically to the decline of that morality. What is 'wrong' is plain for all to see. Furthermore, the 'criminal' is distinctive, and identifiably different from everyone else in society. Overall, the idea is that there is a continuing 'law-and-order' problem in society (Hall 1980b; Downes & Morgan 2007; Mooney & Young 2006), and that things are constantly getting worse. Against this tide of disorder and lawlessness, the police and other crime fighters are generally portrayed as 'superheroes', who are infallible and who use violence legitimately in order to counter the violence of the streets.

The media are important not only in shaping our definitions of crime and crime control, but also in producing legal changes and reinforcing particular types of policing strategies. For example, the 'moral panics' (see Cohen 1972; Poynting & Morgan 2007) generated by the media on problems such as 'youth gangs' may lead to changes in the law (for example, the introduction of youth curfews) and the adoption of certain police methods (for example, increasing the use of 'name checks'—or stop and searches—in particular locales). It has been demonstrated that the interests of the police and the media are entwined; they have a symbiotic relationship, in that the media rely upon the police for much of their information, and the police use the media to portray certain images relating to their work (Dowler 2003; Perlmutter 2000).

The media thus convey a sensationalised image of crime, and a protective view of police and policing practices—and they make unusual events usual events in our lives. As Grabosky and Wilson (1989: 11) comment: 'The most common types of crime according to official statistics, crimes against property, receive relatively little media attention. By contrast, crimes of violence, which are very uncommon in actuarial terms, are accorded much greater coverage.'

Similarly, there is a skewed focus on 'street crime' and bizarre events. Meanwhile, the destruction of the environment, domestic violence, white-collar crimes and occupational health and safety crimes tend not to receive the same kind of coverage or treatment by the mainstream media outlets.

With regard to crime control, the usual implication is that, once a crime has been brought to the attention of the authorities, investigation will generally lead to detection and capture of the offender. This is a far cry from the reality of much police work, and in specific cases of serious street crime a significant proportion of cases do not get to the prosecution stage. In fictional accounts of crime fighting, the police are usually endowed with special qualities (such as big guns and martial arts abilities), and violence is central and always justified because of the nature of the 'criminals' at hand. The nature of actual policing is once again misconstrued, and the mundane aspects—interviewing, looking over file material, research, traffic regulation and so on—are generally absent. Another facet of fictional accounts is that the police are not accountable to anyone; they can even step outside the bounds of the law, because we all know they are on 'our' side. Thus, the police are always honest and incorruptible, even though evidence in real life shows that corruption of the police is a constant challenge. Notable Australian examples include the Fitzgerald inquiry into police in Queensland (Fitzgerald 1989), and the Wood (1997) inquiry in New South Wales, which revealed widespread and systematic corruption.

It is important, therefore, to separate the images and realities of crime in society. The media shape our perceptions of crime, and in the process they define crime in particular ways. One aspect of this process is that the media often portray crime in terms of distinct crime waves. This refers to the way in which increased reporting of particular types of crime (usually street crimes, such as assault, rape, drug offences or homicide) increases the public awareness of this crime. Significantly, there need not have been an actual increase in the crime for a crime wave to occur. The increase exists only in public perception.

Nevertheless, 'crime waves' can and do have real consequences regardless of factual basis. For example, extensive media coverage of child abuse may lead to changes in the law, such as the introduction of mandatory reporting of suspected incidents. Or the fear generated by press coverage of assaults on elderly people may lead to calls for more police, tougher sentences and greater police power. Given the close relationship between the police and the media, major questions can be asked as to who benefits from the selective reporting of specific crimes, especially around government budget time.

measuring crime

Given the limitations and problems of relying upon media definitions and treatments of crime, it is reasonable to accept that any statement made about crime should be tested by referring to the 'facts' about crime. This usually means that we need to confirm particular crime trends and consider official data on criminal activity. However, even here there are difficulties with how crime is defined. For what we 'measure' depends upon how we define crime and how we see the criminalisation process.

In fact, criminologists are not united in their approach to crime and crime statistics (see Nettler 1984; Jupp 1989; Maguire 2007; von Hofer 2000). For present purposes, we can identify three broad strands within criminology that deal with measurement issues:

1\ The *realist approach* adopts the view that crime exists 'out there' in society and that the '*dark figure*' of crime needs to be uncovered and recorded. There are limitations to the gathering of official statistics (such as reliance solely on police records of reported offences), and the role of criminology is to supplement official statistics (those generated by the police, courts and prison authorities) through a range of informal or alternative measures. The emphasis is on the problem of omission—to uncover the true or real extent of crime by methods such as victim and victimisation surveys, self-report surveys, test situations and hidden cameras.

2\ The *institutionalist approach* adopts the view that crime is a 'social process', and it rejects the notion that we can unproblematically gain a sense of the real extent of crime by improving our measuring devices and techniques. Instead, this approach concentrates on the manner in which official criminal justice institutions actually process suspects, and thus define certain individuals and certain types of behaviour as being 'criminal'. Criminologists adopting this approach also argue that statistics tell us more about the agencies that collect the figures than they do about the crime itself. The emphasis is on the problem of bias—to show how some people and events are designated by the criminal justice system as being criminal, while others are not.

3\ The *critical realist* approach argues that crime measurement can be characterised as having elements of both 'social process' and a grounded 'reality'. The task of measurement from this perspective is to uncover the processes whereby the crimes against the most vulnerable and least powerful sections of the population have been ignored or underrepresented. The emphasis is on the problem of victimisation—to demonstrate empirically how certain groups are especially vulnerable to crime and to the fear of crime, and conceptually to criticise the agencies of crime control for their lack of action in protecting these groups.

Thus, there are debates within criminology over how and what to measure, and these ultimately reflect basic divisions within the field regarding the very definition of crime itself. As the preceding discussions make clear, the study of crime is fraught with a wide range of competing viewpoints and perspectives. It is useful, then, to develop an analytical framework that can make sense of these differences and the basis for different points of view on crime and crime control.

criminological perspectives

The style of questions you ask about crime necessarily determines the answers you receive. As we have indicated, there are competing definitions of crime: these produce competing answers or explanations of the causes of crime, and these in turn produce different kinds of responses to crime. Criminologists vary in how they approach the study of crime.

Criminological theory can be presented in abstract fashion as being made up of a series of separate perspectives or approaches. Each approach or paradigm attempts to understand a particular phenomenon by asking certain types of questions, using certain concepts and constructing a particular framework of analysis and explanation. In practice, it is rare to find government departments or academic criminologists who rely solely or exclusively on any one particular criminological framework or approach. Often a wide range of ideas and concepts are combined in different ways in the course of developing policy or in the study of a specific empirical problem.

For the sake of presentation, it is nevertheless useful to present *ideal types* (Weber 1949) of the various theoretical strands within criminology. The use of ideal types provides us with a means by which we can clarify main ideas and identify important differences between the broad approaches adopted in the field. An ideal type does not exist in the real world. Rather, the intention behind the use of an ideal type is to construct abstract concepts from concrete situations, which provide the key elements or components of a particular theory or social institution. In exaggerating these elements, theorists are able to highlight the general tendency or themes of the particular perspective (see Freund 1969). An ideal type is an analytical tool, not a moral statement of what ought to be. It refers to a process of identifying different aspects of social phenomena and combining them into a 'typical' model or example. For instance, an ideal type of bureaucracy would include such things as impartial and impersonal merit and promotion structures, prescribed rules and regulations, and a hierarchical chain of command. We know, however, that people who work in bureaucracies are not always promoted on the basis of their qualifications, nor is decision-making always rational. However, by constructing an exaggerated 'typical' model of a bureaucracy we are able to compare the actual structure of different organisations and how they work in the real world.

If we are to construct ideal types in relation to criminological theory, then it is useful first to identify the central focus of theory, and in particular the level of analysis and explanation at which the theory is pitched. There are three broad levels of criminological explanation: the individual, the situational and the social structural. Different theories within criminology tend to locate their main explanation for criminal behaviour or criminality at one of these levels. Occasionally, a theory may attempt to combine all three levels in order to provide a more sophisticated and comprehensive picture of crime and criminality.

¬ levels of analysis

- *Individual*—The main focus is on the personal or individual characteristics of the offender or victim. A study adopting this level of analysis may consider, for example, the influence of appearance, dress and public image on the nature of crime causation or victimisation (such as tattoos or earrings as indicators of a 'criminal' attitude in men). Importantly, this level of analysis tends to look to psychological or biological factors that are said to have an important role in determining why certain individuals engage in criminal activity. The key concern is to explain crime or deviant behaviour in terms of the choices or characteristics of the individual person.

- *Situational*—The main site of analysis is the immediate circumstances, or situation, within which criminal activity or deviant behaviour occurs. Attention is directed to the specific factors that may contribute to an event occurring, such as how the participants define the situation, how different people are labelled by others in the criminal justice system, the opportunities available for the commission of certain types of offences, and so on. Key concerns are the nature of the interaction between different players within the system, the effect of local environmental factors on the nature of this interaction and the influence of group behaviour and influences on social activity.

- *Social structural*—This approach tends to look at crime in terms of the broad social relationships and the major social institutions of the society as a whole. The analysis makes reference to the relationship between classes, sexes, different ethnic and 'racial' groups, the employed and unemployed, and various other social divisions in society. It also can involve investigation of the operation of specific institutions—such as education, the family, work and the legal system—in the construction of and social responses to crime and deviant behaviour.

The level of analysis one chooses has major consequences for how crime is viewed, the nature of the offender, and how the criminal justice system should be organised. For example, a biological positivist approach looks at characteristics of the individual offender (such as genetic make-up), and sees crime as revolving around, and stemming from, the specific personal attributes of the individual. A situational perspective might consider the interaction between police and young people on the street, and argue that 'crime' is defined in the process of specific types of interactions, behaviours and attitudes. From a structural perspective, the issue might be seen in terms of the relationship between poverty and crime; that is, the elements of social life that underpin particular courses of action. The individualist, the situational and the structural approaches would all advocate quite different policies because of their particular perspective. The vantage point from which one examines crime—a focus on personal characteristics through to societal institutions—thus shapes the ways in which one thinks about and acts upon criminal justice matters.

Most theories of crime tend to congeal into one of these levels of analysis; that is, most rely upon one of these particular areas, advancing different theories relating to the causes of crime. For example, the classical theory focuses on choice—the offender chooses to offend or not offend; the response is punishment. This approach focuses on the criminal act. The biological positivist looks at the offender's personal characteristics, and focuses on treatment. Some researchers—for example, strain and subcultural theorists—attempt to integrate more than one level of analysis into their approach, and focus both on how the social structure shapes the opportunities that individuals have in their lives, and separately consider how those individuals choose to respond to the constraints and opportunities they face. The questions one asks will obviously vary according to the approach or combination of approaches one adopts, as will the consequences.

¬ political orientations

Crime and crime control are inextricably linked with the operation of the state. It is, therefore, important to understand—in addition to the sociological and criminological frameworks—the major political theories and approaches employed to understand the causation, experience, and prevention of crime (Coleman et al. 2009). The political orientation of a writer can be partially ascertained by understanding their overall conception of the 'good' society. For example, consider Brown's (1979) symbolic representations of particular political arrangements:

> ○ *The geometric circle*—This implies society is harmonious, and people share the same values of community and equality. The concept of crime is that perpetrators are deviant, or outside the circle, and thus

they need to be either pulled back into the circle or kept outside the circle's confines.

△ *The triangle*—Society is viewed as a hierarchy, since some people are situated at the top, possessing the wealth and power, and the majority are situated at the bottom. This vision of society implies conflict and inequality. The concept of crime is that it occurs in the context of struggles and hierarchies of control and power. Situated within this perspective are both meritocratic and critical views. A *meritocratic* view of the triangle argues that within the existing structure anyone who plays by the rules of the game is capable of rising to the top of the hierarchy, and that success is a question of ability and hard work. The laws are seen to exist as a means of sustaining the rules of the triangle. A *critical* view of the triangle translates inequality into injustice. The laws are seen to be unequally applied; it is argued that people on the bottom of the triangle are overrepresented in the criminal justice system, and this representation is questioned.

⬜⬜ The *rectangle* or *square*—Society consists of a variety of interrelated rectangles representing different interconnecting institutions, such as the family, work and school. Crime is studied in relation to how these institutions have an impact upon, and reflect upon, crime. The concern here is not with values, as in the circle, but with the smooth running of the interconnected institutions. The issue is one of administrative efficiency and application of the right kinds of techniques to fix the particular social problem.

⚲ *Non-geometric forms such as stick figures*—Here the focus is on individuals, as opposed to society as a whole, and the emphasis is on examining individual creativity and the way individuals construct their realities. The idea is that reality is socially constructed, and that how people act and react in relation to each other has a major impact in terms of defining behaviour and individuals as being deviant. How people think about themselves and each other is a significant factor in how they subsequently behave in their interactions with others.

The manner in which we view society influences the way in which we view crime. The various competing perspectives within criminology reflect different points of view regarding the nature of society. We can identify three major *paradigms* (conceptual frameworks for understanding social phenomena) in criminology. These paradigms inevitably incorporate specific kinds of value judgment. The motivation, conceptual development, methodological tools and social values associated with a specific approach are usually intertwined with one of three broad political perspectives: conservative, liberal or radical.

1\ *Conservative*—A conservative perspective on society tends to be supportive of the legitimacy of the status quo; that is, it generally accepts the way things are, the traditional ways of doing things, and traditional social relationships. Conservatives believe dissenters should be made to conform to the status quo. They believe that there is a 'core value system' to which everyone in society should conform. The function of the main institutions is to preserve the dominant system of order for the good of society generally. The values and institutions of society should apply equally to all people regardless of social background or historical developments.

2\ *Liberal*—A liberal perspective on society accepts the limits of the status quo, but encourages limited changes in societal institutions. This approach tends to avoid questions relating to the whole structure of society. Instead it emphasises the need for action on particular limited 'social problems'. Specific problems such as sexism, racism and poverty can be resolved without fundamental changes to the economic or social structure. Rather, policies and programs that will serve to reform existing institutions and day-to-day interactions can be developed. Problems tend to be studied in terms of their impact on specific individuals (for example, 'the poor' as the focus of research) and the disadvantage suffered by these individuals or groups.

3\ *Radical*—The radical perspective on society wishes to undermine the legitimacy of the status quo. Like the conservative perspective, it looks at society as a whole, but it sees 'social conflict' as the central concern. Society is seen to be divided on the basis of such elements as class, gender, ethnicity and 'race'/ethnicity. The key issue when adopting this perspective is the matter of who holds the power and resources in any particular community. The objective of radical perspectives is to change fundamentally the existing social order. Specific issues, such as poverty, are explained in relational terms (such as the relationship between the rich and poor), and the solution is seen to involve dealing with the structural imbalances and inequalities that lead to the problem (of poverty) in the first place.

If we acknowledge the centrality of politics in criminological analysis, then we must accept that there is no such thing as value-free criminology.

Values of the right (conservative), left (radical), and centre (liberal) are embedded in the criminological enterprise. The political orientation of the particular approach has major implications for how crime is defined. For example, chart 1.1 presents a radical view of how crime can be defined. As opposed to more conservative perspectives, this approach emphasises both the crimes of the powerful and the crimes of the less powerful. Each particular theory of the causes of crime is generally linked in some way to these broad political perspectives, and thus each sees crime as informed by certain values and philosophical principles.

chart 1.1 | a radical definition of crime

crimes of the powerful

typical crimes	examples
economic	breaches of corporate law, environmental degradation, inadequate industrial health and safety provisions, pollution, violation of labour laws, fraud
state	police brutality, government corruption, bribery, violation of civil rights, misuse of public funds

crimes of the less powerful

typical crimes	examples
economic	street crime, workplace theft, low-level fraud, breach of welfare regulations, prostitution
sociocultural	vandalism, assault, rape, murder, resistance via strikes and demonstrations, public order offences, workplace sabotage

Source: adapted from Cunneen & White (1995)

A further aspect relating to the politics of criminological theory is that the dominant paradigm or approach that is adopted by governments and represented in criminological circles (professional journals, conferences) varies over time. That is, there are competing general perspectives within criminology, but in different periods particular perspectives will be ascendant over others. For example, within Australia and the UK the conservative perspectives (within which lie a number of related theories, usually associated with classical and positivist views, and which centre on punishment and control strategies) held considerable sway at the level of policy formulation and action in the 1950s. By the late 1960s, the liberal perspective (centring on labelling and efforts at rehabilitation) informed much of the reform activity related to the criminal justice system. By the mid-1980s there had been a swing back to the right, which persisted into the 1990s, with greater political attentiveness to strident calls for the adoption of tougher measures to deal with issues of 'law and order'. Simultaneous with the conservative push at the level of policy were both liberal and radical critiques of the effectiveness and fairness of such measures. By the late 1990s and early 2000s, the crime debate incorporated conservative elements stressing offender responsibility and strong state action against antisocial and illegal behaviour, and, as well, liberal perspectives that spoke of the need for restorative justice as a key philosophical principle in responding to crime and criminality. Criminological theory is thus always related in some way to specific historical and geographical contexts, specific material conditions and specific political struggles.

The objectives and methods of analysis used in criminology reflect certain underlying ideas and concerns of the writer. In reading criminological material, then, it is important to adopt a 'criminological imagination' (Young 2011). For us, this means doing the following:

1\ Examine the assumptions of the writers—the key concepts they use, and the methods or arguments used to support their theory—to identify their conceptions of society and of human nature, and the kinds of reforms or institutions that they ultimately support.

2\ Identify the silences in a particular theory or tradition; that is, what questions are not being asked, and why not? Importantly, though, you must be aware of how the 'silences' you identify may be the result of your social and historical context—including the questions you want answered.

3\ Consider the social relevance of the theory or perspective. What does it tell us about our society, and the direction that our society is or ought to be heading?

Fundamentally, the study of crime involves the values and opinions of the criminologist, and students of crime must be aware of this if they are to develop an informed view of the issues. Accordingly, each chapter of this book has within it a box entitled 'Then and now' that highlights the theoretical roots of each paradigm, and how each is related to other theoretical perspectives in this book.

what to 'do' with theory and how to 'do' it

Theory and theoretical analysis are not unique to academics or researchers; we all do them as part of our everyday lives. However, unlike the theories influencing everyday life, criminologists consciously frame or bracket a set of concepts in a systemic—ideally, coherent—manner, in order to make general claims about the causes of crime. Until or unless these theories are tested, they remain just theories.

At the same time, however, unlike the disorganised and often contradictory theories that guide us in our micro-decision-making (such as what coffee to buy, what newspaper to read), the theoretical analyses in this book seek to explicitly document the concepts and practices often taken for granted in everyday life and place these within an historical and social context. In this sense, they are more than just theories; they are centuries of argument and debate (and of testing, refuting, and finding contradictions) all congealed into contemporary criminological theory.

The causes of crime and criminality are highly emotional and value-laden topics. If we make claims about these topics based on our unconscious reactions, we will be faced with not only contradictions but also 'exceptions to the rule' that will leave our claims open to criticism. In distancing—though not ignoring—our emotional responses to crime, we are better able to understand what we think, and, importantly, why we think in a particular way. This also assists us in applying and critiquing other's theories and in identifying our own theoretical 'voice'.

Making the transition from just describing a theoretical approach to applying a specific theory to a practical problem is not easy. It is much easier when you are clear about the core values and assumptions that inform your own opinions. In this sense, reflexivity is essential to be able to identify the flaws in our own and others' thinking and theorising. Integrating theoretical analysis in your studies of crime and criminality requires careful application of the 'right' theory with the 'right' crime (or the 'right' causes of crime or practices of crime). To assist you in acquiring these skills, each chapter has a box entitled *From Theory to Practice*, which provides an applied example (or empirical testing) of each theoretical approach.

{conclusion}

The objectives and methods of criminology reflect and are affected by a wide range of ideas and concerns. This chapter has provided an overview of how the study of crime is built upon a variety of different definitions, how it involves recognition of historical and cross-cultural processes, and that it must acknowledge the impact of popular media images on perceptions of crime. The chapter has also indicated the approaches within criminology to measure crime, and the analytically and politically diverse nature of the criminological enterprise.

The main purpose of this book as a whole is to explore how criminology explains the 'causes' of crime. Our concern is not to discuss general social theory as such, although the influence of specific social theorists, implicitly if not explicitly, permeates many of the discussions. For example, the ideas of Foucault (1980) are particularly evident in certain strands of feminist criminology and critical criminology. In a similar vein, we do not deal with the application of general social theory to specific institutional processes, as in the case of Foucault (1977) on prisons, or Cohen (1985) on community corrections. Indeed, the book is not designed to explain issues relating to the 'responses' of society to criminal behaviour and activity, except in a very general sense, and only when directly related to the theories that are discussed. Such questions are considered in greater detail elsewhere, as in the case of Garland (1990) on punishment, Howe (1994) on penality, and White and Perrone (2010) on criminal justice institutions generally.

In providing a broad overview of the major frameworks of analysis within criminology we have structured each chapter in the following way: Introduction; Social context; Basic concepts; Historical development; Contemporary examples; Critique; Conclusion. By organising the material in such a fashion, we hope to offer the reader a useful guide to the background, development and core ideas of each theoretical strand in a way that also makes comparison between the diverse theories relatively easy.

It is our belief that good criminology is that which is self-consciously reflective of the theoretical and political basis of its understandings and analysis. How we view crime, how we define what is harmful or serious, and how we study criminal activity — all have major ramifications for how we propose to deal with crime at the level of policy, institution and strategy. It is our hope that this book will assist the reader in situating the social, theoretical and practical implications of whatever perspective they may draw upon in trying to come to grips with crime and criminology today.

{**further reading**}

Einstadter, W. & Henry, S.
(1995). *Criminological Theory:
An Analysis of Its Underlying
Assumptions*, Harcourt Brace,
New York.

Gadd, D., Karstedt, S. & Messner,
S.F. (eds) (2011). *The SAGE
Handbook of Criminological
Research Methods*, SAGE, London.

Garland, D. (2001). *The Culture
of Control: Crime and Social
Order in Contemporary Society*,
University of Chicago Press,
Chicago.

Jupp, V. (1989). *Methods of
Criminological Research*,
Routledge, London.

McLaughlin, E. & Muncie, J. (eds)
(2005). *The SAGE Dictionary of
Criminology* (2nd edition), *SAGE*,
London.

McLaughlin, E. & Newburn, T.
(eds) (2010). *The SAGE Handbook
of Criminological Theory,* SAGE,
London.

Maguire, M., Morgan, R. & Reiner,
R. (eds) (2007). *The Oxford
Handbook of Criminology* (4th
edition), Oxford University
Press, London.

Muncie, J. & Hughes, G. (eds)
(2003). *Criminological
Perspectives: A Reader* (2nd
edition), SAGE, London.

Nettler, G. (1984). *Explaining
Crime*, McGraw-Hill, New York.

Taylor, I., Walton, P. & Young,
J. (1973). *The New Criminology*,
Routledge & Kegan Paul, London.

Tibbetts, S.G. & Hemmens, C.
(2010). *Criminological Theory:
A Text/Reader*, SAGE, Thousand
Oaks, CA.

Young, J. (2011). *The
Criminological Imagination*,
Polity Press, Cambridge, UK.

classical
theory

{introduction}

—

This chapter provides an outline and review of the classical theory in criminology. It describes the historical context within which classicism emerged, and the basic principles and concepts of the classical model. The contribution of this model to present criminal justice issues and institutions is discussed, along with the strengths and limitations of the perspective.

The foundations of the contemporary criminal justice and legal systems were laid down in the eighteenth century. This was the period when the basic principles and practices of classical theory were developed and institutionalised for the first time in Europe. The emergence of classical thought constituted a radical challenge to the institutional and class relations underpinning the system of justice at that time, and resulted in a departure from previous methods of criminal justice adjudication.

—

social context

The specific contours of legal change associated with the classical perspective in criminology varied greatly, depending upon the national context. For example, in England, the seventeenth century was the epoch of greatest importance in the history of political and legal theory. It was a time when the power of the monarch was directly challenged in a number of ways. One outcome of the conflicts over power, authority and the role of law embodied in this struggle was the development of a body of principles about the supremacy of law, the fundamental rights of human beings, equality before the law and the democratic basis of political authority (Kelly 1992). Major political and legal changes were to occur at different times and in different ways in the other European centres, such as France, Germany, Spain and Italy. These changes were heavily influenced by the Enlightenment, which looked to rebuild social structures on the basis of purely rational principles. Assertion of the rule of law, and of the importance of thinking about society and the state in terms of a social contract, were eventually to prevail. As part of the reform processes taking place across Europe, the basis of criminal law and the nature of punishment were called into question.

The development of classical conceptions of law and the criminal justice system was grounded in the transition from feudalism to capitalism. Major social, economic and political changes occurring throughout Europe were revolutionising the institutions of power and social relationships generally. The 'revolutions' were at two levels: economic and political. In production, economies based primarily on agriculture moved to become commercial market economies and then industrial economies; and in the political sphere, the rule of the landed aristocracy was challenged by the emerging bourgeoisie or capitalist class. Thus, over a period of several centuries to the eighteenth century, there occurred a transition from one mode of production, feudalism, to another dominant mode of production, capitalism.

Under feudalism, land, wealth and power were concentrated in the hands of a small group of people—the landed aristocracy—who maintained their rule through a combination of repression (such as putting down peasant rebellions) and appeal to tradition and custom (such as the idea of a preordained social order with kings and queens at the top). Ideologically, law was maintained by appeal to such notions as the 'divine right of monarchs', which said that monarchs ruled by God-given right.

Since lawmaking was a matter of birthright and religious conviction, the aristocracy was for a time able to rule with absolute power. Disobedience or challenge to that order was repressed. Basic social patterns, in particular the relationship between serf and lord, were cast as 'natural' and permanent social arrangements.

In the feudal era, there was an absence of formal legal status as such. Rights were not acknowledged as being common to all. Rather, any rights that did exist were linked to individual station and class. For example, peasants and (most) women were accorded few formal rights, while members of the aristocracy and the upper levels of the Christian church had special rights associated with their position in society. One's social rank thus determined the nature and extent of the rights one was able to claim or exercise.

The administration of justice tended to be haphazard, localised, irregular and unsystematic (see Hall & McLennan 1986; Walklate 2007). Just as rights and laws were moulded around the specific interests of powerful individuals, so, too, the 'justice' system reflected the personal ties or connections of the powerful (for example, derived from patronage, familiarity or business associations) and the personal whim of the local ruling class. Men (as women were generally not decision-makers, unless part of royalty) held judicial office as an extension of their wealth and rank in society. Furthermore, there was a proliferation of different types of courts, including local manorial courts, ecclesiastical (religious) courts, and the King's or Queen's courts.

Justice was personalised; that is, decisions regarding whether particular acts were deemed to be criminal or not, and the responses to criminal acts, were essentially a matter of the personal opinion or whim of the presiding judge. Decisions were unpredictable. Persons holding legal office could display mercy if they so desired, but this in itself reflected the absolute power they held in their hands to make decisions. There were few institutional checks or balances on this power. The legal system was highly localised, and revolved around the existing power relationships of the landed gentry and church officials.

The penalties for crime were also highly individualised and varied greatly. Torture and death were not uncommon penalties for even minor offences. The brutal nature of the punishment also reflected the fact that the long-term holding of prisoners in particular sites (such as prisons) was not used as a general form of sanction. It also reflected the arbitrary use of draconian or extreme measures when the first priority of the day was maintenance of order and orthodoxy, rather than justice and reform.

The exercise of power was, however, circumscribed by certain customs and traditions that, ultimately, served to legitimise the existing social structure (see Fine 1984). For instance, while the serf or peasant was bound to do extra work or provide an amount of produce for the lord, the lord was in turn obligated to protect his vassals from outside threat or harm, and to ensure that certain social responsibilities were maintained (as in time of famine to provide a share of social goods to the poor).

The rise of the state, initially linked to the extension of monarchical power, saw the legal and criminal justice systems start to change. Over time, if we take the English case, the monarchs were able to fuse local traditions and customs into a general form of law administration—and hence the development of a 'common law' system of justice. In other European centres, such as France, extensive centralised laws (for example, the Code Napoléon) that were to provide a national structure for the legal system were established. Each system of law served to entrench and consolidate the power of the monarch over that of local landowners (especially the barons), so that the monarch was then able to rule much more absolutely than had previously been the case.

The next stage of legal development was linked to the formation of the capitalist class, beginning with the age of mercantile capitalism (merchant trading in the context of nation-states). The absolute power of the monarch constituted a fetter on the activities and aspirations of this new class. For example, the ability of monarchs to grant monopoly trading rights to selected companies (such as the Hudson's Bay Company in North America) was seen to be unfair, restricting the trading activities of the mercantile capitalists. Furthermore, given that the law was still essentially reflective of personal whim and establishment prerogatives (since decision-making at both national and local levels resided in the hands of the landed aristocracy), a political revolution was necessary to change basic relations of power.

This manifested itself in the form of a series of armed struggles and revolutions, including the English Civil Wars, the French Revolution and the American Revolution. The power of the monarchy was circumscribed or replaced by new institutions (especially parliaments), and the aristocracy was pushed to the side as the only or major ruling force in society. For economic reasons (such as long-term planning purposes) as well as political reasons (such as the holding of decision-making power), a new form of law and criminal justice system evolved. A central feature of this system was that it was bureaucratic in nature (rather than personalised), and it provided a more systematic and impersonal method of judicial administration (Walklate 2007).

The concept of individual rights, as opposed to customary and traditional bonds, was central to the political, economic and social project of the new class of capitalists (the bourgeoisie). This new class called for the universalisation of rights (at least to those who had wealth and property) against a regime based solely upon hereditary privilege. Accompanying the demand for recognition of the 'rights of man' was an insistence that the state no longer simply rule on behalf of a monarch, or the aristocracy. Rather, the role of the state was now to preserve the rule of law. In this system the state apparatus acts as a distinct public authority to guarantee 'equality under the law' in relation to freedom, rights and obligations (Walklate 2007). In this conception of law, not only were all equal in the eyes of the law, but the lawmakers themselves were likewise bound by the laws they devised.

The claim for universal and equal rights was relevant to the political domain and, as well, to the law and courts. The idea was that all social attributes, such as class, rank and social background, should be ignored once a person entered the court. People should not be subject to arbitrary judgment and a justice system based upon different rights for different classes of people. Once in court, participants are transformed into 'abstract legal subjects' who, regardless of background, should be treated equally (O'Malley 1983; Massoglia & Macmillan 2002).

Economically, the demand for individual rights was important in a number of ways. According to Fine (1984), it first helped to bolster the idea that 'private property' was a right that did not have to be seen in relation to customary or traditional obligations. For example, ownership of land had been linked to certain social obligations for those living on the land; it was now asserted that the use of property was something that was absolutely and exclusively a matter for the owner to decide. An owner could decide to plant cash crops for the market, rather than subsistence crops for the peasant residents. Any obligations to help the poor, or find work for the peasant who had been dispossessed of land, were effectively transferred from private hands to the state.

Second, the notion of rights was used to justify a breaking of bonds between peasants and the landed aristocracy (Fine 1984). No longer tied by tradition or custom to the land, peasants were allowed the legal right to freely sell their labour. Coupled with the new legal basis of private property, which soon led to the closing of land to the peasant class, the position of individuals as 'free labourers' served to swell the cities as urbanisation gathered pace. This provided the capitalist class with a huge reservoir of labour from which to choose, and with which production could be magnified in ways hitherto not seen in the history of humankind. The 'freeing' of people from the land was, in fact, crucial to the later development of full-scale industrialisation.

The classical approach in law and criminology was thus born of momentous changes occurring across the political, legal, social and economic domains. At the core of these changes was the relationship between individual rights, the state and equality. The rights of human beings, it was felt, should be protected against arbitrary uses of power. Likewise, a rational system of production and exchange (that is, the capitalist market) demanded a legal system that was predictable, systematic and regular (Walklate 2007). Such a system, involving competition between producers, should also ensure that the power of the state be limited, particularly in regard to issues surrounding private property and personal accumulation of wealth. While grounded in the social and political upheavals of the modern era, these approaches to crime and criminality continue to have a commonsense resonance with contemporary political parties and policy makers.

basic concepts

Classical theory is premised upon the notion of individual rights, the human capacity to reason and the rule of law (see chart 2.1). The theory assumes a particular view of human nature, and of the relationship between individuals and the state.

In the classical view, human beings are seen as being essentially self-seeking and self-interested individuals. What we do with our personal talents, skills and energy is a matter of individual initiative and choice; that is, the classical theory has a *voluntaristic* view of human nature that emphasises free will and individual choice. We are thereby seen as ultimately responsible for choosing what to do with our time and energy, and for the consequences that may arise from our actions.

chart 2.1 | **classical theory**

definition of crime	legal
	_ violation of law
	_ rights and social contract
focus of analysis	the criminal act
	_ specific offence
	_ the criminal law
cause of crime	rationality
	_ individual choice
	_ irrational decisions
nature of offender	voluntaristic
	_ free will, self-interest, and equal capacity to reason
response to crime	punishment
	_ proportionate to the crime
	_ fixed or determinate
crime prevention	deterrence
	_ pleasure–pain principle
	_ reform of the legal system to make it more accessible
operation of criminal justice system	legal–philosophical approach
	_ basic principles

Rather than analysing the customary or other links between people, the theory emphasises the status of human beings as *rights-holders*. Individuals are deemed to have an equal capacity to reason and to act in accordance with what is rational from the point of view of their own self-interests. Institutionally, each individual is to be granted equal rights under the law. The fundamental objective of the law is to protect individual rights, and to allow the free exercise of choice among individuals as far as this is possible without leading to social harm.

In order to guarantee both individual rights and some semblance of order, classical theory considers the role of the state to be central. Specifically, the theory rests upon the notion of a *social contract* between individual rights-holders and the state. In this model, there is an implied consensus or agreement: individuals in society give up certain rights to the state in return for the protection of their rights and the security of their person and property from other individuals, and from the state itself. If human beings are seen as essentially self-interested and self-seeking, then there needs to be some kind of mechanism that will, in effect, protect us from the self-interested behaviour and actions of others. Hence, the role of the state is to regulate human interaction, and to be a site where rights in general can be protected by not allowing their infringement in specific instances.

The legal manifestation of the social contract is expressed in the phrase 'the rule of law'. The rule of law means that everyone is to be treated equally, without fear or favour, in the eyes of the law. Further, even the lawmakers are bound by the law set down for the general populace. Thus, the first principle of the justice system is equal protection of rights. A crucial assumption here is that the social contract will protect each individual against the excesses and corruption of institutions and other individuals by treating all people the same way. For this to occur in practice, it is necessary to have a criminal justice and judicial system that is systematic, predictable and regular.

The law is seen to be intrinsically good, and to reflect the reasoned beliefs and values of the lawmakers. The theory assumes a consensus in society regarding what is considered 'good' and what is 'bad', and this is reflected in the specific criminal laws. Crime is defined in the first instance as simply a *violation of the law*. Adherence to the law in general, and to specific laws in particular, is seen to be an essential component of the social contract that protects individual rights generally.

In this framework, criminality is seen as primarily a matter of making the wrong choice, by violating the law. Put simply, individuals are to be *held responsible* for their actions. Since each person is seen to have equal capacity to reason, and given that every effort is made to make citizens familiar with the law, and with its punishments, crime is in essence a matter of free choice. The source of criminality thus lies within the rational, reasoning individual. Crime is the result of individuals either making a calculated decision to do wrong (by weighing up the potential rewards and negative consequences) or engaging in what might be seen as irrational behaviour (by not using their reason adequately or properly).

The social contract is maintained in practice through the use of *punishment* (Carlsmith & Darley 2002). The purpose of punishment is to deter individuals from violating laws, which in effect means an interference with the person or property rights of another. Deterrence should be directed both at the individual (specific deterrence) and at members of society at large (general deterrence) through the use of a wide range of sanctions or penalties appropriate to the offences committed (just deserts). Punishment is based on the pleasure–pain principle, in which the pain of the sentence would outweigh any pleasure to be gained from committing the crime.

The response of the criminal justice system is focused primarily on the *criminal act*. The rule of law demands that each violation of the law be treated in the same way; that is, like cases should be treated alike. To put it differently, the emphasis is on equality in legal proceedings (everyone is equal in the eyes of the law) and equality in punishment of offenders (similar crimes are punished in the same way).

The uniformity of the law is guaranteed by set penalties for particular offences. The punishment is thus meant to fit the crime. For the sake of equality, penalties should be fixed prior to sentencing, and be administered in accordance with the actual offence that has been committed. Punishment, therefore, is to consist of *determinate sentences*, which clearly link specific offences with specific penalties, and which are applicable to anyone who has committed the offence in question.

historical development

The two leading figures in the development of classical criminology were Cesare Beccaria and Jeremy Bentham (see Taylor et al. 1973; Beirne 1993). The work of Beccaria provided a profound critique of the existing systems of law and criminal justice. He opposed the arbitrary nature of judicial decision-making that was characteristic of the courts of his day, and he was critical of the unduly harsh and barbaric forms of punishment, which included extensive use of the death penalty and the routine use of torture.

According to Beccaria (2009 [1767]), the basis for all social action should be the utilitarian concept of the greatest happiness for the greater number in society. Translated into the criminal justice sphere, this meant that crime should be considered an injury to society as a whole (and not explained in terms of 'sin' or dealt with solely on the basis of 'privilege'). The purpose of punishment is not simply social revenge or retribution, but to ensure the greatest overall good for everyone. This means that punishment should be orientated towards deterring individuals and others from committing crime, rather than wreaking vengeance.

It was felt that prevention of crime was more important than the punishment itself. To this end it was important to make sure that everyone knew the laws. Human beings were seen as essentially rational. For punishment to work in a deterrent sense, it needed to be rationally applied (rather than be seen as draconian or unfair). It also needed to be applied in a systematic manner, one that was not subject to the individual whim (including personal granting of mercy) of the judiciary. Further, the deterrent effect of punishment would only be attainable if there were a certainty of punishment, which in turn could be provided only by the establishment of a professionalised police and judicial system.

Ethically, the utilitarian principle demands that the punishment should fit the crime. Hence, the use of torture and the death penalty was condemned insofar as these represented gross violations of individual rights and were disproportionate to the offences actually committed by offenders. Alternatively, incarceration was viewed as a form of punishment that would be particularly effective given the goals of punishment in the classical framework. As Beccaria (2009 [1767]: 43) put it:

> The end of punishment, therefore, is no other, than to prevent the criminal from doing further injury to society, and to prevent others from committing the like offence. Such punishments, therefore, and such a mode of inflicting them, ought to be chosen, as will make the strongest and most lasting impression on the minds of others, with the least torment to the body of the criminal.

Such an approach necessarily was founded upon a heightened importance attached to formal law, which should set out clearly the range of penalties pertaining to particular kinds of infringements. Judicial discretion should be limited to the area of deciding the 'facts' of the case; it should not extend to selection of penalty once guilt had been ascertained.

The classical view was further developed in the writings of Bentham (2001 [1789]). Likewise, seeing human beings and society within a framework of utilitarianism, Bentham argued that all behaviour is reducible to that of seeking pleasure and avoiding pain. Criminal behaviour, in particular, was also seen as reflecting this universal tendency or generalised pleasure–pain principle (see Gottfredson & Hirschi 1990).

Given that human beings were seen as having free will, and having equal capacity to reason, the central question for criminal justice revolved around how to make crime painful and how to reduce the rewards for criminal behaviour. The criminal law reflects a social contract between individuals and the state; a contract that is based upon a rational exchange of rights and obligations. Enforcement of the criminal law should be based on making adherence the most rational thing to do, in the light of the fact that violation would almost certainly mean the experience of negative sanctions. In a nutshell, punishment should offer more pain than the transgression of the law is worth.

To commit or not commit a crime was thus seen as a matter of free choice. Self-interest dictated, however, that if punishment outweighed the potential gain, then crime itself would be the result of either irrational or bad choices. Those who did commit a crime should be punished because the responsibility for doing so in the first place ultimately rests in their own hands.

Although cogent in abstract principle, classical thinking met considerable challenges when put into practice. These came from three directions. The first challenge was to make such general principles serve the interests of justice and equality when faced with a specific defendant in court. Some defendants clearly did not conform to the abstract concept of being rational and equal. Questions could be raised about the rationality of children and people with mental illness, for example. To cope with the reality of life in court, reforms took place (sometimes known as the 'neoclassical' reforms). These developed rules to cope with extenuating circumstances where individuals could be deemed not to be totally responsible for their actions.

The second challenge came from the growing bureaucratisation of the state. As capitalism grew, so did the need for a coordinating bureaucracy to ensure the smooth running of commerce. The state fulfilled such a role. The courts, as part of the state, had to fulfil the bureaucratic criterion of efficiency as much as those of justice and fairness. Where the criteria of efficiency and justice were incompatible, conflict resulted. Changes to the state that result from the demands of bureaucracy have been labelled 'corporatisation', where procedures are put in place to increase efficiency, rather than to emphasise qualities such as justice.

The third challenge to classicism came from vested interests. Those in positions of power viewed classicism as a challenge to their entrenched authority, which they wielded through considerable discretion in application of the law in practice. Codification of legal principles therefore threatened the autonomy of the aristocracy, who naturally resisted such changes. The system that resulted, particularly in the UK and Australia, represents a hybrid of classical and pre-classical models.

then & now

classical theory

Classical theory has provided the benchmark against which other perspectives in criminology have developed; particularly in relation to its basic theoretical assumptions about why people commit crime (for example, because people make a free and rational choice that the gains from offending outweigh the costs) and about what society should do to respond (for example, make sentencing rational so the pain outweighs the gain, and in the process develop a comprehensive criminal code). Challenging or modifying these assumptions has led to changes in criminological thinking over time. Some theories, such as positivist perspectives and strain theory (see Chapters 3 and 4) largely reject, or at least downplay, the idea that free will leads to offending. Rather, and in contrast to classical theory, these theories emphasise how behaviour is determined by factors outside of the actor's immediate control. Other perspectives, such as republican theory, build on the classical understanding of free will and rationality by emphasising the importance to society of such things as trust, loyalty and concern (see Chapter 10). Criminological thinking that ignores free will can find itself marginalised by populist ideas about crime and offending that largely construe crime in classical terms. The strong emphasis on choice and free will in public debate can, in turn, strengthen the appeal of perspectives such as those of the New Right that extend classical conceptions of crime control in more punitive directions (see Chapter 8).

contemporary examples

The classical perspective is reflected in many aspects of the contemporary criminal justice system, and in the general public's commonsense understanding of criminality, despite the three challenges outlined above. Classical thinking is evident in legal doctrine that emphasises conscious intent or choice (such as the notion of *mens rea* or the guilty mind), and in sentencing principles (for example, the idea of culpability or responsibility) and the structure of punishment (for example, gradation of penalties according to seriousness of offence).

Philosophically, the classical view sees its modern counterpart in the supporters of a 'just deserts' approach to sentencing. In this perspective, four basic principles are proposed (see Pettit & Braithwaite 1993):

1\ No one, other than a person found to be guilty of a crime, must be punished for it.
2\ Anyone found to be guilty of a crime must be punished for that crime.
3\ Punishment must be no *more* than is commensurate with, or proportional to, the nature or gravity of the offence and culpability of the criminal.
4\ Punishment must be no *less* than is commensurate with, or proportional to, the nature or gravity of the offence and culpability of the criminal.

Such principles clearly rest on a classical foundation. They encapsulate notions of free will and rationality, as well as proportionality and equality. As we have said, these notions form part of the 'just deserts' understanding of criminal behaviour, and focus on the offence (not the offender) deter the offender from reoffending according to the pleasure–pain principle, and ensure that justice is served by equal punishment for the same crime (von Hirsch 1976; Akers 1990; Trasler 1993). 'Just deserts' philosophy eschews individual discretion and rehabilitation as aims of the justice system. Justice must be done (that is, proportional punishment must be meted out) and must be seen to be done (that is, there should be no exceptions) (Carlsmith & Darley 2002).

The 'just deserts' model has formed the basis for much sentencing reform in Western democracies such as Australia, Canada, the US and the UK. The focus of these reforms has been to rationalise the sentencing structure by specifying more clearly the appropriate penalty for the offence. In reality, this has been seen to reduce the discretion of the judiciary by controlling penalties more closely in legislation (such as mandatory sentencing), dictating length of sentence (or, more accurately, period of incarceration), and removing or reducing parole and other periods of non-incarceration. The intent behind reforms was to codify the sentence for each offence in the legislation itself, and ensure that the actual term an offender served more closely reflected the original sentence handed down by the judiciary (Carlsmith & Darley 2002). The original aim was not necessarily to increase penalties (although this was in fact what happened in most cases); rather, the aim under a 'just deserts' framework was for the penalty to reflect the offence and to be administered without favouring one individual over another (Hirschi 1986; von Hirsch & Ashworth 1992).

Such sentencing reforms revisit many of the debates that surround application of classical principles. In particular, debates concern the fairness of a system that has curtailed considerations of extenuating circumstances of the offender and reduced judicial discretion to a large degree. Those who argue for the need to rehabilitate the offender are particularly troubled by the change in legislation, with rehabilitation being irrelevant to both classical and 'just deserts' thinking (von Hirsch 1976).

It is perhaps misleading, however, to focus on sentencing as the primary concern of classical theory. Classical theorists were equally concerned with codifying and simplifying the law so that it was easily understood by the majority of people. Both these aims have had limited success. For example, codification—the passing of legislation that states exactly what constitutes an offence—is a European rather than Westminster endeavour, and has failed to materialise in several Australian states (for example, Victoria, New South Wales and South Australia do not have consolidated criminal codes). This means that a number of offences, such as manslaughter, are not clearly defined in law but rely on common law judgments as they do in the UK.

Simplification of law to make it open and accessible has faced similar obstacles to codification. Although there have been some attempts to simplify law, and make it accessible to all, many aspects of law remain obscure and impenetrable to the majority. Furthermore, legal expenses often prove prohibitive to all but the wealthy when it comes to pursuing justice through law. To some extent, though, there have been advances in making the law accessible to the general populace. The provision of legal aid, the Community Legal Centre movement, and the provision of small claims courts and tribunals throughout Australia can be seen to have, at least, some origin in these concerns of the classical perspective.

{from theory to practice: deterrence and sentencing}

—

Unlike the theories presented in the proceeding chapters, classical theory is no longer adopted in contemporary criminological research. Instead, those wishing to present classical concepts are more likely to adopt the concepts and theories of the New Right (see Chapter 8). Despite the lack of academic engagement with the older ideas of classical theory, these concepts continue to play an important role in policy development, especially for organisations such as the Victorian Sentencing Advisory Council.

Classical theory emphasises clarity in sentencing, such that an offender must receive a sentence that ensures the pain from the sentence outweighs the gain from the offence. One current example of the move towards more clarity in sentencing has been the decision by the state of Victoria to reduce the judiciary's use of suspended sentences as an option. A suspended sentence is where some or all of a prison sentence can be suspended by a judge provided that the offender does not engage in criminal activity again during that period. The state's Sentencing Advisory Council had found that the wider public mistrusted these sentences, as they appeared to send the 'wrong message' to offenders (they were seen as lenient options in the circumstances). Public concern had risen after a number of high-profile cases in which suspended sentences were handed down for serious crimes (such as rape). From the perspective of classical theory, a reduction in the use of suspended sentences makes sense, since this reduction ensures that everyone is then aware that there is an unambiguous penalty for serious offences. It is important to remember, however, that classical theory does not advocate tough sentences as such; its main concern is that sentences be proportionate to the offences committed (Sentencing Advisory Council <www.sentencingcouncil.vic.gov.au>).

---

critique

The limitations of classical theory have been signalled throughout this chapter. Here they will be summarised for clarity. Concerns with classical theory can be broken down into two groups: namely, problems with fairness in the case of individuals, and neglect of inequalities in the broader social structure (see Young 1981; Taylor et al. 1973; Walklate 2007).

The problem of fairness in individual cases formed an early critique of classical theory and led to the first wave of neoclassical reforms. Despite such reforms, the problem still remains where a system focuses on the offence and not the offender, coupled with principles of equality and fairness when responding to such criminal behaviour. People are not endowed with equal capacity to reason (for example, children and people with intellectual disability or mental illness) or equal knowledge of the law (for example, newly arrived refugees). The decision to offend may or may not be the result of an irrational choice, and classical theory gives no insight into how to deal with cases where offending results from incapacity of reason, or lack of legal knowledge.

The second critique, which follows from the first, is concerned with the classical concept of rationality. If offending results from a temporary irrationality, how is it that the distribution of crime (as measured by official statistics) is not spread equally through the social structure? Such measures place the bulk of offending among those with low incomes. The findings suggest that, for some people, offending may be entirely rational in a manner that is not amenable to the deterrence resulting from punishment (Cornish & Clarke 1986). In a world of deep social inequalities, universal equality cannot be realised by treating everyone equally before the law. Rational choice may lead some to offend precisely because of social inequalities. Equality before the law masks this reality.

On a broader level, it has long been recognised that there are clear differences between formal law (that which is written) and substantive law (that which happens in practice). The way law was written tended to assist some individuals who understood the law and knew how to exploit it, while disadvantaging others who did not have the same access to lawyers nor understand the way law works in practice. It is a common complaint that a powerful individual or organisation appears able to avoid the 'spirit' of the law, while complying with the 'letter' of the law.

The legal process is itself influenced by the broader social inequalities. Some people are more equal than others, and this in turn affects the legal process. The wealthy have access to legal advice that in turn affects how they are dealt with by the justice system. Furthermore, punishments may be proportional to crime, but will be experienced in markedly different ways — the rich may retain income and wealth, while the poor lose out on income and future work opportunities.

Despite these problems, classical theory had a real and positive effect on the justice system. It did promote a more open, systematic system of justice when compared to the previous system based on the arbitrary whim of the aristocracy. Classical principles argue for the rights of an individual within the system, and place limits on judicial discretion. Finally, the theory espouses a humanitarian approach to punishment when compared to the barbaric practices of the previous era. For example, classical theorists such as Beccaria argued against capital punishment, which was very much a radical proposition for the era. This humanitarian sensibility within classical theory points to a tension within the theory, a tension that remains relevant today. This tension centres on classical theory's emphasis on transparency, that there needs to be crime written in law that people are aware of, and the emphasis is on deterrence within punishment. Reforms to criminal law often are influenced by classical theory in that they seek to make the law more transparent, and to reduce discretion of the judiciary. However, disagreements arise about what *severity* of punishment is warranted.

Within criminology, the influence of pure classical theory, and its use in academic research, has waned, in large part due to the emergence of positivist approaches. These new approaches, addressed in the following chapters, fundamentally re-shaped how theorists addressed the issues of crime and criminality. Yet, the more punitive side to Beccaria's ideas remain central to commonsense, popular beliefs about the causes of crime.

{conclusion}

Classical theory was developed at a time of great social change, namely the transition from feudalism to capitalism. Just as that transition challenged the pre-eminence of the aristocracy in economic matters, so classicism challenged the discretion of the aristocracy in matters of crime and justice. Classical theory sought to promote the rights of individuals as equal and rational. According to this perspective, people are inherently self-seeking and endowed with free will. This free will, coupled with a rational system of laws that deter individuals from offending, will ensure few have the motivation to offend. Under this system punishment will be meted out without reference to the 'nature' of the offender, in a manner that ensures the pain of punishment outweighs the gain from the offence.

Classical thinking had a profound effect on the justice system, and can be seen particularly clearly in debates in the 1980s and 1990s concerning 'just deserts' principles in sentencing. However, the focus on the offence (rather than the offender) is problematic when individuals lack the capacity for reason, or when offending can be seen to reflect the wider inequalities in society. Classical theory can have the effect of masking the reality of these broader inequalities in the social structure, and in this way entrench such inequalities through a pretence of equal access to justice through the legal system.

No system has ever reflected the total demands of the classical system. In Australia, the justice system can be seen as only a partial reflection of the classical model, while retaining large areas of pre-classical processes and procedures, such as case law, in which the law is made not by the parliament but by the judiciary. Even where classical principles hold in practice, there have been continuing neoclassical revisions (such as the acknowledgment of individual differences).

The classical thinkers initiated a period of lasting debate and controversy over how we should understand crime and criminal behaviour. Although ostensibly focused on the offence and not the offender, the very process of raising issues concerning law and offending inexorably leads to closer scrutiny of the reasons for offending. It is the reasons for offending that form the basis of the theories in the next chapter, namely the positivist perspective.

{**further reading**}

Beccaria, C. (2009 [1767]). *An Essay On Crimes and Punishments* (5th edition) (trans. P. Marongui, C. Beccaria, & G.R. Newman), Transaction Publishers, New Brunswick NJ.

Carlsmith, K.M. & Darley, J.M. (2002). 'Why Do We Punish? Deterrence and Just Deserts as Motives for Punishment', *Journal*

*of Personality and Social
Psychology*, 83 (2): 284–99.

Fine, B. (1984). *Democracy and
the Rule of Law: Liberal Ideals
and Marxist Critiques*, Pluto,
London.

Gottfredson, M. & Hirschi, T.
(1990). *A General Theory of
Crime*, Stanford University
Press, Stanford.

Kelly, J. (1992). *A Short History
of Western Legal Theory*,
Clarendon Press, Oxford.

McLaughlin, E., Muncie, J.
& Hughes, G. (eds) (2003).
*Criminological Perspectives:
A Reader* (2nd edition), SAGE,
London.

Taylor, I., Walton, P. &
Young, J. (1973). *The New
Criminology*, Routledge & Kegan
Paul, London.

Young, J. (1981). 'Thinking
Seriously about Crime: Some
Models of Criminology', in
M. Fitzgerald, G. McLennon &
J. Pawson (eds), *Crime and
Society: Readings in History
and Theory*, Routledge & Kegan
Paul and the Open University,
London.

Walklate, S. (2007).
*Understanding Criminology:
Current Theoretical Debates* (3rd
edition), Open University Press,
Maidenhead.

biological and psychological positivism

{introduction}

—

This chapter discusses positivism as a central theoretical and methodological approach in the history and contemporary practice of criminology. As will be seen, the development of positivistic perspectives constituted a major break with the classical tradition, which saw crime as primarily a matter of individual choice. For the positivists, crime is explained by reference to forces and factors outside the decision-making ability of the individual. Thus, the classical and the positivist viewpoints are often seen as being directly counterposed.

The rise of positivism represents a shift from what was seen as armchair theorising or philosophising to a more rigorous, hands-on, scientific enterprise. The chapter explores the origins of the 'science' of criminology, and discusses two major approaches within positivism: the biological and the psychological. Central to each of these perspectives is the idea that crime can best be explained by examining individual differences between people and by demonstrating how these differences are, in turn, linked to certain biological and/or psychological factors that predispose certain people towards criminal behaviour.

—

social context

Positivism as a perspective is associated with a very different view of society and human nature from that expressed in classical criminological theory. It emerged in the nineteenth century, a period of further consolidation of capitalism and the capitalist mode of production in Europe. This was a period that witnessed major technological developments and the entrenchment of mass production (rather than agricultural production or merchant trading) as the dominant form of production and source of profit.

The nineteenth century saw the further concentration of peasants and villagers into large cities, the creation and expansion of the factory system, the introduction of new production technologies and sources of energy (such as the steam engine) and expanded communication and transport networks (such as extensive railroad and highway construction). Changes in basic production techniques and relations, and the flow of 'free labour' into employment in the industrial sphere, saw the emergence of a new social class—the working class or proletariat.

The rise of the proletariat as a distinct and growing class was accompanied by major industrial, social and political conflict and upheaval. The previous centuries had been marked by periodic struggles between the aristocracy and the peasantry (in the form of peasant rebellions), and between the established ruling class (the landed gentry) and the bourgeoisie (capitalists). Now the dominant class, the capitalist class, was faced with opposition from the working class over the conditions and nature of work, and in some cases over the very ownership and control of production in society.

Life was hard for the members of the working class: child labour was common, and a thin line separated those who worked for a living from those who were condemned to the poorhouse. Living conditions and working conditions were harsh, dirty and crowded. Meanwhile, the capitalists as a class were amassing huge fortunes and adopting opulent lifestyles. The contrast in circumstances and opportunities was stark.

Not surprisingly, the nineteenth century was also a time when the working class began to organise itself industrially, politically and, in some cases, militarily. Workers began to combine into industrial organisations (trade unions), although they were banned by law. Simultaneously, the material conditions experienced by the working class meant that there was greater analysis of, and sympathetic hearing for, the idea of forging a new type of 'classless' society. This was reflected in the proliferation of alternative working-class publications, pamphlets and daily press, and in the formation of socialist, anarchist and labour political organisations and parties. Over the course of the century a number of compromises were made by the ruling capitalist class. These included, for example, the legal recognition of industrial unions, and the extension of the vote to male members of the working class.

The nineteenth century in Europe was also a time of new thinking about the nature of human beings, and of society generally. The European powers had been involved in carving up the world's resources for several centuries. From Latin America to Africa, the Indian subcontinent to eastern Asia, the Europeans had been extracting resources and exploiting the labour of Indigenous people since the 'voyages of discovery' in the fifteenth century. This was justified initially by the simple expedient that 'might makes right'. However, the justification became more sophisticated with the advent of theories of social and biological evolution.

In particular, the great leaps forward in technology and industrial development, combined with reliance on and appreciation of the importance of 'science', meant that the European nations asserted their pre-eminence in the global economic and political structure on the basis of a presumed national and biological superiority. Science and technology ensured the expansion of European influence and power into all corners of the globe. Domination was seen as a natural outcome of the fruits of a European 'civilisation' founded upon innovation, invention and technological superiority.

Simultaneously, the work of natural scientists such as Charles Darwin, and especially his general theory of evolution (based upon notions of natural selection and competition), were (mis)appropriated to justify and explain the dominance of the white European over the rest of the world's populace. Colonialism and imperialism were seen as a consequence of the natural biological superiority of the white European. White supremacy was thus justified and intertwined with notions of a racist biological determinism, one in which white Europeans were at the top of human hierarchy.

The visible presence of class conflict and social misery in Europe, the rise of scientific interest and industrial innovation, and the idea of evolution and stages in human development were all to influence the establishment of positivism as an approach to human affairs. Positivism was founded upon the belief that society ('civilisation') is progressing ever forward, and that the social scientist can study society, provide a more accurate understanding of how society works, and ultimately provide a rational means of overcoming existing social problems and ills by using scientific methods.

Social scientists were interested in promoting a positive view of the social order, and in providing positive interventions in social life to make things better. This required systematic study of existing social problems, and the development of a wide range of techniques and strategies to deal with issues relating to crime, schooling, poverty and family life.

Institutionally, the development of positivism was closely associated with the rise of the *professions* during the nineteenth century. The passing of legislation in Britain that banned the use of child labour in factories, for example, was accompanied by the introduction of compulsory schooling and expanded welfare concern over the plight of the children of the poor. Under the rubric of positive reform, a wide variety of 'experts'—medical doctors, psychiatrists, health workers, teachers, criminal justice officials and social workers—began to devise 'scientific' ways to raise children better, to professionalise parenting, to deal with personal troubles and individual deficiencies, to deal with young offenders and, generally, to engineer wide-scale social reform.

Liberal reform rested upon the idea of progress, humanitarianism and the active construction of a more caring and supportive society. The main tool of investigation used by professionals and reformers in fostering particular forms of social change was the scientific method. Indeed, the professionals relied for their persuasive power upon the notion that their judgments and strategies were derived from science. Social change was to be managed rationally by use of the scientific criteria of logic and empirical study rather than by appeals to God, revelation, faith or opinion to devise appropriate institutional responses to social problems.

The intrinsic appeal of such an approach is understandable, especially since science and technology played a crucial role in industrial capitalism, and a high level of bureaucratisation and specialisation was a necessary part of an advanced industrial economy. The model of the natural sciences had worked well for capitalist production techniques and manufacturing processes. Now it could be put to use in the social arena as well.

The adoption of concepts and methods from the natural sciences was manifest in several overlapping ideas about the nature of society. For instance, borrowing from the biological sciences, positivist social scientists often viewed society as a type of organism. It was made up of different components, which worked together in order to ensure the proper functioning of the system as a whole. If any one of these components was or became 'dysfunctional', then correction was required to restore the social equilibrium. This could apply to specific institutions (such as school, family, work) and to particular individuals or groups in society (such as the poor, sole parents, the unemployed). Social scientists had the tasks of identifying the nature and source of dysfunctions, and attempting to devise programs and strategies to alleviate them.

The positivist method in the social sciences was guided by certain assumptions regarding the applicability of natural science methods to the study of society. Three premises in particular underpinned the scientific approach as conceived by the positivists (see Taylor et al. 1973; Neyhouse 2002):

– Social scientists were seen to be neutral observers of the world, and their work was 'value free'. This is because the world was seen to be 'out there', as an external reality, and the role of the scientist was merely to record the 'facts'.

– The key method of the positivists was to classify and quantify human experience and behaviours through a range of objective tests. This meant developing various ways to measure human activity.

– As with the natural world, the social world was seen to obey general laws of operation. The task of the positivists was to uncover the causal determinants of human behaviour (for instance, to identify 'cause' and 'effect' relationships), and thus both to predict and to modify future behaviour outcomes.

The development of positivism was thus related to efforts to adopt natural science methods and concepts in the study of society. This meant accepting certain ideas about the human experience, and attempting to quantify and classify this experience in the expectation that expert intervention could forestall or rectify particular kinds of social problems.

basic concepts

Positivism is based on the idea of a scientific understanding of crime and criminality (see chart 3.1). It assumes that there is a distinction between the 'normal' and the 'deviant', and attempts to study the specific factors that give rise to deviant or criminal behaviour.

chart 3.1 | positivist approaches

definition of crime	natural
	_ violation of social consensus _ extends beyond a legal definition _ deviant behaviour with respect to social norms
focus of analysis	the offender
	_ characteristics of the offender
cause of crime	pathology
	_ individual deficiency _ not a matter of individual choice
nature of offender	determined and/or predisposed to certain types of behaviour
	_ biological and social conditioning and individual difference
response to crime	treatment
	_ diagnosis on individual basis _ indeterminate to fit offender
crime prevention	diagnosis and classification
	_ early intervention
operation of criminal justice system	'scientific' approach
	_ measurement and evaluation _ essentially neutral

One of the hallmarks of the positivist approach is the notion that behaviour is *determined*; that is, the activity and behaviour of individuals are primarily shaped by factors and forces outside the individuals' immediate control. Behaviour is a reflection of certain influences on the person, whether biological, psychological or social in nature.

Offenders are believed to vary: *individual differences* exist between offenders, and these in turn can be measured and classified in some way. Rather than seeing people in terms of equal capacities, or equal rights, positivist views emphasise difference, which reflects varying conditions affecting each person.

The focus of analysis, therefore, is on the nature and characteristics of the offender, rather than on the criminal act. Offenders can be scientifically studied, and the factors leading to their criminality can be diagnosed, classified and ultimately treated or dealt with in some way. It is the job of the 'expert' to identify the specific conditions leading to criminality in any particular case.

Similarly, positivists see crime and deviance as phenomena that can be studied in a scientific manner. In other words, the incidence of such behaviour is not assumed to reside only in official violations of the law. This is because the social or moral consensus in society (which can be described and measured independently of the law) can be violated without necessarily being detected or processed formally in the criminal justice system.

Given that deviancy is seen to lie within the (abnormal) individual and is not always reflected in who actually ends up in court or in the hands of the police, the extent of deviant behaviour is an open-ended empirical question. As such, it requires research into the *natural crime* that hitherto has been undetected, but that nevertheless is occurring in society. It is necessary, then, to measure the *dark figure* of unrecorded crime and deviant behaviour, through the use of techniques such as large-scale questionnaires, interviews and various other measures.

A central tenet of positivism is that a moral consensus exists in relation to what constitutes deviant and normal behaviour. Given this, positivists generally see behavioural problems in terms of *individual pathology* or deficiency. Those who do not conform are seen as having personal difficulties related to biological, psychological or social factors. The task of the expert is to identify these factors and to correct or fix the deficiency.

Rather than being orientated towards punishment, the positivist approach is directed towards the *treatment* of offenders. Offending behaviour is analysed in terms of factors or forces beyond the conscious control of the individual. To respond to crime therefore means to deal with the reasons that caused the offending behaviour to occur in the first place.

Since each individual offender is different from all others, treatment must be individualised. This translates at an institutional level into arguments in favour of *indeterminate sentences*; that is, the length of time in custody should not depend solely on the nature of the criminal act committed, but must take into account the diagnosis and classification of the offender (for

example, severe or not severe problem, dangerous or not dangerous), and
the type of treatment appropriate to the specific individual.

historical development

The origins of positivist perspectives in criminology lie in two interrelated
developments in the latter part of the nineteenth century. One strand
of scientific research attempted to provide biological explanations for
criminal behaviour; the other focused on psychological factors associated
with criminality.

¬ biological positivism

Biological positivism was first popularised through the work of Lombroso
(1911; see also Taylor et al. 1973; Rafter 2008; Gibson & Hahn Rafter 2006).
Borrowing heavily from evolutionary theories, Lombroso attempted to
distinguish different types of human individuals, and to classify them
on the basis of racial and biological difference. In a form of 'criminal
anthropology', the argument here was that a general theory of crime can
be developed on the basis of measurable physical differences between the
criminal and the non-criminal. Specifically, Lombroso wanted to establish
a link between criminality and the assumption that individuals exhibit
particular traits that roughly correspond to the various stages of human
evolution.

For Lombroso, the criminal was born, not made (1911). The idea of a
'born criminal' reflected the notion that crime is the result of something
essential to the nature of the individual criminal. In the early formulations
of this view, discussion focused on the concept of the 'atavistic criminal';
that is, a person who was biologically inferior, in that he or she represented
a reversion to an earlier human evolutionary period. To put it in crude
terms, the atavistic criminal was, developmentally, closer to an ape than
contemporary human beings. Such a person could be identified through
a series of physical stigmata, including abnormal dentition (protruding
teeth), asymmetric face, large ears, supernumerary fingers and toes, eye
defects and even tattoos.

Lombroso later modified his views somewhat, although the element of
biological determinism remained. For example, he developed a typology

of criminals that divided the population into such categories as the 'epileptic criminal', the 'insane criminal' and the 'occasional criminal'. In explaining female delinquency and criminality, the argument was put forward that, because of the essential nature of the female sex (which was seen as passive), the female offender in fact was biologically more like a man than a woman.

The emphasis on biological factors in explanations of crime was reflected in a number of subsequent studies. Indeed, the search for a single physiological cause of criminality has persisted to this day. The 'science' of phrenology was popular in criminology for a number of years around the beginning of the twentieth century. This doctrine assumes that the shape and size of the skull correspond to the functions and ability of the brain. A study undertaken in 1912 at the University of Melbourne provides an illustration of this kind of research (Brown & Hogg 1992a; see Rafter 2008 for further examples). The study was conducted on 355 male inmates of Pentridge prison. The skulls of the prisoners were examined and estimates of the cubic capacity of their brains were made in an attempt to correlate the size of skull to intelligence. It was concluded that cattle stealers had the lowest brain capacity, and that forgers and embezzlers had the highest.

Attempts to measure intelligence, and to argue that criminals were innately less intelligent than the general population, were also popular. In 1913, for example, Charles Goring published the results of his work, which involved examining some 3000 convicts. He concluded that people with criminal tendencies were endowed with less intelligence and were of a smaller stature than other people. To measure intelligence, he simply talked to people and decided for himself whether or not they were intelligent.

Another type of study is that which looks to physiology or body structure as a key determinant of criminal behaviour. In the 1940s, William Sheldon (1940) proposed a theory based on body build (somatotype). He wished to establish a link between different body types and criminality. According to Sheldon, human body types can be classed into three broad categories: endomorphic (soft and round), mesomorphic (muscular and strong) and ectomorphic (thin and fragile). Each body type was associated with a particular temperament: relaxed, sociable and fond of eating (endomorphic); energetic, courageous and assertive (mesomorphic); and brainy, artistic and introverted (ectomorphic). It was further argued that mesomorphs were most likely to become criminals. In other words, there was a positive correlation between body type and criminal activity.

As a final example of biological explanation, we turn to research that examined genetic factors (see Taylor et al. 1973; Mednick et al. 1987). According to the XYY chromosome theory, criminality is related to a deviant genetic make-up. The normal female chromosomal complement is XX; the normal male composition is XY. However, an XYY combination was also discovered. It was held that those who had this kind of chromosomal complement were far more predisposed to criminal activity, because of their 'abnormal' height and mental structures. Fundamentally, a central problem nevertheless remained—that is, how genetic differences actually translate into behavioural traits.

Biological explanations of the kind considered above tend to be fairly pessimistic about positive actions to prevent or deal with crime. On the contrary, these explanations have been instrumental in justifying some of the most horrific measures to control human activity, particularly as it relates to the use of eugenics by the Third Reich (Duster 2003). Biological explanations are largely negative because crime is seen to be the result of something *essential to the nature of the individual*. Thus, we are born with certain biological attributes that we cannot change, but that may lock some of us into a life of crime and antisocial behaviour.

¬ psychological positivism

Psychological positivism had different historical origins and a different orientation towards the offender and criminal activity. In this instance, crime was seen as the result of externally caused biological problems (such as war injury) or internal psychological factors (such as mental illness) that were treatable. The criminal was made, not born. And the task of the criminal justice system was to understand the underlying causes of criminality, and to find the appropriate treatment strategy.

This strand of positivism emerged in England from within the criminal justice institutions themselves (see Garland 1988; Forsythe 1995). Doctors and psychiatrists who worked within the medico-legal framework, and who spent most of their working life with inmates, became ever more sophisticated in their classification and diagnosis of offenders. As practitioners within the criminal justice establishment, they had daily contact with a wide variety of 'subjects'. They discovered that there were major differences between individual offenders and, furthermore, that there was a whole range of offenders who did not seem entirely responsible for their actions.

Given their medical background, it is not surprising that these practitioners saw the issue as one of pathology. If offenders were deemed to be 'sick' in some way, then the obvious solution to crime was to find some way to 'cure' them. Thus, an offender might exhibit the conditions of criminality, but these conditions could be dealt with. This could be accomplished by scientific diagnosis, classification of the condition or illness, and devising the appropriate treatment to fit the condition of each offender.

Such ideas and reasoning were reinforced by the experiences of medical practitioners in treating soldiers who returned from the battle fronts of the First World War. Many of these men were shell-shocked and physically disabled. They presented a number of pathological tendencies, ranging from varying forms of mental illness through to antisocial behaviour. Deviancy in this case was clearly related to trauma of some kind. The problem was not with the innate characteristics of the individual, but with the consequences and impact of the trauma on the individual.

Broadly speaking, psychological theories tended to centre attention on the processes of the mind in explanations of criminal behaviour (see Feldman 1993; Bartol & Bartol 2005; Gadd & Jefferson 2007; Jones 2008). They included several kinds of perspectives:

- Some made reference to psychoanalytic theory, such as analysis of the conscious and unconscious, and how basic emotional and developmental processes affect behaviour.

- Some focused on personality traits, such as studies of aggression and passivity, and the psychological structure of personality as these related to behaviour.

- Some dealt with psychiatric issues from the point of view of childhood experiences. An example is analysis that saw deprivation of universal needs during childhood as leading to the formation of certain personality patterns in later life.

then & now

biological and psychological positivism

Biological and psychological positivism largely emphasise how genetic make-up, psychological factors and, to a lesser extent, environmental constraints are associated with antisocial and criminal behaviour. Early work, such as that of Lombroso and Sheldon, emphasised rather arcane connections between biological attributes and offending, while later theories have become more sophisticated, in emphasising 'soft' forms of determinism (how biology and psychology *influence* aggressive or antisocial behaviour) rather than 'hard' determinism (where biology or psychology *determine* such behaviour). However, the impact of positivism on subsequent theories within the discipline of criminology, as a whole, has been rather limited; instead, theories on biological and psychological determinants of antisocial behaviour are debated and developed in the field of psychology; in particular, within forensic psychology. Psychological concerns with individual perceptions and experiences of the world, nonetheless, are central to many theories, such as labelling perspectives (Chapter 5), republican theory (Chapter 10) and postmodernist theories (Chapter 11). However, this concern with the individual in such theories tends not to draw on the work of theorists in this chapter, rather drawing inspiration from other academic disciplines, such as sociology, philosophy and anthropology. Recent work has nevertheless challenged criminology to come to grips with the biological dimension of criminal behaviour and to recognise the positive rewards such research offers for addressing some kinds of criminal behaviour (Anderson 2007).

---

contemporary examples

Two major strands can be found in contemporary examples of biological and psychological positivism. First is the field that can be seen as a contemporary variant of early psychiatric interest in criminality, a field now encompassing both forensic psychiatry and forensic psychology. Leading theorists in this field are most often also practising forensic psychologists or psychiatrists. Second are theories that have, to a greater or lesser degree, taken a more academic turn. As suggested in the previous section, there is a wide range of such theories, all of which focus on the characteristics of offenders, but arguably the two most prominent examples are 'control theory' and 'biosocial' explanations, which, as the name suggests, link biological and psychological factors in explaining criminal behaviour.

The predominant concern of forensic psychologists and forensic psychiatrists is in the provision of services to the criminal justice system. Alongside this practical role they have developed a range of theories, not only to assist rehabilitation but also to interpret culpability of the offender to the court, as well as predict possible reoffending. This knowledge is required within different aspects of the criminal justice system. In the courts, the role of forensic psychologists or psychiatrists is to provide pre-sentence reports and act as expert witnesses. In the corrections area, their role is to manage and treat offenders, as well as provide expert advice concerning parole decisions. The popular perception of the forensic psychologist, that of the 'criminal profiler', who can pinpoint the personality profile of an 'at large' offender as part of the investigation process, remains a small and contentious aspect of the field. Further, criminal profiling is not limited to psychological profiles; a more common and successful approach is that of geographic profiling (that is, the analysis of the spacial patterns of a particular spate of offences).

Control theory can be seen as an extension of psychodynamic theories that emanated from Freud. Psychodynamic theories have a common link, in that a central concern is how individuals learn self-control. As with Freud, the underlying assumption of these theories is that, left to our own devices and desires, humans are necessarily impulsive and antisocial. We only become social by repressing basic desires. According to Hirschi (1969) and later Gottfredson and Hirschi (1990), the basic question criminologists need to answer is not 'Why do some people offend?', but 'Why do most people not offend?' To put it simply, these theorists argue that individuals learn not to offend through developing self-control. By extension, those who do offend lack self-control. Gottfredson and Hirschi (1990) see self-control as a single psychological construct or personal attribute. This single construct is made up of several elements, namely:

- impulsivity, or an inability to defer gratification
- lack of perseverance
- preference for risky behaviour
- preference for physical, as opposed to mental, activity
- self-centredness
- low threshold for frustration.

Gottfredson and Hirschi (1990) argue that child-rearing is critical to the development of self-control, a focus that draws inspiration from the early work of Glueck and Glueck (1960). Poor child-rearing practices, such as lack of supervision (particularly by the mother) and poor attachment to the father, lead to low self-control and higher rates of criminal offending (see also Raine 2002). The theory also asserts that opportunity for offending is important, but only when combined with low social control. Adequately socialised individuals would not succumb to criminal opportunity. It is interesting to note that they see their theory applies as much to white-collar crime as to street offending, since a manager who embezzles company funds has the same problem of low self-control as does a teenager caught shoplifting.

Psychological approaches also include those that focus on 'personality types' (see Farrington 1995), and that present typologies of abnormalities in the psychological structure of individuals (for example, 'over-aggressive', 'highly strung'). Such approaches often see the formation of particular personality types as linked to certain biological predispositions as well as developmental experiences.

The best known of the biosocial explanations is that provided by Eysenck (1984). He argued that behaviour could be explained by a combination of psychological and environmental influences. Human beings are not totally determined by their biology; neither are they unaffected by their social circumstances. Behaviour, and in particular criminal behaviour, can be explained in terms of two key variables:

1\ *The differential ability to be conditioned*—This referred to the way in which genetic inheritance can affect one's ability to be conditioned; that is, the sensitivity of the autonomic nervous system that you have genetically inherited will determine whether you are an extrovert or introvert, and this in turn influences how well you are able to be conditioned in society.

2\ *The differential quality of conditioning*—This referred to the effectiveness and efficiency of the family in using appropriate conditioning techniques; that is, the content and method of child-rearing will have an impact upon the child's subsequent behaviour.

The argument, then, is that biological potentials (such as the ability to be conditioned or socialised) are set through inheritance. These interact with environmental potentials (shaped by parenting practices), and together these factors determine the overall propensity of individuals to commit crime.

Today, the connection between biological and social environmental influences is seen in very sophisticated terms. It is a case of 'nature' plus 'nurture', rather than one or the other as the sole—or even dominant—factor in producing certain types of behaviour. It is generally argued that human beings have a 'conditional free will', and individuals can choose from a range of possibilities that are, to some degree, changeable (Rose

2000; Bartol & Bartol 2005; Gadd & Jefferson 2007; Jones 2008). Human behaviour thus contains biological, psychological and social elements (see, for example, Moffitt 1993). Any potential biological influences we may find will only result in a predisposition towards a particular behaviour. To put it bluntly, 'there is no gene for crime, and none will ever be found' (Anderson 2007: 7), since the 'interactionist and dynamic nature of gene expression tells us that we need to look for multiple causes of multiple crimes' (Anderson 2007: 79).

Present-day positivists define and identify criminality in a manner geared to establishing those people who are 'at risk' of certain behaviour (see Baker et al. 2010 for extended discussion of risk and genetics). There is no longer a one-to-one link between crime and behaviour; rather, certain groups are seen to be more predisposed to crime than others because of biological, psychological and social environmental factors. Individuals are not born criminal, but are exposed to baseline biological and psychological processes that shape their personality in childhood. Once the child is introduced to the school, the personality manifests itself in certain types of behaviour. The social influences encountered in the school environment may then further contribute to antisocial behaviour, depending upon initial personality formation. The rise of 'risk' as a determining factor in contemporary crime governance has led to the increasing use of psychosocial approaches to frame risk assessment tools for frontline criminal justice staff (such as police and prison officers) (Webber 2010).

Contemporary positivists see a dynamic relationship between biological factors (inherited predisposition) and environmental factors (external inputs that modify behaviour). Nevertheless, within this more open and less deterministic framework there has been a resurgence of interest in explanations for crime that are heavily weighted towards the biological (see, for example, Anderson 2007). Recent research has examined the contributions of various factors to criminal behaviour (see Fishbein 1990; Anderson 2007; Rowe 2002):

– *Genetic contributions*—These studies have examined the effect of inheritance on criminal behaviour. Particular traits such as intellectual defects or aggression are seen as genetically given, and as being closely associated with criminal behaviour. Comparisons of identical and non-identical twins, and adoption studies to compare biological and non-biological siblings, are means to test the influence of genetic inheritance (Mednick 1985; Mednick et al. 1984).

– *Biochemical contributions* — These studies look at the impact of biochemical differences on human behavioural patterns. Hormonal activity, metabolic processes and the influence of toxins (such as lead poisoning) are examined in terms of various behaviours, such as aggression, and the overall propensity to commit crime. Another strand of research examines psychophysiological variables such as heart rate, blood pressure, brain waves, arousal and attention levels. It is suggested here that different physiological processes have implications for neurotransmission and psychological impairment.

– *Psychopharmacological inducements* — A third area of research examines inducements such as cocaine, alcohol and amphetamines, and their effects on human behaviour, especially criminal behaviour.

In a number of these areas it is now possible to conceive of some kind of biological 'corrective' being developed to prevent criminal behaviour from occurring. This could take the form of simply removing the source of the problem (such as eliminating lead from one's living environment, or banning alcohol sales) or, in the case of more complex responses, regulating the biochemical and physiological operations of the body through appropriate treatment measures (such as drugs designed to restore hormonal equilibrium or ensure a regular heart rate).

Whether it is efforts to re-jig the biological balance (such as through drug therapy) or to restore a psychological norm or balance (such as through parenting classes), a key emphasis in positivist approaches is that of self-control. In other words, efforts will be made to reinforce external and internal regulatory measures so that individuals will conform to the conventional norms of behaviour.

{from theory to practice: evolutionary psychology}
———

Kanazawa, S. (2009). 'Evolutionary Psychology and Crime', in A. Walsh & K. Beaver (eds), *Biosocial Criminology*, Routledge, New York: 90–110.

In this chapter, Kanazawa introduces the reader to the broad framework of evolutionary psychology, in order to present his theory about universal human nature and sex-specific human nature. He argues that as crime is both historically and culturally universal, and that men universally constitute the majority of offenders, then there must be a 'drive' to criminality that is also universal. At the centre of Kanazawa's theory are Darwin's theories of natural and sexual

continued

selection, and a committed belief in serial, heterosexual polygamy. According to this perspective, those individuals with certain positive traits and psychological mechanisms live longer and are better able to dominate access to reproduction. By dominating sexual selection, these individuals ensure that positive coping mechanisms are passed from one generation to the next, until they become 'part of universal (species-typical) human nature' (2009: 91). The psychological mechanisms for survival and reproductive success evolve in ways that generate particular, unconscious desires, emotions, preferences and values.

Kanazawa suggests that as men and women experience sexual selection in distinct ways, they develop sex-specific psychological mechanisms, and that some of these mechanisms can be considered as the 'proximate causes of [criminal] behavior' (2009: 91). From the central assumption that men are evolutionary predisposed to serial, heterosexual polygamy, Kanazawa argues that most crime can be understood as the result of men's competition for access to women's reproductive capacities. Even where this competition is not explicit, he argues that evidence contained in homicide reports clearly illustrates that these murders are often the result of conflicts over honour, reputation and status. On the flip side, Kanazawa argues that as women are predisposed to selecting men who have high social status, men are compelled to prove their suitability as a mate by engaging in risky conflicts with other men (either to eliminate the competition completely, or to force other men to back down). Either way, this performance demonstrates to any available women present that the men possess the psychological mechanisms required to 'protect' their progeny, and ensure the longevity of their superior genes.

Whether it is consciously appreciated as such, according to Kanazawa, the drive to reproduce is the primary, universal, and fundamental drive to human existence. Men's capacity to control their access to the reproductive marketplace drives their desires and preferences especially in the period prior to the birth of their first child. The universal 'age-crime' curve is provided by Kanazawa as evidence that sex-specific human nature is the primary cause of crime. Once a man procreates, it is no longer necessary to compete in the sexual marketplace; rather, energy wasted in battles over access to women is better directed at the survival of his progeny (and genes). Therefore, as men age they are less likely to need to defend their status or honour, and consider the risks and costs of competition to be too high given their 'parental investment' in progeny. Kanazawa suggests that evolutionary psychology not only assists us in understanding men's physical battles with each other, but also robbery/theft and sexual violence against women. In the case of robbery/theft, the offender is attempting to accumulate (albeit, illegitimately) the resources required to be considered by women as a worthy mate. And in terms of sexual assault against women, Kanazawa suggests that these acts of violence are performed by men who either have failed to compete for reproductive access, or have lost in previous battles over reproductive access, or are attempts at 'mate guarding' (2009: 92) to ensure that no other men are granted reproductive access.

critique

Within the positivist aegis then, there exists a plethora of explanations concerning the factors that predispose individuals to commit crime. However, virtually all such explanations are concerned with 'street crime', predominantly violent crime or juvenile delinquency of one type or another. The reasons behind white-collar crime and state crime are generally left untouched by positivist criminology (however, see Gottfredson & Hirschi 1990 for an exception to this).

Furthermore, many positivistic researchers have based their research on incarcerated populations, or those adjudicated as criminal by the law. This poses a problem of the conflict of definitions: the reasoning is that because criminality is the result of psychological or biological abnormality, someone who is adjudicated as criminal by the judicial process must be psychologically or biologically abnormal (Empey 1982). Thus, all incarcerated populations are, by definition, either psychologically or biologically deficient. This problem results from what is known as circular reasoning where A (criminality) is supposed to be caused by B (impairment), and all those in prison are tested as impaired, and are by definition criminal. Hence impairment is assumed to cause criminality. This conclusion is false for a number of reasons, among them:

- It is not clear whether criminality causes impairment, or impairment causes criminality (problem of the direction of causality).
- It is not clear if the imprisonment was the cause of impairment (confounding variable).

   – It is not clear whether those in the general population who have the same impairment also offend (that is, are the two factors simply correlated, or is there a causal connection?).

All explanations of this type thus face considerable challenges in proving the causal connection between biological and psychological factors and criminal behaviour. These challenges concern defining what exactly is being measured (the specifics of a psychological malfunction or chemical imbalance, for example), and designing and undertaking rigorous studies where extraneous variables are excluded. That is, the study must really measure what it says it measures, and there must be no other plausible explanations for what the study found.

While the problem of circular reasoning outlined above can be eradicated through appropriate use of control groups and application of scientific method, the possibility of undertaking such experiments has considerable ethical implications, and they remain rare. Those that are done face considerable difficulty in matching the variables (such as age, educational attainment or employment status) of the control group with the experimental group. Unless these factors are carefully matched, the claims of the study can be severely compromised.

Many studies that purported to find biological or psychological reasons for offending have been discredited because of the inability to control all variables (Feldman 1993; Bartol & Bartol 2005; Gadd & Jefferson 2007; Jones 2008). A good example of this problem is the purported connection between violence and the genetically controlled abnormal metabolism of neurotransmitters, which was reported in *New Scientist* (26 February 1994). Further research revealed that compounding environmental factors could not be ruled out, and the strength of the relationship between genetics and criminality was greatly downplayed (*New Scientist*, 25 February 1995).

Much critique of positivist theory revolves around the blurred distinction between sickness and criminality. Largely undiscussed are the underlying assumptions behind definitions of criminality or, more specifically, deviation from norms. If criminal behaviour is likened to a sickness, it must, like sickness, be undesirable and in need of therapy and eradication. There is an assumed consensus within positivism concerning what constitutes criminality and deviation from norms, without adequate discussion concerning *whose* norms are used as the benchmark for deviation. However, recent work on biological influences on criminal behaviour is very much aware of problems of criminal definition, and indeed problems associated with biological explanations for social behaviour (such as the eugenics movement) that have been (mis)used to oppress populations, justify genocide and support compulsory sterilisation of particular individuals (see Anderson 2007; Duster 2003).

The analogy with sickness brings further problems. There is a tendency within positivism to reduce the reasons for criminal behaviour to a cause or causes found within the individual, either of a biological or psychological nature. It can assume that adult behaviour and personality are reducible to a single set of overarching factors (such as childhood experiences) that require intervention at specific times in a person's life. This assumption ignores, or fails to acknowledge, that life is a process of continual development, renewal, change and transformation.

This reductionism can lead to both racist and sexist conclusions. Where offending is linked to biology, the logical extension of the line of reasoning can lead to attempts to correlate certain people (for example, Indigenous peoples, poor people) with certain 'biologically determined' traits (for example, intelligence as measured by IQ) and so to criminal offending. Without adequate discussion of the assumptions underlying positivism, the search for the causes of criminal behaviour leads inexorably to racist and unwarranted conclusions (see Haller 1971; Duster 2003).

Once a cause of offending has been isolated, further problems arise. The question of diagnosis, classification and treatment of offenders becomes important. How is treatment to be administered, and on what criteria? Treatment may, for example, require biological 'corrections' (such as chemical castration) that raise considerable implications in terms of human rights and human dignity. Even where treatment seems to be relatively benign, such as enhancing parenting skills, there still may be gross assumptions concerning what constitutes adequate parenting. Because of the intrusive nature of treatment suggested by positivist theories, both the theories themselves and the suggested treatments require close scrutiny. As Duster (2003) suggests, we need to ask: who is making the 'genetic claims', and for what purpose?

With identification of a biological or psychological cause of crime, positivism suggests that early detection of criminal potential is entirely possible, if not desirable. This means intrusive intervention in people's lives may take place long before any crime is committed (see, for example, Goodwin 2008). Such intervention may be extreme, such as sterilisation, or relatively benign, such as pre-school activities in disadvantaged areas. The intrusiveness of the technique must be weighed against the positive outcomes, with each closely analysed. Do pre-school programs or prenatal care really affect behaviour in adolescence and beyond? While there is some evidence that this is the case, should they be conceived of as part of a crime-reduction strategy, with the stigma that entails, or are they simply a normal part of society's responsibility to its citizens? Some intrusions, such as sterilisation, should be disallowed on ethical grounds alone. Alternatively, a focus on the characteristics of an individual also may provide a ready excuse to cut government services; that is, to reduce the level of general state intervention. If violence within schools, for example, can be pinpointed to certain individuals, governments may decide that general programs to help disadvantaged schools are no longer necessary, because the problem has been isolated to individuals and 'dealt with'.

Positivism, with its focus on the scientific method, leads to the production of knowledge that by its nature is inaccessible to the general community. Commonsense understandings of ordinary people are seen as unscientific, and therefore not valid. This reduces the accountability of such professionals, and leaves little avenue for democratic participation in policy that results from positivist research. Specialised knowledge tends to entrench power in the hands of medical or paramedical professionals and other experts. Ironically though, given the inaccessibility of biological and psychological positivism, these approaches are often deployed in commonsense understandings of crime and criminality (such as the popularity of television shows such as *CSI*, *Criminal Minds*, and *Wire in the Blood*, which present largely biological and/or psychological explanations for crime).

As we have seen, it is the forensic psychiatrists and psychologists who are most likely to perform this role of the expert. Judges are particularly sensitive to the concerns of the community regarding the possibility of releasing someone who is a danger to the public at large, and so will draw on this expertise. However, there remain major problems in predicting which person will, and which person will not, pose danger to the community in the future.

The inability to predict dangerousness was dramatically illustrated in New York in the 1970s. A man by the name of Johnnie Baxtrom had been kept in prison after his release date because doctors argued he was dangerous and in need of psychiatric care. All psychiatric hospitals were full, so he remained in prison. Baxtrom challenged the constitutionality of his incarceration beyond the end of his sentence for assault. He won his case, and as a result 967 similarly incarcerated patients were released, all of whom were considered criminally insane (that is, they were considered a danger to the community). A team of researchers, led by Henry Steadman, followed up each of these people after four years in order to ascertain how many had reoffended. Only 2.7 per cent of the original 967 had behaved dangerously and were either in a correctional facility or a hospital for the criminally insane (Steadman 1973). Studies such as this pose tough questions to those who incarcerate individuals deemed to be a danger to the community beyond the term warranted by their criminal offence.

Certainly there have been improvements in the prediction of dangerousness. Forensic psychologists now estimate that they are right in their predictions of dangerousness in about 50 per cent of cases (Litwack & Schlesinger 1999). Nonetheless, significant problems remain. The first is that this percentage still remains the same as chance; that is, in one out of two cases the forensic expert will be wrong. The second is that forensic psychologists will readily agree that they are ascertaining the level of risk a particular offender poses to the community, which is separate from a prediction of actual violent behaviour occurring. This is because the context of violence is an important precursor to a violent crime occurring, and it is these contextual factors that are impossible to predict. No one can tell if an aggressive person will wake up in a bad mood exactly at the same time a number of unrelated events occur (such as a chance meeting with an old enemy, losing a job, or having a car accident), events that tip that person over into violent behaviour. Finally, such assessments can only be made when the person is found and assessed. In many cases, what criminal authorities want to know is the dangerousness of an individual who remains at large—hence the attraction of criminal profiling. This is an entirely separate problem to that of a risk assessment of a person brought to a forensic psychologist or psychiatrist. There remains considerable debate as to the efficacy of criminal profiling. The problem of 'false positives'—bringing under suspicion people who are innocent simply because they match certain personality traits or live in a certain area— remains a major concern.

These criticisms aside, the impact of positivism has been beneficial. It did signal a shift away from hardline classical thinking concerning individual responsibility. People can act for reasons that are outside their own control, and such factors may mitigate their responsibility for their criminal behaviour. Further, punishment must fail if it does not take account of factors that are beyond the control of an individual's free will. Indeed, analysis by Garland (2001) suggests that policies arising out of positivism emphasising the possibility and need for rehabilitation acted as a check on populist impulses towards harsher and harsher sentencing. The decline in faith in expertise since the late 1970s has brought with it a scepticism about rehabilitation, and a considerable increase in imprisonment rates and the length of sentences throughout much of the industrialised world.

{conclusion}

Positivism emerged within a specific historical context that promoted the virtues of scientific reasoning over the philosophical approach championed by the classical thinkers. It was assumed that discoveries about the natural world, and natural laws, would find a counterpart within human behaviour, both individual and social. The emphasis of positivism is on the scientist as neutral observer with the task of uncovering natural laws that regulate human behaviour, including criminal offending. Specific methods, such as experimentation and survey design, are seen to be able to reveal specific causes of criminal behaviour within the individual, causes that are either biologically or psychologically determined. Once causes have been discovered, reduction of offending is seen as possible through treatment programs aimed at ameliorating or eliminating causal agents. Sentencing should therefore be aimed at rehabilitation rather than deterrence. Further extension of investigation into individuals who are 'at risk' of offending may be seen as preferable, since offences may be prevented before they even occur.

Criticisms of positivism centre on the characterisation of criminal offending as akin to a sickness. While criminal behaviour may well be defined as deviation from society's norms, such norms are determined socially, not biologically, and are not universal. Further, society's norms may in fact be the norms of the dominant majority, which marginalise the norms of other social groups within society. In this way positivist research may entrench the current social order by accepting dominant understandings of 'normal' and 'deviant'. Further, positivism has a tendency to reduce the complexities of human behaviour to single identifiable causes, and to prescribe treatments that are intrusive, and in some cases unethical.

Recent writing within positivism has tended to move away from overarching generalisations concerning human behaviour (Moffitt 1993). Fishbein (1990) and, more recently, Anderson (2007) and Rafter (2008) serve as good examples of theorists who seek to establish the place of biological and psychological factors among others as the reasons behind criminal offending. They accept, for example, the very real place of environmental and sociological factors behind offending. It is to these factors that we now turn.

{further reading}

Anderson, G. (2007). *Biological Influences on Criminal Behavior*, Simon Fraser University Publications/CRC Press, Boca Raton, FL.

Baker, A.B., Tuvblad, C. & Raine, A. (2010). 'Genetics and Crime', in E. McLaughlin & T. Newburn (eds), *The SAGE Handbook of Criminological Theory*, SAGE, London: 21-39.

Duster, T. (2003). *Backdoor to Eugenics*, Routledge, New York.

Eysenck, H. (1984). 'Crime and Personality', in D. Muller, D. Blackmann & A. Chapmann (eds), *Psychology and Law*, John Wiley & Sons, New York.

Fishbein, D. (1990). 'Biological Perspectives in Criminology', *Criminology*, 28 (1): 27-72.

Gadd, D. & T. Jefferson (2007). *Psychosocial Criminology*, SAGE: London.

Garland, D. (1988). 'British Criminology before 1935', *British Journal of Criminology*, 28 (2): 1-16.

Lombroso, C. (1911). *Crime: Its Causes and Remedies*, Little, Brown, Boston.

Moffitt, T. (1993). 'The Neuropsychology of Conduct Disorder', *Development and Psychopathology*, 5 (1-2): 135-51.

Rafter, N. (2008) *The Criminal Brain: Understanding Biological Theories of Crime*, New York University Press, New York.

strain theory

{introduction}
—

This chapter provides an overview of various types of strain theory, and includes a discussion of subcultures and the ways in which deviant or criminal behaviour is learned in interaction with others. Rather than focusing on factors relating to the individual, these types of theories are sociological in nature; that is, they point to aspects of social structure and social learning that contribute to the creation of criminal behaviour and attitudes.

While sharing many of the philosophical and political features of biological and psychological positivism, sociological approaches such as strain theory view crime as manifestations of social pathology, rather than individual pathology. For example, tension or strains are seen to be generated by society itself; they do not reside within the individual (as in the case, for example, of a person feeling strained or pressured by circumstance). The chapter discusses the two main wings of strain theory — those that place emphasis on 'opportunity structures', and those that speak about the learning of particular norms, values and subcultural attributes.

—

social context

The social context in which strain theory emerged and developed can be divided into three key periods. The first period was from the middle of the nineteenth century to the beginning of the twentieth, which saw the rise of sociology as an academic discipline. As with comparable social sciences (such as psychology), it was felt that one could apply the approaches and concepts of the natural sciences to the study of society. In particular, society itself could be studied as if it were external to the observer. As with positivism in general, most sociology presumed that there existed a consensus of values and norms across a society (although these may differ between societies). The role of the social scientist was to intervene in shaping the direction of social development by providing positive solutions to identified social problems.

The sociological method adopted at this time was one that constructed broad categories of different types of societies (such as pre-industrial, industrial), and that attempted to show how the structure of a society moulds and shapes individual behaviour. Criminal behaviour, in particular, was seen as a manifestation of a social pathology—the outcome of something wrong in the structures and values of the society generally. Thus, if we are to respond adequately to the incidence of crime, we must go beyond measures that see it as being simply the result of individual malaise. Some type of institutional reform would be necessary if the problem were particularly acute.

The second key period in the development of strain theory was the early 1920s through to the Second World War. The industrial revolution had fostered the development of the professions (including sociology) and was linked to the idea of expert or technical solutions to problems such as poverty and crime. By the early decades of the twentieth century, the conceptual tools of sociology and criminology were being turned to examine problems with a specifically modern character.

In 1917 the Russian Revolution occurred, with long and lasting impact on developments in the West. A series of class struggles and armed conflict occurred throughout Europe in the early 1920s, and the example of a successful workers' revolution was creating alarm in ruling circles in the advanced capitalist countries. Within Russia itself, many people were displaced from their former positions and residences, and later, under the rule of Stalin, a series of purges that cost millions of lives was carried out.

Meanwhile, two further developments were accelerating the tendency towards crisis and war in Europe. On the one hand, one legacy of the First World War was a German nation that had suffered impoverishment and deep loss of dignity as a result of the actions of the victors. As in Spain in the 1930s, and later in Italy, there also arose a strong fascist movement in Germany by the early 1930s. Simultaneously, from 1929 the Great Depression was having a devastating impact on workers and farmers in Europe, North America and elsewhere.

The developments in Europe and the newly constructed Soviet Union, combined with the dramatic changes in economic fortunes, were to lead to mass movements of people. Events such as the counter-revolutionary war in Russia, the purge of selected classes and social groups across different political systems (such as attacks on Jews in Nazi Germany, forced collectivisation of farmers in Russia), and the difficulties of economic survival under rampant inflation and high levels of unemployment created large numbers of war, political and economic refugees in Europe. This led to widescale migration to countries such as the USA and Canada, as well as Australia and New Zealand.

A crucial question emerged within the ranks of those who were studying crime as a social phenomenon: in what ways did the successive waves of immigration have an impact upon crime rates? Furthermore, the issues of unemployment and poverty were put on the agenda in a more systematic and theoretically informed manner by sociologists. These issues were particularly of interest to researchers in the USA. While such people were unlikely to suggest a Russian-style revolution as an appropriate or desirable response to the depression in the heartland of world capitalism, clear links were now being drawn between unemployment and crime. The economic position of the individual in society was now seen as an important factor in the commission of crime.

The third period of note with respect to the development of strain theory was the postwar period of the late 1940s and into the 1950s. By this time, many of the advanced capitalist countries had entered a long boom period of economic growth. People in these countries were generally optimistic about the future, living standards were rising steadily, and capitalism was indeed appearing, for many, to be the 'best of all possible worlds'. The problem, however, was how to explain persistent crime rates even in the face of apparently good general economic and social conditions. The answer, here, was to examine more closely the distribution of opportunities in society, and also the ways in which people interact with and learn from each other.

As with the general orientation of strain theory, the intellectual task was to formulate concepts that would best express the social nature of crime.

It is suggested that we are now entering a fourth phase of strain theory, with a renewed interest in the works of Durkheim (1960 [1893], 1964 [1895], 1979 [1897]), Merton (1938, 1957 [1949]) and Cloward & Ohlin (1960). The core concepts of strain theory have recently been adapted to more adequately capture contemporary strains. Agnew (2005, 2002) and others have used a general theory of crime to investigate how delinquency, cyber-bullying (Hay et al. 2010), terrorism (Agnew 2010; Tiryakian 2005), racism (Hoskin 2011) and hate crime (Walters 2010) can be understood as a consequence of strain.

basic concepts

The starting point for strain theory is the notion that crime is essentially a social phenomenon (see chart 4.1). It is based upon a sociological understanding of individual and group behaviour—one that sees specific activity such as crime as somehow being related to and shaped by wider social processes and structures.

chart 4.1 | **strain theory**

definition of crime	_ natural _ violation of consensus
focus of analysis	_ structure of opportunities _ nature of social learning _ youth subcultures
cause of crime	_ social strain, viz. opportunity structure _ learned behaviour
nature of offender	_ determined (by) social pathology
response to crime	_ provide an opportunity to reduce strain _ resocialise offender
crime prevention	_ expanding opportunity and fostering healthy peer group activity
operation of criminal justice system	_ essentially neutral _ individual rehabilitation combined with social programs

Rather than looking at aspects of personal psychology or individual biological traits, strain theory argues that crime is socially induced. Thus, a 'criminal' or 'deviant' is a product of a specific kind of social order. In essence, the activities and values of the offender are *determined* by wider societal forces and factors, and offenders have few conscious choices regarding their available social options.

Crime tends to be defined in conventional terms. However, rather than viewing it as solely the behaviour that formally violates the legal code (as evidenced by court conviction records), strain theory sees crime and deviancy in wider terms. In particular, crime is seen as any *violation of the general consensus* of values and norms in society. As with positivist approaches, given this definition, and given the high levels of activity that go undetected by the formal criminal justice system, it is important to measure *natural crime* by alternative means. For strain theorists, alternative means might include things such as victim surveys and self-report studies.

The basic proposition of strain theory is that crime is a result of social disjuncture or social processes that represent a *social strain* within a society. The strains or sources of tensions are social, not individual, in nature; that is, the cause of crime is located in social structures and/or value systems that in some way are socially pathological. It is this wider *social pathology* that best explains crime as a social problem.

The main focus of analysis in strain theory is on strains associated with 'structural opportunities' and 'cultural processes'. The cause of crime is often seen to lie in offenders having inadequate or inappropriate means or *opportunities* to achieve certain goals relative to other people in society. Hence this aspect or type of strain theory is sometimes referred to as 'opportunity theory'. It is argued that restricted or blocked opportunities can lead some people to pursue alternative means, including criminal avenues, to gain desired social goods.

A second broad approach examines how, through various social circumstances, people associate with others who share their *cultural understandings* regarding acceptable and unacceptable behaviour. The emphasis in this kind of approach is on how criminal behaviour is learned in social situations. Analysis of particular subcultures and how norms and values are transmitted from one person to another is undertaken. This type of analysis is sometimes called 'social learning theory' or 'subcultural theory'.

According to strain theories, the response to crime and to the reduction of the likelihood of future offending is to *enhance opportunities* in order to reduce social strain. This can take the form of educational programs, employment projects, and leisure and recreation outlets for particularly 'disadvantaged' individuals and groups. A related crime-reduction strategy is to *re-socialise* offenders into conventional goals and means. This may involve removing them from their previous associates in order to minimise the learning and/ or affirmation of deviant norms and values. Overall, the stress is to combine *individual rehabilitation* with a series of social programs.

From the point of view of crime prevention, strain theory leans towards measures that *expand educational, employment and social opportunities* and *foster healthy peer group activity*. The focus is on developing strategies and policies that involve some degree of institutional reform, rather than solely changing or modifying the individual in some way. Since deviance or criminality is related to problems faced by groups of individuals in disadvantaged situations, the solution to crime must be to remedy the disadvantage as far as possible.

historical development

Contemporary strain theories have their origins in the emergence of sociology as an academic discipline and a recognised field of intellectual endeavour. One of the central figures in this process was French sociologist Émile Durkheim, who was writing at the end of the nineteenth and beginning of the twentieth centuries. His work was of great importance, in that he consistently presented analysis of society, and of social problems, in a manner that demonstrated the close relationship between social structure (the organisation of society) and the norms and values of society (social and cultural life) (1960 [1893], 1979 [1897]).

Durkheim's analysis was premised upon the notion that there are 'social facts' that can be studied and used to describe social phenomena (see Lukes 1973; Alexander & Smith 2005). These social facts are seen to be independent of the wishes or actions of individual people. While external to individuals, nevertheless a certain phenomenon has a marked impact upon their behaviours. Thus, for example, one can quantify such social facts as the distribution of population in a certain area or district, or one can ascertain the prevailing norms, rules, regulations, religious beliefs and legal codes of a society. In either case, these kinds of phenomena represent social facts, which can be measured and which exist as independent entities in their own right.

In order to analyse a particular social phenomenon, it is necessary to acknowledge that different societies give rise to different structures, beliefs and sentiments, and thus different behavioural patterns. In his famous study of suicide, for instance, Durkheim (1979 [1897]) demonstrated empirically that suicide rates vary according to whether or not a country is predominantly Catholic or predominantly Protestant in its religious orientation. The point here is that suicide could not be explained simply or solely in terms of individualistic choices or psychological factors. It is a social phenomenon.

More generally, Durkheim employed two basic conceptual tools in analysis of society (1960 [1893]). On the one hand, it was argued that society is structured around a particular kind of 'division of labour', with specific types of work tasks and roles. A distinction is made between mechanical solidarity and organic solidarity as indications of the division of labour. The first describes pre-industrial types of society in which individuals tend to share the same skills, work tasks, customs, beliefs and religion. The second describes an industrial society, which is far more heterogeneous in terms of wealth, ethnicity, religions and beliefs, and which has a high level of work specialisation.

On the other hand, each society was said to be characterised by a particular form of collective conscience (or consciousness). This referred to a set of beliefs and sentiments common to a whole society, which forms a determinate system. What we collectively think is greater than the thoughts of any one individual, and the collective conscience has the feature of shaping and regulating our behaviour as an independent, powerful external force. Crime plays a central role here. Defining a behaviour or event as criminal builds a cohesiveness within a society. Individuals and groups signal their belonging to a society by denouncing certain behaviour as 'criminal'. In this way, crime is a normal, even necessary part of any society. In a very real sense, society defines itself by what it is not—and what it is not is defined as criminal. It is useful to note that this aspect of Durkheim's view was not picked up by strain theory. Durkheim did not, however, see all crime as normal. He argued that when a society is dysfunctional, either through a lack of an adequate collective conscience (which could be either too repressive or not provide an adequate sense of direction for society members) or through a lack of adequate provision of roles for individuals within that society, then abnormal levels of crime would be found. A sick society led to pathological levels of crime.

In a society characterised by mechanical solidarity, the emphasis tends to be on rigid conformity and cultural homogeneity. Alternatively, the organic solidarity of industrial society is one in which people are linked though law and interdependence, rather than similarity of life experience. In applying these concepts to the specific area of criminology, Durkheim was able to argue that the nature of the society in which one lives will determine the manner in which deviants will be dealt with (1960 [1893]; Inverarity et al. 1983; Cladis 2005). A society with mechanical solidarity tends to generate repressive justice, which reaffirms the common beliefs and values by distancing the deviant from the wider collectivity. Conversely, a society with organic solidarity tends to generate restitutive sanctions, which aim to restore the social disruption by reintegrating the deviant back into the network of interdependencies.

Fundamentally, the organisation of society, as shaped by its division of labour and its collective conscience, determines the nature of crime and the regulation of criminal behaviour. Durkheim said that where you have an unhealthy division of labour (based upon force rather than choice) or an unhealthy regulation of the collective conscience (norms not well established), there is greater likelihood of widespread crime, and the level of crime will be greater (1964 [1895]).

A normal, healthy division of labour occurs where occupational relationships are in accordance with individuals' aptitudes. In such a situation, two potential types of deviant can be identified: the biological deviant (who is impossible to predict or prevent), and the functional rebel (who acts as a constructive force for limited social change). Where there is an unhealthy or pathological division of labour, there will be conflict between the individual and the social; that is, it will be difficult to regulate the behaviour of individuals in a society under such circumstances.

Societies vary in their ability to impose social regulation, and this is due in part to the nature of the division of labour. The collective conscience may not be developed sufficiently, or may be skewed in some way, and this can affect behaviour as well. The general condition of society (not the individual) may be one where norms and values are in flux or even partially destroyed. We may thus have a situation in which shared beliefs and values have broken down, and where moral guides to, and constraints on, behaviour have weakened (see Bauman 2005). Applying these ideas to the specific area of crime and deviancy, it is argued that a healthy society is characterised by a collective conscience that regulates behaviour smoothly. An unhealthy society is one in which values are not well established, or where they work against the aims of integration and regulation (Agnew 2006b).

According to Durkheim, individual desires are unlimited; it is the society that gives direction and a limit to desire. Durkheim drew a distinction between 'egoism' and 'anomie', both of which revolve around social norms (1979 [1897]). *Egoism* refers to the desires of the 'pre-social self', desires that society must shape and limit. Dysfunctional societies can be characterised by an overemphasis on egoism, where value is placed on the unrestricted pursuit of individual desires. Here, the norms of society itself can produce deviant behaviour. The concept of *anomie* refers to a lack of social regulation in which the unrestricted appetites of the individual conscience are no longer held in check: we have a state of normlessness in which society fails to impose norms that inhibit such behaviour. This would describe, for example, a society or community at breaking point, where rapid change has destroyed many of the values and norms. Societies experiencing either kind of normative problem would be expected to have abnormal levels of crime.

The most important contribution from Durkheim, within the strain theory tradition, is that he established that crime is essentially a social phenomenon; it is inextricably related to the nature of society itself. Criminality is thus a product of a specific kind of social order. Moreover, it was Durkheim who emphasised that crime is a result of social disjuncture or social strains in a society. These are linked to both the division of labour (later seen in terms of opportunity structures) and the collective conscience (later seen in terms of cultural norms and learned behaviours).

¬ crime and opportunity

These themes were picked up by later theorists in several different ways. Drawing on the early work of the Chicago School (particularly, Park et al. 1967 [1925]), Shaw and McKay (1942) explained crime in terms of social disorganisation theory. The main focus of their work was on the links between a particular kind of urban environment, and the nature and extent of crime associated with this. More specifically, the researchers were interested in undertaking a form of 'social ecology' that examined crime in terms of the changing composition and settlement patterns of the city.

Based in Chicago, Shaw and McKay were writing at a time of great change. The political turmoil and economic hardship experienced by many people in Europe translated at a practical level into mass migration to other parts of the world and, in particular, to the USA. Shaw and McKay (1942) were interested in the way in which the successive waves of immigration were linked to the incidence of crime in American cities. Accordingly, they studied the settlement patterns of migrants, noting the movement first into the spatial grid of the inner-city neighbourhoods and then into outer-city areas.

The process of settling into a new country was accompanied by high levels of chaos and tension, and whole communities were characterised as being in a constant state of change, flux and social disorganisation. Shaw and McKay (1942) examined documents relating to the life histories of juvenile offenders in these areas. They found that crime tended to be associated with particular neighbourhoods, and that it flowed from the cyclical process of social change involving shifts in basic social organisation, towards disorganisation and reorganisation. They argued that delinquency can be viewed as part of the natural process of migrant settlement, because customary social controls that normally produce conformist behaviour are disrupted in such circumstances.

To put it differently, Shaw and McKay (1942) believed that behaviour is regulated via customary social norms and values. In a situation of high social disorganisation, characteristic of concentrated immigrant settlements in the inner city, young people are not subject to the same kinds of controls that customarily produced conforming behaviour in their country of origin. Furthermore, young people in these circumstances will also tend to associate with like-minded individuals who are sharing the same kind of transitional experiences. Since the neighbourhood is in a state of flux, the behaviour of such young people will tend also to include delinquent acts (see Shoemaker 1984).

While Shaw and McKay initially concentrated on the issue of a disorganised and transient population, the impact of the Great Depression prompted them to refine their analysis. They began to look beyond the link between immigration, settlement patterns and crime. They also acknowledged the social strains caused by poverty and unemployment (Shaw and McKay 1942). Economic deprivation meant that, even where mainstream goals had been internalised, people were denied opportunities to achieve those goals. Thus a depressed and stratified economic structure could engender conditions that lead to a greater incidence of crime.

While depressed economic conditions and overall diminished job opportunities seem to provide a reasonable explanation for some types of criminal activity, how are we to explain the incidence of crime in periods of economic growth? This was the dilemma facing sociologists and criminologists in the 1950s.

The first two decades after the Second World War were characterised by low unemployment levels and high standards of living in the advanced capitalist countries. It was a time of general economic prosperity. Politically, the 1950s was stamped by the contours of the Cold War into which the two superpowers—the USA and the Soviet Union— were locked, along with their allies. This manifested itself in virulent anticommunist campaigns in the West, such as the public attacks on the left in the USA by the House Un-American Activities Committee, led by Senator Joe McCarthy, and in Australia the attempts by the Menzies government to ban the Communist Party of Australia. It was a time of general political conformity.

It was in this climate that Merton (1957 [1949]) sought to offer an explanation for the continued existence of crime in the USA. In seeking to explain the prevalence of crime, he embraced the notion that crime rates are related to society's ability to establish norms that regulate the behaviour of the populace. Merton argued that crime can be understood in relation to two main variables: the *culturally defined goals* of a society; and the *institutionalised means* whereby one can attain these goals. 'Mal-integration' occurs when there is a disjuncture between the cultural goals and the institutional means.

Merton argued that all individuals basically share in the same cultural goal—the 'American Dream' of wealth, status and success—but they have different institutional means available to them. In particular, some people experience blocked opportunities, and thus are unable to achieve their goals through normal or legitimate means.

In such circumstances, people are perceived as having the capacity to make meaningful choices as to how to negotiate their futures. That is, depending upon the opportunities available to them, people decide to accept or reject the cultural goals, and to accept or reject the institutional means to attain commonly accepted goals. The decisions one makes are determined or shaped by one's position or status in society. For example, those people at the lower end of the socio-economic ladder will experience a greater likelihood of blocked opportunities than those from better-off or wealthy families. This has an impact on behaviour.

Merton (1957 [1949]) developed an abstract typology of responses to the means–ends equation. The typology described individual adaptations to goals and means. People can respond in five different ways to the structure of opportunities available:

1\ *Conformism*—those who accept the culturally defined goals (such as financial success) and the institutionalised means of attaining them (such as education).

2\ *Innovation*—those who accept the culturally defined goals, but who lack the institutionalised means to attain them. They therefore resort to innovative means to attain the goals, such as turning to crime (for example, robbing a bank).

3\ *Ritualism*—those who accept the culturally defined goals, but who know they cannot attain them. Nevertheless, they continue pursuing institutional means (for example, by staying at school when no jobs are available), regardless of the outcome.

4\ *Retreatism*—those who reject both the culturally defined goals and the institutionalised means of attaining them. They retreat from society in varying ways (such as substance abuse).

5\ *Rebellion*—those who substitute their own cultural goals and institutionalised means in place of the conventional goals and means in society. They create their own goals and means of achieving them (for example, an ecologically sustainable hippie lifestyle).

From the point of view of strain theory, the choices available to people reflect problems stemming from the structure of the society itself. That is, the relationship between cultural goals and institutional means ultimately determines the kinds of opportunities and choices that are available to different groups of people (Rosenfeld & Messner 1995).

¬ crime and culture

The structure of opportunities constitutes one part of the criminal behaviour puzzle. The other part, according to some theorists, is the ideas that people hold regarding what is acceptable or unacceptable behaviour. Specifically, attention was directed to issues of culture and the ways in which young people, in particular, learn certain ways of doing things and certain attitudes towards others.

The work done by Sutherland and Cressy (1974), for example, was directed at explaining the nature and development of youth subcultures. They argued that crime was cultural in nature, in the sense that it is *learned behaviour*. People in particular neighbourhoods, or particular social situations, learn about criminal behaviour by interacting with other people. The most significant interaction occurs within intimate personal groups, which of course includes peer groups.

Sutherland and Cressy developed the concept of *differential association* to describe a process by which behaviour is differentially associated, insofar as some individuals will associate with carriers of criminal norms, while others will not.

They discussed the process that occurs when a criminal association does take place. The learning of criminal behaviour includes:

- the techniques of committing a crime (for example, how to hot-wire a car in order to steal it)

- the motives, drives, attitudes and rationalisations associated with crime (for example, stealing only Porsche cars, because 'the owners can afford it anyway')

- the definition of the legal code within particular criminal subcultures (for example, car theft is not seen as wrong since no one gets hurt (as in the case of assault), and car owners commonly have insurance).

Differential associations may vary in frequency and duration, priority and intensity. Those persons who become delinquent or persistent offenders do so because of a greater number of definitions favourable to violation of the law over definitions unfavourable to violations. This in turn is shaped by group interaction. For example, an individual may associate with a delinquent group, and then later change that orientation by associating with a non-delinquent group.

The essential point of the theory is that criminal behaviour is learned. Because learning takes place in the context of specific types of group formation, and particular types of definitions of behaviour and attitudes, the issues of peer group pressure and offending cultures are seen as of central importance.

The idea that people learn to associate certain classes of conduct, either legal or illegal, with the group's approval or disapproval has obvious links to analysis of subcultures *per se*; that is, deviant or criminal behaviour is collective in nature, and is based on shared experiences and perceptions. From within the strain theory tradition, various writers have argued that the strain between cultural goals and institutional means is reflected in specific class cultures.

Albert Cohen (1955) argued that working-class subcultures can be seen as a product of a conflict between working-class and middle-class cultures. That is, such a subculture is an alternative cultural system that develops as a result of the blocked opportunities and low self-esteem experienced by working-class young people. Instead of measuring 'success' in conventional terms, then, the group focuses on alternative goals that are more directly related to their own class experiences. Whereas Merton's typology spoke of the disappointed individual, Cohen saw crime and delinquency in terms of collective behaviour associated with the different aspirations, expectations and lived experiences of two different class groupings. For Cohen, the school was the point at which lower-class youth understood their choices were constrained by society.

Going one step further, Cloward and Ohlin (1960) put forward the view that, in fact, all classes have the same basic cultural goals (wealth, success, security), but that the working class as a class is disadvantaged in gaining these desired ends. Crime is indeed collective in nature (you learn from your peers), and some groups of working-class children who consider their opportunities to be blocked will adopt criminal or alternative opportunity structures as a result. In other words, illegitimate opportunity structures will develop in those situations where the culturally defined goals are still sought, but legitimate opportunities are blocked or absent. The issue here is not a conflict between middle-class and working-class cultures, but the relationship of certain subcultural practices to specific class backgrounds (that is, a sense of injustice at the lack of opportunities).

Other explanations of subcultural form were provided by both Matza (1964) and Downes (1966). These writers argued that working-class young people neither rejected nor inverted the dominant culturally prescribed values of society. Instead, they saw working-class youth subcultures as simply accentuating particular 'subterranean values' (risk, adventure, fun) that are part of normal society, but which are sometimes taken too far. In response to restricted access to opportunity, the response of young people is to resort to forms of 'manufactured excitement' of their own.

then & now

strain theory

Strain theory can be understood as part of a range of theories that look to society as the starting point for understanding crime. These theories include *social ecology*, which emphasises social disorganisation and the built environment; *opportunity theory*, which emphasises the disjunction between societal goals and individual means to attain these goals; and *subcultural theories*, which emphasise group responses to social strains generated by inequality and social marginalisation. Each of these theoretical contributions retains a strong presence within criminology. For example, the work of Elijah Anderson (1999) and William Julius Wilson (1996) in their research on Black neighbourhoods in the USA emphasise lack of opportunities, social dislocation and, for Anderson, subcultural mores that are ultimately self-defeating. This emphasis on responses to social conditions and, in particular, the recent work emphasising the centrality of 'respect' has seen these theories draw on themes that are also present in labelling perspectives and cultural criminology, in particular the work of Katz (Chapter 5), and in critical criminology (Chapter 11).

---

contemporary examples

The appeal of strain theory is that it attempts to provide a sociological explanation for the causes of crime. As we have seen, crime is usually related to blocked opportunities, combined with the activities of particular subcultural groups. While several theorists addressed the criticisms of strain theory (as it developed from Merton, Cloward and Ohlin, and Cohen)—in particular, Greenberg's (1976) work on autonomy, and Messerschmidt's (1993) research on masculinity and crime—it was not until Agnew's work on general strain theory (GST) that the concept of strain was reconstituted. This contemporary development of strain theory went beyond the *objective* strains identified in early research (such as those events or conditions that were thought to be a universal) to include those strains that were stressful or negative for the individual (Agnew 2006b). For example, the closure of a large employer in a small town could be considered an objective strain; however, on closer investigation, some individuals may not be so badly affected or strained by this event (perhaps because other employment opportunities are available to them, or it may give the individual a chance to return to education to retrain in another field).

Further, Agnew identified that beyond the *experience* of strain, individuals could be affected by *vicarious* strains (such as those imposed on friends and family), and *anticipated* strains (such as those generated out of *fear* of crime) (Agnew 2002). He also identified three categories of strain:

1\ loss of legal avenues to attain goals (such as loss of secure employment, or autonomy)
2\ loss of positively valued stimuli (such as friends, romantic partners, money)
3\ experiences of negatively valued stimuli (such as verbal and physical abuse).

According to Agnew & Brezina (2010) strains are most likely to result in criminal behaviour if they are thought by the individual to be

(a) insurmountable, (b) unjust, (c), subject to limited social control, and (d) subject to pressure or incentive to act negatively. Within this framework, importantly, strains do not inevitably lead to crime or criminality. Some individual- and social-level factors 'immunise' individuals from responding to strain through crime. Those who are not able to react to strain positively are more likely to have:

- high criminal coping skills and resources (such as criminal self-efficacy)
- high negative social capital (such as criminal associations and/or family networks)
- low conventional social capital and support (such as positive role models, access to social workers/lawyers)
- low social control (such as negative emotionality, loss of conventional moral and ethical guidelines)
- exposure to high 'benefits' and low 'costs' of crime (such as an absence of moral entrepreneurs and target hardening, use of drugs and alcohol) (Agnew & Brezina 2010).

There are several broad strands to contemporary strain theory that seek to investigate the factors identified in Agnew's general strain theory. For example, there is a growing body of work in the area of *social ecology*. Part of this research looks at how aspects of the physical and social environment at the local level influence patterns of offending and the fear of crime. The emphasis is on exploring the spatial features of offences and offending by examining the natural and built environments, studying the actions of individuals and groups within certain places at certain times of the day or week, and evaluating the processes of social regulation as these pertain to specific city sites, residential areas and commercial districts (see Evans et al. 1992; Bottoms & Wiles 1997; Taylor 2001; Bottoms 2007; Zahn & Browne 2009; Agnew 2011; Bichler et al. 2011). The intention of such research is to explain the uneven distribution and impact of crime, and to develop crime prevention and policing strategies that take into account characteristics of the local environment.

Another related approach is that which provides a theory of crime based upon analysis of community-level *social disorganisation* (Kubrin & Weitzer 2003). Again, the main focus is on particular kinds of neighbourhood areas, such as inner-city ghettos. It is argued that, for example, persistent high crime among African-American youth is a result of both structural and cultural factors. Specifically, a 'culture of violence' is sustained among the new urban 'underclasses' through 'structural disorganization and cultural social isolation that stem from the concentration of poverty, family disruption, and residential instability' (Sampson & Wilson 1995: 14; see also Sampson et al. 1997; Sampson et al. 2002; Sampson & Laub 2004). More generally, such perspectives stress the importance of considering the impact of 'neighbourhood effect' when it comes to crime. That is, the social status and crime rate of a neighbourhood have been shown to have an effect on a person's chances of becoming involved in offending behaviour regardless of his or her specific socio-economic status (Reiss 1986). For instance, a young person from a low-income background living in a high-crime area is far more likely to engage in offending behaviour than an identical person living in a low-crime neighbourhood. Thus, community context is seen as an integral part of why some unemployed and marginalised young people have a greater propensity to commit crime than other similarly positioned young people.

Social ecology and social disorganisation perspectives combined can provide important insights into how and why certain communities are stigmatised and disadvantaged as communities. For example, research undertaken in the USA (Wilson 1996), Germany (Heitmeyer 2002) and Australia (Collins et al. 2000; Poynting et al. 2004) has pointed to the fusion of class and ethnic dynamics that have direct and indirect negative consequences for ethnic minorities. A crucial factor appears to be the location of specific minority groups in segregated ghettos, a process exacerbated by selected government policies and programs. The result of a concentration of ethnic minority groups in heavily disadvantaged areas is the systematic exclusion of these groups from mainstream social, economic and political life. It can also be associated with alternative forms of gaining social status, including the use of violence and reliance upon criminal or illegal activity.

An area of particular and growing interest to criminologists today is that of the study of *youth gangs* and youth in groups. This research has concentrated on providing detailed descriptions of specific types of youth group formations in places such as the USA (Klein et al. 1995; Huff 1996), Europe (Klein et al. 2001; Taniguchi et al. 2011), Australia (White 2002b, in press; White & Wyn 2008) and Canada (Gordon 1995; Gordon & Foley 1998). This kind of work has generally attempted to provide more precise definitions of different types of youth groups, to examine the kinds of activities and associations associated with diverse group formations, and to explain the origins, dynamics and changes in group formation as these relate to social, economic and policing factors. Significant issues include not only those of poverty and unemployment, but racism and the impact of ethnic divisions and inequality on group behaviour. Attention is also directed at patterns of policing, and how these impinge upon different populations of young people in different ways.

A large body of literature that is informed by what can be called *social development* theories has also emerged. This literature deals with the personal, family and social factors that influence the life chances and life decisions of young people. This research and theorising draws upon elements of strain theory, as well as ideas and findings more closely associated with biological and psychological research. For example, in a review of empirical research on the predictors and correlates of offending, Farrington (1996) provides a systematic outline of the key 'risk factors' associated with youthful offending. Among the many factors cited are:

- prenatal and perinatal factors (such as early child-bearing, substance use during pregnancy, low birth weight)
- hyperactivity and impulsivity (such as hyperactivity–impulsivity–attention deficit, inhibition)
- intelligence and attainment (for example, low non-verbal intelligence, abstract reasoning, cognitive and neuropsychological deficit)
- parental supervision, discipline and attitude (for example, erratic or harsh parental discipline, rejecting parental attitudes, violent behaviour)
- broken homes (for example, maternal and paternal deprivation, parental conflict)
- parental criminality (for example, convicted parents, poor supervision)
- large family size (for example, insufficient parental attention, overcrowding)
- socio-economic deprivation (for example, low family income, poor housing)
- peer influences (for example, male group behaviour, delinquent friends)
- school influences (for example, use of praise and punishment, classroom management)

- community influences (for example, high residential mobility, neighbourhood disorganisation, physical deterioration, overcrowding, type of housing)
- situational influences (for example, specific opportunities, benefits outweigh expected costs, seeking excitement).

The combination of these factors, and their association with certain categories of young people, are seen to explain variations in the propensity for criminal behaviour and criminalisation among young people (see also Sullivan & Hirschfield 2011; Tapia 2011). However, these risk factors are seen to coincide and to be interrelated in complex ways, and as such they do not yield easy or simple answers to the question of crime causation.

Researchers within this broad framework attempt to identify not only the range of 'risk factors' (such as drug abuse), but also those 'protective factors' (such as family cohesion) that influence whether or not an individual engages in criminal or antisocial behaviour (Catalano & Hawkins 1996; Hwang & Akers 2003; Morash & Chesney-Lind 2009). More generally, there is seen to be an overlap between offending behaviour and other types of problem behaviour, and a close connection between immediate social context and the developmental pathways of, in particular, serious and violent young offenders (Loeber & Farrington 1998; see also Rutter et al. 1998; Sellers et al. 2003; Simons & Burt 2011). This type of multifactoral perspective leans towards a quantitative and empirically based analysis of offending. As such, it pitches causal explanations not at the more general level of wider social structures, but at the immediate and observable features of society and behaviour (Agnew & Brezina 2010). For instance, poverty is treated as a risk factor, rather than a phenomenon stemming from, and requiring investigation in terms of, systemic social inequality.

The sophistication and complexity of the explanations broadly influenced by strain theory are mirrored in the incorporation of elements of the theory into other distinctive explanatory models. For example, the notion that there are distinct criminal subcultures is an important component of republican theory (discussed in Chapter 10).

{from theory to practice: cultural strain, race and violence}
———

Hoskin, A. (2011). 'Explaining the Link between Race and Violence with General Strain Theory', *Journal of Ethnicity in Criminal Justice*, 9 (1): 56–73.

Hoskin argues that Agnew's (1992; 2006a) general strain theory (GST) can assist in understanding the strain of race-related discrimination. In adopting Agnew's theory, Hoskin attempts to map the relationship between unjust strains and serious violent offending. According to the GST, life circumstances can create high levels of stress and strain, and, in some circumstances, illegal coping techniques (such as serious interpersonal violence) are employed.

African-Americans, when compared to White Americans, are more likely to encounter the three types of strains identified in GST (failure to achieve positive goals, withdrawal of positively valued stimuli and presentation of negatively valued stimuli) (Agnew 1992). Further, those strains perceived by individuals as unjust are more likely to lead to illegal coping mechanisms such as violent crime. In the case of race discrimination, the tendency towards the use of illegal coping mechanisms is exacerbated because the source of this unjust strain is other-directed and non-specific. Research into GST indicates that this can lead not only to frustration, anger and desire for revenge, but also to despair, hopelessness and depression (Hoskin 2011: 58). These strains are more likely to emerge during the adolescent years, with social and individual interactions in school and in the family strongly determining the likelihood of delinquency and interpersonal violence. These strains are evidenced in the African-American community by lower levels of education, increased chances of repeating a school year, higher dismissal rates, higher numbers of serious and fatal workplace injuries, increased subjection to of stop and search powers, higher levels of detention (even when other variables are taken into account), harsher sentences, and higher levels of police-involved homicide (Hoskin 2011: 59).

On the basis of these findings, Hoskin developed a hypothesis to test the relationship between serious offending and race discrimination. Importantly, in Agnew's GST, race discrimination is a specific form of only one of the three types of strains; that is, presentation of negatively valued stimuli. Using the first wave of data collected by the National Longitudinal Study of Adolescent Health (which is a national survey of students in the 1994–95 school year, in grades 7 to 12, who are followed through to adulthood), Hoskin (2011: 62) sampled all students who identified as African-American. He further sieved the data based on the mother's level of education to source respondents with fairly high socio-economic status (N = 726). He subjected the data to a logistic regression using the question, 'In the past 12 months, how often did you hurt someone badly enough to need bandages or care from a doctor or nurse?' as the dependent variable (Hoskin 2011: 62).

Just over a fifth of the respondents reported that they had seriously hurt someone at least once in the past 12 months (Hoskin 2011: 63); however, boys were much more likely to respond positively to this question (31 per cent compared to 14 per cent for girls). While gender was significantly related to violent behaviour, age and residential mobility were not significant predictors for African-American students. This result contradicts earlier research into GST, as does Hoskin's finding that only moodiness relates to violent behaviour (and not fearfulness, depression or getting very upset). Further, in this analysis of the data, high self-esteem was found to have a reverse effect on violent behaviour: that is, 'students who do not like themselves are significantly *less* likely to be in a fight that involves seriously injuring someone' (Hoskin 2011: 65, emphasis in original). Respondents who reported that students in their school were prejudiced were also significantly more likely to engage in violent offending.

Hoskin's research offers partial support for Agnew's general strain theory. However, it also highlights the problems that arise when unified theories attempt to capture universal human processes. Hoskin's research provides a much-needed critique of the GST in light of the race-specific strains and coping mechanisms encountered by African Americans.

critique

Strain theory represents a broad array of differing perspectives. In the light of this, the critique offered here highlights some of the problems with the main thrust of strain theory. In general, for example, a critique is possible of strain theory's almost exclusive focus on working-class crime.

Despite understanding the need to gauge levels of crime not reported to police within communities, strain theorists largely accepted the 'shape' of the official crime statistics, namely that the majority of offences are perpetrated by the working class. An exception to this was Sutherland (1983), who undertook groundbreaking work in the area of white-collar crime. The majority, however, accepted that the crime in working-class neighbourhoods was that which needed explaining and eradicating.

This reflected an acceptance of a consensus of values in society. Ultimately all people in society wanted to achieve the same goals and share the same lifestyle (again there are exceptions to the general view; see, for example, Miller 1958; Rosenfeld & Messner 1995; Young 2007). In this way, strain theory accepts the status quo. Rather than seeing the goals and aspirations of society as moulded by those in positions of power, strain theory sees such aspirations as a genuine consensus of values. Others argue that this is not necessarily the case at all. The acceptance of the genuine nature of the consensus is subject to challenges today, for example, by many churches, which argue against the materialistic nature of the 'American Dream'. Still others argue against the notion of any consensus by looking at entrenched conflicts of values and interests, as indicated for example in the work of Marxist, feminist and radical environmentalist writers (see for example, Jock Young's (2007) critique of strain theory in light of Bauman's notion of liquid modernity).

The concept of a general social consensus has several consequences. First, it denies pluralism of values in society. By definition, since there is consensus, a conflict of values must mean that one group's values are wrong. Second, strain theorists tended to accept that the gender roles in society were part of this consensus. Working in the 1950s, Cohen, for example, felt that the major strain in the lives of young women was the tension associated with wanting an ideal husband (Cohen 1955; Naffine 1987). It did not occur to him that the roles of young women in the 1950s were imposed, or that, given the choice, women might have a genuine desire to pursue a career outside the home. Furthermore, Cohen's view was distinctly middle class, since many working-class women needed to work to bring money into the family home. In working-class areas the strain of unemployment could be as great on working-class women as on their male counterparts. Fifty-five years after Cohen's work on delinquent boys, strain theorists (such as Agnew 2010; Zahn et al. 2009) are still arguing that research into gender differences of strains and coping strategies is required.

It can also be argued that, by accepting the status quo, in terms of 'core values', strain theory fails to take account of structural inequalities—the way the capitalist system by its very nature renders some people 'marginal' and so criminalises their activities. As theories in later chapters suggest, the system itself can be responsible for labelling some people and their activities criminal, while leaving alone other individuals whose activities are equally, or even more, harmful to society as a whole. The process of criminalisation is such that only those who challenge the status quo are labelled as criminal.

Without tackling issues relating to the inequalities of the system itself, some argue that strain theory simply attempts to adapt the individual to a system where, structurally, he or she has no place. Furthermore, there is often inbuilt resistance to this kind of change. Periodically, for example, the system will actively react against any (limited) attempts to 'adapt' marginalised groups and to provide them with equal opportunity. A good example of this 'reaction by the system' or 'backlash' is shown by the eventual collapse of the 'War on Poverty', a major initiative by the Kennedy and later the Johnston administrations in the USA. The aim of the initiative was to empower the poor in order to enable them to assimilate into the opportunity structure of American society. Part of the reason for the lack of effectiveness of this program was the resistance by those in power to the new realities created by the movement towards empowerment. While various factors led to the demise of the 'War on Poverty' (including some ill-conceived programs), the resistance to the status quo—and particularly politicians who were now faced with an organised, aggressive inner-city urban population—was certainly a major factor in sealing its fate.

Finally, it can be argued that some variants of strain theory oversimplified the link between lack of opportunity and crime. Subsequent studies have shown the link between unemployment and offending to be a very complex one (see especially Weatherburn & Lind 2001). There are also numerous additional factors (such as attachment to school, and family and peers who also offend), which are not accounted for in many of the theories discussed above. While there may indeed be some generalised strain that underlies offending, how this affects individuals, and why some individuals respond with offending behaviour and others do not, is not explained fully by strain and subculture theories. And while Agnew's 'work-in-progress' (Agnew & Brezina 2010) on a general strain theory (GST) has begun to resolve some of the issues identified above, these theoretical approaches remain embedded in notions of universal values and norms and, therefore, universal responses to strain.

Having said this, these theories highlight aspects of offending that were clearly absent from psychological and classical perspectives. They raised the level of debate away from a focus on the individual, to the influence society has on the criminal behaviour of some members of the working class. In doing so, it established a strong link between societal context and the nature of criminal or deviant activity. Furthermore, it recognised that criminal activity for those who lack opportunities is meaningful, given their reduced opportunities and/or peer group supports. Finally, it opened the way for more progressive reforms politically, and against kneejerk punitive approaches or intrusive psychological rehabilitation.

{conclusion}

From a strain theory perspective, crime is seen to be more a matter of 'normal' people in 'abnormal' situations, rather than disturbed individuals acting out their pathology (Gibbons 1979). This is clearly a sharp break from individualistic perspectives that locate deviant behaviour squarely in the choices or defects of each offender. These theories took, as a base, the sociological concepts of Durkheim (1960 [1893], 1964 [1895], 1979 [1897]), which steered them away from individual characteristics, and towards the social processes of anomie and social solidarity.

Within the aegis of strain theory there is a wide range of perspectives that share some similarities, yet also clearly differ in their detail and emphasis. Early theorists such as Shaw and McKay (1942) emphasised the disorganisation of the poor and lack of cohesive identity that lead to offending. Later theorists, such as Merton (1957 [1949]), emphasised the strain between goals and means, and the way criminality would be used to attain goals in the absence of legitimate avenues, such as access to employment and a career. Sutherland and Cressy (1974) shifted attention to the social interaction that leads to offending behaviour, and looked at the way criminal associations supply the techniques, motivations and rationalisations necessary to act criminally. Subcultural approaches, such as the work of Cohen (1955), and Cloward and Ohlin (1960), took association between individuals a step further, emphasising the formation of subcultures as a response to the lack of opportunity supplied by society to working-class youth.

The relationship between lack of opportunity, alienation and criminal behaviour is, if anything, more important in the current economic climate (see Agnew's work in this area as an example of the increased use of strain theories to understand contemporary social strain). Levels of youth unemployment are high, the inequalities between rich and poor continue to grow at an alarming rate, and strains have become global. If strain theorists are right, then the levels of youth crime and the levels of gang formation should also increase. These concerns are, in fact, being reflected in the formation of new international networks of researchers. The Eurogang Research Network (2011), for example, comprises researchers from over twenty-four different countries spanning Europe, Russia, North America and Australasia. A key task of this network is to provide grounded, specific research into the nature of youth group formations within the context of global processes relating to consumption, immigration, youth identity, employment trends and educational opportunities (see also White & Wyn 2008).

Strain and subculture theories began to move away from a concentration on the conditions of the offender, to the circumstances of criminalisation itself — that is, crime as a social process in response to the

··· inequalities in society. What was left unchallenged was the legitimacy of basic structures of society, and the way society itself influenced the way some activities were criminalised, and others not. This 'labelling process', the process of being seen as criminal, is the subject of the next chapter.

{**further reading**}

Agnew, R. (1992). 'Foundation for a General Strain Theory of Crime and Delinquency', *Criminology*, 30: 47–87.

Agnew, R. (2010). 'A General Strain Theory of Terrorism', *Theoretical Criminology*, 14 (2): 131–53.

Agnew, R. & Brezina, T. (2010). 'Strain Theories', in E. McLaughlin & T. Newburn (eds), *The SAGE Handbook of Criminological Theory*, SAGE, London: 96–113.

Anderson, E. (1999). *Code of the Street: Decency, Violence and the Moral Life of the Inner City*, W.W. Norton, New York.

Bottoms, A.E. (2007). 'Place, Space, Crime and Disorder', in M. Maguire et al. (eds), *The Oxford Handbook of Criminology*, Oxford University Press, Oxford, UK: 528–74.

Cloward, R. & Ohlin, L. (1960). *Delinquency and Opportunity: A Theory of Delinquent Gangs*, Free Press, Chicago.

Eurogang Research Network (2011).
'Eurogang Home Page', available
at <www.umsl.edu/~ccj/eurogang/
euroganghome.htm>, accessed 11
July 2011.

Farrington, D. (1996). 'The
Explanation and Prevention of
Juvenile Offending', in
J. Hawkins (ed.), *Delinquency
and Crime: Current Theories*,
Cambridge University Press,
Cambridge.

Merton, R. (1938). 'Social
Structure and Anomie', *American
Sociological Review*, 3: 672–82.

Merton, R. (1957 [1949]). *Social
Theory and Social Structure*,
Free Press, New York.

Polk, K. (1994a). *When Men Kill.
Scenarios of Masculine Violence*,
Cambridge University Press,
Melbourne.

Reiss, A. (1986). 'Why Are
Communities Important in
Understanding Crime?', in
A. Reiss & M. Tonry (eds),
Communities and Crime,
University of Chicago Press,
Chicago: 1–34.

Shaw, C. & McKay, H. (1942).
*Juvenile Delinquency and Urban
Areas*, Chicago University Press,
Chicago.

Sutherland, E. & Cressy, D.
(1974). *Criminology*, Lippincott,
New York.

Wilson, W. J. (1996). *When Work
Disappears*, Knopf, New York.

chapter 5

labelling perspectives

{introduction}
—

The aim of this chapter is to discuss how issues of crime and criminality are viewed from the perspective of labelling theories. Borrowing conceptually from sociological approaches such as 'interactionism', the labelling perspective introduces us to the idea that to understand crime we have to explore both objective and subjective dimensions of the criminal justice experience.

In the previous chapter we examined how strain theory explains crime in terms of blocked opportunities and cultural or learned behaviour. One of the hallmarks of positivist criminology — whether biological, psychological or sociological — is that crime is basically seen as a given; that is, it is assumed that crime exists 'out there' in the real world, and that all we have to do is record it, through classifying behaviour and searching for determining causes. Such criminology assumes that much criminal behaviour is caused by forces beyond our control (genetic, psychological, institutional). Generally speaking, it is further assumed that there is a consensus in society regarding core values and norms, and that the role of the social scientist is to provide an objective investigation into the factors that underpin why certain people commit crime.

The labelling perspectives challenge this view of crime and criminal justice. Instead, it is argued that crime is a *social process*. As such, it involves different perceptions of what constitutes 'good' or 'bad' behaviour (or persons), and particular power relationships that ultimately determine what (or who) is deemed to be 'deviant' or an offender. Crime is not an 'objective' phenomenon; it is an outcome of specific types of human interaction.

—

social context

The development of labelling perspectives within criminology was a result of a combination of the influence of certain intellectual currents, and wider changes occurring in society generally. We shall explore the intellectual foundations of labelling theory in greater depth further on in the chapter. For now, suffice it to say that a central concern of the 'new deviancy' theory was the issue of subjective meaning, and how this impinged upon objective social relationships. Or, to put it differently, the concern was with how human beings actively create their social world.

The impetus for the rise of labelling perspectives, in large part, lies in the changes that were taking place in the advanced capitalist countries, particularly the USA, in the 1960s and 1970s. The dominant image of the 1950s was one of shared collective interests, consensus on core values, economic prosperity for everyone, and standards of 'deviance' and 'conformity' that were clear for all to see. Consequently, the social order was viewed as monolithic—everyone was dedicated to common goals, and had a stake in the status quo. Any problems that did arise could be dealt with through adequate research and application of appropriate technical responses and programs.

By the 1960s, however, the presumed consensus was disintegrating. The phenomenal popularity of Elvis Presley in the 1950s signalled a new cultural form that was premised upon energy, separateness, novelty and rebellion. The birth of rock-and-roll music in the postwar period saw the creation of a leisure-based 'youth culture', one that generally represented a sharp break with the existing 'culture' of their parents. Music, fashion, language, appearance and activities were all forged in a manner that departed from existing conventions (and, yet, in the end were linked to the creation of new youth-related and commercialised conventions). 'Deviancy' in the youth cultural revolution was consciously perpetrated and, simultaneously, hotly contested by the young themselves. In this sense, the deviant behaviour was not necessarily, or solely, reactive. It was also a positive act of identity formation and social change.

If conventional family relations involving the generations were undergoing massive change, so too they were under pressure by the public campaigns of women, and gay men and lesbians, to have their collective needs and human rights acknowledged in society. The Second Wave of feminism, in the form of a militant Women's Liberation Movement, actively challenged traditional, conservative notions of the female role and place in society. Similarly, conventional ideas regarding sexuality and sexual preference were subject to increasing analysis and condemnation by feminists and by gay and lesbian activists. Conflict went to the heart of mainstream society and, in particular, the basic assumptions concerning the 'American way of life'.

The idea of a uniform social consensus was further de-mythologised by the coming to prominence of the civil rights movement. The radicalism of Malcolm X and Martin Luther King Jr, and the dream of a more just, equal and free society for African-Americans, were crucial components in the creation of a mass social movement that sought fundamental social transformation. The movements for equal rights, and Indigenous rights, were echoed in Australia with the establishment of the Aboriginal Tent Embassy on the lawns of Parliament House in 1970. People of colour, Indigenous people and migrant groups could no longer be easily silenced, nor could their demands be ignored. Social division was now on the political agenda.

The breakdown of convention, and the elevation of social difference to cultural and political prominence, was further entrenched through the fierce public resistance to the Vietnam War, particularly among the young, in a number of countries, and especially in the USA and Australia, where conscription into the conflict was an ever-present reality for young people. The events of May 1968, in which students and then workers took to the streets of Paris and paralysed France for a period of weeks, underscored the fact that social change was unavoidable and was happening then and there.

One consequence of these great movements for change and reform was that social scientists started to rethink their conceptions of society, social order and deviancy. Society was now seen as *pluralistic* in nature, made up of a number of diverse interest groups and classes. It was not immutable, but subject to constant pressures to change. Furthermore, what was deviant one day might not be the next. Likewise, what one group thought of as deviant might well be acceptable to another. Social reality thus is contingent—how we view the world very much depends upon where we are situated within that world.

One of the characteristics of the social movements of the time was the emphasis and stress placed upon human creativity, liberation and free will. The libertarian ethos emphasised choice and rebellion over passive acceptance and conformity. Translated into social theory terms, this broad orientation was reflected in the idea that *meaning* is part of an ongoing social process. Social life is not fixed and immutable. It is made up of constant interactions between groups. The meaning we give to events and situations depends upon how we negotiate definitions of each event or situation.

basic concepts

Labelling perspectives generally start from the premise that crime and criminal behaviour are social processes (see chart 5.1). The focus of concern is with the nature of the interaction between 'offender', 'victim' and criminal justice 'officials'. What counts as a 'crime' is, in essence, determined by the activities of the criminal justice system and its officials; that is, the definition of particular behaviour or an individual as criminal depends upon who does the labelling (Plummer 1979). Official designations of 'crime' are thereby conferred by those who have the power to label.

chart 5.1 | **labelling perspectives**

definition of crime	_ defined by social action and reaction _ conferred by those who have power to label
focus of analysis	_ relationship between offender and those with power to label
cause of crime	_ stigmatisation and negative effects of labelling
nature of offender	_ determined by the labelling process
response to crime	_ diversion from formal system
crime prevention	_ decriminalisation _ radical non-intervention
operation of criminal justice system	_ system should not have stigmatising effect _ greater tolerance and minimal intervention

The measurement of crime is a process in which the particular actions of certain people are defined by those in power within the criminal justice system as being 'deviant' or 'criminal'. This *institutionalist* perspective on crime measurement stresses that crime is not in fact 'objective': it is shaped by the nature of interactions and selective labelling by members of the criminal justice system in their dealings with the general public (Becker 1963; Tannenbaum 1938, cited in Muncie 2010).

The broad interactionist perspective thus focuses on how people typify one another (such as 'mentally ill' or 'young offender'), how people relate to one another on the basis of these typifications, and what the consequences of these social processes are (Muncie 2010).

From the point of view of criminology, the influence of perspectives that wish to examine the 'social construction of reality' is manifest in two major questions:

1\ How do individuals come to be labelled deviant or criminal?
2\ How do individuals come to be committed to a deviant or criminal label and, ultimately, career?

A key area of analysis is the relationship between the offender and those who have the power to label. The consequence of this relationship, and especially of the labelling process itself, is that stigmatisation can occur. Negative effects can arise from labelling, such that the person labelled takes on the role prescribed in the label. In other words, if a person is branded officially as a 'deviant', 'offender' or 'criminal', then this may result in the person acting in a manner that fits the label (Lemert 1951; 1974).

Once a person has been labelled a particular kind of person, he or she is liable to be treated in a different kind of way from others who may engage in the same kind of behaviour, but who have not been so labelled. This general process can be represented as follows:

1\ negative labelling
2\ stigmatisation
3\ new identity formed in response to negative labelling
4\ commitment to new identity based on available roles and relationships.

Labelling perspectives in general are based upon this kind of processual model (Berard 2003; Muncie 2010). In essence, this says that, in association with labelling, stigmatisation occurs. Others see a person who is stigmatised predominantly in terms of one particular character trait or behavioural pattern, based upon the content of the initial negative labelling.

For example, the negative label may be 'juvenile delinquent', because the person was alleged to have stolen an item from a shop. The person becomes subject to stigmatisation when the negative 'juvenile delinquent' label becomes a master public definition of 'what they are like'. Everyone then responds to the person according to the terms of the label, regardless of what such people may now actually be doing with their life, and with little regard for the other positive qualities they possess. Over time, if the stigma attaches, young people may commit themselves to the new label and hence change their identity to fit the label. Within labelling perspectives, labelling is usually seen to produce negative consequences.

In effect, the labelling perspective points to the impact of labelling on the psychological and social development of offenders. The self-concept and social opportunities of the offender are determined or influenced by the labelling process. The stigma sticks to offenders, and it affects how others see them, as well as how they perceive themselves.

One result of stigmatisation is that some people who have been negatively labelled not only engage in further criminal, offending or deviant activity, but they also seek out or find comfort in the company of others who have likewise been cast as outsiders. Another consequence of the labelling process, therefore, is that it creates an impetus for similarly labelled people to associate with each other — generally, in the form of delinquent or criminal subcultures.

From a labelling perspective, the potentially negative outcomes of the labelling process are seen to outweigh the necessity to intervene in the first place. That is, for young people in particular, the stigmatisation of official criminal justice intervention may well propel them into a criminal career for activity that, for most people, is generally transitory in nature (Matza 1964; Lemert 1967).

The response of the criminal justice system to offending behaviour therefore should be based upon a policy of diversion from the more stigmatising aspects of the criminal justice system. The idea is that every attempt must be made to divert certain offenders from contact with the more formal elements of the system, and thus to reduce the chances of stigmatising them.

Less serious offences, for example, should not warrant arrest, court appearance and incarceration. Rather, the response should be based upon the principle of (radical) non-intervention, or at the least minimal intervention. In a similar vein, in order to reduce the possibility of unwarranted or unnecessary stigmatisation there may be calls to decriminalise certain 'victimless' or 'non-predatory' activities.

Overall, there is a general demand that many different types of behaviour and activity should be tolerated by criminal justice officials. The power to label is substantial, and has lasting impacts. Therefore, it should be used judiciously and only where absolutely necessary.

historical development

Broadly speaking, labelling perspectives have strong links to the 'symbolic interactionist' perspective in sociology, especially the early work of the Chicago School (such as Mead, Cooley, Znaniecki and Blumer). These early symbolic interactionists were influenced by the newly emerging approaches of social psychology, phenomenology and ethnomethodology (see Muncie & Fitzgerald 1981; Taylor et al. 1973). While the work of these sociologists continues to be central to understanding this approach, it was not until the work of Edwin Lemert in the 1950s and Howard Becker in the 1960s that labelling perspectives came to dominate the theoretical analysis of criminal and deviant behaviour. The early symbolic interactionists employed the concepts of 'self' and 'symbol' in order to explain social behaviour and social action. The logic of such a perspective revolves around the innumerable and diverse individual responses available to social situations and interactions (see, for example, Berger & Luckmann 1971).

The *self* is not a psychological concept (like personality), but refers to how people see themselves. According to Mead (1962 [1934]) and others, this *self* is built through social interaction. In this sense, we can talk about the 'looking-glass self', which is the self-image reflected in those around us (see discussion of the work of Cooley and Mead in Coser 1977). Further, all human beings learn how to respond to different social interactions by accurately 'reading' the symbols (for example, a badge, gesture, words) around them. Building on these ideas of self and symbol, other sociologists, including Goffman, began to develop a theoretical framework for understanding the function of *role-playing* in human interaction (Goffman 1959). For role-playing to occur, each individual has to be able to 'take the role of the Other'—to see things as others see them. In other words, interaction can occur only because each person is able to attribute appropriate meaning to the symbols—words, gestures and so on—of the other.

But the 'self' does not simply passively respond to events and people around it. It also plays an active part in selecting how it responds. How we respond to other people in our social interactions depends upon how we *define the situation*. The symbolic nature of behaviour means that the first stage of any interaction is one of definition. When people share the same definitions, communication is likely to be straightforward and clear, and they can move on to interpreting the significance of the interaction itself.

The taken-for-granted world may appear to us as the 'real world' that exists outside us—as hard, concrete, objective fact. Yet, according to symbolic interactionists, we are collectively involved in constructing reality through the use of signs and symbols, and each of us generally interprets these in the same way. The basis of our interaction with other people is the use of *typifications*, which are drawn upon as part of our recipe knowledge that we use in order to make sense of the world (Berger & Luckmann 1971).

From these types of propositions, it can be concluded that, at one level, it does not matter what the actual situation is: what matters is how we define it. The first step in communication therefore is one of defining situations in a process of interaction. Situations and social interactions, however, can be misinterpreted, either when we define them incorrectly, or when we do not share a common definition. For instance, a blazing light in the sky could be seen as a comet, or as a sign from a supernatural being. In either case, how we collectively define the situation will have real consequences for our behaviour and actions.

Importantly, human beings are not passive in their social interactions. Nevertheless, how other people perceive us has real and immediate effects on how we see ourselves and how we behave. And this social process can be negative or positive—as was clearly demonstrated in Goffman's early studies of hospitals, asylums, schools and prisons (Goffman 1959).

In early versions of the labelling perspective, it was asserted that deviancy is not an inherent property of behaviour. Rather, deviancy is something that is conferred upon an individual by society. According to Becker (1963: 9), the impact of *social reaction* to certain types of behaviour or particular categories of people is crucial to explaining the criminalisation process:

> Social groups create deviance by making the rules whose infraction constitutes deviance, and by applying those rules to particular people and labeling them as outsiders. From this point of view, deviance is not a quality of the act the person commits, but rather a consequence of the application by others of rules and sanctions to an 'offender'. The deviant is one to whom the label has successfully been applied; deviant behaviour is behaviour that people so label.

The focus of his research was people considered to be on the margins of society, and on the margins of conformity (such as the homeless, alcoholics, prostitutes). According to Becker (1963), the key reason why these people are placed on the 'outside' is because their particular behaviour has been labelled deviant by more powerful interest groups in society. There is nothing in the behaviour itself that is necessarily 'deviant' or 'conformative': it only becomes so in the actual process of labelling.

The importance of this view was twofold: first, it called into question the social nature of the definitions of crime by alerting us to the variability in human behaviour; and second, it showed us that 'crime' is as much as anything a matter of who has the power to officially label behaviour or persons as criminal (see Cicourel 1976). According to labelling theorists, the use of self-report and victim surveys indicates that crime and victimisation are ubiquitous—that is, they are found in all social classes and across gender and ethnic boundaries. Hence, the crucial issues are who gets labelled by whom, and what are the consequences of this labelling.

An important concept here is that of the *self-fulfilling prophecy*. The idea behind this is that who I am is determined by who defines my reality and how this is done. People who are labelled 'stupid', 'bright', 'dumb', 'genius' and so on will respond accordingly. For example, in the so-called Pygmalion experiment, a group of school students was split into two. One half of the group was publicly labelled 'slow and stupid', while the other half was told they were 'brilliant'. After a while, the school grades of the two groups began to deteriorate and to improve respectively. The argument was put forward that each group had internalised the self-concepts framed for them, and had responded to the public labels by playing the role of 'stupid' or 'brilliant' (Rosenthal & Jacobson 1968).

One explanation of the importance of labelling on people's future behaviour was provided by Lemert (1967, 1969). In this case, the main focus is with the social-psychological level of analysis. That is, we want to know the reasons why a person engages in a deviant act to begin with and, furthermore, what maintains their commitment to deviant activity. According to Lemert, in order to describe the process of labelling we can distinguish between primary deviation and secondary deviation.

Primary deviation refers to initial deviant behaviour. The proposition here is that most of us at some stage in our development engage in activities regarded as deviant (such as underage drinking, smoking cannabis, petty shoplifting), but we do so because of a wide variety of social, cultural and psychological reasons. Little is said about the primary causes of deviant behaviour, except that these are wide-ranging and involve a multitude of individual factors. However, the important point is that at this initial stage of deviation, when people engage in deviant activity they do not fundamentally change their self-concept; that is, the individual's psyche does not undergo a symbolic reorientation or transformation (for example, we do not see ourselves as a drunk, a pothead or a thief). There is no change in identity, and deviance is seen as nothing more than a passing event.

The main focus of labelling perspectives is with *secondary deviation*. This occurs when the individual engages in some kind of primary deviation (such as shoplifting) and there is an official reaction to that behaviour (for example, the police are called in). If a person is apprehended by the police, they may be officially labelled as 'deviant' (that is, 'young offender') (Lemert 1951). The individual may begin to employ a deviant behaviour or role based upon this new status, which has been conferred upon them by state officials, as a means of defence or adjustment to the overt and covert problems created by the public social reaction to their original behaviour. For example, the person may start to 'act tough' to counter ridicule from peers, taunts from neighbours and persistent surveillance by police when he or she goes out. Secondary deviation is said to occur when, because of the social reaction to primary deviation, the person experiences a fundamental reorientation of self-concept, and thus behaviour.

Labelling perspectives were to have most application in the area of juvenile justice. It was argued that young people are particularly vulnerable to the labelling process, and thus more likely to respond, for better or worse, to official social reaction. In their work on juvenile delinquency, for instance, Sykes and Matza (1957) and Matza (1964) described the motivational accounts provided by young people themselves as to why they engage in certain types of activity. They argued that young people use certain *techniques of neutralisation* as a way of denying the moral bind of law (such as 'they started it' or 'no one got hurt'). Furthermore, Matza argued that the actions of the juvenile justice system, and especially youth perceptions of the competence of officials and the application of sanctions, also affect the 'will to crime' of young people, and form part of the ways in which they neutralise their moral restraint.

In studying the values, perceptions and emotions of young people, Matza (1964) explored the reasons that propelled some youth into further criminal activity. Although most people at some stage engage in some form of criminal, antisocial or deviant behaviour, not all young people experience offending and criminal justice in the same way. Matza found that juveniles generally 'drift' between the two poles of conventional and unconventional behaviour (including crime), without being fully committed to either. In the end, most young people drift towards conventional lifestyles and behaviours as their permanent pattern. However, if during the teenage years of drift there is official intervention and social reaction to specific kinds of unconventional behaviour, this may well precipitate the movement of the juvenile into a more permanent state of delinquency.

The idea that young people subjected to public labelling may be propelled into criminal activity or careers also features in the work of Schur. The solution, according to Schur (1973), is to adopt a policy of *radical non-intervention*. This means that we should take a hands-off attitude to juvenile offending as far as possible. Young people should be free from official intervention, and they should be diverted from the formal systems of juvenile justice in order to avoid stigmatisation.

then & now

labelling

Labelling perspectives raise a range of important issues for understanding why people offend and, critically, the ways 'onlookers' can stigmatise and isolate people who don't 'fit in' with what they see as normal behaviour. Labelling is part of a number of related sociological perspectives, including symbolic interactionism (a broader theory that includes labelling, but looks at social interaction and the development of identity and social categorisation more broadly) and phenomenology (a theoretical perspective that emphasises the emotional and personal experience of life). Labelling remains an important theoretical perspective and has also influenced many others. The importance of how stigmatisation can lead to further offending is important to republican theory (Chapter 10), and the importance of the creation of outsiders or 'other' individuals or groups is a central element to postmodernist theories and critical criminology generally (Chapter 11). From the perspective of the New Right, on the other hand, negative labelling may well in fact be lauded as appropriate social control rather than being seen as problematically reproducing deviancy (see Chapter 8). For cultural criminology and the sociology of emotions, labelling embodies more nuanced understandings of human behaviour and social action, with an emphasis on the irrational as well as the instrumental in shaping the choices that people make.

contemporary examples

Labelling perspectives have become an ingrained part of how we think about juvenile justice institutions and processes (see Cunneen & White 2011). As will be explored in more detail later on, many of the core ideas of labelling perspectives have spurred further conceptual development in the areas of 'restorative justice' and 'reintegrative shaming', which are at the heart of the republican theory of criminal justice (Chapter 10).

In addition to having a major influence on other theoretical perspectives (such as Marxist, feminist, republican and cultural criminology), the labelling approach has had a marked impact at the level of policy development. This is particularly the case with respect to young people and children. For example, diversion programs now operate in many jurisdictions. These take the form of pre-court programs (such as police cautioning schemes) and alternatives to court (such as juvenile conferencing projects). The emphasis here is to divert the young person away from the more formal aspects of the criminal justice system, and therefore to reduce the likelihood of stigma and negative labelling (Woolford 2009).

Another example of the systemic response to labelling perspectives is the way in which a number of jurisdictions attempt to protect the young person from being stigmatised and penalised for the rest of his or her life for offences committed when young. This can take the form of the destruction of official records once a juvenile has reached a certain age and has not reoffended. Limitations on publicity in cases heard before the Children's Court, and restrictions on the taking of bodily samples and fingerprints from children and young people, are similarly designed to keep the young person at arm's length from the official criminal justice system.

One of the more unusual applications of labelling theory was the Tattoo Removal Scheme operating in Victoria in the 1980s. This was part of a young offender program in the state of Victoria, in which attempts were made to reshape the public image of certain young people. The presence of tattoos was seen as part of the problem for these young people. They were too easily branded as 'crims' or 'toughs', and this fed into a long-term scenario of heightened police intervention, offending activity and criminal careers. In order to reduce the stigma attached to these young people, the detention centres introduced a scheme whereby they could have their tattoos removed (Ross 1985). Again, the idea here is that how 'others' respond to a person is an integral part of how people see themselves and how they behave. This example also points to the changing nature of symbols. Tattoos were once a symbol of deviance, but are now highly desirable, with tattoos common among young people— not only those who are viewed as 'troublemakers'.

These policy and structural applications of labelling theory draw heavily on two contemporary strands of this approach: criminalisation of deviance and moral panics (Cohen 1967, 1972; Young 1971), and cultural criminology (Katz 1988).

¬ moral panics

One of the most significant and widely adopted contemporary approaches to labelling theory was that provided by Jock Young and Stanley Cohen in the late 1960s and early 1970s. While Young is attributed with first using the concept of moral panic—in his study of drug-takers—the clear articulation of the process of a moral panic is most commonly attributed to Cohen's ground-breaking study of Mods and Rockers (1967), which was later published as the much cited, *Folk Devils and Moral Panics* (1972).

In this research, Cohen documented the social and structural responses that arose out of the labelling of a group of youths who were thought responsible for 'a day of terror'. According to Cohen, the demonisation of small groups of young people for relatively minor incidents of harassment and threatening behaviour became a symbol for the social disorder created by the shift in norms and values between generational cohorts at this time. This clash of values was amplified and criminalised by the media in their reporting of 'outsiders' invading the town. Although Cohen found no evidence of organised gang activity—Mods or Rockers—the over-reporting of this one-off event created a set of social and structural responses that further demonised and criminalised youth.

In response to the media amplification of the public disorder, the state via its policing services was forced to react by increased policing of the two youth subcultures, which in turn heightened the animosity and antagonism between the two groups—which had the unfortunate consequence of formalising membership of the groups. This increased animosity was instrumental in creating further occasions for the two groups to 'mark their territory' and refine their subcultural identity through clashes with each other. As a consequence, the groups' actions were subject to further media attention and over-reporting, state action and marginalisation.

Importantly, both Young and Cohen recognised this as a product of the changing social order at this time. Young people were finding new ways in which to engage with their world. Their parents and grandparents— happy in the familiar patterns—attributed the disorder to Cohen's 'folk devils'. As a symbol of all that was wrong with the world, these folk devils become the scapegoats of their parents' and grandparents' desires for the social order and harmony they had come to expect.

Although Cohen's formulation of labelling theory has been subject to critique from many perspectives (including self-critique, Cohen 2002)— for being atheoretical (Plummer 1979), ignoring the reality of crime (Lea & Young 1984) and simplifying complex processes (Poynting & Morgan 2007)—it remains an important analytical tool for understanding the consequences of labelling. Since the publication of Cohen's third edition of *Folk Devils and Morals Panics* in 2002 to mark the thirty year anniversary of its original publication, the theoretical framework offered by Cohen has been applied to a variety of social and criminal contexts (such as antisocial behaviour, 'ethnic' gangs, drug misuse, hooning, transmission of sexual diseases, sexual violence and same-sex families). In Poynting & Morgan's (2007) collection on moral panics, the contributors offer critical—some, almost ambivalent—analyses of how and when the concept of 'moral panic' serves to better understand the power and consequences of labelling. Importantly, as with other authors (such as Feeley and Simon 2007), contributors to Poynting and Morgan's *Outrageous!*, highlight that the single one-off moral panic documented in Cohen's 1960s research clashes with the climate of a permanent moral panic in the early twenty-first century.

¬ cultural criminology

The idea of reaction being important to crime is also found in the work of Katz (1988). In an unusual twist to the labelling perspective, Katz has argued that knowledge of labelling processes (and, in particular, the notion of shaming) may itself constitute part of the impetus to engage in deviant or offending behaviour. Katz was interested in the relationship between crime and the emotional states of offenders. He turned his attention to the *seductions of crime* and the compulsions that are felt by people as they engage in various types of criminal projects. Crime, in emotional terms, is exciting and exhilarating. It represents a transcendence of the mundane, an opportunity to creatively explore emotional worlds beyond that of 'normal' rational behaviour. Part of the thrill of crime is seen to lie precisely in the risk that one will be shamed if caught. Thus, being successful in activity such as shoplifting or joyriding is not only about 'getting away with it'; it is also about avoiding the shame they would feel if they did get caught. These risks thus constitute an important part of the excitement of the deviant experience. If an arrest does occur, this is seen by Katz as a kind of 'metaphysical shock', in that it implies that persistence in the activity would now signal a commitment to a deviant identity. This, in turn, would undermine the emotional impact of knowingly being deviant, particularly since such thrill-seeking deviance is seldom tied to the notion of criminal identity or criminal career.

As with the themes and issues raised by Matza, for Katz (1988) it is important to examine the lived experiences of criminality, to consider the emotional and interpretive qualities of crime. Emotions such as humiliation, arrogance, ridicule, pleasure and excitement are often central to why we act as we do. Indeed, the study of the emotions of crime is capturing greater interest within criminology, particularly since criminal behaviour is deeply and ambiguously emotional. It is argued that different states of emotional arousal, from fear and anger through to pleasure and excitement, have major bearings on individual and group behaviour, and for the policies and practices of criminal justice institutions (see de Haan & Loader 2002). Locating activity within an emotional universe is one of the characteristic features of what is broadly known as cultural criminology.

Cultural criminology refers to a body of scholarship that tends to focus on the pleasures, excitement and opportunities for 'psychic resolution' involved in certain modes of criminality (Ferrell et al. 2004; Hayward 2002; Ferrell & Sanders 1995; Spencer 2011). The focus, therefore, tends to be on the varied emotional dynamics and experiential attractions that constitute an essential element of much crime and antisocial behaviour. For example, Presdee (2000) writes about the dynamics of the spectacle of violence in popular movies, sexual activities such as sadomasochism and the attractions of rap and rave. Ferrell (1997) describes the liberating feelings and sense of power and resistance associated with writing graffiti. A common theme in much of this work is that deviance offers the perpetrator a means of 'self-transcendence'—a way of overcoming the conventionality and mundanity of everyday life (Hayward 2002).

The contribution of cultural criminology to the understanding of youth violence, for example, is that violence is not only a rational or strategic activity—it can be exciting and thrilling as well. Thus, there is increasing evidence that some types of violence stem from the efforts of young people themselves to engineer situations and events with the intended aim of increasing the likelihood of violence occurring (Jackson-Jacobs 2004; Schinkel 2004). From this perspective, the 'gang' provides a forum or ready-made opportunity structure within which to engage in what is felt to be exhilarating activity. Fighting is fun; and gangs provide an avenue to increase the thrill factor beyond the norm. Violence can thus be seen to be attractive and desirable in its own right, as well as being linked to instrumental purposes (such as defending male honour, defending oneself). Such violence thus achieves a number of rational, emotional, psychological and social purposes, simultaneously (White in press; White & Mason 2006).

More sophisticated accounts also make the link between the loss of ontological security (a sense of place and belonging) at an individual level that makes people feel at risk in an unstable world, and achieving a 'controlled sense of loss of control' by engaging in risky practices (see Hayward 2002). Consider planking and car surfing, for example. These acts of 'controlled loss of control' involve people using their bodies as a prop in their risky behaviour. In the latter, by standing on top of a speeding car, the individual puts him- or herself at considerable personal risk. So why do it? The emotional answer is that it is fun and exciting; the analytical answer is that it represents a choice to engage in a 'controlled sense of loss of control'. According to cultural criminologists, as everyday life becomes more routinised, sanitised and criminalised, so too there will be greater propensity among people to transgress the boundaries of what is deemed to be acceptable behaviour.

{from theory to practice: labelling and drug use}

——

Homan, S. (2007). '"Why Are They All Drinking Water?" Raves, Ecstasy and the Death of Anna Wood', in S. Poynting & G. Morgan (eds), *Outrageous: Moral Panics in Australia*, ACYS, Hobart: 82–98.

In his contribution to this collection, Homan tests and critically analyses Cohen's (1972) theory of moral panics. As with others in this collection, Homan seeks to document the ways in which the media, the state and the 'public' colluded in creating 'folk devils' out of those who participated in, or organised, raves. As with Cohen's earlier study of Mods and Rockers, the rave moral panic(s) of the 1990s coalesced around a catalytic event that created a feedback loop, which amplified, demonised, and, eventually, criminalised this particular form of music and culture. The catalytic event—the death of fifteen-year-old Anna Woods after the use of ecstasy at a rave—brought the subterranean (perhaps, subaltern) culture of raves to the attention of local moral entrepreneurs, and through media representations of this 'tragedy' of 'lost innocence' created a public outcry, and later a bidding war over tough law-and-order responses from the state.

As Homan suggests, law and order (its philosophy, its funding, its approach to accountability) is a common political tool in New South Wales's elections (2007: 84). However, the death of Anna Woods came at a time in state and national politics that facilitated the amplification of this single event, and the development of kneejerk, at times, contradictory legislation, policy and practice. In particular, at the national level, in 1996, the Hawke-Keating Labor government was replaced by the Howard Coalition government. With this new conservative leadership, Australia's commitment to the research-driven policy of drug harm minimisation was replaced with prohibition, 'just say no' and heavier policing and punishment, At the state level, the Carr Labor government had won a hard election on the basis of tough law-and-order promises.

Homan documents that, in addition to this political landscape, the tabloid reporting of Anna's death—particularly from the Murdoch-owned *Daily Telegraph Mirror* (along with several Sydney-based 'shock jocks', such as Alan Jones)—amplified the process of criminalisation, in part, by drawing on discourses of the 'lost innocence' of middle-class Australian suburbia, and the sexualised, predatory nature of the inner-city night-time economy (2007: 85). Homan argues that as with Cohen's study, despite empirical evidence to the contrary (in this case from the Australian Medical Association), these catalytic events are used (or appropriated) by moral entrepreneurs (in the media, state, and community) to facilitate harsher social control measures.

In the case of rave culture in New South Wales (as in the UK at the same time), the government responded to the public outcry and media amplification by introducing a range of measures to control the inexplicable attraction to this form of anarchic music and culture. In addition to subjecting the club attended by Anna (the Phoenician Club) to judicial review by the Director of Liquor and Gaming (which initially led to its license to operate being suspended), the government also amended regulations governing the access of minors to registered clubs for alcohol-free events. This was to ensure that rave parties were 'professionally organised, legal and hassle-free dance parties in suitable locations' (NSW Ministry of Police cited in Homan 2007: 92). Homan suggests that in controlling the organisation of rave culture—to be more in line with acceptable, commercialised practices—the government also increased the opportunities for controlling cultural production itself.

critique

One of the first criticisms that often comes to the mind of students is the fact that the labelling perspective does not provide any explanation as to why people offend in the first place—the so-called 'primary deviation' (although cultural criminology does in fact do this). Labelling theory, however, concentrates on *social reaction* to deviant behaviour. Those using the labelling perspective argue that this criticism is misguided since they did not in fact set out to explain why primary deviation occurred. They do not see labelling theory as a discrete theory but rather as a perspective, a part of the overall picture that is able to explain the negative consequences of criminal justice intervention.

Some would argue, however, that there is a problem with focusing exclusively on crime as defined by social reaction. There are crimes that are characterised by a high level of social agreement concerning both their harmfulness and their criminality. Crimes such as rape and murder are seen to possess intrinsic qualities that make them a part of criminal law across cultures (Hagan 1987). Focusing exclusively on social reaction with respect to such crimes would seem to distort the reality of such criminal behaviour.

So, while labelling theory seems plausible in explaining minor delinquency, there are some crimes, such as rape and murder, where the labelling perspective is less useful. It is hard to conceive of these crimes as defined purely on a subjective basis, or as simply a by-product of the confirmation of a 'criminal identity' by the state. While some serious offences, such as murder, are committed by those with an extensive history within the criminal justice system, and could be seen as a result of secondary deviation, for others murder is a first offence. It is hard to conceive of these as resulting entirely from secondary deviance.

Nonetheless, even under the terms of the labelling perspective itself, it is not always clear what gives people the capacity to reject particular labels. While some seem to succumb to labels and easily slip into deviant identities, others reject the labelling process even after repeated contexts where 'labelling' has taken place. There is extreme variability in how people respond to labels in practice. This has many implications for labelling theory, and republican theory, which we shall consider in Chapter 10. Fundamentally, labelling is unable to explain what gives one person the capacity, or the will, to reject the label, while another lacks such a capacity.

There is, then, considerable variability in how people respond to a labelling process. For example, an individual may persist in shoplifting in the absence of overt or immediate social reaction. This same individual, when caught, may cease shoplifting precisely because of the stigma of being caught (and possibly not even because the person thinks that what he or she was doing was 'wrong'). Others, such as political activists, may be arrested several times for their activities, yet continue to protest. This is because they see official policy—such as the destruction of the rainforest or bias against gay and lesbian lifestyles—as the deviance, not their behaviour. They actively reject the labelling of the criminal justice system. Finally, for some people the act of going through the criminal justice system and its labelling processes may be seen as an important rite of passage, as has been suggested is the case with some young people (McRobbie & Thornton 1995), in particular Indigenous young people in northern Australia (see Johnston 1991). However, the labelling perspective cannot explain this phenomenon on its own, since it is bound up with broader social issues. In the case of Indigenous Australians, these social issues include colonial relationships, and in particular the relationship between Indigenous people and the police.

However, it is important not to oversimplify the labelling process, for example, by suggesting that it only takes one event and a person is labelled for life. The process of acquiring labels is far more subtle, and, as Plummer (1979) points out, labels are used by a wide range of institutions, such as family and school, that extend far beyond the reaches of the criminal justice system. By the time some people reach the criminal justice system they may well have an entrenched set of negative labels. It may be this labelling process—not the labelling that occurs in the criminal justice system—that determines the fate of a young person (Braithwaite 2002). Labelling by the criminal justice system remains important, however, since as Polk (1993, 1994b) points out, it can wield only negative labels—'graduating' from a criminal justice institution has very different connotations in mainstream society from graduating from high school.

For this reason there has been much discussion of the concept of 'net widening' in the literature. Those with concerns about the policies that emanate from labelling theory argue that diversion, rather than turning people away from formal involvement in the criminal justice system, actually draws more people into its purview. Thus, the negative labels wielded by the system reach further into the juvenile population. This is particularly the case where diversion results in greater intrusion into individuals' lives, for example, through the use of juvenile conferencing in cases of minor offending (see Alder & Wundersitz 1994; Cunneen & White 2011). 'Failure' in the context of such diversionary programs can mean re-entry into the justice system, possibly with harsher penalties involved. Alternatively, this possibility is minimised where diversion involves no further action, such as in the police cautioning program in New Zealand.

The concept of diversion then needs critical evaluation. Cohen (1985) argues that analysis of diversionary programs reveals several recurrent problems. First, diversionary programs can be more intrusive of individual lives (denser nets). Second, people may be brought into the criminal justice system where previously they would have had no contact (broader nets). Finally, while the institution of social control may change, the nature of social control may remain—that is, control that marginalises and alienates the person (different nets). For example, some form of medical or psychiatric control may replace the criminal justice agencies.

Ultimately, however, to explain criminality it is necessary to go beyond interaction at the level of individuals and social groups. Explanation of how power is wielded within the labelling perspective is limited to the immediate institutional level (such as the individual police officer), which begs analysis of the wider distributions of power in society. The analytical gaze of the labelling perspective is on the 'underdogs' and their reaction to their position, not on how they are positioned and regarded by the more powerful in society.

{conclusion}

The labelling perspective can be seen as a radical break from earlier positivist and classical explanations of criminality and criminal behaviour. For the first time the notion of a consensus in society was challenged by criminologists and sociologists. With this challenge came the understanding that 'crime' and 'criminal' were themselves subjective and depended as much on context and social reaction to give them meaning as on the nature of the actual behaviour.

Labelling theorists were ultimately concerned with the nature of action and reaction that resulted in an individual taking on a deviant identity, and pursuing a deviant lifestyle. The central problems that inform the labelling perspectives have been usefully summarised by Plummer (1979: 88) and include:

- What are the *characteristics* of labels, and their variations and forms?

- What are the *sources* of labels, both societally and personally?

_ How, and under what *conditions*, do labels get applied?

_ What are the *consequences* of labelling?

Through these questions, crime is seen as a process. Becoming successfully labelled as 'criminal' involves taking on a negative label that is primarily applied by the criminal (or juvenile) justice system. This system is full of symbols, or cues, that denote who is criminal (the one in the dock) and who sits in judgment on the person (those on a raised platform, the judge or magistrate). The consequences of this process include an individual taking on a criminal identity and then acting according to the expectations of that label; that is, committing more offences. Labelling theory has important issues to raise about the social reaction process and how best to intervene or not to intervene.

Finally, the labelling perspective raises the importance of power and competing interests in society. This combination of the power differential and conflict of interest between some groups in society often results in the powerless being labelled as deviant. Those without power are thus more vulnerable to the labelling process. It is this issue of the power differential in society that is taken up in radical and feminist theories.

{**further reading**}

Becker, H. (1963). *Outsiders: Studies in the Sociology of Deviance*, Free Press, New York.

Braithwaite, J. (2002). *Restorative Justice and Responsive Regulation*, Oxford University Press, New York.

Cohen, S. (2002). *Folk Devils and Moral Panics* (third edition), Routledge, New York.

Ferrell, J., Hayward, K., Morrison, W. & Presdee, M. (eds) (2004). *Cultural Criminology Unleashed*, Glasshouse Press, London.

Hayward, K. (2002). 'The Vilification and Pleasures of Youthful Transgression', in J. Muncie, G. Hughes & E. McLaughlin (eds), *Youth Justice: Critical Readings*, SAGE, London.

Katz, J. (1988). *Seductions of Crime: Moral and Sensual Attractions in Doing Evil*, Basic Books, New York.

McLaughlin, E., Muncie, J. & Hughes, G. (eds) (2003). *Criminological Perspectives: A Reader* (2nd edition), SAGE, London.

Muncie, J. (2010). 'Labelling Social Reaction and Constructionism', in E. McLaughlin & T. Newburn (eds), *The SAGE Handbook of Criminological Theory*, SAGE, London: 139–52.

Plummer, K. (1979). 'Misunderstanding Labelling Perspectives', in D. Downes & P. Rock (eds), *Deviant Interpretations*, Martin Robertson, Oxford.

Poynting, S. & Morgan, G. (eds)
(2007). *Outrageous: Moral
Panics in Australia*, Hobart,
ACYS.

Presdee, M. (2000). *Cultural
Criminology and the Carnival of
Crime*, Routledge, London.

Sykes, G. & Matza, D. (1957).
'Techniques of Neutralization:
A Theory of Delinquency',
American Sociological Review,
22: 664-70.

marxist criminology

{introduction}

—

The labelling perspective represented a major challenge to existing orthodoxies of crime, particularly positivist assumptions regarding the straightforward existence of crime as fact. Labelling perspectives instead saw the creation of crime as an active social process. When such notions were first mooted in the 1950s and 1960s, a number of significant questions that created further critical waves within criminology were raised. For instance, why are some groups in society labelled more than others, and why are some groups more vulnerable than others to the labelling process? One answer to such questions was provided by perspectives that analysed the structure of society itself as a major source of inequality and differential treatment. These were the Marxist and broad conflict perspectives in criminology.

This chapter will focus predominantly on the Marxist perspective in criminology. The key aspect of this approach is that it views crime as an outcome and reflection of basic class divisions in society. The focus of analysis, therefore, is on power and inequality, especially insofar as these embody class-related processes associated with the overall distribution of social wealth.

The chapter begins with a brief discussion of the differences and similarities between a Marxist and a broad conflict perspective within criminology. This is followed by a review of the core concerns of Marxist writers, and the particular attention they pay to crimes of the powerful, as well as crimes of the less powerful. The relationship between economic, political and criminal processes is a central theme of the chapter.

—

social context

Terms such as 'critical', 'conflict' and 'radical' have all been applied interchangeably to theories that acknowledge the importance of power and social inequality in the construction of criminality. However, the terminology can be misleading. Regardless of the label, there exist important conceptual boundaries between liberal–conflict theories and Marxist analyses of crime.

The work of social scientists in the 1950s was largely conservative in nature. Writers of the period had either overtly adopted the Cold War ideology, which defended the 'American way of life' (based upon defence of capitalism), or were afraid to voice a critical response to such ideology. Their fear was created by state-sponsored attempts to stifle social criticism that bore any resemblance at all to communist ideas, such as the House Un-American Activities Committee in the USA. This situation was similarly reflected in the criminological writings of the time, many of which were premised upon the idea that there was a consensual social order and a core set of universal values. Deviance meant deviation from consensus and the presumed accepted core values and norms.

This *consensus perspective* adopted a functionalist approach, in which everything was conceived as operating to sustain society as a whole. According to this perspective, we all have shared values and shared interests in society. If individuals deviate from the social norm, then we bring them back into line, thus restoring the equilibrium. In this fashion, individuals are socialised into the core set of values and common interests. This view of society characterised most criminological perspectives until the 1960s.

The 1960s was a period that saw sustained critique of many of the dominant social institutions. There was a general rebellion against the norms, values and activities of mainstream society. This took such forms as resistance to the Vietnam War in Australia and elsewhere, student militancy, the rise of the Women's Liberation Movement and demands for civil rights by Black and Indigenous minorities. By this stage, the anticommunist fervour had died down, thus permitting a more open and critical analysis of society. The readiness to adopt a conflict perspective of society is reflected in the literature of the time. It is essential to note that a conflict perspective is not necessarily radical; it does not necessarily have to question the status quo, including the processes and institutions of society.

In the 1960s, labelling theory emerged as the precursor to more profound critiques of the existing orthodoxies; it questioned the prevailing world views, and emphasised that not all was as it appeared to be. Indeed, some of the writers who had subscribed to the consensus view of society, such as Lemert, changed their views and began conceiving of society in *pluralistic* terms (see Pearce 1976). Society was no longer seen as a homogeneous, unitary whole, but one made up of various competing interest groups. One could identify diverse ethnic, class and religious groupings; divergent economic and political interest groups; conflicting lifestyle approaches; and subcultural values.

The recognition of social difference was translated at the level of theory into several conceptions of the relationship between social interests and power. Some theories suggested that competing groups are more or less equal in power, and that power is more or less evenly distributed throughout the social structure. Other theories, particularly those developing from the ideas of Max Weber, suggested that conflict exists between different groups in any society (O'Connor 1998). These theories argued that there will always be less powerful and more powerful groups in society. Further, the capacity of elite groups to wield influence is related to both their economic and ideological resources (those based in values). Several questions arise. What is the nature and composition of these groups in society? How did elite groups entrench their world view as the 'right' one within a society and how did they respond when their authority was challenged? What caused changes in dominant values in society, and how was this related to changes in the status of particular groups?

While these *conflict perspectives* acknowledged the competitive nature of society, they did not necessarily argue for a replacement of the central institutions in a society, as ongoing conflict and power struggles were seen as inevitable. For a society to survive, then, it had to provide a forum for *resolution (or accommodation) of such conflicts*. In many cases, for example, they argued that existing institutions, however imperfect, provided the most appropriate means of dispute resolution. The basic institutions of society therefore were not necessarily challenged. Broadly speaking, conflict theorists argued that the current institutional structure within an industrialised democracy and the norms that underpin that state are a reflection of that power struggle, and reflect the interests and values of the elite. For these theorists, the influences of different groups wax and wane over time. The semblance of movement up and down the status ladder, though, was an important way elites could stay in control.

Others argued for a different view of competing interest groups in society. Becker (1963), for instance, observed that there is not a constant movement up and down the power ladder. Instead, it is always the same composition of people on the bottom: always the poor, the Blacks and the disadvantaged. A key concept here is that of the 'underdog' (see Pearce 1976). According to this view, the solution to the problem was to *assist the disadvantaged*—who were locked out of the process of acquiring wealth in society—via piecemeal management programs. This strategy does not challenge society's basic institutions, however; it merely tries to ameliorate the more blatant negative aspects and inequalities of the system.

In contrast, *Marxist* conceptions of society are rooted in the analysis of *social power*. A crucial aspect of the theory is the notion that power is concentrated increasingly into fewer and fewer hands, and that there is a ruling or capitalist class (Chambliss 1978). There is, therefore, not a plurality of power. Those who ultimately wield power are said to be those who own the means of production (and consumption): the factory owners, landowners and media owners. These individuals will dictate the nature and shape of society.

A liberal–conflict conception sees the state as a coordinating body within society. It recognises that conflict exists within society between competing groups, but sees the state as critical either to resolving conflict, or, if that is not possible, maintaining the legitimacy of that society and keeping violent civil conflict at bay. Marxist theory disagrees with this view. For Marxist theory, power is concentrated in a capitalist society and is a product of the economic system. The state and its personnel reflect the interests of the capitalist elite. The argument here is that if one conducts a class analysis of the state's personnel and analyses critically the state's policies, including economic and military ones, it becomes apparent that the state does not reflect a plurality of values and economic interests, but those of the capitalist class.

Ultimately, the instruments of the state apparatus (the courts, judiciary, police, prisons and community programs) operate in the interests of capitalism (Chambliss & Seidman 1971; Chambliss 1973; Chambliss & Mankoff 1976). Questions were therefore raised in relation to the criminalisation process: structurally, if the state reflects the interests of capitalism and the capitalist class, then who is subject to what kind of state sanctions, and why?

basic concepts

Marxist conceptions of society are based upon an analysis of structural power in society (see chart 6.1). As mentioned, those who wield decisive power in a society are those who own and control the means of production. An individual in a class society is defined not so much by personal attributes or by reference to universalising statements regarding 'choice' and 'determinism', but by their position and opportunities in society as dictated by class forces.

chart 6.1 | marxist criminology

definition of crime	– human rights conception – class interests
focus of analysis	– economic and state crimes of the powerful – economic and sociocultural crimes of the less powerful
cause of crime	– institutionalised inequality, exploitation and alienation – marginalisation and criminalisation of the working class
nature of offender	– choices of offender dictated by structural imperative to maximise profit, or by subsistence pressures – alienation
response to crime	– challenge state repression of working class – expose extent and nature of social harm by the powerful
crime prevention	– radical democracy – collective ownership and control over means of production – redistribution of societal resources according to need
operation of criminal justice system	– democratisation of institutions – public accountability – upholding of human rights – law reform to reflect working-class interests

To understand crime, we need to examine the actions of the powerful in *defining and enforcing a particular kind of social order*, and the activities of the less powerful in the context of a social structure within which they have fewer resources and less decision-making power than the owners of the means of production. Power is concentrated in a capitalist society, and the activities of the state reflect the interests of capital-in-general; in fostering the accumulation of capital, maintaining the legitimacy of unequal social relations, and controlling the actions of those who threaten private property relations and the public order. The general tendency of state institutions (such as the police, the judiciary, the prisons and community programs) is to concentrate on specific kinds of behaviour (usually associated with working-class crime) as being more 'deviant' and 'harmful' than other kinds of destructive or exploitive behaviour (usually associated with crimes of the powerful), which is deemed to be less worthy of state intervention.

In determining what is 'crime', the initial difficulty is that if the laws reflect the interests of the ruling class, then many types of social harm may not be incorporated into the criminal law if they go against capitalist interests (Chambliss 1973). In such circumstances, there is a need to establish wider criteria relating to the nature of offences. Thus, for example, crime has been redefined in a broader sense to encompass any activity that interferes with *basic human rights* and causes *social injury* (Hillyard & Tombs 2004, 2007).

Marxist criminology directs attention away from an exclusive focus on 'street crimes' or working-class crime, towards the social harms perpetrated by the powerful within society. It attempts to demonstrate how the *class situation is linked to specific types of criminality*.

According to the Marxist view, a broad distinction can be made between the crimes of the powerful and the crimes of the less powerful (Pearce 1976; Pearce & Snider 1992):

- *Crimes of the powerful* are linked to both a personal desire to augment one's wealth and a structural imperative to get an edge in the overall capitalist economic competition. They include economic crimes (such as fraud, violation of labour laws, environmental destruction (Pearce & Tombs 1993; Brill 1982; White 2008b, 2009a, 2009b) and state crimes (such as misuse of public funds, violation of civil rights, corruption).

_ *Crimes of the less powerful* stem from a combination of economic
and social motivations. In the first instance, they are related to
efforts to bolster or supplement one's income relative to subsistence
levels (Gordon 1971; Linebaugh 1976; Field 1990); in the second,
they may represent antisocial behaviour linked to varying types of
sociocultural alienation. They include subsistence-related crimes (such
as shoplifting, workplace theft, welfare fraud) and sociocultural crimes
(such as vandalism, assault, public order disturbances) (Morgan 2007).

Thus, the cause of crime is found in the structure of unequal class
relations in a society. It is institutionalised inequality, the intrinsic
economic exploitation of workers by the capitalist class, and the alienations
associated with consumer capitalism that form the context for criminality
under capitalism (Gordon 1971; Chambliss 1975c; Colvin & Pauly 1983;
Lea & Young 1984; Field 1990; White 2002a; de Giorgi 2006). In essence,
where you are located in the class structure will influence the kinds of
criminal activity you engage in, the propensity for you to engage in such
activity, and the intensity of that involvement.

The pressures and limits of circumstance—and thus *offender choice*—
vary according to class position. For example, economic forms of
criminality involve different motivations, propensities and characteristics,
depending upon class background and circumstance. Crimes perpetuated
by the working class are largely the result of a need to ensure economic
subsistence; that is, a need to live. This situation can be contrasted with
motivations based on accumulation rather than subsistence. Hence, the
choices open to an offender are dictated by wider structural imperatives to
maximise profit, or by immediate subsistence pressures. In addition, both
individuals who are powerful and those who are less powerful in society
can be deeply alienated from other members of the human community.

For a Marxist, to respond to crime is to expose the extent and nature
of the social harm perpetrated by the powerful in society (see Tombs &
Whyte 2006; Hillyard & Tombs 2007). It is argued that crimes of the
powerful have a much greater economic and social impact than 'street
crime' and working-class crimes generally, and that if coercion is to be
used it should be directed at those doing the *most harm*.

Simultaneously, effort is put into challenging the manner in which the
state apparatus is used to *repress the working class*. This extends to such
issues as public-order policing—especially of the unemployed, poor and
minority groups—and the policing of class conflict in the form of union
strikes and industrial disputes. Further, other theorists have sought to

investigate the differential policing and punishment of industrial, rather than criminal, manslaughter (Tombs 2008).

In ideal terms, the operation of the criminal justice system should be based upon full *public accountability* of each apparatus of the state (such as the police, courts, prisons); a genuine upholding of human rights; law reform that is designed to protect the interests of the working class (for example, enshrining the right to strike); and a *democratisation of institutions* (by a combination of participatory involvement of citizens and election to decision-making positions within the criminal justice system).

The best form of crime prevention is one that addresses the basic problem of a concentration of wealth and power into a small number of hands in society. Crime is seen to flourish in a context of inequality and structural pressures towards capitalist accumulation and profit. Alternatively, it is felt that much crime can be eliminated or reduced through the extension of radical democracy throughout society and its institutions, the *collective ownership and control over the means of production* (such as various forms of nationalised industry), and a redistribution of societal resources according to *human need*.

historical development

Within the Marxist framework it is argued that history can be seen in terms of a succession of different 'modes of production' (see, for example, Cornforth 1987). Each mode of production encompasses particular forces of production (for example, tools, techniques), relations of production (for example, lord–serf, capitalist–proletariat) and social institutions (for example, monarchy, parliamentary democracy). So, as societies move from, for example, feudalism to capitalism, we see a shift in the mode of production across these areas: from agriculture to industry; from power concentrated among the aristocracy to power concentrated among the bourgeoisie or capitalist class; from institutions built upon the notion of the divine right of monarchs to those based upon rule of law that binds the ruler as well as the ruled.

The emergence of different modes of production has been associated with the rise of different kinds of class societies, where the central dynamic of each society is that the surplus wealth created by its direct producers is expropriated by those who own and control the overall means of production. For instance, in a slave-based economy (as in ancient Greece or Rome), the slave-owner appropriates the surplus product of slave labour; in a feudal society, the lord appropriates the surplus product of the serf; and, in capitalist society, the factory owner appropriates the surplus labour of the worker. Hence, the concept of economic exploitation and class struggle are central to the Marxist view.

In order to place the rise of conflict approaches and Marxist criminology into perspective, we need to acknowledge the impact of recent historical developments. In the last century and a half, for example, we have witnessed the birth and growth of a new class—the working class or proletariat—and with this the rise of distinctively working-class political organisations (such as trade unions) and theories (such as social democracy and socialism). In particular, the philosophies and analyses provided by Marxism and anarchism voiced the concerns of working people to forge a new kind of social order in which the working class, rather than the capitalist class, was in power. Revolutionary ideas were in a number of instances accompanied by actual revolutions. Some of these were successful (as in the overthrow of the Tsar in Russia in 1917) and some were not (as in France in 1871 and Germany in 1918–19).

As the twentieth century unfolded, rebellion and revolution were to be features of many peasant and working-class revolts around the world. Class conflict was an ingrained part of life for many people. Class conflict was manifest in the form of periodic economic recessions that disproportionately affected the working class (as in Australia in the mid-1800s, the 1890s, the 1930s and the mid-1970s), and in the form of struggles over industrial issues (such as strikes and lockouts) and political activism (the formation of the Australian Labor Party and, later, the Communist Party of Australia). It was a time of conflict, revolution and change.

Early Marxist writings on crime in the first few decades of the twentieth century discussed the ways in which crime is an outcome of the precipitating economic and social conditions of capitalism. Bonger (1916) and Sellin (1937, 1938), for example, argued that 'criminal thought' is generated by the conditions of want and misery foisted upon sections of the working class, and is also the result of the greed that underpins the capitalist competitive process. In Australia, the work of Wood on convict history provided an important stepping stone for later radical historians, who likewise saw crime as stemming from the twin evils of poverty and a savage and unjust criminal code (cited in Garton 1991). However, generally speaking, these writings went against the mainstream of criminology of the time. It was not until the 1970s that Marxist criminology was incorporated into the field as a significant and popular perspective in its own right.

During the 1960s and 1970s, American criminologists such as Quinney and Chambliss directly challenged the prevailing approaches in criminology. Clear distinctions were drawn between a conservative ('functionalist') and a radical ('conflict') perspective on the nature of crime and law enforcement. It was argued that where there are class divisions in a society, you will find different capacities to determine the content of the laws of that society (Chamblis & Seidman 1971; Chambliss 1973). The powerful ruling class will be able to shape the criminalisation process in such a way as to protect its own collective interests, which reflect the interconnection between this class and a particular state form (see Chambliss 1975b; Chambliss & Mankoff 1976; Quinney 1970, 1974a, 1974b).

How issues are constructed, how crime is defined and how crime is responded to all relate directly to one's position in the class structure. If social power is concentrated in the hands of those who own the means of production, then they will influence and generally dictate what behaviour will be defined as criminal and what will not. For example, shoplifting may be considered theft, but false advertising may be viewed as only a trade practices violation. Similarly, those with power are capable of influencing the nature of societal reaction to behaviours deemed to be socially harmful. For example, whether to prosecute industrial homicide as murder or simply to see it as accidental or a product of workers' negligence is dependent upon the perspective applied to the issues of workplace crime (Pearce & Tombs 1993, 1998; Tombs 2008; Tombs & Whyte 2008).

In developing a new typology of crime—one that dealt with both crimes of the powerful and crimes of the less powerful—Quinney (1977) argued that analysis of the relationship between class, state and crime is essential. It was put forward that, on the one hand, there are *crimes of domination*. These are crimes committed by the capitalist class, the state and the agents of the capitalist class and the state. They include crimes of control (such as police brutality, violation of civil liberties), crimes of government (such as warfare, political assassination) and crimes of economic domination (such as pollution, price-fixing). On the other hand, there are *crimes of accommodation and resistance*, which are associated with the working class. These include predatory crimes (such as burglary, robbery), personal crimes (such as murder, assault, rape), and crimes of resistance (such as workplace sabotage, protests).

Criminality is intimately tied to class position, and the logic of a system that is geared towards capital accumulation rather than the meeting of social need (Quinney 1974b; Greenberg 1993). According to Quinney

(1977: 60), crime must be understood from the point of view of the political economy of capitalism:

> Those who own and control the means of production, the capitalist class, attempt to secure the existing order through various forms of domination, especially crime control by the capitalist state. Those who do not own and control the means of production, especially the working class, accommodate to and resist capitalist domination in various ways.

A crucial concept within the Marxist framework is that of *surplus population*, in that much of the existing forms of criminalisation and public concern with 'street crime' are seen to be targeted at those layers or sections of the population that are surplus to the labour market and the requirements of capitalism generally (Bonger 1916; Spitzer 1975; Field 1990; Colvin & Pauly 1983). A broad political economic analysis of capitalism set the scene for research and writing on more specific aspects of class conflict and class processes relating to crime.

For example, arising from concerns with class and class analysis of society, attention was drawn to the specific ways in which the activities of working-class juveniles have been subject to particular processes of criminalisation. The research of the Birmingham Centre for Contemporary Cultural Studies in England, for instance, re-examined the issue of youth subcultures from the point of view of the unequal material circumstances of working-class boys and girls (Hall & Jefferson 1976). It was argued that class was central to any explanation of the experience of 'growing up', and that the relationship between young people and social institutions such as school, work and the legal system was characterised by different forms of class-based resistance to the relations of power and domination. Certain youth subcultures were seen to 'solve', in an imaginary way, problems experienced by working-class young people (such as unemployment, educational disadvantage) that at the material level remained unresolved (Clarke et al. 1976; Brake 1985).

From the point of view of social control and policing, various studies pointed to the ways in which the media portrayed certain types of youth subcultures, which in turn led to a form of 'deviancy amplification' (Cohen 1972; Young 1971). That is, the sort of public labelling that pertained to some groups of young people actually generated further 'deviant' behaviour in the group so labelled. More generally, the link was made between the actual experiences of working-class young people — culturally, socially and economically — and the manner in which the state, particularly the police, intervened in their lives both coercively (such as arrest rates) and ideologically (through the promulgation of 'moral panics' over their behaviour and attitudes).

By providing a structural perspective on social institutions, social processes and social outcomes, Marxist approaches argued that revolutionary or profound social transformation is needed if 'crime' is to be addressed in a socially just manner.

then & now

marxist criminology

The influence of capitalism and power on crime was first analysed from a Marxist perspective by the Dutch criminologist Willem Bonger in his text *Criminality and Economic Conditions* (1916). Marxist criminology has often been connected to activism and protest. Willem Bonger was a fierce critic of Nazism and was personally affected by the rise of Nazism in the 1930s. He argued that the capitalist system, with its focus on individual success over the collective good, led to both crime and brutalisation of the poor. These themes were further emphasised in the Marxist criminology that flourished in the 1970s. Marxism is important to some feminist theories (Chapter 7) and some theorists working in critical criminology (Chapter 11). Marxist criminologists in the 1970s wrote at a time of protest and rebellion, particularly around civil rights and anti-war issues. However, Left Realist criminology (Chapter 9) was to criticise Marxist criminologists for not having practical responses to the problem of crime, especially responses that would help those most affected by aggressive violence: the poor. The entrenchment of global inequality and the overarching power of transnational companies has, however, rejuvenated interest in critical class analysis in recent years, especially as it relates to workplace crime. Further, there has been a renewed interest in class differences in the experience of victimisation, and critical analyses of 'fear of crime' measures.

contemporary examples

In Marxist criminology, the concern is to highlight the inequalities of a class society (such as wealth and poverty; business profits and low wages), and to show how these have an impact upon the criminalisation process. The powerful are seen as designing the laws in their own collective interests, while having greater capacity to defend themselves individually if they do break and bend the existing rules and regulations. The less powerful in society are propelled to commit crime by economic need and social alienation. They are also the main targets of law enforcement and wider criminal justice agencies. This is reflected in statistics that show an overrepresentation of the unemployed and poor in prisons, in police lock-ups and in the courts.

Because of a range of academic institutional factors (such as the rise of postmodernism as a perspective) and external political changes (such as the collapse of Stalinism and the demise of large Marxist-orientated political parties in the West), the Marxist perspective waned within criminological circles in the 1980s. In its stead, there developed a broader and more inclusive radical approach that we describe in Chapter 11 as critical criminology, and various liberal strands of criminology, such as Left Realism and republican theory. Nevertheless, there are ongoing attempts to restate and make applicable the basic propositions of Marxist criminology today, especially in the light of the increasing polarisation of wealth and poverty on a world scale, internationalisation of crime, and the further concentration and monopolisation of production.

The ongoing contribution of a Marxist framework to understanding contemporary developments in society, and criminal justice specifically, has long been highlighted in the work and writings of Jeffrey Reiman (1998). Reiman first published his book *The Rich Get Richer and the Poor Get Prison* in 1979, and as the title suggests, the book is an analysis of the economic biases, ideological processes and social inequalities associated with the criminal justice system. In later editions, the book includes an appendix that provides a detailed outline of the Marxist critique of criminal justice. Marxism as an analytical framework may have declined in popularity among academic intellectuals, but Reiman argues (1999) that the issues with which it is concerned have not lost any of their potency or relevance.

As Reiman (1999: 1) puts it: 'Economic bias is still with us. What has changed is that the attention and concern that was once focused on economic bias as a serious problem that threatened to undermine the legitimacy of the criminal justice system has steadily diminished.' For Reiman, economic bias has continued and, in some respects, deepened. The lack of attention to the contours and dimensions of this bias among social scientists and political leaders is explained in terms of the power of ideology, and specifically what he refers to as the 'angle of moral vision'. Reiman says that the 'awareness' of economic bias may well still be there, but its 'acceptance' indicates that differences in wealth are perceived simply as morally irrelevant differences (1999: 4). Thus, analytically, Marxism is seen to continue to provide important insights into class inequality, and the ideologies and institutions that sustain this. The political attractiveness and criminological implications of the perspective, however, tend to be bound up with the degree of social upheaval and social movement within society at large. In other words, the social context within which Marxist analysis takes place forms an important part of how it is received in the wider intellectual and political communities.

The works of White (2008a), White and van der Velden (1995), Hillyard & Tombs (2004), Tombs & Whyte (2008) and Pearce & Tombs (1993, 1998) provide examples of contemporary Marxist writing on issues of class and criminology. Each of these theorists argues that there are typical patterns of crime associated with specific classes. This is because class position embodies diverse material circumstances and variable capacities to marshal economic and political resources, and this in turn depends upon one's relationship to the means of production. To put it differently, the wealth and power one has determines the kind of crime in which one might engage or, alternatively, the kind of crime in which one is victimised. Thus, the crimes of the capitalist class are linked both to augmentation of personal wealth and to attempts to secure an advantage in the process of 'doing business'. This translates into various types of criminal fraud and illegal business transactions. By way of contrast, working-class criminality is seen as based on subsistence, designed to supplement income or in some cases to be of a survival nature (such as theft, shoplifting). Further, working-class crime also includes a range of activities that reflect the various alienations experienced by workers, such as vandalism, rape and racist attacks.

The impact of the crimes of the powerful is often diffuse, yet they affect a large number of people directly or indirectly simply because of the capacity of the capitalist to do harm on a large scale. For example, tax avoidance or environmental destruction (White 2008b, 2009a, 2009b, 2011) may have a considerable social cost, but not be 'visible' in the public domain in the same way as 'street crime'. In defending themselves against prosecution, the powerful have greater social resources at their disposal with which to protect their interests. Furthermore, the sheer costs associated with investigation and prosecution of white-collar and corporate crime often make it prohibitive for the state to proceed, or to cast a wide net to catch other violations similar to the exceptional few that are prosecuted (Tombs 2008; Alvesalo et al. 2006; Tombs & Whyte 2009;

Haines 2011; Sutton & Haines 2011). Crimes of the powerful may have significant structural effects in terms of lives lost and financial impacts (Brill 1982; Pearce & Tombs 1993, 1998). Because such crimes are usually directed, in the first instance, against other capitalists or against the rules governing the marketplace, they are rarely perceived by the general public as being of special interest to them personally (except in the case of events such as industrial homicide).

By way of contrast, the crimes of the less powerful tend to be highly visible and to be subjected to wide-scale state intervention involving police, welfare workers, social security officials, tax department officials, the courts and prisons (Hunt 2004; White 2009b). A feature of relative powerlessness is that the crimes committed tend to be individualised, and thus to have a discrete impact. There is usually one victim (or a few), whether personal or business or household, and the impact of the offence is limited to the actual household or person violated (White & van der Velden 1995). Crimes relating to welfare fraud and tax fraud, while institutional in nature, tend to involve relatively small amounts of money that supplement rather than substantially augment an individual's income. The response of the major institutions in society is largely orientated towards stopping these kinds of crimes, regardless of the comparatively greater amount of damage caused by crimes of the powerful. The lack of access to resources, such as control of the media and legal experts, means that working-class people are more vulnerable to apprehension, prosecution and punishment at the hands of the capitalist state. They are exposed to societal control mechanisms in such a way that they feel the full force of the state for any transgression they might commit.

In this analysis, issues of the regulation of an 'underclass' and the policing of working-class communities are bound up with the cyclical and long-term deterioration of the social and economic conditions of life for the majority in capitalist society (see Spitzer 1975; White & van der Velden 1995; Antonaccio & Tittle 2007). The structural conditions producing working-class crime (such as unemployment and cutbacks in welfare spending) are seen to have implications, as well, for the capacity of the state to respond other than coercively to 'street crime'. When the state faces a fiscal crisis (a crisis around a real or perceived lack of government funds), it cannot use welfare-type measures as the only means to deal with the social fallout arising from capitalist restructuring. The harsher 'law-and-order' strategies most commonly adopted to manage the working class (which can be seen in any election campaign, and in the current imprisonment rates across the world) will only make worse the political isolation, socio-cultural alienation, and economic decline of the marginalised layers of the working class, thus causally feeding the very criminality that the campaign for enhanced social control is designed to overcome.

Most criminological theories focus their attention on those crimes perpetrated by the working class. Marxist theory, however, redirects our attention away from 'street crimes' and compels us to examine crimes of the powerful. The question then arises of how we are to do this, given the concentration of power and the ability of the powerful to define crime in their interests. For example, within capitalist society there are contested definitions concerning criminal behaviour (what ought to be criminalised), and instances where criminal offences exist but are not enforced (what is actually criminalised). In other words, the criminality of this behaviour is perceived as ambivalent within the capitalist system—there is uncertainty whether or not an activity is really criminal—and whether or not the powerful in some instances should be labelled as criminal, as in the case of industrial homicide (Tombs & Whyte 2008; Pearce & Tombs 1993, 1998; White 2009b).

Alternatively, Marxists argue that there is a need to broaden the definition of crime. This entails establishing wider criteria relating to the nature of offences (see Schwendinger & Schwendinger 1975), including a more critical understanding of harm and risk (Tombs & Whyte 2006; Hillyard & Tombs 2007). The definition of crime would accordingly extend to encompass any activity that interferes with one's human rights, including things such as racism, sexism and so on. Ultimately, Marxists argue that wherever economic exploitation exists, a crime has occurred.

{from theory to practice: corporate crime}

Tombs, S. (2006). '"Violence", Safety Crimes and Criminology', *British Journal of Criminology*, 47 (4): 531–50.

To date, mainstream criminological approaches to violence have largely ignored those harms generated within the workplace, and as a consequence of the production process. According to Tombs (2006: 531), even a cursory glance at the costs and harms created by 'safety crimes' demonstrates that 'one is more likely to be a victim of a fatal ... injury related to work than one is to be a victim of so-called conventional violence'.

Tombs concedes that many of these workplace injuries may not be crimes, as they are commonly understood. Yet, most involve the violation of occupational health and safety laws. As such, even within the most conservative definition of crime—as a breach of the law—these workplace injuries constitute a criminal act. Tombs asks therefore: why are safety crimes not considered within mainstream criminology, and what would criminology look like if these crimes were integrated into models of criminal behaviour and criminal justice administration?

As a means to illustrate the problems criminology has had in integrating safety crimes into the research agenda on violence, Tombs initially assessed and evaluated how the issue was addressed by three significant sites of agenda-setting in the UK. In his study of the primary criminological textbook used in the UK—*The Oxford Handbook of Criminology* (Maguire et al. 2002)—Tombs found that despite the authors' commitment to critically analyse (and be more 'imaginative' about) the limitations imposed by some definitions of violence, they proceeded as if violence were only interpersonal and not an outcome of institutional practices. This 'authoritative' reading of violence marked out the field of study, and delimited the imagination of most British undergraduate and postgraduate students. Second, Tombs analysed the definition of violence used by the Economic and Social Research Council's Violence Research Programme. Again, while the coordinators set out to expand conventional ideas about what constituted violence, the stated aims of the research programme explicitly limited the research endeavour to 'the various forms of violence to the person' (cited in Tombs 2006: 534). The conflation of violence with interpersonal violence in the guiding documents of the program inevitably led to projects that ignored the collective/institutional violence of safety crimes.

In the final area of evaluation, Tombs analysed the research generated from the British Crime Survey's data on 'violence at work'. In this burgeoning field, Tombs hoped to find the theoretical and methodological tools required to expand the meaning of violence to include safety crimes. However, in key reports, the definition of violence at work adopted by the Home Office included only those 'assaults or threats which occurred while the victim was working and were *perpetrated by members of the public*' (Budd 1999 cited in Tombs 2006: 536, emphasis in original). The field of research was immediately narrowed to exclude those acts of violence perpetrated (deliberately or by omission) by employers or organisations.

Tombs argues that each of these considerations of violence share two characteristics: namely, the primacy of intention, and the focus on individual (rather than collective or institutional) sources of violence. Apart from the work of a few criminologists (such as Bowie 2002 and Reiman 1998), Tombs argues that the study of 'violence at work' continues to be framed by individualism—both in terms of individual intent, and of 'mad, bad, or sad' individual perpetrators (Tombs 2006: 542). However, he suggests that innovations at the margins of criminology (such as 'green' criminology, and genocide studies) offer opportunities to break from this criminological tradition of individualism. In particular, Tombs advocates the adoption of Salmi's (2004 cited in Tombs 2006: 544–5) framework, in which the issue of violence is considered through four dimensions of violence: direct, indirect, repressive and alienating. In adopting this approach, Tombs suggests we are better able to evaluate the harms of all violence, and can begin to question the core assumptions underlining mainstream criminology's violence, pathology, and agency.

critique

Despite the overview given above, it is clear that Marxist criminology—like many other strands of criminology—has variations on a particular theme. The theme here is that capitalist exploitation leads to criminal behaviour and criminalisation of one group (the workers) to a greater extent than the powerful in society. While there are considerable areas of agreement between Marxist criminologists, there are also considerable areas of disagreement.

One concern of some Marxist criminologists relates to the use of the term 'criminal'. For example, Steinart (1985) argues that the term 'crime' has lost any useful meaning it might once have held. It is too imbued with the capitalist ethos, so that the symbolic emotive aspect of the label cannot be separated from its capitalist connotation. For this reason, the term is of no use to Marxists. Rather, he argues that the term should not be used; instead, the aim of Marxist criminology should be to highlight those who are harmed the most (the proletariat) and devise policies that have the sole aim of reducing harm, without recourse to criminal law or criminal process. Such a position is labelled as 'left idealist' by those advocating Left Realism, a theory discussed in Chapter 9.

While some would see this position as extreme (including many Marxists), it does overcome a central problem in Marxist criminology: namely, how to define crime. Is there a qualitative difference between the harm that is labelled 'criminal' and other sorts of harm? Traditional perspectives in criminology insist that crime consists of both 'the harm' and 'the guilty mind'. One of the problems with this definition is that 'the guilty mind' takes actions out of context, in particular a context where the powerful dictate the conditions under which the powerless act. Furthermore, harm in the white-collar area results, in many cases, from many negligent minds rather than one guilty mind. For these reasons Marxist criminologists have moved away from the notion of *mens rea* and criminal motivation, and focused on the degree of harm. In an era of risk management, some authors such as Hillyard & Tombs (2004, 2007) have been able to revisit the very notions of crime, harm and risk, without the often inherent idealism of earlier radical and Marxist criminologists.

The problem then becomes what harm to define as criminal (Moxon 2011). This has led, as we have seen, to very broad definitions of what constitutes criminal activity; for example, 'any activity that interferes with one's basic human rights', or 'wherever economic exploitation exists' (Russell 2003), a crime has occurred. Some would argue such definitions are so broad that they lose any useful meaning (Cohen 1993), and alienate wide sectors of society that may be sympathetic to the general thrust of Marxist criminology. This raises big issues for criminology generally; that is, the terms 'crime' and 'non-crime' are dichotomous, whereas in reality degrees of harm can be considered along a scale. Definitions of crime that are broad (or narrow) do not solve this problem of trying to squeeze a variable that exists on a continuum (such as harm) into dichotomous categories, such as criminal/not criminal.

Furthermore, Cohen (1988) argues that there is a tendency for those who argue for greater use of the criminal law against white-collar crime, such as the Marxists, to forget the problems associated with using the criminal law to curb harmful behaviour. Earlier research has mapped out a multitude of problems associated with processing people through the criminal justice system, such as the problems associated with stigmatisation and the costs involved in criminal prosecutions. There is also the issue of the politics of criminalisation. Any push to criminalise behaviour is subject to political contingencies that result in unintended consequences of reform; instead of ameliorating the harm, it may indeed exacerbate it.

Marxists have been subjected to further criticism as well. It has been argued that aspects of Marxist writing in criminology have a romantic image of the criminal as 'primitive class rebel' (Sparks 1980). These conceptualisations understate the real harm caused by such 'rebels'. Those who are the victims of antisocial behaviour, often poor themselves, suffer considerable hardship at the hands of those who commit 'street crime'.

Some Marxists have been criticised for conspiratorial overtones in their analyses regarding, for example, the direct involvement of members of the ruling class in dictating the operational activities of the police (Hall & Scraton 1981). Critics argue that there are many examples where laws are enacted to fetter the activities of specific capitalists (such as anti-trust law, particularly in the United States). Further, there are many laws in existence that restrain the activities of individual capitalists, which would seem to refute the Marxist argument that the criminal law always defines the activities of the powerless as criminal and never those of the powerful (Sutton & Haines 2011).

This criticism, however, highlights a debate within Marxism itself concerning the precise nature of the state. Some, such as Miliband (1969), have argued that the state can be viewed as an instrument of class rule by virtue of the close social relationship between the top members of the state apparatus (such as high-level bureaucrats and members of the military establishment) and members of the capitalist class (such as bankers, media owners, industrialists and other corporate leaders). Others, such as Poulantzas (1972), have argued that the state exists to promote the interests of capital-in-general, not individual capitalists. In the end, both Miliband and Poulantzas would be unfazed by the criticism above that laws have a negative impact on individual capitalists. They would see that the state exists to maintain conditions for capital accumulation, and defend those conditions, whether threatened by individuals of the ruling class or the proletariat. However, the state, by defending the conditions of capital accumulation, ultimately enhances the prospects of the ruling class as a whole.

In terms of crime, it is clear that one cannot reduce crime to a simple equation with poverty or alienation. If this were so, then we would need to explain why it is that not every person living in poverty commits crime, and why some people who appear to be well-off do engage in crimes such as vandalism and homicide. This does occur. Nor can a simple class-based equation help us understand violence against women and children (Simpson & Ellis 1994) or homophobic violence. However, Marxists are more interested in general trends and broad predictions, based upon the notion that social context shapes the choices or options actually available to a person. The choices for the poor concerning whether to steal or not are categorically different to the choices for the rich; furthermore, these conditions are structurally determined.

Some criminologists, such as Carson (1979) and Sparks (1980), although sympathetic to a Marxist analysis, argue that the approach is too broad and sweeping. While it may provide a good basis for understanding the basic direction societies take, it is less useful at helping us understand the complexities along the way. In short, Marxism provides a useful sense of the destination towards which capitalist societies are headed, but little in the way of a road map with which to make sense of the twists and turns of how crime and harm are experienced and struggled over within communities over time.

Importantly, not all criminal laws can be defined as 'class' laws, as some deal with class-neutral questions, such as sexual assault, intimate partner violence and hate violence against gay men, lesbians, and the disabled and/or elderly. This suggests that power may not be totally encapsulated or explicable in class terms. Power and powerlessness can exist in a sense outside the class structure, such as the power of men over women. Similar concerns have been expressed in relation to issues of racism and the relative position of different ethnic groups in society. In either case, however, there are usually strong class factors that shape the contours of the power relationship between men and women, and different ethnic and 'race' groups. The same cannot be said, though, in relation to homophobic or heterosexist offending and victimisation.

There are many diverse interpretations and explanations for crime from within the broadly Marxist framework. Some of them offer rather simplistic formulations (for example, the ruling class directly defines what is criminal or not) and some of them provide detailed, sophisticated accounts as to how class power is exercised via the state to enforce basic class rule (for example, through analysis of personnel, decision-making processes, limits to reform). Overall, however, it can be said that the strength of such approaches is that they attempt to locate social action within the wider structural context of a class-divided society. In doing so, they elevate the issue of power and control to the foreground of criminological analysis, and they stress the ways in which social background and social processes give rise to certain propensities (on the part of the powerful and on the part of the less powerful) to engage in criminal activity.

{conclusion}

Marxists argue that, within contemporary capitalist societies, the capitalist mode of production operates at many levels, both national and global, and this has an impact economically, socially and politically. There is a concentration of wealth and power into the hands of transnational corporations, which control both material and cultural production. The penetration of capitalist relations and enterprises (as in Russia), and the concentration of economic power into fewer hands (for example, Murdoch), is apparent on a world scale. Internationally and at the national level, the number of poor is growing and the rich are getting richer.

Marxist criminology argues that the concentration of wealth and power into the hands of a small capitalist class has ramifications for the definition of, and responses to, crime. If power is concentrated in the hands of those who own the means of production, they will influence, and to a certain extent dictate, what behaviour will be defined as crime and what will not. Those with power are likewise capable of influencing the nature of societal reaction to behaviours deemed to be criminal. There is thus an ability here to influence how the state will intervene, for example, on issues relating to environmental destruction.

According to a Marxist perspective, if we wish to examine crime and class in the global context, we must determine who it is that controls the finances (such as the banks or the International Monetary Fund); we must evaluate trade agreements that define how the benefits of trade are to be distributed, and the conditions of trade that will be adhered to; and we must consider the

⋯ impact of mass production and technology (including new information technology) on the lives of workers. Class divisions exist both within and between countries. The existence of the rich and the poor, the divide between the North and the South, are symptomatic of processes of polarisation that fundamentally determine the distribution and definition of crime. For a Marxist, the fundamental questions revolve around the implications of such divisions for the nature and causes of crime, and for the manner of state intervention into people's lives. These ideas were essential in the development of feminist criminology.

{**further reading**}

Chambliss, W.J. (1975c). 'Toward a Political Economy of Crime', *Theory and Society*, 2 (2): 149–70.

Chambliss, W.J. & Seidman, R. (1971). *Law, Order, and Power*, Addison-Wesley, Reading, MA.

Greenberg, D. (ed.) (1993). *Crime and Capitalism: Readings in Marxist Criminology*, Temple University Press, Philadelphia.

Lynch, M.J. & Stretesky, P.B. (eds) (2011). *Radical and Marxist Theories of Crime*, Ashgate, Surrey, UK.

Pearce, F. & Snider, L. (1992). 'Special Edition: Crimes of the Powerful', *Journal of Human Justice*, 3 (2).

Quinney, R. (1977). *Class, State
and Crime: On the Theory and
Practice of Criminal Justice*,
David McKay, New York.

Reiman, J. (1998). *The Rich Get
Richer and the Poor Get Prison*,
Allyn & Bacon, Boston.

Spitzer, S. (1975). 'Toward a
Marxian Theory of Deviance',
Social Problems, 22: 638-51.

Tombs, S. & Whyte, D. (2008).
*A Crisis of Enforcement: The
Decriminalisation of Death and
Injury at Work*, Centre for Crime
and Justice Studies, London.

White, R. & van der Velden, J.
(1995). 'Class and Criminality',
Social Justice, 22 (1): 51-74.

White, R.D. (2009b). 'Toxic
Cities—Globalizing the Problem
of Waste', *Social Justice*,
35 (3): 107-19.

feminist perspectives

{introduction}
—

The intention of this chapter is to discuss and review issues pertaining to feminist perspectives in criminology. To do this adequately, we need to know something about the position of women and girls generally within the broad criminological discipline, and how gender differences or similarities have been theorised within the field.

The previous chapter outlined the impact of class structure on the construction of criminality, and fundamental motivational distinctions were drawn between crimes of the powerful and those of the powerless. This chapter shares some themes in common with Marxist criminology. Namely, feminist criminology has been centrally concerned with issues of power, the distribution of economic and social resources, and the differential position of selected groups in society, which has implications for their activities as both 'offenders' or 'victims'. Feminist criminology, in most of its forms, seeks to address the absence of women from much of the early theorising about crime, especially those approaches that sought answers to the 'causes' of crime through the study of men alone. From feminist perspectives, the focus is on the sexist operation of the criminal justice system, girls' and women's experiences of crime and criminality, and the role that gender plays in criminological theory.

—

social context

Marxist criminology put questions of power on the agenda in a forceful way during the 1970s. Feminist criminology also looks at who holds and wields power in society, and questions how this has an impact on women. Feminist criminology developed in the late 1960s and into the 1970s, and was closely associated with the emergence of the Second Wave of feminism at this time. History reveals that women have long been oppressed as a group, denied rights and subjected to violence. The new movement was called the Second Wave of feminism in recognition that the First Wave of feminism had surfaced in the form of the suffragette movement towards the end of the nineteenth century. This movement had been expressly concerned with attaining political power through gaining the vote for women.

The advent of the Second Wave of feminism in the 1970s saw the formation of a dynamic social movement that projected many issues into the public domain, highlighting both the structural oppression of women and the general abuses and crimes directed at them. In its radical phase, the Second Wave of feminism was called the *Women's Liberation Movement*. The social agenda was radical social transformation. The key demands were:

- equal pay
- equal education and job opportunities
- free contraception and abortion on demand
- free twenty-four-hour nurseries, under community control
- legal and financial independence
- an end to discrimination against lesbians
- freedom from intimidation by the threat or use of violence or sexual coercion, regardless of marital status
- an end to the laws, assumptions and institutions that perpetuate male dominance and men's aggression towards women (Feminist Anthology Collective 1981).

In any discussion of feminism, there is a fundamental distinction to be made between sex and gender. This distinction is likewise at the nub of explanations of male and female offending and victimisation. *Sex* (male/female) is a biological classification indicated primarily by genital characteristics. *Gender* (masculine/feminine) is a social construct, not a biological given. Concepts of masculinity and femininity are part of the learned culture and can be indicated by dress, gestures, language, occupation and so on.

In a review of feminist thought and criminology, Daly and Chesney-Lind (1988: 504) describe what they see as the key defining elements of feminism as a mode of analysis:

– Gender is not a natural fact, but a complex social, historical and cultural product; it is related to, but not simply derived from, biological sex difference and reproductive capacities.

– Gender and gender relations order social life and social institutions in fundamental ways.

– Gender relations and constructs of masculinity and femininity are not symmetrical, but are based on an organising principle of men's superiority, and social, political and economic dominance over women.

– Systems of knowledge reflect men's views of the natural and social world; the production of knowledge is gendered.

– Women should be at the centre of intellectual enquiry, not peripheral, invisible or appendages to men.

Feminism has much to contribute to our understanding of both biological and social constructions of the female (see, for example, Eisenstein 1984). Early feminist works, for instance, looked at sex roles and distinguished the differences between males and females in a biological and social sense; they essentially sought to explore whether sex roles are biological or social.

This questioning was followed by a period in which feminists looked not at the polarisations between men and women, but rather at the similarities. The focus of analysis here was on androgyny. Males and females were said to exhibit characteristics that were similar as a whole. For example, musicians such David Bowie, Grace Jones, Michael Jackson and Lady Gaga have at times presented an androgynous image that combined elements of 'femininity' and 'masculinity'.

Another approach adopted a women-centred analysis, which explored the specifically different characteristics of women stemming from their biology or physiology. The emphasis here was on the fundamental, special divisions that separate men and women. For instance, the ability of women to give birth—to perpetuate the human race—was viewed as rendering women essentially superior to men in regard to aspects of caring, sharing and loving another person.

Regardless of specific orientation, feminism deals with the structural position of women in society. For example, there is a call for greater autonomy and the advocacy of rights for women in social, political and economic spheres. Feminist movements were initially motivated for change because of a perceived inequality of autonomy and rights. This can be generalised to all women in society or can be applied to specific categories of women. Indigenous women, for instance, tend to be overrepresented in the criminal justice system. Some groups of women therefore experience specific concerns related to or stemming from their ethnicity, class position and national background.

Feminism is not a single theoretical approach; rather, it consists of a variety of perspectives, each of which has implications for how we view the world and respond to it. There are a number of competing explanatory frameworks focusing on the place of women and girls in society (see, for example, the differences between de Beauvoir 1952 [1949]; Daly 1978; Eisenstein 1984; Tong 1989; Segal 1987; Butler 1990; Haraway 1991; Woolf 2002). These various feminist strands are primarily concerned with autonomy, rights and power. The different perspectives within feminism broadly include the liberal, Marxist, radical, socialist, cultural and postmodernist/poststructuralist approaches, which are each discussed below.

¬ liberal feminism

This approach views the individual as the most important part of society. There is talk here about rights, dignities and freedoms of the individual. The hallmark of this perspective is the need to value reason, and not to discriminate against anyone. In the view of liberal feminists, the question of rights is paramount in the context of competitive views of the individual. Hence, the laws should be changed to ensure that women have equal rights. For example, it is seen as necessary to change legislation in order to provide equal opportunities in the sphere of paid work. There was a recent example of the assertion of such rights in a Western Australian case of female construction workers. The argument was that sexist violence (such as pornography and abusive language) existed in many forms on the worksite, and that female workers should not be exposed to this. The Equal Opportunities Board decided in this instance that the women were being denied the right to participate in the workforce.

¬ marxist feminism

This perspective is not so much concerned with traditional rights, but instead analyses the structural position of women in society in terms of paid and unpaid labour. The key category of employment for women is seen to be that of domestic labour, which is unpaid. This situation is viewed as exploitative. Even in those instances where women participate in the paid workforce, they tend to be lowly paid relative to their position and their male counterparts, and to be concentrated in insecure positions such as part-time and casual work. The argument advanced here is that if we want to deal with gender inequality then we need to do something to fundamentally transform class societies, such as capitalist ones, that are organised around the exploitation of female (and male working-class) labour.

¬ radical feminism

This approach stresses the common experiences of women; it is basically involved in collective consciousness-raising about the oppressions shared by all women. The assertion here is that all aspects of women's lives (both personal and political) are touched and shaped by patriarchal relations. The personal is viewed as inherently political. Women are viewed as an oppressed class, and all women are said to be subject to the oppressive structures of male domination. At the same time, all men share in some way in the benefits of that oppression. This approach examines the historical exclusion of women from political, social and economic spheres. The social institutions of home, the law, the workforce and the courts are examined in order to expose the victimisation of women across all spheres and institutions of life. The issue of male violence—physical, verbal and psychological—is of major significance.

¬ socialist feminism

This perspective agrees that in both the public and private spheres women have been, and continue to be, exploited and oppressed, but this is viewed within the framework of capitalist society. There is an emphasis here on the necessity of examining the commodification of women's bodies as a capitalist enterprise—for example, the pornography and advertising industries. It is contended that the nature of a class-divided society and the issue of male domination need to be considered in tandem. Women as a broad social category are subject to oppressive images and practices, but the specific nature of concrete instances of exploitation and inequality needs to be examined from the point of view of capitalist accumulation. In essence, the social and economic needs of women have been subordinated to the requirements of profit-making institutions, a process that directly affects many men as well. It is possible, therefore, to think of alliances with certain sections of the male population on some issues as a means to institute social change to the benefit of women.

¬ cultural feminism

This adopts a women-centred analysis that is often not tied to any specific economic or political program. It concentrates instead on the development of a separate women's culture and the special nature of women's relationships to each other and to society. This perspective manifests itself philosophically in the appeal of New Age religion, magic and mysticism. Women are seen as intrinsically and fundamentally different from men. They are seen to exhibit a number of gender-specific traits (such as caring and sharing attitudes) that are positive feminine features that make them somehow superior morally to their male counterparts. Alternatively, male traits, such as violence and egoism, are constant dangers to women individually and collectively. Hence, for many women, the solution is to separate themselves from male society, and thus domination, as far as they can. As part of this, it is also important to develop and expand a 'female discourse' or construction of the social world that sees things in specifically female gender terms.

¬ postmodern feminism

The standpoint perspective of earlier feminisms—such as the development of a body of knowledge relating to women's unique characteristics, experiences and shared oppression—is critiqued in postmodern feminism. From the late 1980s, feminism, as with many other social theories at this time, was subject to critique in light of newly emerging postmodern and poststructuralist concepts. In the case of feminism, this theoretical shift led to the dismissal of modernist notions of gender. In particular, by the mid-1990s, the very definition of what constitutes a woman became problematic. In understanding gender as a performance (rather than fixed by social or biological roles), this approach enabled feminists such as Butler (1990) to uncover the multiple, contradictory and complementary ways in which we 'do' gender. Rather than fixed categories of masculinity and femininity—men and women—these new approaches sought to move beyond gender as *the* explanatory tool. In adopting this approach, postmodern feminists do not seek to provide grand narratives or universal theories to explain women's experiences. Rather, they suggest that these experiences of gender are variable and fluid, and that our gendered experiences are the result of bio-power rather than structural inequalities.

⌐ women and crime

Each of the feminist perspectives identified in the previous section has implications for how we view and respond to female criminality. We must further understand that how we respond to 'crime issues' is determined by the way in which the law positions women in society. It is essential here to note that the language adopted within the law is generally gender-exclusive, which clearly advances the rights of 'man' but makes little if any mention of the rights of 'woman'.

Criminological theorising did not escape this gender-based critique (see, for example, Allen 1990). A couple of important observations in that regard can be made:

- There has been sheer neglect of women in criminological thought and enquiry, in part because of the male domination of academic criminology, both historically and in the present. This is an important point, since what results is necessarily a male perspective on the world, and the selection of issues perceived to be important by men.
- The criminal justice system is also dominated by male personnel: judges, barristers, solicitors, prison officers and police. Again, it can be argued that the composition of institutional workforces can have a significant impact on how that workforce pursues its tasks in practice.

Hence, in terms of theory and research and at the level of the practitioner, the system is dominated by men, and there is an obvious hegemonic masculinity informing the structures of the criminal justice system. While individual men (such as judges, magistrates and barristers) have, at particular times, challenged overtly sexist practices, this has not necessarily produced changes in the overall structural domination (that is, the way institutional practices themselves are systematically biased against women). Similarly, individual women have been directly involved in policing and other justice-agency practices, but in doing so may simply serve to reinforce the conservative views of ideal female sexual behaviour. For example, the policing of morality and behaviour of female children during the period of the 'child savers' movement at the turn of the nineteenth century was both conservative and spearheaded by women (Platt 1977). Such practices did not radically challenge the position of women in society.

The neglect of women within the discipline of criminology is a reflection not only of the composition of the criminal justice system, but also of women's relative absence from the criminal statistics. Women do not appear to be as statistically significant a problem as men. They appear generally to commit fewer crimes, and the crimes they do commit appear to be less serious than those committed by men, and they are less violent. Furthermore, in examining victimisation statistics, although there are female-specific categories of victimisation such as rape and domestic violence in which women appear overrepresented, women and girls do not appear to be victims of homicide to the same extent as men. As a consequence of such observations, investigators within the criminological field have often regarded it as unimportant to look at female offending or female victimisation.

When seeking to examine female offending, there has been the additional problem of applying male correlates. Theories of offending have generally been conducted within a male framework and constructed in male terms, with male research participants. Since mainstream criminological theories reflected a male experience, it was difficult to apply them to women or girls. For example, strain theory's concept of opportunity structures and cultural goals do not account for the gendered nature of both opportunity and culture (see Naffine 1987; Becker & McCorkel 2011). The limitations of mainstream criminology are discussed further below. For now it is important to acknowledge the need for, and significance of, a perspective that rejects theories of the 'causes' of crime when these approaches are the result of studying male criminality alone.

basic concepts

The feminist perspectives are based on the premise that women are structurally disadvantaged in the present society (see chart 7.1). That is, male domination and female subordination are an entrenched part of patriarchy, which expresses fundamental inequalities between the sexes. Sexual inequality and the disempowerment of women are embodied, as well, in the legal and criminal justice systems.

chart 7.1 | **feminist perspectives**

definition of crime	_ male violence _ institutionalised inequality and discrimination
focus of analysis	_ unequal position of women in society _ victimisation of women _ victim status of female offenders
cause of crime	_ criminality is a function of patriarchy _ result of social oppression and economic dependency on men and state
nature of offender	_ sexualisation of offences and victimisation according to gender criteria (such as 'femininity')
response to crime	_ social empowerment of women _ confrontation of institutions of male domination
crime prevention	_ economic, social, political power and equality _ antisexist training programs for judiciary and other sections of criminal justice system
operation of criminal justice system	_ provision of gender-specific services and support systems _ within criminal justice (such as jails) and welfare spheres (such as refuges)

Feminist criminology defines crime in terms of gender-based and gender-related types of activities. Specifically, a major concern is with the nature of *male violence*, as this has an impact upon both female offenders and female victims, and the ways in which forms of *gendered inequality and discrimination* are institutionalised throughout society. A substantial part of feminist criminology has been directed at exposing the 'hidden' levels of violence against women, and the structural oppressions that they have had to face over long periods of time.

The main focus of analysis, therefore, is the unequal position of women in society, the specific kinds of crimes committed against women as women, and the status of female offenders in the context of wider social inequalities and gender-based oppressions. Crime against and involving women is seen to be the result of *social oppression* and *economic dependency* upon men or the welfare apparatus of the state.

The way in which women, as victims and offenders, are processed by the criminal justice system is described in terms of the *sexualisation thesis*. This refers to the notion that when the criminal justice system and its agents deal with women (in whatever capacity) they do so on the basis of certain gender-related criteria; that is, the behaviour, marital status and appearance of women are constantly linked to particular ideas regarding the preferred forms of 'femininity'. In this way, what is labelled 'criminal' or an act of 'victimisation' depends to a large extent upon the perceived sexual behaviour and social status of the woman in question.

It is argued that there is a *double standard of morality and power* with respect to women in the criminal justice system. Men and women are treated differently on the basis of gendered stereotypes. Furthermore, in many cases this leads to inequitable and unfair treatment of women who present themselves as offenders or victims before the system. One manifestation of this double standard is the fact that the senior members of the police, judiciary and correctional apparatus are men, and that generally speaking they reflect existing prejudices regarding women's roles, status and position in society.

From the point of view of feminist criminology, there needs to be major changes to the existing criminal justice system and to society as a whole. The problem is ultimately seen as one of *social empowerment* of women as a broad category, and of confronting the negative and restricting nature of male domination as evident in the present institutional set-up.

To prevent crimes against women, and to forestall many of the crimes committed by women, it is necessary to have greater economic, social and political equality. Institutional reforms could include affirmative action policies to advance the position of women within the criminal justice and judicial systems; antisexist training for lawyers and judges; and law reforms that recognise and acknowledge the gendered nature of the social world. The criminal justice system needs an overhaul with respect to the provision of gender-specific services (such as trauma counselling and skills training) and support systems in areas such as detention, and more resources are needed in the wider 'welfare' domain (for example, rape crisis centres, refuges).

historical development

In the historical development of feminist criminology there are two points to note at the outset. The first is that, while female offenders were generally ignored in mainstream analysis, there were instances when they were specifically examined. However, this was a rather small and neglected area of criminological theorising. Second, the critique offered by feminists was that such theories as did exist were either overtly sexist in nature, or extremely limited in what they could say about the nature of female involvement in the criminal justice system.

When attempting to explain female crime as a distinct and specific social phenomenon, the mainstream theories accepted the narrow, conservative view regarding the place and position of women in society, and more often than not did so on the basis of a form of *biological reductionism*. This refers to instances where female experiences and behaviour are reduced to the imperatives of biology—the (biological) sex of a person is seen to dictate or determine appropriate social roles and practices in terms of one's gender (social constructions of femininity).

A key contribution of feminist criminology has been to critique one-sided, distorted views of women in the traditional literature that did exist on female offending. The basis of the critique had to do with the conflation of sex and gender (failure to distinguish the biological from the social) in much of the analysis on offer, and the misogynous (women-hating) character of some of the writing. Here we can point to several different theories that have ultimately based their conclusions upon the idea of innate female social characteristics linked to female biology.

¬ biological explanations

These explanations view female crime as stemming from biological causes (see, especially, Smart 1976; Naffine 1987). Most focus on sex-specific biological differences as the standards by which to compare men and women, and as explanations for particular kinds of activity (see Naffine 1987, Smart 1990a, Daly & Maher 1998 and Walklate 2004 for critiques of these perspectives). They vary in substantive emphasis, but the overall message of biological determinism remains the same:

–   Early theories argued that the true, biologically determined nature of women was antithetical to crime. Such views were based upon stereotypical notions of women as being passive and non-aggressive.

Criminality was linked to 'maleness' and 'masculine' traits such as aggression and physicality. Therefore the female offender, who was seen as exhibiting male traits, was considered doubly deviant, both socially and biologically—she was an exception to the usual sex of the offender and, as a woman, she went against her biological nature and thus was not fully female.

- Some theories discussed female criminality in terms of the physiological differences between the sexes. In this case, women conceal their offending behaviour (and thus have lower rates of report and detection than males) and use their sexuality to attain (presumed) greater leniency by the police and the courts; they do this because their nature is inherently deceitful and manipulative. This in turn is linked to their physiological make-up, in that women are capable of concealing their sexual arousal (unlike men) and thus in the most intimate human acts they have the opportunity and ability to manipulate those around them.

- In some recent theories, research on hormonal disturbances and social behaviour has tried to establish a link between pre- and postmenstrual activity, and the propensity of women to engage in criminal activity. In a similar vein, it is sometimes argued that postnatal depression is responsible in some instances for infanticide. In other words, as the female body fluctuates in terms of hormonal activity, women may engage in a wide variety of antisocial and criminal activity.

¬ socialisation theories

A common way to explain female crime is to point to differences in the ways in which men and women are, or should be, socialised. These types of explanations are generally closely tied to specific notions of appropriate sex roles. The problem is usually seen as inadequate socialisation, leading to a violation of the behaviour appropriate for members of the female sex (see Smart 1976, Daly & Maher 1998 and Walklate 2004 for critiques of these perspectives). Again, very often the approaches reduce crime causation to essentially biological or psychological factors.

- Some theories see deviancy or delinquency as a form of 'acting out' on the part of young women. It is stated that women have traditionally been socialised to be passive and need affection, and that this explains their lower crime rates. However, if they have been abnormally or poorly socialised, then they may be susceptible to manipulation by men, and this manipulation can result in sex-related deviancy, such as prostitution.

- A variation of this theory argues that the key issue is the undersocialisation of individual female offenders. The maladjustment of the offender to mainstream social norms manifests itself in the form of sexually inappropriate conduct, such as promiscuous sexual relations. The desire of girls and women for acceptance and approval may result in gratuitous sexual relationships, because this is seen as the only way in which the young women can assert themselves (through their sexuality).

- Some theories begin by arguing that crime is a result of the disconnection felt by some women. The psychological absence of love produces instability in these females, and this in turn leads to various 'acting out' behaviours of an antisocial or deviant nature. The argument assumes that emotionality is an inherent biological feature of the female sex. Women are said to have a need for dependencies because they are primarily emotional creatures—again a biological reductionist argument.

¬ feminist responses

The response of feminist writers to these kinds of biological explanations and socialisation arguments is that they represent a 'double standard' in terms of morality and power. Underpinning this double standard is a blurring of the distinction between 'sex' and 'gender'. Women and girls are presumed to have a fixed biological nature that is indistinguishable from their fixed social role. Any maladjustment to this stereotypical femininity is said to be the consequence of biological defect or inherent biological weaknesses of the female sex. Women's social nature is given naturally by her biological being.

A crucial issue from a feminist perspective is that of relative social power and access to social and economic capital (Alder 1994). The criminalisation process itself is heavily laden with sexist assumptions that reinforce and reproduce structural inequalities of gender in society (Gelsthorpe & Morris 1990; Pearson 1997; Morash & Chesney-Lind 2009; Hamilton & Worthen 2011). Sexist assumptions determine how offending behaviour is constructed (Zahn et al. 2009), and how victims are portrayed (see chart 7.2) (Burman 2009; Lievore 2004). The central proposition of much feminist analysis is that women are treated differently in and by the criminal justice system because of the persistence of traditional gender-role expectations regarding 'appropriate' and 'feminine' behaviour for women (and men) (Chesney-Lind 2010; DeKeseredy 2010).

chart 7.2 | women and crime

	women as offenders	women as victims
nature of crimes	sex-specific offences; for example, prostitution, infanticide	sex-specific offences; for example, rape, sexual assault
	sex-related offences; for example, shoplifting, fraud	sex-related offences; for example, consumer rip-offs
mainstream explanations	related to issues of female sexuality; for example, biological drives and hormonal activity	categories of 'deserving' and 'undeserving' victims based upon sexuality and relationship to men; for example, married
	related to notions of gender, for example, constructions of 'feminine' behaviour, and socialisation into these	related to notion of 'weaker' sex and dominant sex roles and social functions; for example, housewife
	categories of 'mad' and 'bad' based upon essentially passive and/or deceitful nature of women	sex-specific victimisation explained in terms of male biological drives, such as sexual aggression (leading to rape) and susceptibility to 'provocation' (leading to men to respond aggressively)
feminist explanations	double standard of morality; for example, sexualisation of offences for women but not for men	emphasis on women as victims of male violence generally
	prior status of women as victims; for example, of persistent abuse, of economic dependency	sex-specific victimisation linked to patriarchal cultures and institutions
	attempts to control and regulate female behaviour by criminalising certain offences as sex specific	relative powerlessness of some women to protect themselves from personal and property crime
	different social opportunities linked to male-dominated institutions and cultures	traditional gender-role expectations shape victimisation process

Underpinning this gendered division of the sexes is *power*; that is, society is male dominated, and this is reflected in a myriad of social institutions, including the law and the criminal justice system (Jensen 2001; Chan et al. 2010). Thus, feminist jurisprudence has been concerned to demonstrate the gender biases built into the very processes of the law (for example, the 'reasonable man' argument in legal reasoning), as well as specific overt instances of gender inequality (for example, laws that allowed rape in marriage). The status of women as 'property' and as 'rights holders' has been examined historically, and as part of an ongoing struggle to assert women's place and position in a patriarchal system and society (Smart 1991, 1992; Scutt 1990; Graycar & Morgan 1990; Naffine 1990; Chesney-Lind 2006).

The nature of *female offending* is placed into a wider social, economic and political context, rather than one that reduces female experience to biological or psychological determinants. Women who commit homicide, for instance, have often been victims of violence themselves. Similarly, women who commit social security or other minor forms of fraud and theft usually do so, not for themselves, but to support children and dependants. Hence, the generalised violence against women as a social category, and the relative disadvantages they suffer economically, are explored as vital preconditions to any personal or individual offending behaviour.

In terms of activities pertaining to young offenders, historically young men have been picked up for certain 'conventional' violations of the law (such as street assaults and robbery), while young women were seen as delinquent because of their presumed immorality or promiscuity (see Alder 1985; Cunneen & White 2011; Chesney-Lind & Shelden 1992; Zahn et al. 2009). It is thus presumed that men are in court because of their criminal offending, while women are there because they have slept around—clearly there are double standards operating.

In the case of *victimisation*, much attention is paid to the ways in which crimes against women have historically either not been considered as crimes (as with domestic violence) or are subject to trivialisation and sexual bias (for example, rape trials involving sex workers). It has been argued in some cases that a woman who has been victimised is herself judged in relation to a man, rather than a specific offensive action. For example, a married woman subjected to injury may be seen in terms of a 'serious crime' insofar as it affects her status as her spouse's 'sexual property' or 'homemaker'. An unmarried woman who has a sexual history of multiple partners may be treated by the courts as having actually provoked a criminal assault. Questions of what is an 'offence' and who is a 'victim' are thus often intertwined with gender stereotypes and biases that reflect a general inequality between the sexes in society.

A fundamental question assessed by feminist criminology is how the *sex variable* has been dealt with by the various perspectives:

- There are theories that ignore the sex variable altogether; the vast majority of traditional criminology appears to do this, since it deals only with male criminality, and ignores the specific conditions under which women exist in society; that is, the female experience.

- There are theories that conflate or blur the distinctions between sex and gender. Girls and women are presumed to have a fixed biological nature and/or role(s), and any maladjustment to this stereotypical femininity is said to be the consequence of biological defect. A woman's criminal nature is seen as an extension of her sexuality and genitals.

- There are theories that ignore the impact of gender relationships. There is a discussion here of women, but the male/female experience is presented as androgynous. These theories neglect the impact of gender on people.

Feminist criminology wanted to explore issues relating to women, and looked initially at sex-role differences. Smart (1976, 1990a, 1990b) stated that there was a double standard operating in society in relation to morality and power. This was particularly indicated in the nature of offences with which women were charged: primarily sex-specific offences such as infanticide and prostitution (women's crime). The legal framework— both historically, and as revealed by the official statistics—has similarly treated the category of prostitution as relating only to women in spite of the existence of male sex workers.

With the shift in feminist politics and theory over the last twenty years, approaches to the issues of women and crime also shifted from *sex* roles to *gender* and *gendered* roles (Walklate 2004). From these critical perspectives, criminologists began identifying the nature of gendered criminality, including *gender-related offences*, such as shoplifting. Of the total number of crimes reported in official statistics, a proportionately higher incidence of shoplifting offences are committed by women and girls. The nature of the goods stolen also appears to be gender-related; for example, perfume, lipstick and tampons. Gender is also tied to other offences; for example, passing fraudulent cheques and social security fraud tend to be female offences.

However, as Daly (2010) and Zahn et al. (2009) point out, the meaning of gender and sex in relation to crime, and the role of feminism, has fundamentally changed in the last twenty years. For Gen Y, the landscape of feminist criminology is not as obvious as it was in the early days of its development. In addition to the critical theories generated out of Messerschmidt's (1993) and Connell's (2002, 2005) work on masculinities, feminist theories, methodologies and critiques have been integrated—to various levels—throughout criminology.

then & now
feminist criminology

The development of feminist criminology needs to be understood in the context of Second Wave feminism in the 1970s, with its emphasis on equal rights and personal security. To a considerable extent, the concerns of Second Wave feminists were central to criminology; in particular, raising consciousness of the problem of domestic violence and male violence generally. The provision of 'safe houses' for women and children escaping family violence was a key demand of many feminists in the 1970s. The academic trajectory that arose from this activist base has taken a number of forms, each with distinct ideas about the causes of and solutions to the subordination of women in many societies. Today, different women are seen to be positioned in society in quite different ways, and gender issues are conceptualised in a much more complex manner than suggested in earlier times. The diversity of feminist perspectives is further evidenced in cases where feminists have drawn on postmodernist theorists to understand the continuing marginalisation of and violence against women (see Chapter 11). The impact of feminism is apparent in contemporary criminological perspectives ranging from the New Right (Chapter 8) to Left Realism (Chapter 9) to critical criminology (Chapter 11), particularly in relation to matters surrounding victims and victimisation.

contemporary examples

If we examine contemporary female offending, some interesting pictures emerge:

- A significant proportion of offenders are single parents, of low educational standing and unemployed, and many have been victimised through male violence, such as rape, sexual abuse and incest. There is also an overrepresentation of Indigenous women in the system.

– Feminist theorists state that there are obvious double standards operating in terms of how women and men are treated, both as victims and offenders. This can be highlighted once again by referring to the example of prostitution. Why is it that the female service providers are charged with solicitation and offences associated with prostitution, while the male service user is rarely criminalised? While there is a dual relationship between the sex worker and her client it is uncommon for the male patron to be implicated in criminal activity (exceptions to this exist in Sweden and Canada).

– With respect to the offence of rape, again for many years and still today, there are many myths relating to the nature of rapists. The stereotypical rapist has customarily been portrayed as a violent sexual psychopath and serial offender. Thus the individual is disturbed, and/or the victim has been seen to act to arouse the uncontrollable desires of the male attacker (for instance, by wearing inappropriate clothing. This understanding of sexual assault is captured by comments made by a Canadian police officer in 2011, when he suggested that female students would be safe from sexual assault if they would only stop 'dressing like sluts'). This image reduces rape to an individualistic biological problem, disregarding societal explanations that view rape as relating to social power (Lievore 2004, 2005).

– Likewise, in terms of victims, there has been a league table established in relation to the worthiness or otherwise of the victim status; distinctions are made as to who is or is not to be believed. As conveyed in a judge's comments in Victoria, claims of rape made by a nun or married woman are to be believed, while those made by a prostitute are to be treated as dubious. Such distinctions misconstrue the nature of the crime, which is linked to violence and power, and not sex or sexuality.

Such double standards of power and morality are represented as the *sexualisation thesis* by feminists. According to this perspective, women who deviate from what is construed to be the norms of sexuality and morality are seen to be offenders (see Chesney-Lind 1974; Smart 1976; Zahn et al. 2009).

In particular, when such offenders are young, they are viewed as being immoral or in moral danger. This has been a traditional way of bringing young women into the system; that is, through a category of welfare provision (what are called 'status offences' in the USA) rather than criminal offence. Hence, they did not necessarily have to do anything illegal to warrant state intervention. Young women who were considered to be sexually promiscuous (thus 'exposed to moral danger') were incarcerated in juvenile institutions 'for their own welfare' (Smart 1990a, 1990b, 1991). Historically, intervention was often followed by physical examination and subjection to 'treatment' regimens. Institutionalisation aimed to impart necessary instruction in domesticity; adolescent girls were taught to play their 'natural' subservient role as the servers of men. They were released when considered to be 'of a marriageable age'. Men have not been classified, diagnosed and treated in the same way. Their sexuality has been encouraged, because it is viewed as a 'natural' part of manhood.

The clause in child welfare provisions concerned with 'moral danger' has historically resulted in long periods of incarceration for considerable numbers of young women in Australia (Jaggs 1986). It is important to recognise that in Australia such provisions were not part of the criminal law as such, but were part of the child protection legislation. In reality, such treatment regimens translated into harsher penalties than those given for offending behaviour. Such provisions, it should be added, no longer exist, but they form an indelible part of the history of women's involvement with the criminal justice system.

It should be noted that not only the justice system, but also psychiatric, welfare and other bio-medical professions have tried to reinforce these conventional boundaries and distinctions. Women who transgressed the boundaries of dominant conceptions of femininity were seen as falling within one of two categories: they were either *mad* or *bad* (Koonin 1995; Harris & Crocker 1997; Summers 2002; Appignanesi 2008; Chesney-Lind 2010). The policing of female behaviour occurs not only in the legal and medical arena, but also in the wider social community. This is evident, for example, in the examination of the nature of the interactions between men and women in youth centres (Nava 1984). The policing of females is widespread, with the objective of preserving the good sexual reputations of the women.

There have been several critiques of the sexualisation thesis, including Carrington's (1993, and with Periera 2009) argument that from the mid-1970s there has been an equal number of men and women appearing before the courts. She discusses the notion of the sexualisation of offending, but looks also at the nature of penalties imposed. She examines the notion that young women are prosecuted primarily on the grounds of their immorality, and are dealt harsher sentences because of this (see also, for example, Sandler & Freeman's (2011) research into gender differences in arrests and outcomes for sexual offences). She argues instead, however, that when welfare intervention occurs, irrespective of whether the offender is male or female, harsher sentences are received, because the actions are initiated by the welfare–helping professions.

Carrington & Pereira (2009) also challenge the sexualisation thesis on another ground. If the sustenance of male patriarchy is the objective of the legal system, then one would expect the system to be dominated by men. She claims we should instead look at the composition of all those seeking to control women's behaviour, such as welfare workers, youth and community workers and social workers. If we do, we see that a large proportion of those who are the gatekeepers and custodians of female behaviour are women. And among those who wield derogatory and negative labels are young women themselves. Research by Lees (1989), and later Payne et al. (2009), for example, found a liberal use of derogatory terms by adolescent girls within the schoolground setting, as well as stereotyped labelling by women teachers of their students. Further, hate speech—such as 'slut', 'slag' and 'lesbo'—is commonly used as a tool to regulate female behaviour (Asquith 2007, 2008).

The impact of 'race' or ethnicity on female offenders is also raised by Carrington & Pereira (2009) as part of the critique of the sexualisation thesis. In particular, concern is expressed regarding why working-class and Indigenous young people are overrepresented in the crime statistics (Bartels 2010). These are the types of questions asked by a number of contemporary feminist criminologists (see Gelsthorpe & Morris 1990; Walklate 2004; Burgess-Proctor 2006), which has led to the development of more sophisticated and complicated analyses that focus not just on sex differences, but also on differences of class and ethnicity (Harris & Crocker 1997; Daly 1997; Burgess-Proctor 2006).

Carrington & Pereira's (2009) rejection of the sexualisation thesis has not been entirely convincing, however. In a review of Australian feminist criminology, Alder (1994) argues that the sexualisation thesis itself should not be oversimplified. While acknowledging differences between women's experiences, Alder argues that the power of the sexualisation thesis lies in linking the similarities of women's experiences. Female offending behaviour, and their involvement in the criminal justice system, forms but one part of their lives. If we were to examine the totality of women's lives, in all their complexities and diversities, both the similarities as argued by the sexualisation thesis, and the differences as argued by Carrington & Pereira

(2009), can be supported. Alder (1994) goes on to argue that contemporary feminism cannot be oversimplified and parodied any longer as somehow merely advocating a simple relationship between gender and experience (Daly 2010). Nonetheless, exploration of the diversity of women's lives reveals consistent themes of surviving, coping and thriving within patriarchal structures, all of which demand further attention and analysis.

Feminist work since the 1990s has tended to focus on two key substantive areas for investigation (Daly & Chesney-Lind 1988; Daly & Maher 1998; Daly 2010). These are, first, explaining and responding to *men's violence* towards women (which encompasses issues such as pornography, rape and prostitution); and, second, thinking about the problems associated with *equality and difference* as these manifest in the legal and criminal justice systems (which encompasses issues such as legal equality, affirmative action and specific needs of female prisoners). In analysing these kinds of issues, feminist criminologists have employed a wide array of analytical methods and concepts, as shown in accounts that utilise postmodern analyses of knowledge and power relations involving men and women (for example, Carrington 1993, 1994, and with Pereira 2009; Smart 1990b; Walklate 2004), and those that focus on 'deconstruction', a technique to explore the workings of language—including non-verbal communication—in conveying meaning (see Young 1996; Asquith 2010; Miller & McMullan 2010). As suggested by Naffine (1997) early in the development of postmodern feminist approaches, contemporary feminist criminology cannot ignore these recent theoretical and methodological insights into the social world, but nor can it ignore the limitations (and strengths) of any one particular perspective or approach (Howe 2000).

Feminist criminology is diverse, particularly when reviewing the contemporary debates about sex, gender and criminality. Feminists continue to focus on the nature of female offending, but also seek to explore the area of victimology, particularly in relation to sexual assault and intimate-partner violence. Feminists have long been associated with activism, as well as theoretical debate. In particular, feminist criminologists are concerned to change the law to promote recognition of the issues of violence directed against women. This has led many to argue for the harsher enforcement of laws against perpetrators at the operational level, and a call for greater sensitivity of police to these crimes. However, others see limitations to this, arguing that calling for greater use of the criminal law in a patriarchal system to defend and protect women is fraught with problems (Edwards 1990).

{from theory to practice: female serial killers}

Thompson, J. & Ricard, S. (2009). 'Women's Role in Serial Killing Teams: Reconstructing a Radical Feminist Perspective', *Critical Criminology*, 17: 261–75.

According to Thompson and Ricard, traditional radical feminism has failed to account for the existence of, let alone growth in, numbers of women serial killers. The authors argue that in focusing on men's patriarchal violence, and ignoring the presence of women in some serial killing teams, this theoretical approach has yet to provide a complete analysis. In addition, they suggest that 'justifications' used by radical feminist theory to explain women's violence (such as victim-precipitated or self-defence) (2009: 262) are unable to explain the absence of both these in the actions of serial killing teams, and the agency claimed by the women involved in these teams.

Using case study data extracted from newspaper stories, court proceedings and evidential documents, and biographies, the authors set out to reconstruct central concepts employed by radical feminism in order to make sense of the crimes of violence committed by Martha Beck (1940s), Myra Hindley (1960s), and Karla Homolka (1990s). The central premise of radical feminism is that, under a system of patriarchy, both individual sex-based characteristics and institutional systems and practices are designed in order to support and 'recreate male power and female subordination' (Rowland & Klien 1996, cited in Thompson & Ricard 2009: 264). From this perspective, all violence against women seeks to control women's autonomy and subordinate them to men. However, in analysing the issue of serial killing, radical feminist theory has, in the past, been gender blind, preferring only to consider these as sexually motivated crimes of men against women and children. When they have addressed the existence of women in these serial killing teams, their presence has been reduced to passive participant with no control over the crime, or with 'good reasons' to participate (such as threats to children).

Thompson and Ricard extend the theoretical basis of radical feminism to account for not only the effects of sexual objectification, but also an active female subjectivity. In each of the three case studies, the authors clearly demonstrate that an 'emphasised femininity' (Connell 2005) can be as dangerous and violent as hegemonic masculinity. Beck, Hindley and Homolka were all fixated on securing a relationship, and each illustrated that they would do anything for their man, if it meant retaining the relationship. All three women participated in the killing, and in the case of Beck and Homolka, both women actively killed to eliminate any competition for their partners' attention. In the case of Homolka, this included murdering her own sister.

Unlike the traditional presentation of passive women responding to men's violence, Thompson and Ricard's women know what they want, and are prepared to organise and participate in extreme acts of violence to please their sexual partner. In avoiding the essentialism of earlier theory, they are able to fully account for the active subject, while remaining cognisant that the micro-expressions of power within these serial killing teams are informed by larger structures of patriarchy.

critique

Various issues have been the subject of intense discussion and debate within feminist criminology. For example, it has been noted that some feminist approaches do not deal adequately with questions relating to class, ethnicity and 'race' in discussions of the female offender and the female victim. Yet, as various studies show (for example, Carrington & Pereira 2009; Bartels 2010), the 'race' of a person is a crucial factor in terms of overall representation of some groups within the criminal justice system. Likewise, the class background of the offender or victim has significant consequences with regard to the actual nature of the criminalisation and the victimisation process (Harris & Crocker 1997; Daly 1997; Burgess-Proctor 2006).

A second area that is generating more attention is the notion that feminist criminology needs to do more than provide a woman-centred analysis: it needs to foster a non-sexist criminology that focuses more broadly on gender relations in their entirety (Walklate 2004). Specifically, it has been suggested that issues of female and male criminality need to be examined in terms of the social constructions of both 'femininity' and 'masculinity', and with regard to the relationship between each of these social constructions (Gelsthorpe & Morris 1990; Cunneen & White 2007). Naffine (1997: 91) makes the telling comment that:

> As feminist criminologists have shifted our understanding of women, repudiating the female stereotypes, revealing the differences between

women's understandings of their own lives and the orthodox (male) accounts of them, so man (whose meaning is so intimately linked with woman) has been altered too.

The idea that women and men need to be understood in terms of their mutual relationship to each other is evident in the literature associated with contemporary feminism. It is also apparent in the criminological work that has been influenced by feminism but focuses specifically on men and the male experience (see Polk 1994a; Messerschmidt 1986, 1993, 1997; Jefferson 1997). There has been burgeoning interest in, and debates over, how best to conceptualise the relationship between men and violence. Work by theorists such as Connell (2000, 2005) has consistently pointed to the ways in which certain forms of 'hegemonic masculinity' are played out, and resisted, in specific historical situations. In many instances, how these diverse masculinities are positioned in relation to each other (and in relation to various femininities) has been shown to have major implications for youth crime, homophobic violence, violence against women and children and male-on-male violence (see Connell 2002; Tomsen 2002; Mason 2002).

Generally, as Walklate (2004) and Naffine (1997: 2) argue, the message conveyed in mainstream criminology is that 'feminism is about women, while criminology is about men'; but the analytical and political challenges of feminism are nevertheless highly influential throughout the field. One area where this influence has been greatly felt is in victimology. For example, notions of 'women-as-victims' have been subjected to various feminist critiques. From these perspectives, victims should not be viewed merely as passive, but need to be empowered by extending to them the alternative term of 'survivors'. This term is said to imply active response. Hence, debate within the feminist movement has served to push the boundaries as they relate to women, both as victims and as offenders.

As a consequence of the increased use of postmodern and post-structuralist feminisms, theorists have also questioned the 'dual edged sword' that comes with the continuing use of theoretical approaches that negate women's autonomy, including their active choices to offend. For example, Allen (1987) argues that feminists need to take account of how their analyses affect those in different roles in the criminal justice system (as victim or offender). She suggests that seeing women as victims undermines their autonomy, since they are portrayed as 'weak', 'passive' or 'vulnerable' rather than as survivors and resilient. On the other hand, for those women charged with serious violent offences, an understanding that somehow they are less responsible for their offending (and thus deserving of a lesser penalty) can undermine the notion that women, too, make choices, and that not all their actions are socially determined by forces beyond their control (see also Koonin 1995; Jensen 2001; Pearson 1997; Sandler & Freeman 2011; Thompson & Ricard 2009). At a broader level, this likewise can perpetuate myths about women's autonomy, and may have challenging implications for the cause of promoting women's rights and integrity more broadly in society.

More generally, the issue of power, and how this is manifested institutionally and interpersonally, remains an area where feminist debate appears to be stalled. While many younger theorists have welcomed the conceptual tools offered by postmodernism and poststructuralism (including, but not limited to, the Foucauldian notions of governmentality and bio-power), these approaches appear to be antithetical to the modernist goals of earlier feminist theorists (see for example the debates in the 1990s between Fraser and Butler, Benhabib and Young, in Benhabib et al. 1995; Young 1997; Fraser 1997; Butler 1998). This impasse may be a product of changes in sociological and criminology theory more generally, and is a concern not only for feminist theory. Importantly, the continuing debate about power within feminist theory has led to more sophisticated analyses from both sides of the modernism/postmodernism divide. Equally, this new research agenda for feminist criminologists has produced a wealth of research that seeks to address the concerns with feminism listed above.

However, an immediate problem confronting many feminist theorists and activists is the conservative backlash (such as the campaigns of 'men's rights' groups) against many of the feminist concepts and issues raised in relation to women and crime (Chesney-Lind 2006). The profile of female victims, and the dilemmas and inequities surrounding the processing of female offenders, have been actively raised by feminist criminologists. But in the light of contemporary calls for greater 'law and order', there is a fear that such work will be subverted and/or swamped by the moralising, and individualised responses to crime generated out of the New Right.

{conclusion}

In summary, the feminist perspectives within criminology challenge the male biases and neglects of mainstream criminology. It is identifiably part of Second Wave feminism, which has been part of the social landscape since the 1960s. Within criminology, criticism is levelled at historical and contemporary examples of the double standards applied to women and men in the criminal justice system. As well, active intervention has been called for in areas such as inappropriate responses to female offenders (such as imprisonment), law reform that prevents discrimination against women (such as equal employment opportunity), the legal recognition of certain crimes against women (such as sexual harassment), and active enforcement of laws to protect women from male violence (for example, domestic violence, incest, rape).

Feminist criminology cannot be seen, however, as a single theoretical perspective. As outlined in this chapter, there are many strands of feminism, from radical feminism and socialist feminism through to liberal and cultural feminism, each having a distinctive voice within criminology. Further, it is a field that is continually changing, and has developed extensively by drawing on postmodernist perspectives (see Chapter 11). Taken as a whole, feminist criminology has radically altered the nature of the criminological debate. Challenges highlighted by feminists have influenced debates within left-leaning perspectives such as Left Realism

... and Critical Criminology, as well as conservative and liberal theories such as New Right criminology and republican theory. Thus, as well as constituting an identifiable perspective within criminology in its own right, feminist criminology has significantly influenced the wider criminological debate.

{further reading}

Carrington, K. (1993). *Offending Girls*, Allen & Unwin, Sydney.

Carrington, K. & Periera, M. (2009). *Offending Youth: Sex, Crime and Justice*, Federation Press, Annandale, NSW.

Daly, K. (2010). 'Feminist Perspectives in Criminology: A Review with Gen Y in Mind', in E. McLaughlin & T. Newburn (eds), *The SAGE Handbook of Criminological Theory*, SAGE, London: 225–46.

Daly, K. & Chesney-Lind, M. (1988). 'Feminism and Criminology', *Justice Quarterly*, 5 (4): 497–538.

Naffine, N. (1997). *Feminism and Criminology*, Allen & Unwin, Sydney.

Scutt, J. (1990). *Women and the Law*, Law Book Company, Sydney.

Smart, C. (1976). *Women, Crime and Criminology: A Feminist Critique*, Routledge & Kegan Paul, London.

Smart, C. (1990a). 'Law's Power,
  the Sexed Body and Feminist
  Discourse', *Journal of Law and
  Society*, 17 (2): 194-210.

Smart, C. (1990b). 'Feminist
  Approaches to Criminology: or
  Postmodern Woman meets Atavistic
  Man', in L. Gelsthorpe &
  A. Morris (eds), *Feminist
  Perspectives in Criminology*,
  Open University Press,
  Buckingham: 70-84.

Tong, R. (1989). *Feminist
  Thought: A Comprehensive
  Introduction*, Unwin Hyman,
  London.

Walklate, S. (2004). 'Women and
  Crime or Gender and Crime?',
  in *Gender, Crime and Criminal
  Justice* (2nd edition), Willan,
  Cullompton.

new right criminology

{introduction}
—

The 1960s and 1970s were broadly characterised by rapid social change and heightened political conflict, which manifested themselves in the rise of radical theories about society in the social sciences, including criminology. By the 1980s, however, a major change in thinking had occurred in society at large. Conservative politicians and political ideologies dominated the electoral landscape across many countries, and 'law and order' emerged as a predominant issue, along with that of high levels of unemployment.

The aim of this chapter is to outline the main currents of *New Right criminology*. This particular approach or perception of crime has both a populist dimension (related to the political process) and an academic dimension (related to the work of criminologists). The fundamental ideas of New Right criminology are based on two themes: placing responsibility for crime squarely on the individual, and reasserting the importance of punishment in responding to crime.

The chapter makes a broad distinction between 'right-wing libertarian' views and those of 'conservatism'. These describe essential differences in the political perspectives contained under the New Right criminology umbrella. The chapter also discusses those traditional academic approaches within criminology' itself that reflect and are reflected in the general New Right perspective. In particular, the ideas of 'social control theory' and of 'opportunity-rationality theory' will be discussed.

—

~~social~~ context

The phrase 'New Right' refers to a particular political orientation, rather than to a systematic, coherent theory in its own right. A conservative perspective in criminology—directly opposed to the liberalism of strain theory and labelling perspectives in particular—arose at a time when the long boom of economic prosperity in the advanced capitalist countries was coming to an end. The mid-1970s saw a world economic recession, followed over the next two decades by periodic, and in some instances devastating, economic slumps.

In these new times there was likely to be an increase in property and personal crime at both corporate and street level. The alienation and marginalisation of a significant layer of the population, many of them young people, were associated with a range of antisocial and deviant behaviour. For example, during the mid-1970s punk rock began to emerge and, with it, the overt rebellion of many young people against both the commercial music industry (for its insipid conformity and slick production values), and the powerbrokers and 'respectable' members of society who had done so little to stem the tide of youth unemployment and yet condemned the ripped shirts of the poor.

Politically, by the 1980s there had been a swing to the right at the level of policy formulation and development, regardless of the political party in power. The economic ideas of Margaret Thatcher in the UK and Ronald Reagan in the USA, the advent of 'Rogernomics' (named after the Treasurer) in New Zealand, and the approach adopted by Hawke and Keating in Australia all signalled an *economic rationalist* platform for dealing with contemporary issues. This emphasised the notion of 'economic efficiency' above all else in policy development, and in each case led to tax cuts for both individuals and corporations, while at the same time universal provision in the allocation of the welfare services and benefits was curtailed. According to the economic rationalists, the wealth created by these measures would benefit both rich and poor. Many argue, however, that the net effect was to exacerbate the growing distance between the rich and the poor in society.

Simultaneously, efforts were made to neutralise any resistance to the economic restructuring that aimed to increase competitiveness and efficiency. Conservative parties, in particular, made concerted attempts to drastically reduce trade union power. For example, Reagan smashed the air traffic controllers' strike in the USA, while Thatcher took on the miners' union in the UK. In Australia, union power initially was curbed more subtly and, some would argue, more effectively. The Prices and Incomes Accord between the Australian Labor Party and the Australian Council of Trade Unions was used to defuse any possible union militancy. Nonetheless, strong-arm tactics were also used against 'recalcitrant' elements; notably, the army was used to break the airline pilots' strike, and the police and courts were used to deregister the Builders Labourers Federation. More recently in the 2000s, however, the Howard government took a more explicitly anti-unionist stance, moving away from an accord between union and government and towards an emphasis on individualised contracts as the most efficient form of workplace contract between employer and employee.

The 1980s saw an emphasis on controlling union power and enhancing wealth creation. In the 'decade of greed', much media prominence was given to business entrepreneurs, many of whom gained near folk-hero status. Labour and financial markets were deregulated, and the idea of a 'free economy and a strong state' (Gamble 1988) was entrenched in places like the UK through the rhetoric of defending the 'people's capitalism'. Market structures were opened up in order to stimulate greater economic activity. In reality, in most cases it was the strong who stood to benefit most, while the rest would have to work that much harder to gain a share of the societal wealth. State agencies that were seen to impede economic growth were more closely scrutinised. Welfare provisions were often downgraded or targeted at a minority of the most impoverished in society, and those institutions that maintained public order and protected private property, such as the police, were strengthened. In the late 2000s, after decades of clawing back some of the lost social and economic measures that protected the poor and disadvantaged, these types of political and economic approaches were to re-emerge after the Global Financial Crisis in 2009.

The increased uncertainty created by these economic policies, combined with a reduction of welfare support (for example, in the area of old age pensions and in a lack of support for free higher education), albeit in a context where overall government spending has increased, has not been entirely problem free for governments. Governments have lost traditional sources of support, and are often viewed as self-interested and manipulative. In short, they have lost legitimacy and, with this, the trust of the public (Habermas 1979; Garland 2001), and have thus often resorted to short-term popular policies to increase their appeal.

In the context of increasing economic hardship, growing scepticism about governments and an ideological swing to the right, supported largely by an economic rationalist mentality, there was a rise in 'law-and-order' politics, both domestically and internationally. For example, internationally, the former concern with the preservation of 'human rights' propounded by world leaders was quickly transformed into an emphasis on the 'war on terrorism' and the 'war on drugs', and the necessity to combat these 'by any means necessary'.

Domestically, the law-and-order push assumed the tone of a 'war on crime' and an attack on the disorder of society. This translated into a call during the 1980s for increased police personnel, powers and resources; longer prison sentences; the provision of more prisons; stronger discipline within families and schools; and a return to more traditional values generally. For young people there was the demand for 'greater responsibility', which translated into more punitive attitudes in the area of juvenile justice.

New Right criminology tends to revolve around the individual in society, and to provide a moralistic and punitive approach to issues of crime and criminality (Young 1981; Tame 1991; Mooney 1998; Mooney & Young 2006). While academic studies have provided sophisticated defences of these ideas (Roshier 1989; Tame 1991; Buchanan & Hartley 1992), in the public domain the get-tough approach has generally been associated with populist appeals to the public at large with their commonsense classical ideas about crime and criminality. This has proved to be electorally expedient and attractive, even if the consequences of the adoption of such measures have proven to be both socially and economically costly in the long term (such as the costs of an ever-increasing prison population).

Populism is not a political ideology as such, but is a loosely defined mood. It appeals to people on the basis of 'us' versus 'them'. The 'us' is always viewed as virtuous. The 'them', whoever they are, are viewed as being parasites and destructive to the social body. In terms of crime, the essence of populism exaggerates the dangerousness (and risks) of crime, and the foreign or alien nature of the criminal. The criminal is seen to be outside the society—its networks, institutions, communities, mores, values, methods of income and ways of life. Insofar as the criminal is not seen to be bound by normal social rules of conduct, so too it is argued that normal rules of order should not necessarily be adhered to if criminals are to be brought to book for their offensive activities.

The rhetoric of populism is one that reduces all crime problems to simple solutions. Offenders are made entirely responsible for their actions, particularly since they exist outside the mainstream institutions of society. They are not seen as members of the 'community' and, indeed, are sometimes presented as not being members of the human race (described as 'animals' or 'savages'). Insofar as this social distancing occurs at the level of rhetoric and policy development, it is not a great leap to encourage ever more draconian solutions to the crime problem. If the problem is constructed as being one of 'us' against 'them'—as a 'war', which implies violence and destruction—then redemption of the situation is seen to lie in enhanced state power (Jones & Novak 2009).

Since the 1980s, populist rhetoric about crime has been used actively as a major electoral tool, particularly in the UK and US. *Authoritarian populism* refers to a process in which crime is ideologically conveyed in a series of moral panics about 'law-and-order' issues (Taylor 1981; Hall 1980a, 1980b; Hall et al. 1978). The extent and seriousness of crime are highlighted (but not necessarily backed up by statistical or other research findings) and this, in turn, is used to justify harsher penalties, and the assertion of state authority in more and more spheres of everyday social life. As part of this process, specific groups or categories of people are singled out for special attention: young people, Indigenous peoples, welfare recipients, striking workers and sole parents. Thus, 'we' are protected by having ever greater state intervention into the affairs of 'them' who are the most likely candidates for membership of the criminal class. Again, the rationale behind such intrusion is usually a combination of protection of private property, and the differential treatment that should be meted out to the moral and immoral in society.

The broad appeal of authoritarian populism is in part a result of the pervasive influence of the print and electronic media in conveying particular types of images regarding crime in society (Grabosky & Wilson 1989; Ericson et al. 1991; Males 1996; Young 1996; Mason 2009; Greer 2010). For example, Hogg and Brown (1998) have identified the key assumptions in what they call 'law and order commonsense', many elements of which are perpetuated by the media. The assumptions include:

- crime rates are soaring
- crime is worse than ever
- the criminal justice system is 'soft' on crime
- the criminal justice system is loaded in favour of criminals

- there should be more police
- police should have more powers
- courts should deliver tougher penalties
- the greater satisfaction of victims demands more retribution through the courts.

More recently, with the increased media attention on forensic processing of crime (such as *CSI*, *Waking the Dead*, *Silent Witness*, *Bones*, *Wire in the Blood*, let alone the news reporting of forensics), the elements of Hogg and Brown's (1998) 'law and order commonsense' could be expanded to include:

- forensic science is instrumental in assigning guilt
- forensic evidence is irrefutable proof of guilt.

These general elements of law-and-order commonsense are seemingly routine aspects of the way in which the electronic and print media portray crime. By and large, crime is sensationalised in and by the media. The flooding of the media with stories of 'street crime' has, however, real and pertinent effects: heightening the fear of crime, feeding the stereotypes regarding the 'typical offender', exaggerating the extent of extremely violent and serious crimes, and fostering acceptance for policies that appear to 'get something done' about the crime problem. The politically important role of New Right criminology is thus related to the basic electoral appeal of authoritarian populist rhetoric.

basic concepts

The main elements of New Right criminology include a combination of conservative moralising and free-market competitive ethos. These sometimes contradict each other at the level of specific policies. However, the overriding message is that there is a need to 'get tough on criminals', to hold them responsible for their actions and to punish the wrongdoer in a consistent manner.

New Right criminology is opposed to perspectives that emphasise 'treatment' and 'reform' rather than punishment (von Hirsch 1976). It opposes the views of orthodox positivist criminology, which have a deterministic view or model of the causes of crime; rather, it asserts that *people do make choices*, and that they therefore must pay for these choices.

In a nutshell, the argument is that if you 'do the crime', then you must 'do the time'.

The New Right criminological perspective includes several strands: some deal with more philosophical views regarding the nature of human activity (such as rational choice theory), and some with specific areas of interest such as retributivist concerns with sentencing. The range also extends to economic analyses of the causes and social responses to crime. For present purposes, however, we will illustrate the broad orientation of these kinds of perspectives by examining two general views on the nature of crime and crime control—right-wing libertarianism and traditionalist conservatism. Each is concerned with the *punishment and disciplining of offenders*, but the overall analysis of crime in society does nevertheless differ.

¬ right-wing libertarianism

The right-wing libertarian perspective harks back to the days of classical liberalism, characterised by competitive free-market capitalism and minimal state intervention, including welfare provision (see chart 8.1). In this approach, human beings are conceived of as rational entities with free will. It is based upon a moral philosophy of egoism (selfishness), in which the only constraints on behaviour are those that limit the use of force over others.

The notion of a *competitive ethos* pervades this perspective. This is usually tied to the idea of rights to private property as being the first virtue of the legal and criminal justice system. Accordingly, crime is defined in terms of the infringement of private property, including infringements of one's physical self. Generally this approach defines crime in restrictive terms, as only those acts that violate the 'natural rights' of others.

Since human nature is conceived of as being possessive and individualistic, and since crime is conceived mainly in terms of private property, then the role of the state should be restricted to dealing with those instances where other people actually come to harm. In other words, there should be *minimal state intervention* in one's life, and that intervention should be tightly focused on enhancing and protecting individual liberty and protecting private property (Tame 1991).

The cause of crime is seen to lie with the individual. In reinforcing notions of individual selfishness, rights and individuality, this perspective simultaneously asserts that criminological theorising of the recent past has made excuses for individuals, by taking away people's *responsibilities for their actions*—their agency. It is argued, for example, that to speak of biological drives or social determinants such as poverty takes away any notion of choice in the selection of behaviour and activity.

Thus, individuals should be held fully responsible for their actions. Crime is seen fundamentally as a matter of *rational choice*, involving various incentives and disincentives. Since individual liberty is highly valued, however, the perspective believes that so-called 'victimless crimes' should be *decriminalised*, insofar as they do not harm any other person than the participants in the criminal behaviour. In other words, people should have complete liberty to do as they want, as long as they do not infringe upon the property or person of others in an illegal way.

Where harm to another individual does occur, as in the case of the commission of an offence, then the offender should be punished. The perspective generally favours the promotion of retribution, deterrence, incapacitation and punishment in its response to crime. It is informed by a *just deserts* philosophy, whereby punishment should be proportional to the crime. Furthermore, it favours the enforcement of *restitutive measures* with respect to the victims of crime; that is, compensation should be paid by the offender to the victim for any harm that he or she may have caused in the course of the offence. In order to quantify the harm caused to the victim, criminal justice agents must be able to assess the dangers and risks of both offending and victimisation.

In response to perspectives that see behaviour mainly in terms of psychological or social influences, this approach calls for a *moralising* of society. Morality is seen in this context to be rooted in the individualistic ethos of personal responsibility and self-control. In return for minimal state intervention, it is essential that people use their liberty in accordance with the law. If individuals choose not to comply with norms, values and laws, they should shoulder the penalty themselves.

In line with a general libertarian philosophy that de-emphasises the state, this approach also supports the idea that security, law enforcement and prisons should be *private* rather than public institutions. This reflects a broad ideological commitment to the so-called free market as the best and most efficient avenue for the provision of social services, including punishment.

chart 8.1 | **right-wing libertarianism**

definition of crime	– (restrictive) only those acts that violate the 'natural rights' of others
focus of analysis	– individual liberty and protection of private property rights
cause of crime	– matter of rational choices involving incentives and disincentives
nature of offender	– fully responsible for their own actions
response to crime	– retribution, deterrence, incapacitation and punishment insofar as individual held responsible
crime prevention	– decriminalisation, minimal state intervention, moral call for taking of personal responsibility and self-control
operation of criminal justice system	– reduction in number of laws relating to 'victimless crime' – greater use of incarceration and detention – use of restitution to compensate victims – support for privatisation of security, law enforcement, prisons

¬ traditionalist conservative

The traditionalist conservative perspective on what constitutes a crime (see chart 8.2) takes a broader view than the right-wing libertarian one. The conservative view of crime includes not only activity that endangers property or the person, but also activity that offends morality. Hence, attacks on certain traditional values and people's general respect for authority may be viewed as criminal.

From this point of view, crime is not only a matter of 'free choice', but also is linked to certain intrinsic aspects of humanity. In particular, people are seen to possess certain 'natural urges' that go against the more civilised or divine purposes of society. Whether it be a concept of 'original sin' or a secular theory of human nature that sees people in a negative light, the idea is that all people are somehow *inherently evil or flawed*.

chart 8.2 | conservatism

definition of crime	_ (expansive) violations of law, and acts that offend morality as well
focus of analysis	_ personal discipline and self-control
cause of crime	_ lack of self-discipline, undermining of traditional loyalties, lack of respect for authority
nature of offender	_ inherently 'evil' or flawed
response to crime	_ need for strong coercion, general deterrence strategies, assertion of authority
crime prevention	_ importance of traditional morality in maintenance of social authority, emphasis on self-discipline and submission to authority
operation of criminal justice system	_ expansion of laws relating to 'moral' issues, such as pornography _ harsher penalties to enforce the legal and moral code _ order to take priority over justice _ emphasis on conformity to established traditions and social roles

In order to constrain the 'natural' urges to do wrong, it is necessary to establish a strong order based upon personal sacrifice, self-discipline and submission to authority. *Order* must take precedence over all else, including justice. Crime is said to be caused by the unwillingness of people to accept discipline, the undermining of traditional loyalties—such as to the (patriarchal) family—and the pursuit of immediate individual gratification without appropriate hard work.

According to this approach, punishment is an essential part of deterrence. This is not only because it establishes personal responsibility for one's actions, but also because it has an important *symbolic impact* on society as a whole. That is, punishment has to be seen in terms of its effect on the establishment of moral solidarity through stigmatisation. Punishment is, in effect, a form of social *retribution*, and may thus represent a response that is not proportional to the offence (in fact, it may be much greater) because of the important symbolic role of punishment in bonding community members together.

Strong emphasis is placed upon the importance of *morality* in the maintenance of social authority. Thus, if someone does something deemed to be wrong or harmful, then that person must be punished swiftly and appropriately in order to set the moral standard. Simultaneously, it is important to set clear moral standards and guidelines to appropriate conduct.

The traditionalist conservatives generally possess anti-libertarian views with respect to pornography, sexual behaviour, drug use and abortion. Unlike right-wing libertarians, they favour intervention in areas regarded as victimless crimes. Indeed, the conservative point of view often favours *increased state intervention* in everyday social life, because it is felt that only strong coercive measures will ultimately keep people in line and teach them the discipline they require to live as members of a civilised community.

then & now

new right criminology

As is clear from this chapter, New Right criminology refers more to a political orientation (see Chapter 1) than a distinctive theoretical tradition. For this reason, the perspectives here draw somewhat selectively on classical theory (Chapter 2) and biological and psychological positivism (Chapter 3). This presents somewhat of a problem, as classical theory emphasises individual free will and rationality, while positivism emphasises the way individuals are driven by biological and psychological tendencies outside of their control. One result of this is that classical theory's emphasis on proportional punishment has transformed into the need for harsh punishment. So too, classical theory's emphasis on the social contract has been individualised with policies aimed at making individuals sign contracts with the state regarding their antisocial behaviour or imposing conditions that individuals need to follow if they are to receive unemployment benefits. While developed during the conservative years of the 1980s, the neo-classical and New Right perspectives have re-emerged in the early twenty-first century, particularly in the forms of rational choice, routine activities and opportunity theories.

historical development

The New Right perspective has historical links with several different traditions within criminology. The right-wing libertarian approach is clearly identified within a classical criminological perspective. The emphasis on individual choice and responsibility, punishment and proportionality, and protection of liberty and property all have their echoes in the previous discussions of the social contract.

The traditionalist conservative approach has also been reflected in sociological and criminological theorising. For example, the emphasis on punishment as a means of reinforcing moral boundaries echoes aspects of Durkheim's work. Durkheim (1964 [1895]) saw punishment as a social institution intimately concerned with morality and social solidarity. As Garland (1990: 28) suggests, 'the existence of strong bonds of moral solidarity are the conditions which cause punishments to come about, and, in their turn, punishments result in the reaffirmation and strengthening of these same social bonds'. Durkheim was thus concerned with exploring conceptually the nature of punishment, particularly in relation to the ideas of the 'collective conscience' and the role of passion and sentiment in social life. However, unlike Durkheim, traditional conservatives promote a single moral 'rightness' that pertains to society as a whole, whereas Durkheim was at pains to point out that morality varied between different societies.

More recent work has elements of both descriptive and proscriptive analysis. The emphasis on discipline, coercion and self-control in the traditionalist conservative approach, for instance, is mirrored in the concerns of control theory (ranging from the early work of Shaw & McKay (1942), through to Wilson and Kelling's (1982) ideas about 'broken windows', and later Sampson et al. 1997, 2002). Whether it emphasises bio-psycho-social processes (such as Eysenck 1984) or socialisation processes (see Hirschi 1969), a social control perspective argues that the nature of crime is intertwined with the connection between individual and society.

Control theory, as formulated by Hirschi (1969), for example, is premised upon the idea that it is an individual's bond to society that makes the difference in terms of whether or not the person abides by society's general rules and values. From this perspective, all people are inherently antisocial, and thus all people would commit crime if they so dared. It is the nature of the bond that children have with their society that ultimately determines their behaviour (Paternoster & Bachman 2010).

In rejecting the competing explanations for the causes of crime (such as strain and differential association theories) Hirschi (1969) suggested that his social bond theory was better able to capture the 'lifecourse' of criminality (with its peak in early years) without 'widening the net'. In constructing his social bond theory, he identified four major elements:

1\ *attachment*—the ties of affection and respect to significant others in one's life, and more generally a sensitivity to the opinion of others

2\ *commitment*—the investment of time and energy to activities such as school and various conventional and unconventional means and goals

3\ *involvement*—the patterns of living that shape immediate and long-term opportunities; for example, the idea that keeping busy doing conventional things will reduce the exposure of young people to illegal opportunities

4\ *belief*—the degree to which young people agree with the rightness of legal rules, which are seen to reflect a general moral consensus in society.

It is the combination of attachment, commitment, involvement and belief that shapes the life world of young people, and that essentially dictates whether or not they will take advantage of conventional means and goals of social advancement, or whether they will pursue illegal pathways to self-gratification.

It is up to society, and its agents, to step in and ensure that its younger members are imbued with the right bonds. In other words, there is a high degree of intervention necessary if children and young people are to be guided the right way, and if they are to follow paths that uphold social values, but that ultimately go against their essential antisocial nature. Without adequate socialisation—a strong social control presence of some kind—criminal behaviour would be common.

contemporary examples

In related and later work, Hirschi (1986), and Gottfredson and Hirschi (1990) argue that the central issue in explaining crime is that of self-control; that is, people differ in the extent to which they are restrained from criminal acts (see also Wilson & Herrnstein 1985). This, in turn, is linked to the question of social bonding, and especially the problem of ineffective child-rearing (Akers 1990). This theory has been adopted as the basis for most contemporary social control, opportunity reduction and routine activity crime prevention approaches, and incorporates elements of other theories and perspectives:

- classical theory, in its acceptance of the idea that people are basically self-seeking
- bio-psycho-social positivism, in its focus on the importance of proper 'conditioning' or training of the young
- sociological perspectives, which look to the nature of the family as a key variable in the development of self-control
- some elements of strain theory, especially those related to social learning theory.

The theory does not analyse specific social divisions (such as class, gender and ethnicity), but rests upon a conception of human nature that sees all people as essentially driven by the same kinds of 'universal tendency to enhance their own pleasure' (Gottfredson & Hirschi 1990). Given this, the crucial issue is then one of how best to socialise all people to conform to society's values and to engage in conventional law-abiding behaviour.

In policy terms, the answer to juvenile crime lies in redressing the *defective social training* that characterises offenders who have in some way 'lost control'. In other words, the emphasis from a practitioner's perspective will be to re-attach the young people to some kind of family, to recommit them to long-range conventional goals, to involve them in school and other constructive activities, and to have them acquire beliefs in the morality of law (Empey 1982: 269; Akers 1990).

Importantly, the control perspective is premised upon the idea that 'deviancy' stems from lack of self-control (Akers 1991; Bouffard et al. 2000; Tibbetts & Gibson 2002), and that this is fundamentally a matter related to the processes of socialisation. Whereas Gottfredson and Hirschi (1990) emphasised the significance of relationships within the family, other contemporary criminologists have concentrated on social control, and making changes to the costs and benefits of crime.

For example, New Right approaches to crime and criminality have expanded particularly in the area of *opportunity–rationality* and *routine activities* theories (see, for example, Cohen & Felson 1979; Cornish & Clarke 1986; Clarke & Felson 1993; Cornish 1993; Felson & Clarke 1998; Trasler 1993). This approach reflects the libertarian emphasis on choice and responsibility for one's actions. It is postulated that crime cannot be understood apart from the nature and distribution of opportunities for both crime and non-criminal behaviour. Thus, when people find themselves in situations in which they have opportunities to commit crime, the decision to do so (or not to do so) is a rational one (see Barlow 1993; Massoglia & Macmillan 2002).

In fact, from the point of view of rational choice theory, we need to assume that most 'criminals' are rational agents who can be deterred from committing additional crimes by an increase in the punishment they might expect to receive (von Hirsch 1976; Buchanan & Hartley 1992). In economic terms, the idea here is that individuals will always act in such a way as to maximise their own benefit. They are responsive to incentives and disincentives. From an economic rationalist position, therefore, the best criminal justice policy is one that prevents the commission of crime at the least financial cost. For example, according to the advocates of this approach, the most economically efficient way in which to manage the crime problem is to privatise institutions such as prisons, and to increase the probability of detection and conviction of offenders. Or, in the case of the UK 'ConDem' (Conservative-Liberal Democrat) government elected in 2010, the most economically viable option is to privatise punishment into the hands of the 'community' (such as the policy for increasing numbers of offences to be punished with community (rather than penal) sentences, and antisocial behaviour orders) (Burney 2005).

The broad philosophical orientation of rational choice theory also has been related to the adoption of crime prevention techniques directed primarily at *opportunity reduction* (see Wilson 1975; Brantingham & Faust 1976; Clarke 1980; Felson 1994; Felson & Clarke 1998), rather than the structural reasons for offending behaviour or the criminalisation process itself. From this perspective, it is not the severity of punishment that compels acceptable behaviour; rather, it is the likelihood of detection and detention. Analysis of particular activities and locations can form the basis of a strategy designed to change the risks and costs associated with certain behaviours. In this way, the potential offender is deterred from making the decision to commit crime in certain areas, against certain targets. However, care should be taken in assuming that opportunity reduction is necessarily a conservative approach (see Sutton et al. 2008; Hancock 2009). Opportunity reduction measures in public housing estates can make a significant difference to residents. Obtaining the necessary resources from government to fund such initiatives, however (particularly when there is little widespread public support for such measures or the housing is not located in a marginal electorate) can prove challenging.

A third perspective identified with New Right criminology is that of *underclass* explanations (Murray 1990; Herrnstein & Murray 1994; Wilson & Herrnstein 1985; Murray 1994). In this view, the problem resides in the behaviour of certain population groups, particularly the poor, the homeless, single mothers and, in the case of the USA, African-Americans (see Mooney 1998; Fraser 1995). The problem of crime and deviancy is thus seen to lie within the identified populations themselves. The 'underclass' comprises those sections of the poverty-stricken who, through their own volition or choice, or by genetic default, engage in criminal activity, substance abuse, and deliberate non-participation in paid employment. Essentially, the so-called underclass is presented here as a 'moral' category, given that the emphasis is on behaviour (rather than structural conditions, such as lack of jobs) and disapproval (rather than understanding of social hardship).

One of the most (in)famous and widely adopted approaches that draw on both the underclass and opportunity reduction theories is that of Wilson & Kelling's '*broken windows*' (1982). In this early formulation of community policing theory, Wilson and Kelling (1982) argue that 'signs of *disorder*' (such as a broken window and beggars) are 'signs of *crime*', and that, unless these signs of disorder are remedied quickly, they will reduce the community's informal controls.

From one broken window, not fixed, 'strangers' to the community (or even some on the margins of the community) may feel empowered to break another window. With no sign of a moral guardian or entrepreneur to care that the windows are broken, harder criminals (rather than just deviant individuals) may believe that their crimes will go undetected and without penalty. Before a community knows it, they are living in a high crime area.

Wilson and Kelling (1982) argue that a logical response to this transition from vulnerable to high-risk community is a proactive 'quality of life' policing program. In isolation, or in conjunction with other welfare and social services, the police clean up the physical and behavioural signs of disorder such as graffiti, rubbish, broken windows, beggars, sex work, drugs, or even young people hanging out in public places.

In contrast to the massive shift in criminal and social laws over the last forty years, which sought to decriminalise many moral and behavioural crimes—such as public drunkenness, offensive language and begging— the broken windows approach sought to empower police to become the primary agents of social control, not just society's crime fighters.

A summary of common themes in New Right writings on the underclass is provided by Lind (1995). The nature of the problem, from a right-wing perspective, is a combination of lack of economic incentives (such as welfare dependency), a culture of poverty (such as familial breakdown and inappropriate role models), intellectual deficiencies (such as hereditary genetic inferiority) and low standards of morality (such as sole parenting). The proposed solution is to make members of the 'underclass' more responsible and accountable for their own welfare and lifestyle choices (Jones & Novak 2009). In effect, the demand is for the withdrawal of government support for the disadvantaged, coupled with efforts to re-socialise people into new value and moral systems.

Whatever the specific theories that have been developed over the years, it appears that some writers have adopted a New Right criminological position simply because of the perception that 'nothing else has worked'. The so-called new realists, for example, have observed the deficiencies of a system partly built upon 'treatment' and positivistic assumptions, and concluded that it is time to reassert order and authority across our social institutions (see Wilson 1975; Tame 1991; Murray 1990). However, as we see from the argument above, there are other reasons for the rise in the popularity of criminological perspectives that emphasise individual responsibility and the need for a tough authoritative approach. These perspectives fit well with a political context that emphasises individual effort and negotiation at work, downplays the importance of collective action to generate change, and in which people are concerned about their economic and emotional well-being and are cynical about their government's motives.

From the point of view of crime control and public order, the direction of policing and punishment fostered by New Right criminology is towards more active containment of, and control over, what are seen to be *criminogenic populations*—the 'dangerous classes' of the late modern era (Karstedt 2010). The practical implementation of criminal justice policy is based upon the regulation of those population groups most closely identified with the 'underclass'. For instance, intervention is increasingly concerned with identifying, classifying and managing groups in the community that are assessed on the basis of 'risk' and 'dangerousness' (see Feeley & Simon 1994; Ericson & Shearing 1991; O'Malley 2010). This is associated with various kinds of pre-emptive action and incapacitation strategies, such as 'zero tolerance' policing and 'three strikes and you're out' punishment. The emphasis is on attacking the 'signs of disorder' through confrontational policing strategies (in which any behaviour, activity or group deemed to be antisocial is not to be tolerated by authorities), and by locking up those who transgress the criminal and moral norms of society (through committing them to long prison terms or, in the absence of a criminal offence, placing individuals on antisocial behaviour orders and subjecting them to a behavioural contract). Getting 'tough on crime' is part of a generalised escalation in the punishment ethos.

This conservative turn to criminological theory is despite an avowed emphasis by governments on 'evidence-led' policy-making. For all the criminological talk about 'rationality' and the need for research to guide policy-making, it is clear that criminal justice policy is far too important to contemporary governments to be left in the hands of criminologists who seek positivist and/or sociological answers to crime and punishment. Criminological perspectives that are sympathetic to the government agenda appear at the present time to be those most heeded (Walters 2009). New Right perspectives often fulfil these requirements.

{from theory to practice: punishment, punishment-
avoidance and deterrence theory}

Sitren, A.H. & Applegate, B.K. (2007). 'Testing the Deterrent Effects of Personal and Vicarious Experience with Punishment and Punishment Avoidance', *Deviant Behavior*, 28 (1): 29–55.

Deterrence theory has long been a central plank of classical and New Right theories of criminal behaviour. In this article, Sitren and Applegate test Stafford and Warr's (1993) reconceptualised deterrence theory. In classical theory, deterrence is conceived as two distinct processes: general deterrence (which aims to deter the community as a whole through the symbolic punishment of an individual) and specific deterrence (which aims to deter a specific individual from future offending). The 'audience' of these two practices of deterrence differs. For general deterrence, the 'audience' is a would-be offender 'who somehow witnesses or vicariously experiences punishment' (Piquero & Paternoster 1998: 3). This would-be offender is swayed against criminal behaviour after rationally weighing the costs and consequences of criminal behaviour. On the other hand, the audience of specific deterrence has already had their behaviour judged as criminal and, having not appreciated the consequences of this previous act

continued

of criminal behaviour, must be subject to customised techniques of deterrence to ensure future compliance with norms and rules.

In the early 1990s, Stafford and Warr (1993) proposed that deterrence theory needed to account for the relationship between these two processes. In particular, they argued that all individuals (offenders and would-be offenders) could be influenced by direct (or personal) and indirect (or vicarious) experiences of punishment *and* punishment avoidance. In this new framework, Stafford and Warr combined the forms of deterrence while simultaneously foregrounding the importance of punishment avoidance, which they suggested 'may do more to encourage crime that punishment does to discourage criminal behaviour' (Sitren & Applegate 2007: 31). Unlike earlier formulations of deterrence theory, the inclusion of punishment avoidance also attempts to account for classical theory's central arguments about the importance of certainty and swiftness of punishment.

Building on three earlier studies that have tested Stafford and Warr's (1993) reconceptualisation of deterrence theory, in this article Sitren and Applegate used a scenario-based survey to elicit information from 860 university students about cheating on an exam. The scenario required respondents to make a series of decisions about whether they would participate in criminal behaviour. The questions related to variables such as certainty of punishment, punishment severity, personal and vicarious experiences of punishment and punishment avoidance, and likelihood of offending (Sitren & Applegate 2007: 37). Students were asked about the number of times they had been caught cheating, and the number of times they had cheated and not been caught. Similarly, students were asked about the proportion of people they knew who had been caught cheating, and the proportion of people they knew who had cheated and not been caught. Each of these sets provided a numeric scale to measure the effect of personal and vicarious punishment avoidance.

Sitren and Applegate reported that 42 per cent of the respondents admitted to prior exam cheating, with 10 per cent having done so on more than six occasions. The average likelihood of offending was 17 per cent and the estimated likelihood of getting caught was 64 per cent (2007: 40). Students indicated that they would not cheat when there was certainty and swiftness of punishment: however, the certainty of punishment was modulated by students' vicarious experiences of punishment avoidance (Sitren & Applegate 2007: 41). Importantly— and in contradiction to Stafford and Warr, and all previous models of deterrence theory—Sitren and Applegate found that there was a *positive* relationship between previous personal experiences of punishment and likelihood of offending. The authors argued that the results from this study have important consequences for the application of deterrence theory in policy and sentencing, especially the long-held belief that 'experiencing punishment deters offending' (2007: 46).

---

critique

A critique of New Right criminology stems from the way in which theories within this perspective ignore issues of power in their assertion of choice and free will. In this way the critique of New Right criminology mirrors, to some extent at least, criticisms of classical criminology. On 'rational' criteria, there is much to criticise in New Right criminology, particularly in its populist political guise.

On a theoretical level, New Right criminology does not analyse the nature of choice within a society that is characterised by inequality. It does not address concerns about the ethnic and 'racial' divisions in society, and the way in which certain groups, such as Indigenous people, are systematically overrepresented in the criminal justice system. The explanation that such overrepresentation can be explained purely by a 'choice' to offend does not seem to take us very far. Much New Right criminology simply ignores issues of 'race', ethnicity, gender and class by prioritising the individual, along with individual choice and individual values.

Where levels of analysis other than that of the individual are evident, it is clear that they rest on a particular set of values that does not include significant sectors of society. For example, control theory talks unproblematically about inculcating majority values, expressed through belief in the rightness of legal rules that are seen to reflect a general moral consensus in society. The interdependence of individuals that prevents criminal behaviour is premised upon adherence to the moral consensus. Non-adherence predisposes an individual to criminal offending. Within multicultural societies such as Australia, Canada, the USA and the UK, there are major problems if the notion of consensus is defined in the narrow terms that traditional conservatives tend to use (Burnett 2009).

Many of the policies proposed by New Right theories have themselves been discredited. In particular, the capacity of harsh, or even proportional, punishment to deter individuals from reoffending has been the subject of long debate. There is substantial evidence that imprisonment, in particular, is counterproductive, serves only to exacerbate, not diminish, rates of offending and provides an apprenticeship in crime for young offenders. As the Conservative Home Secretary of the UK government recently suggested, prison is both ineffective and expensive.

Furthermore, the debate concerning the need for harsher penalties has negative consequences in and of itself. For example, it engenders a fear of crime that is out of all proportion to the realistic possibility of victimisation. The problem of how to deal with the fear of crime—independent of how to deal with crime *per se*—is an urgent issue facing many people today, and in some cases 'drives' many operational policing decisions.

Finally, crime itself is defined narrowly. For the majority of New Right theorists, the major concern is with 'street crime'. Crimes of the powerful and crimes of the state are hardly mentioned. Where they are mentioned, the state is seen as able to deal adequately with the problem, since there is no conception that the state itself may favour the powerful over the powerless.

The popularity of the law-and-order debate, and with it the popularity of New Right criminology in general, cannot be accounted for adequately by reference to a rational 'scientific' debate. It is best explained by the need of societies for symbolic assurances of certainty in the face of growing economic uncertainty. The symbolic and political nature of the crime debate is well evidenced through the popularity of New Right criminology. It provides government with a justification to capture the emotional needs of an electorate within a capitalist democracy. The potency of the symbol of 'law and order' is not lost on governments increasingly at the mercy of unpredictable and often unpleasant financial and employment trends in the economic sphere.

A further, and worrying, aspect of the authoritarian strand within New Right circles is the merging of global and international developments with national and domestic concerns. This is most evident in the ways in which the so-called 'war on terrorism' has seen even greater collaboration between military, police and secret services; a greater propensity to do away with long-established human rights and civil rights protections (in the name of homeland security); and the putting into place of informal and formal sanctions designed to ensure public 'unity' in support of war efforts (both within and without national borders) (Gill 2009). Politically, the pursuit of 'security' has been accompanied in the USA by what has been called 'prescriptive patriotism', which is an orchestrated patriotism that aims to close down 'debate and dissent through the imposition of a prescribed allegiance' (O'Leary & Platt 2001: 42). Crime and deviance are thus defined almost exclusively in terms dictated by ruling elites, who mobilise public opinion in ways that allow for the silencing of dissent, the imprisonment of those who have not been formally charged with a crime and the vilification of minority groups.

Similar types of processes are also apparent with regard to immigration controls and border protection. Once again, the treatment of asylum seekers, especially in countries such as Australia, has frequently been characterised by systematic denial of human and legal rights, an emphasis on illegality of entry, the selective rejection of refugees by possible host nations and the enforced detention of those who survive the journey to new lands (see Weber 2002; Pickering & Lambert 2001). The symbols of the New Right are basically constructed around notions of social difference, which are in turn interpreted as evidence of social deviance. This applies to 'deviants' inside a country, as well as those outside.

Despite the negative aspects of New Right criminology, there are elements that are of importance to the criminological debate. It is clear that criminological theories (at least at the present time) need to take account of individual action to be seen as legitimate. This clearly contains a number of elements, not all captured by a New Right perspective. For example, while New Right perspectives assert issues of individual responsibility, they also highlight individual rights and, in particular, the right to feel safe and secure (Walklate 2009). The rights of victims, which had been ignored by the majority of criminologists, also are brought to the fore within this perspective. Victims' rights and needs can no longer be ignored within criminological theory. Further, the popularity of some New Right perspectives points to the need to go beyond a view of human activity as purely rational in the sense of formally logical. Values, emotions and ideas evident in the debate about crime clearly point to the need for criminological theory to understand both the political and cultural role crime plays in societies, as Durkheim pointed out over a century ago. Finally, the phenomenon of New Right criminology is a timely reminder of the political nature of crime and crime policy. Criminological theory has to come to grips with political realities if its policy proposals and strategic plans of action are to go beyond mere conjecture.

{conclusion}

New right criminology refers to a particular political orientation, rather than to a systematic, coherent theory in its own right. For this reason there is a broad range of theoretical perspectives that are brought together in this chapter, from authoritarian populism and right-wing libertarian perspectives through to traditionalist conservatism and control theory. Despite the differences of these approaches, all can be characterised by a focus on the rights, responsibilities and free will of the individual who offends. Each has a particular moral stance that upholds the status quo of society and the right of those with power to dictate what constitutes the moral consensus.

Each strand of New Right thinking also tends to see human nature as ultimately depraved. Without sufficient deterrent measures put in place by the state, or strong social bonds as defined by control theory, human nature would automatically lead to antisocial and criminal behaviour. Overlaid on this pessimistic perspective of human nature is the need for society to define clearly right from wrong, to reward the right and, more importantly, to punish the wrong. Without such an approach, a general breakdown in law and order would result.

Like many criminological theories, the popularity of New Right criminology cannot be divorced from the broader political environment. The political popularity of the law-and-order debate and calls for tougher punishment on a political level are legitimised through many of the perspectives outlined above. The prominence of the law-and-order debate, as fostered by New Right ideas, led directly to the emergence of a new theoretical

perspective on the left, namely Left Realism. It was
the success of the New Right at a popular level that
led sections of the left to 'take crime seriously'. To
do so they recognised that issues such as victims'
rights and the popularity of a strong response to
criminal behaviour resonated with community concerns,
and were thus important.

{further reading}

Buchanan, C. & Hartley, P.
(1992). *Criminal Choice: The
Economic Theory of Crime and Its
Implications for Crime Control*,
Centre for Independent Studies,
Sydney.

Coleman, R., Sim, J., Tombs, S.
& Whyte, D. (eds) (2009). *State
Power Crime*, SAGE, London.

Cullen, F.T., Wright, J.P. &
Blevins, K.R. (eds) (2009).
*Taking Stock: The Status
of Criminological Theory*,
Transaction Publishers, New
Brunswick, NJ.

Feeley, M. & Simon, J. (1994).
'Actuarial Justice: The
Emerging New Criminal Law', in
D. Nelken (ed.), *The Futures of
Criminology*, SAGE, London.

Gottfredson, M. & Hirschi, T.
(1990). *A General Theory of
Crime*, Stanford University
Press, Stanford.

Herrnstein, R. & Murray, C.
(1994). *The Bell Curve*, Basic
Books, New York.

Lind, M. (1995). 'Brave New Right', in S. Fraser (ed.), *The Bell Curve Wars: Race, Intelligence and the Future of America*, Basic Books, New York.

McLaughlin, E., Muncie, J. & Hughes, G. (eds) (2003). *Criminological Perspectives: A Reader* (2nd edition), SAGE, London.

Murray, C. (1990). *The Emerging Underclass*, Institute of Economic Affairs, London.

Nettler, G. (1984). *Explaining Crime*, McGraw-Hill, New York.

Piquero, A.R. & Tibbetts, S.G. (eds) (2002). *Rational Choice and Criminal Behavior: Recent Research and Future Challenges*, Routledge, New York.

Roshier. R. (1989). *Controlling Crime: The Classical Perspective in Criminology*. Open University Press, Milton Keynes.

Simpson, S. & Agnew, R. (eds) (2000). *Of Crime and Criminality: The Use of Theory in Everyday Life*, Pine Forge Press, Thousand Oaks, CA.

Tame, C. (1991). 'Freedom, Responsibility and Justice: The Criminology of the "New Right"', in K. Stenson & D. Cowell (eds), *The Politics of Crime Control*, SAGE, London: 127–45.

chapter {9} | |
left realism

{introduction}
—

        Left Realism is best seen as a response to two conflicting perspectives on crime that emerged strongly in the mid-1980s: New Right criminology and Marxist criminology. The previous chapter outlined the political popularity of the conservative political perspective, with its strong emphasis on 'law and order'. Left Realism was concerned that the political debate was being dominated by the right wing, which had a destructive impact on the lives of the working class. It attempted to capture the political debate by focusing, like the conservatives, on the victims of so-called street crime. However, Left Realists wanted to highlight the fact that the majority of victims of street crimes were from the working class, not the middle and upper classes. In doing so, Left Realism wanted to reorientate the law-and-order debate—away from the middle-class fear of the working class, and towards a consideration of how the working class itself suffers from crime.

    Left Realism saw radical criminology as unable or unwilling to ameliorate this suffering of the working class because it failed to take crime seriously (Young 1981). This failure further meant that such criminological analysis was unable to provide the antidote to the conservative 'law-and-order' politics that dominated crime policy. Left Realists contrasted the political popularity of the conservative Thatcher government in Britain with the political marginalisation of the radical perspective, or 'left idealist' view (as it was labelled by the Left Realists). The reason for such marginalisation, they suggested, was the lack of practical suggestions put forward by Marxist criminology to deal with crime in the inner city.

    This chapter will outline the origins of Left Realism, and the nature of the response it made to 'law-and-order' politics from a left perspective. It has received considerable criticism, mainly from the left, and has undergone considerable revision. The major revisions within Left Realism will also be outlined in this chapter. What is central to the Left Realist endeavour, and common to all permutations of the theory, is its pragmatic core. Left Realism sees itself as both a reasonable and practical response to the problem of crime in inner-city communities.

—

~~social~~ context

Left Realism can be seen as a response within (initially) British criminology to the policies of neo-conservatism in general, and the Thatcher government in particular. It was avowedly political, in that it saw itself as a political response to the law-and-order agenda of the right. It was this response to the law-and-order debates of the early 1980s that galvanised the thinking of Left Realists (Brown & Hogg 1992b). Before this time they had been writing as predominantly Marxist or radical criminologists debating with other radical criminologists from within the same paradigm.

In attempting to enter into the political discussions of law and order, the Left Realists joined in the conservative debate about *crime control*, which was less concerned about the causes of crime (Garland 2001). In doing so, they confirmed that conservative politics had successfully defined the crime problem as one where there were clear distinctions between those who were criminal and those who were not. In this conception, crime was a unitary phenomenon defined by commonsense. With this in mind, crime policy was properly concerned with controlling crime, not with reducing conditions that might give rise to criminal behaviour, such as inequality and unemployment.

This emphasis on controlling crime, rather than on dealing with the causes of crime, could be seen clearly in the contribution Left Realist writers made in response to the riots experienced in Britain in 1981. These riots occurred in areas of poverty and high levels of unemployment, such as Brixton, but it was not this unemployment and deprivation *per se* that captured the imagination of the Left Realists. These theorists argued that while poverty and deprivation were a precondition of riots, and more generally of increases in crime, they were not a sufficient cause. Poverty and unemployment could be associated with quiescent fatalism and the acceptance of adversity, as much as with rebellion and violence (Lea & Young 1982). Left Realists argued that the riots had their genesis in three factors: West Indian counterculture; the political marginalisation of the inner city; and, crucially, the police methods of dealing with people who lived in deprived neighbourhoods.

The explanations by the Left Realists for the existence of a violent and aggressive counterculture are similar to the explanations of the strain theorists, which were outlined in Chapter 4. Left Realists argued that countercultures thrive where the expectations of material rewards engendered by the education system and the mass media are manifestly not available to certain sectors of society. In particular, successive generations of West Indian immigrants in the UK saw themselves as discriminated against and alienated from the mainstream culture. In the face of this lack of opportunity, a counterculture developed—based on a 'hustling' mentality and street culture—that was competitive, disorganised and antisocial. Along with poverty and unemployment, the existence of this counterculture produced extremely high rates of inner-city crime. In opposition to Marxist criminologists, who downplayed or denied the existence of rising rates of street crime, Left Realists argued that street crime was much higher than police figures suggested.

Those who lived in the decaying inner city lacked access to an effective voice within the political process; this exacerbated the alienation that people in those neighbourhoods experienced, and spawned the counterculture. Those marginalised within the inner city had no access to traditional centres of power within society, such as those controlling capital or the trade unions. Such people were locked out of the world of production and, with this, access to the political system was also denied. Left Realism suggested that the return to violence, epitomised by the riots, was the politics of last resort. Economic marginalisation exacerbated political marginalisation.

The marginalisation felt by people in these neighbourhoods was not addressed by government or state agencies. Rather, the methods used by the arm of the state that had the greatest impact in the area, namely the *police*, were disastrous. Left Realists argued that in deprived neighbourhoods police deliberately shifted away from 'consensus' policing (policing for the community), which might have at least gone some way to reducing alienation in these communities. Instead, police used military tactics, 'swamp' procedures and 'stop-and-search' provisions that allowed on-the-street searching of any suspicious-looking person. These tactics had the effect of blurring the distinction between offender and non-offender to a point where, Left Realists argued, any action by police became perceived as a symbolic attack on the community as a whole. It is at this point that any consensual relationship that existed between the police and the public breaks down, and actions by police can trigger rioting (Lea & Young 1982).

The analysis of the riots in the UK set the scene for the early formulations of Left Realism, and defined the theory as one primarily concerned with the control of crime, rather than the preconditions of crime. Relief of the preconditions of the counterculture, for example, was not the primary policy goal of these theorists. Rather, they took as central planks the second and third strands of analysis outlined above—political marginalisation and policing reform. The political dimension was addressed by alignment with the British Labour Party and the production of policies with which the left could intervene effectively in the law-and-order debate (Lea & Young 1984). The substance of the policies provided by Left Realism predominantly addressed the third strand of analysis, that of policing reform, and the creation of consensus-style policing within inner urban areas. It was this newly emerging 'public criminology', where links were created between academics and governments, which transformed criminological theory into criminal justice studies and practices.

The focus on policing was seen as justified because of perceived omissions by Marxist criminology concerning the reality of crime in working-class areas. From this approach, Left Realists argued that the major concern of the working class and marginalised poor in the city was not the crimes of the powerful, as suggested by Marxist criminology, but the property offences, robbery and domestic violence that were experienced as an everyday reality. The victims of such crimes, as well as the perpetrators, were predominantly the poor and vulnerable sections of society. The radical criminological focus on crimes of the powerful and crimes of the state 'missed the point', and failed to represent accurately the needs of the working class. Furthermore, when 'street crime' was mentioned by radical criminology it was too often romanticised: street criminals were characterised as 'latter-day Robin Hoods' rather than as perpetrators of criminal behaviour that was seriously antisocial and destructive. So, for Left Realists it was the street crime of inner-city neighbourhoods that should form the predominant focus of this new form of public criminology.

then & now

left realist criminology

Left Realism is a good example of an eclectic theory that draws together diverse strands. As this chapter makes clear, it began as a 'practical' Marxist alternative, and so shared Marxist criminology's analysis of capitalism (see Chapter 6). It also was inclusive of feminist concerns about women's victimisation and social marginalisation (Chapter 7) Yet the emphasis on practical policies means that the theoretical analysis shares much with strain theory (Chapter 4), a perspective that also emphasised the possibility of reform within the existing economic order. The continuing challenge of implementing a genuine alternative to 'law-and-order' policies within contemporary Western societies has seen recent proponents of Left Realism (for example Jock Young) move back towards a more in-depth analysis of why social exclusion remains so entrenched—a concern that is central to critical criminology (Chapter 11).

~~basic~~ concepts

Left Realist criminology is characterised by its pragmatic focus on crime control (see chart 9.1). Because of this, it is not concerned with lengthy analyses of what actually constitutes crime. Rather, it is content to define crime as that contained in the legal code. This can be seen as partly a result of the major means of data collection used by the Left Realists—namely, local crime victim (or victimisation) surveys (see, for example, Sparks et al. 1977; Jones et al. 1986; Young 1988). Local crime victim surveys target specific inner-city locations and ask residents about their victimisation from criminal activity and what residents would like done about it. As a result, the definition of crime is driven by the definitions of crime that are reported on the survey. Local residents are more likely to see crime as defined in traditional terms, and so Left Realism itself defines crime in traditional terms.

chart 9.1 | **left realist perspectives**

definition of crime	_ as contained in legal code, with main focus on street crime
focus of analysis	_ as crime by and against working class, with working class as both offender and victim _ use of crime victim surveys
cause of crime	_ relative deprivation _ ineffective methods of policing
nature of offender	_ most crime is intra-class _ offenders must be held responsible to a degree for their own actions
response to crime	_ develop more effective policing, and greater community control over criminal justice agencies
crime prevention	_ reduce alienation of community from the criminal justice system _ adopt problem-solving approaches _ take crime seriously
operation of criminal justice system	_ active cooperation between police and community members _ meeting of victim needs _ crime prevention programs

The local crime victim survey is the major tool of analysis of Left Realists. Because the emphasis is on addressing the concerns expressed by inner-city populations, analysis is directed towards concerns raised about crime in local areas as expressed through the crime surveys. In particular, this perspective is concerned about *intra-class crime*; that is, criminal behaviour by the working class against the working class.

More recent analysis has focused on the 'square of crime' (Young 1992). This consists of two dyads. One is concerned with the *criminal act*, which comprises offender and victim. The other is concerned with *social control*, which comprises social action (especially the actions of police and 'multi-agencies') and social reaction (especially the reaction of the public). A complete analysis of crime, according to Left Realists, should focus on both dyads (Young 1991).

figure 9.1 | the square of crime

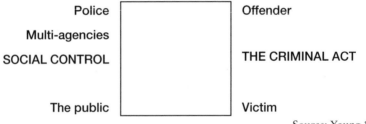

Police		Offender
Multi-agencies		
SOCIAL CONTROL		THE CRIMINAL ACT
The public		Victim

Source: Young 1992

The causes of crime, as perceived by the Left Realists, span both the conditions endemic to inner-city working-class areas, such as poor facilities and lack of jobs, and the response by the criminal justice agencies, notably the police, which exacerbate the problem of crime by their heavy-handed responses. The cause of crime, according to Left Realism, results from the amalgamation of three aspects:

1\ the *relative deprivation* of those in working-class areas, which gives rise to countercultures
2\ the lack of access to the political sphere, which spawns *feelings of powerlessness*
3\ *dissent and police responses*, which antagonise local populations and cause further breakdown in these communities.

This leads to rising crime rates in these areas. The level of crime, according to Left Realists, is higher than that in official figures, and is rising in areas of high social breakdown (Young 1991).

Concern with the suffering of the victims of crime has led Left Realism to adopt a less-than-sympathetic view of the offender. As with most theory generated out of a classical view, offenders are *responsible for their behaviour*, which is antisocial and destructive, and causes great hardship within already impoverished areas of society. However, unlike New Right criminology, Left Realists do not see offenders or offending totally as a result of free will. The motivation to offend springs from the relative deprivation in these areas; that is, external influences shape criminal action, which is a central claim of traditional positivist theory. Young people and ethnic minorities are led by the broader culture to expect material reward, yet their situation within the social order prevents them achieving that reward. Further, social cohesion in these areas has broken down. Left Realists argue that in other times of great hardship, such as the depression of the 1930s, there was a working-class solidarity and working-class culture that saw people pull together. Today, inner-city areas with a high crime rate lack *social solidarity* that could insulate against feelings of deprivation. The result is anger and frustration, particularly in young people.

According to Left Realists, the primary response to these problems has been in the area of *police and policing*. In line with the Peelian traditions of policing, crime can be better controlled by a police force that is responsive to the needs of the local community, and wields this power by consent of the community (not by force or coercion) (Kinsey et al. 1986). Furthermore, local communities need effective political responses to their concerns, which can be brought about by giving greater power to local councils to control criminal justice agencies (Hancock 2009). More recent writing in the area of Left Realism has dealt with what to do once offenders are apprehended. However, in areas such as penology (the study of corrections), Left Realism has largely 'borrowed' from the liberal analysis, which emphasises the need for *community-based corrections*.

Crime prevention, then, will be achieved by reducing the alienation of the community from the criminal justice system. This will not be achieved, though, by the agencies themselves deciding what is in the best interests of these high-crime areas. Policies are needed that will reduce the alienation of the community from the criminal justice system. These policies will give the *local communities an active voice* in how the police, in particular, go about dealing with people in local areas. Local communities should be able to decide what the problems the police should tackle, and then should be able to work cooperatively with police to solve these problems.

The criminal justice system under a Left Realist policy agenda would involve active cooperation between community members and police; commonly referred to as the 'co-production' of law and order. The system would be geared towards the concerns of local communities rather than driven by a broader, and more partisan, political agenda. The law-and-order debate would then be immune from capture by political concerns aimed at providing a 'quick fix', such as military-style policing, which is ultimately a symbolic and destructive solution.

historical development

The historical development of Left Realism can be seen as two 'waves'. The first came out of the analysis of the Thatcher years by Left Realists in the mid-1980s; the second, more comprehensive, theory arose in response to a critique of early formulations of the theory, mainly from the so-called Left Idealists. Before describing these two waves, it is important to describe the way in which data is gathered for analysis and theorising under a Left Realist perspective. Left Realism prides itself not only on the development of a paradigm with which to understand the problem of crime and criminality, but also on the development of the research instrument that underpins this theorising—the local crime victim (or victimisation) surveys. In this sense, Left Realism is closely wedded to the goals of early positivist criminological theory (Pawson 2006).

Local crime victim surveys can be differentiated from broad-based crime victim surveys undertaken at state or national levels. The aim of these local surveys is to understand the problem of crime and victimisation within specific locations (Evans 1992). These research locations were often the poorest and most marginalised. In the UK, for example, the first survey was undertaken in Islington, a predominantly Black working-class area in London (Jones et al. 1986; MacLean 1993). The aim of the surveys was to monitor people's needs concerning crime, and then develop policies that accurately reflect those needs. Questions in the surveys were broadly concerned with issues of victimisation and the respondents' relationships with criminal justice agencies. The surveys purported to measure some 550 variables (MacLean 1993).

Importantly, victimisation surveys are seen as a complete method, in themselves, of obtaining the necessary information on which to base theory and policy. This can be contrasted with the traditional methods of radical research, case studies and ethnographies (interview and participant observation). Left Realists claim that victim surveys generate better empirical data, which is then more authoritative in the public sphere. In an era when governments wanted 'the numbers' (a task well suited to the twin disciplines—sociology and psychology—of criminology), victim surveys provided Left Realists with the opportunity to shape government responses, policies and practices in relation to crime and criminality.

There are, however, significant shortcomings in victim survey data. Among these shortcomings is the problem of reporting only on those crimes reported by respondents of the survey. As a consequence, white-collar crimes, for example, were omitted from early studies. Furthermore, other crimes, such as domestic violence and sexual assault, pose problems for those using a survey format because of the sensitivity of the material. In addition, victim surveys were not used to explore the various meanings of the label 'criminal', and terms such as 'violence', 'vandalism' and 'sexual assault'. While there may be consensus regarding their seriousness, Hogg (1988) argues that there may be little agreement concerning what these terms actually mean. Further, survey methods are not helpful in understanding the *nature* of family violence or child abuse. Nor are these approaches suitable for respondents who do not speak the primary language of the nation, or those who have difficulty in reading and/or comprehending the survey information. Ongoing forms of criminal activity are unlikely to be usefully represented when relying on answers to survey questions. Finally, asking people what they want done about crime may not elicit the most useful response. Organised burglaries may result from the actions of the receiver of stolen goods, not the actual burglar. Arresting one burglar is unlikely to stop burglaries from happening, if it is the receiver of stolen goods who provides the primary influence for the offending (Hogg 1988).

Left Realism has attempted to deal with some of these criticisms, primarily through redesigning the survey instrument. In turn, successive waves of victim surveys have resulted in Left Realist theory being refined to better represent the process and practices documented in crime surveys. It is to the major developments of Left Realist theory that we now turn.

¬ early versions of left realism

Left Realism is distinct from its ideological predecessor, radical criminology, in many ways. According to Hogg (1988) and other early

Left Realists (see, for example, Sparks et al. 1977; Young 1981, 1986; Lea & Young 1984), the main points of contention between these approaches are:

- Crime is a major problem, especially personal violence and property crime, and is a problem of growing proportions of people.

  By denoting 'crime' as the major focus, Left Realists were reasserting the centrality of 'crime' as a unifying focus for criminology. Although Marxist criminology, as well as labelling theory, had gone to great lengths to highlight the contextual nature of labelling an event 'criminal', Left Realists saw crime as a unitary concept, something 'out there' and measurable. Furthermore, unlike Marxist criminology, Left Realism emphasised 'street crime' and played down white-collar and state offences. Finally, this differed from Marxist criminology, in that it saw crime as increasing. Some Marxist criminologists are less convinced of an increase, and see the rise shown by statistics as more likely a result of a 'law-and-order' panic than of any real increase in the rate of offending.

- Official crime statistics considerably underestimate the problem, because of the levels of unreported crime, which is in large part a result of public alienation and frustration with the ineffectiveness of criminal justice agencies, particularly the police.

  Here Left Realism is somewhat similar to mainstream radical theory in that it asserts that the community is alienated from the criminal justice system (in this case, the police). However, unlike radical criminology, Left Realism argues that there is even more crime, defined in traditional terms, than suggested by police statistics, and that this can be measured.

- Most personal crime (such as robbery, assault and burglary) is intra-class, and disproportionately afflicts the poor and their neighbourhoods, thus compounding the inequalities and exploitations they already suffer.

  The similarity with mainstream radical theory here is that it is the working class that primarily suffers exploitation and hardship. However, unlike some Marxists, Left Realists argue that the victimisation is primarily intra-class: that is, the working class preys on the working class. This is a marked diversion from traditional Marxist criminology, which emphasises that the ruling class preys on the working class.

  — The police are both extremely inefficient at dealing with inner-city crime and are endemically hostile and discriminatory with regard to the inner-city populace (especially youth and ethnic minorities).

Much of this resonates with a traditional radical view with respect to the endemic hostility between police and the working class. Unlike traditional Marxists, who see police as an instrument of class control and, for the maintenance of the status quo, Left Realism sees possible positive roles for police. Police might well be useful, if only they were more effective.

  — The mutual antagonism between police and local communities sets in train a vicious circle of non-cooperation, whereby the alienated community does not report crime to the police, and the police respond by heavier proactive and discriminatory police strategies, which alienate the community further.

This underscores why the police are ineffective and the futility of current policing methods in attempting effective control of crime. Marxist criminologists would argue, however, that the purpose of discriminatory policing is not crime control, but control of the working class. For Marxists, then, such discriminatory policing is fulfilling its purpose if it is effective in 'quieting the masses'.

  — Inner-city working-class communities are deeply concerned about local crime, want effective policies to control it, and see the police as central to crime control.

This is crucial to the Left Realist position. Left Realism takes the working-class communities' opinion at face value and reasserts the position that the communities themselves see police and police response as key elements of crime control in inner-city areas. Left Realists argue that these sentiments must be listened to, and acted on, if radicals are to claim any credibility in attempting to help these communities. If the communities say police are potentially useful, the task for criminology is to assist in making police more responsive to the communities' needs, not to decry the existence of the police.

  — Effective policing requires that police concentrate on those crimes that the public see as most serious, that they cease alienating the public by heavy-handed intrusive strategies, and that they be brought under local democratic control through elected police authorities.

This is the last major argument of the early formulations of Left Realism. It argues that crime can be controlled within working-class communities to some extent. This must be achieved through active cooperation between the police and the policed. This differs from the general thrust of Marxist criminology, since it places prime emphasis on the possibility of reform within the capitalist system that would benefit the working class in the long term, and also argues that reform of police is possible.

This early version of Left Realism caused much debate (see Schwartz & DeKeseredy 1991; Carlen 1992; Matthews & Young 1992; Sparks 1992; DeKeseredy et al. 1997; Matthews 2009). It became clear that the theory was too narrow, and too fixed on issues of policing. The key criticisms of this first attempt hinged around four major areas, and arose in part from weaknesses in the research instrument, the local crime victim survey.

The first criticism concerned the problem of using 'crime' as the unifying focus. While Left Realists asserted the need to 'take crime seriously', critics asked which crime should be the major focus and, more importantly, what was meant by the term 'crime'. Critics argued that the theory treated definitions of crime as if they had common meanings that were universally accepted. Such an assumption is anathema to many on the left, who assert that the term 'crime' has no common meaning. Further, popular definitions of crime are too heavily influenced by the state to be of constructive use (Brown & Hogg 1992b; Brown 2002). Terms such as 'vandalism' and 'graffiti' are used in the political sphere for political ends. The theory failed to take account of the political dimension of terms concerned with crime and criminality.

Furthermore, the use of politically tainted terms allows popular misconceptions of crime and criminality to continue. In particular it exacerbates the problem of stereotypic impressions of who 'we' are (the goodies), as opposed to 'them' (the baddies). Critics argued that Left Realism tended to treat the results of the victim surveys as if they represented a true picture of crime, and what constituted crime. Public concern must be understood as the result of a political process, and in particular a result of the active influence of the police and the media in shaping popular conceptions of crime and criminality (Greer 2010).

Critics also pointed to the narrow scope of victimisation covered by Left Realism, quite apart from the problems of the definition and meaning of the term 'crime' (Walklate 1992; Rock 2010). Concern was expressed that only certain forms of victimisation were considered as important. The most notable omissions were in the area of white-collar crime (Pearce &

Tombs 1992). Certain forms of white-collar crime also disproportionately affect the working class, most notably industrial pollution and negligence, loan sharking and false advertising; yet, these were largely ignored by early Left Realists.

Great criticism was also levelled at the narrowness concerning effective responses, notably the almost exclusive focus on policing. This partly resulted from the emphasis of the surveys themselves. Early surveys placed a great weight on what the victims felt should be done about crime. Critics argued that this allowed the assumption that in order to reduce crime one must necessarily focus on police action to remain unchallenged. Effective reduction strategies may mean something else entirely: in particular, solutions may lie with non-policing crime prevention, or from outside the criminal justice system itself. A good example of this arises within Australia. Indigenous communities recognise that the problem of violence within their communities is a result, in part, of the availability of alcohol. From the mid-1990s, some of these communities have taken action to limit the availability of alcohol, including restricting sales in multiracial towns such as Tennant Creek (Gray et al. 2002). This is seen to be far more effective than direct police action. Police action, however well intentioned, may simply exacerbate the violence, since the cause lies outside police control.

Critics also argue for greater attention to the possible consequences of greater cooperation between the public and the police. Police responding to complaints may be ineffective in solving burglary, as mentioned above, if the primary problem is one of receiving stolen goods. Left Realists argue that changes in policing style—so that it is reactive, cooperative and accountable (community or reassurance policing styles)—will increase the flow of information to police and dramatically improve clear-up rates. However, the opposite might occur if, for example, clear-up rates were substantially boosted by coercion or verballing (untrue police testimony).

If policing strategies did lead to greater numbers of arrests, Left Realism had also left open the question of what to do with offenders once they had been apprehended. Early Left Realists had not considered what was appropriate in dealing with offenders in terms of a humane penal policy. Furthermore, penal policy—in particular, the greater use of prisons—is very expensive, and Left Realism had not come to terms with methods of funding an increase in the size of the both the policing and penal systems. There were fears that this vacuum in theorising would result in the familiar conservative plea for harsher penalties. Or, as is the case in the

UK since the election of the 'ConDem' (Conservative-Liberal Democrat) government in 2009, that penal punishment is too expensive and that this expense should be shared with the community through the greater use of community-based sentencing.

¬ the second wave of left realism

Left Realism has made attempts to come to terms with the criticisms levelled at the theory as it was initially expressed. In collection of data, analysis and policy-making there has been considerable revision of the original theory.

In terms of data collection, Left Realists have undertaken a second wave of surveys. They argue that the notion of 'victim surveys' is now a misnomer, since they now attempt to deal with a far broader range of issues (Young 1988). Among the new questions considered are those concerning the use of self-reported data, public evaluation of police service deliveries, police–public encounters, public attitudes to adequate punishment and avoidance behaviour with respect to some crimes. Left Realists have also retreated from seeing the survey as the sole focus of data collection (Pawson 2006). They now argue that, while these surveys are important, it is necessary to triangulate the data gathered in this manner with other forms of empirical and discursive enquiry. Positivist methods of data collection (such as psychological testing, for example) are seen as relevant, along with traditional radical research methods (such as case studies and ethnography). More recently, theorists have also supplemented their analyses using discourse analysis (such as document and content analysis of media reports, legislation, policy and practice).

In theory at least, Left Realism has widened the focus beyond exclusive concentration on the offender towards a broader emphasis, which they conceptualise as the *square of crime* (Young 1991). The square of crime, as we have seen, involves two dyads. The first concerns social control, and comprises police and other agencies of social control on the one hand, and the public on the other. The second concerns the criminal act, and comprises the offender and the victim. The current aim of Left Realism is to address all parts of the square, in that all aspects need to be addressed in theory, research and policy (DeKeseredy et al. 1997; Ericson 2007; Matthews 2009, 2010). Further to this, each aspect should not be taken as a separate entity, as the interaction between each element is crucial to understanding crime and crime control. Crime rates are, according to Left Realists, a product of the interrelationship between the four aspects of the square of crime.

This proposal by Left Realists of the centrality of the 'square of crime' directs attention to the criminal act and its context, by its emphasis on four separate but interrelated dimensions: the police, the public, the victim and the offender. They argue there needs to be analysis of the state and the problems of defining crime within a political system, as the left argues, but there also needs to be a realistic account taken of the 'reality' of crime and the offender–victim dyad (Brown & Hogg 1992b). This means researching appropriate responses that can address the needs of victims, as well as supporting programs and policies that both reduce offending before it occurs (crime prevention) and respond effectively when offences do occur (Pawson 2006).

Left Realism has also broadened its focus in terms of the crimes that are considered of major concern. Recent volumes contain analyses of white-collar offending, and issues of gender are more explicitly brought into the Left Realist fold (Smart 1990b; Carlen 1992; Lowman & MacLean 1992; Pearce & Tombs 1992; Schwartz & DeKeseredy 1991; Garland 2001). Importantly, Left Realism has also acknowledged the need to discuss penal reform.

However, much of this writing has not come from the Left Realists themselves, but from authors with particular research interests that are used to 'fill the gaps' of earlier versions of the theory. In addition, when theorising in relation to punishment is undertaken by those readily identified with Left Realism (such as Matthews 1989; Pratt et al. 2005), the suggestions that are mooted do not differ significantly from liberal suggestions in the same area; an exception to this is the more recent work relating to citizenship and penal punishment (Brown 2002, 2008, and with Wilkie 2002).

Left Realism has then shifted ground from identifying with radical or Marxist criminology to a position that is more easily described as social democratic or liberal (Walters 2009). That is, it is more concerned with a reform agenda that deals with the issues of crime and crime control within the current social system than with suggesting that the system itself is the root of the problem and should be changed. In doing so, it borrows heavily from theories and research that are characteristic of the middle ground, such as strain theory, labelling and certain strands of radical criminology. By shifting ground in this way, Left Realism loses some of its identity, and at times becomes indistinguishable from the theories it replaces, or purports to supersede.

~~contemporary~~ examples

It is important to point out that Left Realism *per se* does not exist as an independent entity outside of the UK. In the US, Australia and Canada, Left Realists are more likely to be part of Critical criminology (see Chapter 11). In Australia, it is interesting to note that a Left Realist perspective was initially taken up in New South Wales at a time when that state was experiencing a strong political emphasis on law and order by the (then) Liberal (conservative) government in the late 1980s. The government of that period promoted a law-and-order policy that purported to take crime seriously by increasing police powers and increasing the use of prison as a sentencing option, as well as increasing the time spent in detention (Dixon 1990, 2008; Brown 2008; Hogg 2008).

A group (known at the time as the Campaign for Criminal Justice (CCJ)) challenged the 'law-and-order' rhetoric of the Liberal government, and proposed a new direction for crime policy. The group comprised not only academics but also youth workers, left lawyers and those working in the criminal justice system. Like Left Realists in the UK, the CCJ argued that crime was rising, and that those who were the victims were the most vulnerable—in this case, old people, women, children and the Indigenous population. Furthermore, the group also advocated the use of the local crime victim survey and, in the early 1990s, undertook a survey of inner-city Sydney. This survey was concerned with the fear of crime and its connection to the local social and economic organisation of particular communities.

It is important to note that the expression of Left Realism within Australia is much broader than the predominant focus on policing that characterised Left Realism, in early UK versions of this approach. In addition to the work of Hogg and Brown, many feminist criminologists (see, for example, Carrington 1993) have adopted a left realist approach to crimes against women and children. From the perspective of these theorists, it is deeply problematic that just as women were beginning to name and document the violence against them, other theorists derided the validity and uses of this type of research, especially as it related to 'fear of crime'. Under the framework of Left Realism, contemporary analyses of violence against women—and victims more generally—have developed critical policy responses that aim to ameliorate the harms caused by these types of violence, including, importantly, risk assessment tools and pro-arrest/pro-prosecution strategies for intimate partner violence (Lievore 2004, 2005; Winter 2006).

An additional area of contemporary Left Realist research is that relating to rural crime. While early versions of Left Realism were focused on documenting the experiences of crime in inner-city communities, more recent research has investigated the experiences of victims and offenders in rural and regional Australia (see, for example, Hogg & Carrington 2006; Scott et al. 2007). In line with the foundational objectives of Left Realism, this later work attempts to define and measure rural crime, and offer policy options to remedy the unique conditions of rural crime.

Importantly, 'Left Realism' outside of the UK is not constructed as a radical break from critical or radical criminology generally. However, like Left Realists in the UK, the CCJ sought to influence the political process directly. In particular, it worked with the Labor opposition in the formulation of policy that could neutralise the conservative 'law-and-order' rhetoric. In terms of policies, the CCJ proposed such measures as:

- all new government policy be accompanied by a crime impact statement
- crime-related social impact be a factor built into urban planning
- local safety strategies be developed
- staffing on public transport be maintained
- development of strategies be built around community participation, using local action groups such as tenants groups, refuges and residents groups.

These measures sought to place 'crime' on the political and academic agenda in a way that recognised the social and political motives of crime and crime policy. They sought to engage government in dialogue about reforms to reduce the victimisation of vulnerable groups.

The fate of this policy was considerably undermined, if not abandoned, after the 1995 New South Wales elections. Instead of promoting a broadly Left Realist agenda, the Labor Party was in the forefront of a renewed conservative law-and-order debate, promoting tough new crime policies aimed at increasing imprisonment, especially for 'serious' offences. As with other Western democracies, the trend to law-and-order policies became even more firmly entrenched in Australia as the 1990s progressed (Brown 2002). Rather than bring criminal justice agencies under greater community control (as has been the case in the UK), the trend has been in the opposite direction. This was exemplified by the privatisation of a large proportion of the nation's prisons, replete with secrecy provisions precluding adequate public scrutiny of the financial details of contracts between prison owners and the government. Like their US counterparts, under pressure from the media and the voting public, the New South Wales government (along with most other Australian state governments) has used the 'war on crime' and 'war on terrorism' as a means to expand the net of criminal justice agencies (Hogg 2008).

Interestingly, there is some question as to which political debate needs to be captured by Left Realists. In recent years there has been a re-evaluation of the split between Left Idealism and Left Realism, in which some argue that the debate was from the beginning fraught with inaccuracies and misleading characterisations (Cottee 2002; for a response, see Cohen & Young 2004). Similar concerns about accuracy and representation also have been seen in discussions of law-and-order politics and policy in Australia. The political debate in this instance is within criminology itself, and those on the receiving end are the Left Realists. For example, Weatherburn (2002) has argued that researchers such as Brown and Hogg, who are closely identified with Left Realist concerns in Australia, have not taken crime seriously enough, and that they do not appreciate fully the seriousness of the crime problem. The latter writers, who have been accused of lack of methodological rigour and political disinterest, have responded with a spirited defence of their empirical work (Brown 2002). They also have distanced themselves from a purely 'evidence-driven' policy formation approach, and reaffirmed their commitment to examination of the normative and political nature of law-and-order politics (Indermaur et al. 2002; Brown & Wilkie 2002; Hogg 2001, 2008; Pratt et al. 2005; Scott et al. 2007; Brown 2010). How debate is carried out is perhaps one of the more salient lessons from our review of Left Realism as a criminological development. The review also highlights the continuing commitment of those willing to translate their concerns about crime into practical forums without necessarily compromising political critique.

{from theory to practice: policing racist violence}

Iganski, P. (2008). 'Hate Crime' and the City, The Policy Press, Bristol, UK.

As with many Left Realists attempting to connect the experiences of victimisation with policing policy and practice, Iganski provides a study that brackets the definition of 'hate crime' in order to take seriously the experiences encountered by hate crime victims. There is a long Left Realist tradition of using the British Crime Survey (BCS) as a basis for developing critical insights and policy options for policing organisations. However, in the case of Iganski, the results of this substantial victim survey are not taken for granted. Rather, he subjects this empirical evidence to a critical quantitative analysis, which is part of Iganski's wider theoretical critique of 'hate' and policing practices.

As documented by Iganski, 'hate crimes' have become embedded in crime policies, often without a clear and practical definition, and commonly in response to a critical incident (in the case of the UK, this was the murder of Stephen Lawrence and, in the US, the murders of James Byrd and Matthew Shepard). As with others in this field of study, Iganski is concerned with how emotionally laden terms such as 'hate' come to inform the dominant discourses about prejudice-related violence. While he acknowledges that we need to be cognisant of the problems associated with this form of criminalisation, for the sake of comparability and consistency, he retains the term—with caveats. His analysis of the BSC data (and his evaluation of the Race Hate Crime Forums) points to three significant areas requiring further investigation.

In relation to victims' perception of hate, Iganski critically reflects on the victim-centred approach adopted in UK law and policing, especially the consequences of labelling some actions as 'hate'. In the UK, anyone can claim that an incident is a hate crime. In this formulation, as Iganski documents, the perception of 'hate' stems not from the motivations or intent of the offender, but rather from the perception of the victim/witness/police officer. However, when asked in the BSC what would lead an individual to believe that this was related to 'hate', respondents most commonly reported cultural (or racial) differences between the offender and victim. In this way, if the victim was Black, and the offender was White, then it was a 'hate crime'.

Second, in Iganski's analyses of the BSC data on hate crime, he documents how the dominant discourse on hate crime offenders (neo-Nazis or Fascists) belies the fact that most incidents recorded in the survey are far more familiar and closer to home. Unlike the cliché of an offender that is totally and wholly motivated by hate of the other, this study finds that 'hate' is something that aggravates everyday interactions with people in the neighbourhood, and in the transit zones between home, work and leisure. Crime, in this sense, is a predicate for hate; this is unlike the cliché of the organised hatred of the British National Party, where hate is a predicate for crime.

Third, in explicitly adopting a harms-based approach, Iganski offers an alternative reading of 'hate crime', one that respects the harms experienced by individuals (and communities)—where he takes their experiences of 'crime seriously'—while retaining a critical eye to the ways in which we attempt to remedy the harms caused. In studying the operation of the Metropolitan Police Authority's Race Hate Crime Forums, Iganski makes the responses to this form of crime much more social (rather than individual), and highlights the problems that arise when victims' rights to live free from discrimination and violence trump offenders' right to free expression.

critique

An adequate critique of Left Realism has to encompass both early and later versions in order to get a clear picture of the strengths and weaknesses of the theory as a whole. It will be remembered that the criticisms of early versions of Left Realism were as follows:

_   The theory treated *definitions of crime* as if they had factual, uncontested meanings.

_   The *scope of victimisation covered by Left Realism was very narrow.* It omitted certain offences, most notably white-collar offences, and then presented the results as if this gave a total picture of crime.

_   The *focus of response was very narrow.* The theory was almost exclusively concerned with issues of police and policing style.

_   There was a *lack of any realistic penal policy.* The theory had not considered to any degree how to deal with offenders once they were apprehended.

_   Finally, there were concerns, mainly expressed by radical criminologists, that *Left Realists accepted the notion that the criminal law could be liberating.* Critics argued that the problem in working-class areas was not crime, but community breakdown. This being the case, the criminal law could only exacerbate problems, not ameliorate them.

As stated, Left Realists made a concerted effort to address these problems. In particular, they broadened the scope of their analysis to include white-collar offences in their victim surveys. They also began to look at the issues surrounding an adequate penal policy. Rather than being a narrow, single-issue theory, Left Realism now attempts to look at what it calls the 'square of crime' concerned with both social control and the criminal act, as outlined above. But their success—theoretically and practically—is questionable.

In broadening its focus, Left Realism could be said to have lost its defining parameters, and with them any claims for being a separate theoretical entity. Many elements of Left Realism appear in similar form elsewhere: for example, elements of strain theory deal with the formation of antisocial cultures; and liberal forms of criminology also seek to redress the inequities of the system. Left Realism is an eclectic mix of criminological theory of a generally liberal nature, which sees society as based on conflicting, but ultimately not irreconcilable, differences.

There is nothing wrong with an eclectic theory or one based on 'multi-factorial explanations'. However, when a theoretical perspective draws together theoretical insights from diverse traditions, the question of compatibility of ideas arises. For example, Left Realism identifies itself with a Marxist tradition. However, this tradition sees attempts to democratise sections of the state apparatus (such as the police) as being linked to wider political strategies that go directly to the heart of who controls production and government in a capitalist society. Indeed, attempts to democratise the police through local councils in the UK initially kindled the ire of the conservative national government; it responded by substantially reducing the power of local government in that country, effectively neutralising police reforms. However, since the election of the Conservative Liberal Democrat government in 2009, conservatives have rekindled their faith in the 'local'; going so far as to offer local communities control over not only their police, but also their schools and health services.

The point is that eclecticism is acceptable if the theory links diverse traditions in a way that is ultimately productive and without irretrievable conflict. Some would argue that Left Realism has failed to do this. It retains a notion of consensus concerning crime that many would argue is not sustainable. Furthermore, the aims of the theory itself may be incompatible. For example, to enlist the cooperation of police in 'fighting crime' while at the same time attempting an adequate critique of the role of the state in perpetuating crime would be seen by many as a contradiction in terms.

It is notable, therefore, that one of the leading proponents of Left Realism has in more recent years turned his attention to structural issues rather than those relating to policy implementation as such. Jock Young (1999, 2007) appears to have abandoned the quest for pragmatic criminal justice responses in favour of a more sustained analysis and critique, in which the dynamics of social exclusion, antagonism and conflict once again become central. In doing so, Young is also challenging previous approaches that fail to take into account the existential and experiential dimensions of crime. In other words, cultural criminology is accorded an important place in the new understandings of social division, and the world of crime is interpreted in the light of emotional and structural factors (Young 2003). If this is Left Realism, it is now Left Realism with 'attitude'.

Left Realism correctly identifies the central place of crime in society. People are concerned about crime. Perhaps what has been ignored by this perspective, though, is the multifaceted nature of that concern. Drawing from Durkheim, it would be possible to argue that this concern reflected, at least in part, anxiety about the state of our society as well as anxiety about the actual chances of victimisation (Ericson 2007). Further, it is this concern that is most amenable to manipulation for political ends. Fears and insecurities about jobs, education and so on can be allayed (at least in part) by governments espousing strong law-and-order rhetoric in order to secure their political popularity. This tactic is well illustrated in Australia, as well as in the USA and the UK, in recent years.

Importantly, many theorists on the left are often required to adopt Left Realism in their work, especially research undertaken with, or for, government organisations (Walters 2003, 2009). In a world where governments (and their individual agencies of law and order) fund or partly fund the research undertaken by academics, compromises on theoretical frameworks and policy provisions are often inescapable. As such, contemporary left criminology can be usefully divided between the publicly funded research of Left Realism, and the independently funded research that is more appropriately designated as critical criminology.

Nonetheless, Left Realism has contributed positively to the criminological debate. It has reasserted the need to take account of those most affected by crime—the marginalised and the working class—and has been essential in the uncovering of hidden crimes, especially those affecting women and children. It has sought to take the views of these people seriously and to translate their views into a workable policy agenda. This has been particularly important at a time when 'law-and-order' policies dominate the political debate.

{conclusion}

Left realism can be seen as a left-wing response to the law-and-order debate, which has been dominated by the right in politics. As such, it sees itself in contrast to that criminology that sees the discipline as a value-free and neutral exercise. Left Realism identifies itself as part of a socialist strategy to democratise the state apparatus and other areas of social and economic life. Responding to crime is a political process, not a neutral research exercise. However, Left Realists argue that doing something practical in the current environment means much more than simply raising class consciousness or working for 'the revolution' sometime in the future.

Left Realism has stimulated much debate, with most of it from other radical traditions. The response to the criticisms has been for Left Realism to broaden its focus, use a wide range of empirical research and borrow from other theoretical perspectives in order to 'fill the gaps' of its initially narrow focus. There have been some successes in this attempt, and it has spawned useful debate, in the Australian context, with the work of the Campaign for Criminal Justice.

In the next chapter we focus on another recent theory that is generally eclectic in nature. In this case, however, the theory starts from a very different philosophical base, that of republicanism.

{further reading}

Brown, D. (2002). 'The Politics of Law and Order', *Law Society Journal*, 40 (9): 64–72.

Brown, D. (2010). 'The Limited Benefit of Imprisonment in Controlling Crime', *Current Issues in Criminal Justice*, 22 (1): 461–72.

Hogg, R. (1988). 'Taking Crime Seriously: Left Realism and Australian Criminology', in M. Findlay & R. Hogg (eds), *Understanding Crime and Criminal Justice*, Law Book Company, Sydney.

Hogg, R.G. (2008). 'Resisting a "Law and Order" Society', in T. Anthony & C. Cunneen (eds), *The Critical Criminology Companion*, Hawkins Press, Sydney: 278–89.

Lea, J. & Young, J. (1984). *What Is to Be Done about Law and Order?*, Penguin, London.

Lowman, J. & MacLean, B. (eds) (1992). *Realist Criminology: Crime Control and Policing in the 1990s*, University of Toronto Press, Toronto.

McLaughlin, E., Muncie, J. & Hughes, G. (eds) (2003). *Criminological Perspectives: A Reader* (2nd edition), SAGE, London.

Young, J. (1986). 'The Failure
of Criminology: The Need for a
Radical Realism', in R. Matthews
& J. Young (eds), *Confronting
Crime*, SAGE, London: 9–30.

Young, J. (1991). 'Left Realism
and the Priorities of Crime
Control', in K. Stenson &
D. Cowell (eds), *The Politics of
Crime Control*, SAGE, London.

Young, J. (1999). *The Exclusive
Society: Social Exclusion,
Crime and Difference in Late
Modernity*, SAGE, London.

Young, J. (2007). *The Vertigo of
Late Modernity*, SAGE, London.

republican theory and restorative justice

{introduction}

—

This chapter discusses the republican theory of criminal justice. As a relatively new theoretical perspective, republican theory draws upon a wide range of concepts and trends that we have previously examined. The hallmark of the republican approach is its stress on the need for a restorative form of justice, rather than a punitive one.

The strength of republican theory is that it provides a comprehensive view of crime and society. In moving towards a general theory of crime, republicanism offers a *normative* framework, based on the premise of how to make a good society by outlining the values that should underpin the ideal operation of the criminal justice system. With respect to this, the theory seeks to reform or reshape our major institutions in accordance with the ideals of republican liberalism. The theory thus stands as a systematic critique of authoritarian populism (which it views as wrong and dangerous), in that it claims we can use reason and justice to inform institutional practices rather than refer to base emotions such as hatred and fear.

The theory also offers an analysis and outline of how the criminal justice system could be reorganised *in practice* to reflect restorative justice. It is here that the theory has gained much prominence, insofar as the notion of 'reintegrative shaming' has received much international attention. The theory argues that we need to emphasise positive ways in which to deal with offenders, and victims, and that a punitive response to crime will lead only to negative social consequences.

social context

Some criminological theories commence with a broad conception of the society we live in and what the society as a whole should be striving to achieve. Such theories usually begin with a theory of society, and a vision of 'the good'. Within the radical framework (Marxist and feminist theory), for example, society is characterised by profound inequalities, such as poverty, racism, sexism and other exploitative situations created by imbalances of power. The solution sought is for a revolutionary change in the core structures and nature of society generally, requiring collective mobilisation for change. There is an attempt to raise the consciousness of those most affected by the discriminatory actions of the capitalist state, to expose the evils and injustices built into the system, and to expand democratic participation and economic redistribution.

Conservative theories (New Right and other populist versions of this) also start with a conception of society as a whole. Here society is characterised as comprising self-interested individuals, some of whom are particularly evil or bad. This perspective asserts that crime results as a consequence of the disorder in society. It therefore seeks to re-establish discipline, order and authority. The aim is to restore society to the way things used to be; in this sense, it often appeals to a mythical 'golden age' of aberrant crime. These theorists argue that the society requires a strong state that will assert its authority in a moral way, in order to maintain the free economy. In this system, law and order must take precedence over justice. The focus is on 'street crime' and crimes committed by the less powerful; for example, social security fraud. Crime is seen to result from a breakdown in the societal moral fibre, hence the stress on morality, liberty and authority.

As we saw, Left Realism emerged as a response to the conservative backlash of the 1980s. This perspective has tended, however, to move away from a theory of society *per se* (that is, based upon socialist principles) to focus specifically on crime, which is viewed as a problem that needs to be taken seriously. There has been a consequent shift away from the big picture (that is, structural causes) to focus on specific issues, such as the victims of crime and the effects of crime on the less powerful, such as the working class, the poor, ethnic minorities and women. It is argued that, because the community is concerned about crime, the focus should be on fighting crime at the local level, and the main concern is with developing an effective form of policing that is responsible, responsive and democratic.

The conservative push to get tough on offenders through concerted law-and-order campaigns spurred the particular response adopted by the Left Realists. Republican theory likewise is a response to the conservative push of the last three decades (see Braithwaite & Pettit 1990; Marshal 1998). Many conservatives were critical of the crime prevention strategies of treatment and rehabilitation being pursued by the positivists in dealing with offenders. The *retributivists* claimed treatment, rehabilitation and preventive measures had not worked, and had, in some instances, been grossly unjust, and pointed to cases where indeterminate sentences had been wrongly applied. They highlighted the injustice and futility of strategies adopted by the *preventivists*, who sought to rehabilitate and deter offenders through incapacitation (von Hirsch 1976). The retributivists called for punishment of the offender in accordance with their 'just deserts'; that is, offenders should get what they deserve in proportion to the gravity of the offence and the culpability of the offender.

The alternative theory proposed by Pettit and Braithwaite is the *republican theory* (Braithwaite & Pettit 1990; Pettit & Braithwaite 1993). This theory seeks to link up with older republican traditions of thinking that sought to promote the notion of liberty. These theories extend from Roman times, through the philosophies of republicanism developed in the northern Italian republics, to those apparent in the course of the English Civil War and in the American Revolution in the eighteenth century. In this historical thinking about liberty, freedom was perceived as the social status enjoyed by someone other than a slave; someone so protected by the law and culture of their community that he or she did not have to depend upon the grace of another for the enjoyment of independent choice. Liberty was conceptualised as the negative good of not being interfered with by others.

This republican notion of negative liberty was displaced in the nineteenth century by a new, different sense of liberalism. Here the main objective was to avoid interference by the state and the law altogether, and thus, as well, to exclude the enjoyment of being protected against possible interference. This right-wing libertarian perspective promoted the notion of the free market, and sought to remove government constraints, especially on trade and the labour market. The enjoyment of non-interference in our lives was thus at the mercy of those who chose to interfere. Based upon a competitive 'law of the jungle' notion, this perspective is premised on the belief that we are all free and should be able to do what we want without any interference whatsoever.

The republican conception of liberty differs from this nineteenth-century conception. It involves the concept of personal liberty constituted by *protection of liberty by the law*. Non-interference should not be enjoyed only as a matter of contingent luck; instead, it should be extended to all by the law and its related institutions. The non-interference involved is to be of a resilient or secure nature; that is, the person who enjoys non-interference is thereby protected from the predations of the potential interferer. Should someone choose to interfere, then the law or other protective institutions would move to block that interference and provide whatever compensation is necessary in order to restore the person to their former status.

The law and its related institutions are seen to play a central role in maintaining republican liberty. There has to be equal knowledge that we collectively enjoy that status of being guarded from interference.

basic concepts

In the republican view, crime is seen as the denial of personal dominion—evil is always represented by this denial (see chart 10.1). Three characteristics of the denial of dominion are identified (Braithwaite & Pettit 1990; Braithwaite 2000):

1\ Denial of dominion is a negative challenge to the *dominion status* of the victim, which is a threat to, or disregard for, the dominion of an individual, and constitutes an attack on the status of that individual (as someone who holds a protected dominion status in society). If someone commits a crime against an individual, then the criminal act asserts the vulnerability of the victim to the will of the criminal, nullifying the protected status of the victim.

2\ If the negative challenge is successful, the criminal act not only disregards the victim's dominion, but also undermines, *diminishes* and perhaps even *destroys the victim's dominion*. For example, kidnapping or murdering someone will *destroy* that person's dominion, while stealing a person's property will *diminish* his or her dominion by undermining certain exercises of dominion that person might otherwise have pursued (for example, it diminishes the liberty to use that property).

chart 10.1 | republican theory

definition of crime	_ denial of dominion, largely reflected in legal code
focus of analysis	_ victim, community and offender dominion, particularly in areas where shaming may be appropriate (drink driving, white-collar crime, juvenile justice)
cause of crime	_ lack of self-sanctioning conscience and appropriate social connections (lack of interdependency) _ broader society characterised by mobility and a focus on individualism (lack of communitarianism)
nature of offender	_ partly voluntary, partly determined, responsibility and opportunity
response to crime	_ reintegrative shaming, least restrictive measures
crime prevention	_ promotion of valued norms, fostering of communitarianism
operation of criminal justice system	_ expansion of reintegrative shaming into social life of community through family group conferences, victim–offender meetings

3\ Finally, every criminal act represents a *communal evil*; it does an evil to the community as a whole. A crime not only affects the dominion status of the individual victim, but also endangers the community's notion of resilient status. Every act of crime represents a challenge to the dominion of people in society generally, who will begin to doubt that they really do have the capacity to positively respond to crime.

If every act of crime represents damage to dominion, then it is the responsibility of the state (through its criminal justice system), to promote dominion, by rectifying or remedying the damage caused by the crime — for example, how the state uses the legal system to respond to a convicted criminal.

Retributivists have tended to focus on sentencing, as they believe that treatment and rehabilitation are not working. However, Braithwaite and Pettit (1990) challenge the retributivist perspective on a variety of levels. They argue that:

_ the criminal justice system should be organised so as to promote the goal of republican liberty, which is construed as personal dominion (control over one's life); and

— a theory of criminal justice needs to cover a broad range of issues
(including what should be criminalised; what guidelines should cover
police surveillance; what initiatives should be possible in the pursuit
of offenders; and what procedures should be followed in prosecution
and adjudication, and the sentences imposed for given offences).

Braithwaite and Pettit (1990) argued that the retributivist theory does
not address these levels of analysis adequately and, instead, focuses solely
on sub-questions. They argue that, if a theory deals only with questions
of sentencing, as the retributivist theory does, then any initiatives taken
in respect to this area of the justice system are likely to flow on and affect
other parts of the system. Hence, they argue that we cannot simply tinker
with only one part of the system: we need to look at the system as a whole.

Republican theorists are also critical of other goal-orientated approaches,
such as *utilitarianism* (an approach that suggests we should promote the
greatest good for the greatest number), because injustices can lead to good
for the greatest number. Further, they are critical of the prioritisation
within the criminal justice system of crime prevention, as this can lead
to increased intrusiveness (such as holding parents totally responsible for
their children's actions).

In contrast, republican approaches to the sentencing of a convicted
offender consider three philosophical elements. First, the offender must
recognise the personal liberty of the victim in order to restore the victim's
status. To achieve this, the offender must withdraw the implicit claim
that the victim did not enjoy the dominion that was challenged by the
crime. Second, in order to restore the victim's former dominion—which
may not only have been disregarded, but also may have been diminished
or destroyed—there must be some form of *recompense* for the damage
done to the individual's personal dominion. And third, there must be a
general *reassurance* given by the convicted offender to the community that
restores the community's resilient status.

The republican theory thus assumes an equilibrium model of criminal
justice, because it seeks to *restore the dominion status of the victim* by
reintegrating the victim back into society so that he or she can once again
exercise personal dominion. Abstractly, the recognition of dominion of
the victim by the offender requires a mix of measures, both symbolic and
substantive.

From a republican point of view, the causes of crime lie in a combination
of social and psychological factors. Part of the problem is the lack of a

self-sanctioning conscience. This is where an individual has not learned to interpret and accept societal norms as being right and just. One of the results of a punitive and stigmatising system is that it propels people into associating with other similarly ostracised individuals (for instance, in a criminal subculture) who individually and collectively do not develop this conscience.

The lack of adequate and appropriate social connections is expressed in the concept of *communitarianism*. This describes interdependency at a societal level involving relationships of loyalty, trust and concern. Interdependency is itself reflected in a person's relationship to school, work, marriage and stable residence. The issue of social opportunity is important insofar as it affects the interdependencies, and eventually the moral development, of an individual.

The response to crime in a specific sense is to utilise the least restrictive measures possible, and to undo the wrong that has been committed. The republican theory of criminal justice is intended to deal with the victim so he or she can once again exercise public dominion, and the community can be reassured. The focus is on *maximising personal dominion* for the victim. However, there is also the assumption that the offender should be reintegrated, so that his or her dominion also can be reinstated. The theory seeks a minimalist response on the part of the state to the offender. A reintegrative equilibrium needs to be established where the victim, the community and the offender are considered.

The republican response to crime therefore bases itself on the concept of *reintegrative shaming* (Braithwaite 1995a). This involves a process in which the offender is shamed for the action, but is not 'cast out' as a person. It describes a process whereby the offender is publicly rebuked for the harm caused, but is then forgiven and reintegrated into the mainstream of society. As part of the reintegrative shaming process, the victim is directly involved in proceedings and is able to be compensated in some way for the harm done (de Greiff 2006).

From a crime prevention perspective, steps should be taken to *promote valued norms* (which, in turn, become the basis for the formation of a self-sanctioning conscience) and to *foster greater communitarianism* by enhancing educational, work and social opportunities (Pavlich 2007). The criminal justice system ought to incorporate a broad range of informal and more formal institutional arrangements (such as conferences of the offender and victims), and be orientated towards the least intrusive kind of punishment possible (Schiff 2003).

~~historical~~ development

The historical development of republican theory is undoubtedly tied to the liberal tradition, outlined earlier in the chapter. It can be traced to the eighteenth century concern with crime and criminality as championed by Montesquieu, which aimed at 'lessening the burden of fear in the minds of ordinary citizens' (Shklar 1987, cited in Braithwaite & Pettit 1990: 61). Its philosophical roots clearly can be seen within the classical tradition, and its practical application can be traced to a range of processes adopted by Indigenous cultures (including Maori justice and Native American sentencing circles) (Marshall 1998).

Furthermore, however, republican theory can be seen as a liberal response to the changing shape of capitalism and the ensuing uncertainty and opportunities this engenders. Positivism was developed out of the challenges posed by the industrial revolution, including its emphasis on positive reform. So too, republican theory can be seen to have a similar emphasis on attempting to construct changes based on contemporary research especially as it relates to the challenges posed by the fragmentation and fluidity of contemporary capitalism.

The advent of significant social and economic transformation in the late twentieth and early twenty-first centuries, and the existence of evidence-led approaches to crime and criminality, mean that current theories can, in part, be measured by their ability to provide solutions to immediate contemporary concerns. These include issues such as white-collar crime (Simpson 2000) and the plight of victims of violent crime, particularly of family and sexual violence (Daly 2006). In fact, republican theory has had a longstanding concern with white-collar crime. In contrast to Marxist criminology, however, with which it shares many similar concerns, republican theory is essentially optimistic about changing business practice within the current capitalist structure. Fundamentally, the principles applied to the control of 'street crime', republican theorists argue, have equal applicability in the white-collar sphere (Braithwaite 1995b).

The concern with victims evident within republican theory can be seen as part of a much broader shift within criminology in recent years (see Braithwaite & Pettit 1994; Mawby & Walklate 1994; Walklate 2008). Victimology, the study of victims of crime, is a recently established sub-discipline within criminology. It has gained considerable popularity at a theoretical level, and also in government policy (Braithwaite 1995a).

An example of its acceptance by governments is the introduction of victim impact statements (written statements by victims handed to the judge at sentencing) in a number of jurisdictions (White & Perrone 2010; Rock 2010). Republican theory shares common ground with a number of perspectives that aim to integrate the needs of both victims and offenders within the same system (Walklate 2008).

¬ restorative justice

The overarching name usually associated with these perspectives is that of *restorative justice*. The aim of such perspectives is to develop policies whereby the offender makes reparations for wrongdoing and, in doing so, restores the victim's and the general population's faith in society. Conceptually, restorative justice sees crime as fundamentally a violation of people and interpersonal relationships, and the point of action is to seek to heal and put right the wrongs (Zehr 1990). In line with 'third way' politics, the justice process, in this framework, is seen to belong to the community, rather than exclusively to the state (Walklate 2003). The emphasis is on reparation of harm to victims, addressing the offender's needs and competencies, and sending offenders a message of disapproval about the impact of the crime (Bazemore 1997).

Translated into specific assumptions and principles, the restorative justice lens can be usefully summarised as being based upon three interrelated propositions (Zehr & Mika 1998; van Ness 2003):

1\ *Crime is fundamentally a violation of people and interpersonal relationships.* The key issue is that victims and the community have been harmed and are in need of restoration. Importantly, victims, offenders and the affected communities are seen as the key stakeholders in justice and, as such, ought to be directly involved in the justice process.

2\ *Violations create obligations and liabilities.* It is felt that the offenders' obligations are to make things right as much as possible for the harm they have caused. However, it is also argued that the community's obligations are to victims and offenders, and for the general welfare of its members. Obligations are thus both individual and collective in nature.

3\ *Restorative justice seeks to heal and put right the wrong.* The starting point for justice is the need of victims for information, validation, vindication, restitution, testimony, safety and support. The process of justice ought to maximise the opportunities for exchange of information, participation, dialogue and mutual consent between victim and offender, and the justice process ought to belong to the community. The offenders' needs and competencies also are to be addressed. In the end, justice needs to be mindful of the outcomes, intended and unintended, of its responses to crime and victimisation.

There are various specific models of restorative justice, ranging from, for example, circle sentencing, family group conferencing and reparative probation through to victim–offender mediation (see Bazemore 1997, 1998; Wright 1991; Schiff 2003). Each model has different key objectives — from citizen involvement to meeting victims' needs — and these objectives shape the manner in which restorative justice is institutionalised in practice. Generally speaking, however, each program or model tends to focus on the 'victim', the 'offender' and the 'community', and each attempts to respond to the immediate harm, and to the specific situation and individuals that are linked by a particular criminal harm. Some approaches are based upon moral categories (such as reintegrative shaming), where the aim is to shame the offence, while offering forgiveness to the offender (Braithwaite 1989, 1995a). Others are based upon strategic assessment of offenders and events (for example, balanced restorative approach), in which case the aim is to design interventions that best address issues of offender accountability, competency development and community safety (Bazemore 1991; Bilchik 1998). Some approaches focus almost exclusively on meeting victim needs (usually via some method of restitution or compensation involving the offender); others place emphasis on widespread community engagement in dealing with underlying problems and issues, of which specific offending is but one manifestation.

Under the restorative justice umbrella, there are differences between those who see restorative justice as, essentially, a form of diversion from the formal criminal justice system (Walgrave 2007), and those who view it as a potential *alternative* to that system, and thus as something that could supplant the existing system *in toto* (see Bazemore & Walgrave 1999; Harris 2008). Whatever the specific differences, it appears that the central thread underlying restorative justice is the spirit within which 'justice' is undertaken — the intent and outcomes of the process are meant to be primarily orientated towards repairing harm that has been caused by a crime, and this means working to heal victims, offenders and communities that have been directly injured by the crime (Bazemore & Walgrave 1999; Zehr & Mika 1998; Clarkson 2008; Cunneen 2008).

¬ republican liberty

A crucial aspect of republican theory, as a particular model of restorative justice, is that it attempts to provide a normative theory of crime and society. It comes from a particular value stance in relation to criminal justice that seeks to maximise personal dominion, which is construed as republican liberty (Pettit & Braithwaite 2000).

The main elements of the theory were developed in the light of differences between republican and retributivist perspectives on sentencing (Braithwaite & Pettit 1990; Roche 2007). Retributivists argue that, in sentencing an offender, the motivation of the criminal justice system is to ensure that no crime goes unpunished. The republican theorists agree that convicted offenders need to be sentenced. However, instead of 'just deserts', sentencing is necessary because the criminal justice system should be promoting dominion of the victim, the offender and the community. This view leads to different conclusions regarding the operation of the criminal justice system (see also Zehr 1990 and Roche 2007 on the difference between retributive and restorative justice).

While retributionists seek some sort of repayment for the offence and argue for penalties proportional to the crime, republican theorists argue for a *rectification of the offence*: that is, to put the harm right. Hence, while the retributivist concentrates on the offender, the republican examines the harm done both to the victim(s) and the community. In terms of the kind and degree of penalty to be imposed, the two perspectives also differ. The retributivists look for harsh treatment as the appropriate form of response, on the grounds of proportionality and a guarantee of deterrence. Thus, retributivists tend to impose upper and lower limits on sentences that are available to the courts, and generally ignore circumstantial and mitigating factors.

Like the retributivists, republican theorists seek to impose upper limits; however, they disagree with the imposition of lower limits, arguing that there should be a whole range of measures available at the lower levels. Furthermore, they argue against long sentences and capital punishment.

In response to 'just deserts' retributivist perspectives, the republican theory supports four main assumptions of systems operation (see Braithwaite & Pettit 1990):

1\ *Parsimony*—This assumes that the onus of proof must always rest on the side of justifying criminal justice intrusions, not on the side of justifying their removal.

2\ *Checking of power* — Controls should be established and constraints placed upon those who have the power in the system to intervene in individual and collective lives. In this way the required accountability can be achieved.

3\ *Reprobation* — The criminal justice system should be designed to expose offenders to community disapproval in a constructive way.

4\ *Reintegration* — The system should seek to restore the full dominion of those who have been deprived of it by either crime or punishment.

Republican theorists argue that the practical theory can be introduced 'bit by bit', in a strategy of incremental implementation, including measures such as a codification of rights; a system supporting the right to a fair trial; a system that guarantees the right to protection of the person (that is, against capital punishment and corporal punishment); and a presumption in favour of punishments against the property rather than the person (that is, fines, restitution and community service rather than imprisonment).

The kinds of principles that republican theorists support in practice include such things as rendering police more accountable for surveillance of suspects, and decrements to all layers of criminal justice intervention, such as less criminal law, less police surveillance, less prosecution and less punishment. Hence, republican theorists support a system that is as unobtrusive as possible, where consideration is extended to victims, offenders and community alike.

then & now

republican theory and restorative justice

Republican criminology is of recent origin; however, both its philosophical roots and policy initiatives have a much longer history. It shares a philosophical orientation with classical theory (Chapter 2), although with an emphasis on 'positive' ('republican') rather than 'negative' liberty. The emphasis on considering both the broader societal impact on offending as well as the influence of peers means it reflects an analytical frame of reference similar to that of opportunity and subcultural theory (Chapter 4). In terms of the emphasis on community-based problem-solving, the history of conferencing can be traced to traditional forms of conflict resolution within (among others) Maori societies of New Zealand. More recently, republican theorists have moved in the direction of peace building and other forms of conflict resolution (see the 'from theory to practice' box). In this it shares some common concerns with critical criminology (Chapter 11).

contemporary examples

The republican theory is built upon responding to crime in a manner that is unique and, theoretically, positive for all parties. As Braithwaite and Pettit (1990: 2) see it, 'we need a theory of criminal justice which allows us to respond in the best way to harmful conduct, where responding in that way sometimes will, and more often than not, entail punishment'. In broad conceptual terms, republican responses to crime entail symbolic measures plus substantive measures that involve material actions necessary to give credibility and sincerity to the symbolic measures. The measures adopted in practice depend upon the immediate circumstances of the players.

The substantive nature of recompense involves *restitution*, compensation or reparation. Restitution means to return to the victim whatever it was that was lost in the commission of the offence. For example, it may involve giving back stolen property. *Compensation* occurs where restitution is not possible. This entails an attempt to make up for the loss the victim has experienced (de Greiff 2006). *Reparation* is where neither restitution nor compensation is possible; for example, in the case of murder or genocide (Gallant & Rhea 2010; Cunneen 2008). This is an offering of compensation to those close to, and dependent upon, the victim of the offence.

At a theoretical level, the remedies and responses put forward by the republican theorists reflect their overall concerns with personal dominion and restorative justice. According to Pettit and Braithwaite (1993), the actual response to crime should reflect the following concerns:

- The offender must *recognise* the personal liberty of the victim in order to restore the dominion status of the victim. This can be achieved through some type of symbolic measure, such as an apology on the part of the offender for their behaviour, a commitment not to reoffend, reconciliation with the victim.

- In order to restore the victim's former dominion there must be some form of *recompense* for the damage done to the individual's personal dominion. This can be achieved through a range of substantive measures, such as restitution, compensation, or reparation.

- There must be a general *reassurance* given that the community will be protected from future acts. For instance, through a process of reprobation, the criminal justice system should be designed to expose offenders in a constructive way to community disapproval, and to reintegrate the victim and the offender back into community life.

An explanatory theory of republican justice is one that moves from a normative view of the criminal justice system (what *ought to be*) to a discussion of practical intervention measures (what *can be* put into place). Here the republican theory argues strongly that reintegrative shaming is the key to crime control (Braithwaite 1989; Ashworth 2002). In arguing this line, Braithwaite integrates the key lessons from labelling theory, in order to minimise the undesirable effects of shaming.

According to labelling theorists (Chapter 5), when an individual is termed 'bad', that label can stigmatise the individual. There is a need, however, to distinguish between stigmatisation, which increases the risks of reoffending by the shamed actor, and reintegrative shaming. In terms of the latter, preferred approach, disapproval of the behaviour (not the individual) is extended while a relationship of respect is sustained with the offender; (Ashworth 2002). Stigmatisation is disrespectful—it is seen as a humiliating form of shaming, where the offender is branded an evil person and is cast out permanently. Reintegrative shaming, by contrast, seeks to shame the evil *deed* but sees the offender in a respectable light. The shaming is finite, and the offender is given the opportunity to re-enter society by way of recognising the wrongdoing, apologising and being repentant. In this way, shame is seen as a useful means of combating crime as long as it is not applied in a stigmatising fashion.

Braithwaite (1989, 1995a) argues that we need a culture where we promote a self-sanctioning conscience. If we can develop certain norms and cultures, then individuals will not engage in certain activities, because their conscience will prevent them: they will feel ashamed for doing the wrong thing (Sherman 2010). In this respect, republican theory links up with older conservative theories that look to the internalisation of controls in addition to societal imposition of controls. Thus, the theory looks to both external processes of shaming (as expressed in official institutional intervention) and also internal self-sanctioning forms of shaming (as expressed in the ideas of control theory) (Braithwaite 2000).

The concept of reintegrative shaming has been employed in a number of different ways. The importance of combining formal and informal processes of social control is seen to be relevant in such areas as corporate crime (Braithwaite 1995b; Haines 2011), domestic violence (Strang & Braithwaite 2002) and juvenile justice (see Braithwaite 1991, 1992; Calhoun & Pelech 2010).

The theory asserts that we need a fair degree of community shaming before the offender reaches the stage of requiring formal institutional shaming. In this manner, we need to ensure that a 'public' conscience exists in society, along with a culture that develops this kind of conscience within each person. For example, if *domestic violence* is deemed intolerable by the community, then potential violators will stop themselves because they imagine wider community disapproval. This informal shaming process occurs outside the criminal justice system in order to prevent the crime from occurring. It is argued that formal sanctions should not be imposed until further down the track. Recent research has also identified that it is the informal shaming of friends, family, mentors and neighbours (rather than the formal shaming from criminal justice agencies) that is most likely to change behaviour, or prevent criminal behaviour in the first place (Simpson 2000; White 1994).

¬ peacemaking criminology

The reluctance of republican theory to impose formal sanctions is shared by another important strand of restorative-based criminology, in this case 'peacemaking criminology' (see Pepinsky & Quinney 1991). It is argued in this perspective that the criminal justice system fails at every level. The criminal justice system represents a state-sanctioned means of inflicting pain under the guise of reducing criminal activity and, yet, the imposition of punishment and repression never solves—and never will solve—social problems (Cohen 1993). The basic philosophy is that we cannot solve violence or human suffering with more violence and more human suffering. Instead, it is argued that humanistic and restorative principles need to be adopted at the level of dealing with the offender, and in dealing with wider social conflicts as well. The emphasis is on transformative strategies that are themselves premised upon participatory forms of conflict resolution (Walklate 2003; Harris 2008).

Drawing upon various peacemaking traditions—such as religious, humanistic and feminist approaches to understanding and responding to violence—peacemaking criminology criticises models based upon the idea of winners and losers. Rather, and in contrast, the approach speaks about openness, trust and cooperation (Moyer 2001). In many cases, it is argued that, literally, peace begins at home; that is, it is important that each individual lives his or her everyday life based upon love, forgiveness, kindness and hope (see, for example, Quinney 1991). These principles and concepts are also pertinent to developing a critique of a society that is class divided, racist and sexist, and that predominantly operates on the basis of power, domination, exploitation and control over others.

Not surprisingly, peacemaking criminology tends to stress mediation, conflict resolution and reconciliation as preferred methods with which to deal with human suffering and wrongdoing (Skelton & Sekhonyane 2007). Non-violent ways of thought and action are essential to the peacemaking conception of restorative justice. The intent is to understand how and where people make peace (Pepinsky 1991) in order to supplant existing criminal justice models that are based upon the 'war' on crime.

One of the key challenges of peacemaking criminology has been to translate a philosophy of 'being nice' into the practical realities of actual conflicts and instances in which social harm is occurring (Acorn 2004). To put it differently, how does one move beyond expressing the sentiments of compassion and empathy to addressing concretely real sites of conflict? Part of the answer to this is provided in recent work by McEvoy (2003). Based upon grounded interventions with paramilitary groups in Northern Ireland, McEvoy (2003) argues that a 'new' peacemaking criminology might include:

– an explicit focus on jurisdictions where actual political or ethnic conflicts are occurring, or have occurred (such as the work being done in post-conflict societies such as the former Yugoslavia and South Africa)

– a recognition of the idea that political engagement is necessary and that conflict transformation be based upon the objective of trying to make a difference

– a substantive engagement with human rights discourses, particularly as a counterweight to those sorts of moral relativism that can impede practical intervention (Skelton & Sekhonyane 2007)

– a reframing of the evaluation of 'what works' into a political rather than a technical exercise, thereby acknowledging the profound transformations in individuals, groups and communities that peacemaking criminology, somewhat ambitiously, wishes to make manifest.

An important observation of peacemaking criminology generally is that very often war and the war on crime are interlinked, and share many of the same attributes and institutional dynamics. Philosophically, and increasingly at a practical level of intervention, peacemaking criminologists wish to challenge violence, repression and humiliation as preferred modes of conflict resolution—whether this be at the level of individuals, groups, families, communities or nation-states (Arsovka et al. 2008). Conversely, drawing upon human rights discourses and restorative justice activities such as community mediation, and by stressing the positive value of nonviolent alternatives and the vital need to address the material reasons for social differences, peacemaking criminology aims to transform social settings in more profound ways than traditional criminal justice approaches. Similar to republican theory, it suggests the possibility of both a normative theory of crime, war and violence, and potential practices that might reflect and reinforce the restorative justice ethos.

{from theory to practice: poverty, crime and peacemaking criminology}

———

Wozniak, J.F. (2008). 'Poverty and Peacemaking Criminology: Beyond Mainstream Criminology', *Critical Criminology*, 16 (2): 209–23.

While most criminologists consider the impact of poverty on criminal behaviour, Wozniak suggests that this attention to economic inequalities is most commonly considered as a single variable within a much larger multivariate analysis. He argues that once criminologists accept poverty as a 'master status' to all social action (including criminal behaviour), appropriate policies can be developed to diminish suffering, and reduce the prevalence of economic inequalities. Policies and practices created from a peacemaking perspective do not focus on the criminal behaviour after it has happened. Rather, as Wozniak suggests, this approach aims to prevent the conditions that foster criminal behaviour from arising in the first place.

In this article, Wozniak documents the ways in which mainstream and peacemaking criminology address the issue of poverty. He initially contextualises the study through the lens of Kozol's (1991) ethnography of school children in America. In *Savage Inequalities*, Kozol (1991) illustrates the vast differences in children's experiences of school. Kozol's study of over thirty neighbourhoods in inner-city America provides the data and evidence for Wozniak's advocacy of peacemaking criminology.

Given the 'savage inequalities' (Kozol 1991 cited in Wozniak 2008) experienced by American children and the symbiotic relationship that exists between these inequalities and crime, Wozniak argues that poverty should necessarily be a significant topic in criminology teaching and learning. Yet, in his document analysis of mainstream criminology, criminological theory, and juvenile delinquency textbooks (twenty-six in total), he found that none addressed the issue of poverty as a standalone issue, or as a key concern in the introductory chapter, and only four included poverty in the subject index (Wozniak 2008: 212). And while poverty was discussed in relation to a variety of other topics and theories—such as its relationship to some forms of criminal behaviour (e.g. theft), and as a shaping force in state policy (e.g. 'war on poverty')—as a concept, it was not utilised systematically, nor did the textbooks place 'poverty at the center of an understanding of criminology' (Wozniak 2008: 212).

Wozniak advocates a new type of analysis that draws on the best characteristics and practices of contemporary critical criminology. In particular, he argues that current criminological practices that seek quantifiable answers—where poverty is reduced to a single variable in a multivariate analysis—cannot grasp the texture and force of 'savage inequalities'. To reduce these experiences of suffering to a measure fails to account for the thick narratives (and deep data) that emerge from immersion in the everyday lives of those living in poverty. Instead of asking questions about 'whether or not, and in which way or not, poverty measures are linked to crime', Wozniak (2008: 213–4) suggests a peacemaking criminology would begin with, 'How does poverty make people suffer?' Wozniak's 'visionary criminology' attempts to see those things others 'won't or don't see' (Barak 2003 cited in Wozniak 2008: 214). To do so, he argues that peacemaking criminology must draw upon three theoretical traditions and methods: religious, feminist and critical. These intellectual traditions share a commitment to criminology as an 'active vocation, one that is grounded in a particular moral stance toward human existence' (Quinney 2000: 194).

The translation of these theoretical and methodological traditions into criminal justice policies is guided in peacemaking criminology by six concepts: nonviolence (avoid coercion and force), social justice (elimination of prejudice and discrimination), inclusion (participation by all concerned parties), correct means (due process), and ascertainable criteria (agreement over procedures), and categorical imperative (decisions based on moral reasoning) (Wozniak 2008: 217). Wozniak suggests that these tools enable peacemaking criminologists to develop a systematic method for studying the suffering imposed by 'savage inequalities', and provide a better account for the relationship between poverty and crime.

critique

A number of criticisms can be levelled at republican theory, and restorative justice has been subject to sustained critique since its adoption by criminal justice agencies (see von Hirsch & Ashworth 1992; Morris 2002; Muncie et al. 2002; Daly 2003; von Hirsch et al. 2003; Acorn 2004; Bennett 2006; Clarkson 2008; Friedrichs 2008; Harris & Maruna 2008; Walklate 2008). One weakness of the theory is that it does not really look at the causes of crime. What it does is provide a whole range of variables that are associated with crime, at the level of both the individual (interdependency) and society (communitarianism). The theory thus provides a description of 'background' characteristics of the 'typical offender' (such as young, unemployed, male, transient) without really exploring how these factors interact with the given environment that leads to offending.

Furthermore, the societal-level variable 'communitarianism' needs greater analysis if it is to be a truly useful concept in analysing potential levels of criminality within a given society. It is one thing to link variables by way of association to an underlying construct, but it is quite another to map out, in any given society, how each is ordered, and the 'flow' of these variables. It is important to do this in order to explain why some parts of society are more vulnerable to crime, and in particular to locate the individual offender within society in a way that provides a meaningful explanation for the pressures to offend. Thus far, republican theory has tended to remain at the level of description when dealing with the way the world actually is, with the theory outlined in its fullest extent with respect to some notion of an ideal society.

When dealing with a less than ideal society, further problems arise. The notion of exercising self-control and the concept of the self-sanctioning conscience raise a number of questions when they are applied to a society that has a great divide between rich and poor. The theory assumes that individuals make incorrect choices that ultimately lead to their criminal behaviour. However, if the social and economic world of the individual is falling apart, the offender is obviously in a difficult situation. The theory has little to say about the structural characteristics of offending and policing, nor how family group conferencing aims to account for these structural effects. The policies that have been suggested thus far appear unable to deal with real clashes of interest between wealth and poverty, issues of racism and sexism, and the wider issues of class structure. The policies emanating from the theory do not address the degree to which young people may be brought into the system because of institutional biases, such as over-policing, or bias in decision-making of the courts.

These problems arise partly because the theory works on the idea of a presumed consensus within society. In particular, there is a consensus concerning the nature of criminal activity: crimes are those predatory acts that are accepted by all as criminal. From previous chapters we have seen that many would agree with this. The concern is that the definition of crime and the application of criminal law are subject to political interests; as a result, both the definition and the application are biased. The theory does not take adequate account of these biases within the system itself. Rather, it relies on a policy of minimal intervention, expressed through the underlying principles of parsimony and checking of power, as a way of attempting to deal with such problems.

Interestingly, and by way of contrast, peacemaking criminology has been criticised for going too far in the other direction. That is, the problem in this perspective is that the presumed consensus is biased and socially negative: the dominant social values and ideals revolve around violence as the key means of conflict resolution. Thus, it is the systemic reliance upon violence (as manifest in institutional practices and cultural values) that is viewed as destructive, wasteful and inhumane in contemporary societies. However, it has been argued that this particular philosophical stance provides little more than a utopian vision of society, and that, in the end, it does not provide for an adequate empirical and theoretical understanding of crime and crime control. As Akers (1997: 183 in Moyer 2001) puts it: 'This is a highly laudable philosophy of criminal justice, but it does not offer an explanation of why the system operates as it does or why offenders commit crime'. Similar types of criticism have also been noted among supporters of peacemaking criminology. For example, as discussed above, McEvoy (2003) is highly conscious of the fact that too often the tendency in peacemaking criminology is to stimulate interest in the perspective but to pay much less attention to practical application. The perspective is pitched at a level of abstraction and philosophical reflection that offers a different way of framing and thinking about crime and criminality, but as an emerging form of criminological theory it has some way to go in providing more specific, grounded analyses of relevant issues and trends. Moreover, big questions remain with respect to analysis of different types of violence, whether and under what conditions violence can be seen as liberating or repressive, the legitimacy or otherwise of violence that enables the state or community to wield authority and to enforce collective decisions, and the moral basis upon which to condemn (or support) those who utilise violence to achieve social goals. Resolution of these practical and conceptual issues is most likely through specific case studies and strategic interventions, as illustrated, for example, in McEvoy (2003).

The translation of theory into practice, and of understanding into action, is more transparent and integral to republican theory than has been, to date, generally demonstrated in peacemaking criminology (Daly 2003). However, in the case of republican theory the notion of reintegrative shaming also raises a number of issues. It is not clear from the model which comes first: effective shaming or low crime rates. It may be that low crime rates are a precondition for the success of a criminal justice process that relies on shaming a transgressor so he or she does not reoffend. Following on from this, it is possible to argue that it may not be possible to shame successfully in a society that is low on communitarianism. Put another way, if an offender was never integrated into society in the first place, it makes no sense to rely on 'reintegration' to solve the problems and costs of crime. Reintegrative shaming loses its meaning when faced with someone who is marginalised from society and not repentant in the least (Acorn 2004; Bennett 2006).

The difficulties of trying to 'repair the harm' in the context of social disintegration and inequality have been implicitly acknowledged in other types of restorative justice approaches. For instance, rather than being based upon a concept of 'shaming', the balanced restorative approach is based upon a 'balanced' assessment of the offender's needs and competencies (Bazemore 1991). This approach relies not so much on what is essentially a moral category (shaming), but rather on situational assessment (involving close scrutiny of offender capabilities). As such, it attempts to explore the specific requirements related to each case of offending and to respond variably to each offender in terms of his or her immediate situation and capacities. Such an approach appears to offer more scope in dealing with issues relating to the marginalisation and alienation experienced by young offenders in particular.

Problems also arise with the way shaming works in practice. For example, how, in practice, do we distinguish between reintegrative shaming and stigmatisation? It may be that a wider form of stigmatisation occurs because so many more people are involved in situations such as a juvenile conference. There are further problems with the concept of shaming and compliance, in that there is a need to distinguish between compliance with

chap. 10.
p.241.

republican
theory and
restorative
justice

what the group wants, which is not internalised, and conformity, which is internalised (Potter 1992). Presumably, the ideal is for shaming to lead to changes internal to the individual that will reduce the chance of future offending. Shaming, then, is ultimately a concept that is internal to the individual, and yet the theory does not detail how successful shaming is to be measured, so that we can avoid stigmatisation or mere external compliance, both of which may lead to future offending. Further, in pluralistic societies, where there are multiple perspectives on crime and criminality, how can we ensure that each family or juvenile conference is not biased to local norms and values that are unrepresentative of the wider societal values (Acorn 2004)? This is especially the case for restorative justice initiatives in heavily divided communities (Arsovka et al. 2008), where the moral entrepreneurs of the late twentieth century have become the community members on restorative justice panels in the early twenty-first century.

Furthermore, the practice of reintegrative shaming is used with certain types of offenders, mainly young people. There is little discussion regarding the success or otherwise of reintegrative shaming as it might be applied to white-collar offenders (though Simpson 2000 provides an exception to this). There are yet other crimes, state crimes for example, that do not lend themselves easily to the concept of reintegrative shaming, which focuses on individual transgressions. And, in some cases the very thought of reintegrating offenders is beyond the norms and values of a particular society (for example, in cases of paedophilic violence and genocide). In fact, as Acorn (2004) argues, the ironic twist on restorative practices is that a sincere transformative apology has a limited impact in anything but the most unforgiveable crimes. To forgive an offender for anything less is patronising, net-widening, and naive about the role, objectives and human practice of forgiveness.

It can also be argued that the practical examples of republican theory, such as juvenile conferencing, involve a denial of due process. It is problematic if the offender does not plead guilty as these programs can be seen to be attempting to shame someone before due process. In practice, then, those *accused* of offending who participate in such programs either plead guilty before due process, or have their guilt assumed before participating. This can be seen as a denial of due process of the law, which presumes people are innocent until proven guilty (Ikpa 2007; Foley 2008). Many pre-court (or diversionary) processes come up against this difficulty. The problem is that, if a given body is granted the power to punish an individual, the state has to be satisfied that the individual in question really committed the offence. The traditional way for this to happen is for the case to be tried in a court. However, these programs attempt to avoid the court process (as it is seen as stigmatising and also expensive), but in doing so they deny the accused the right to have his or her case proved in the appropriate manner in open court.

Without the mechanism of the court ensuring those who receive punishment are guilty, it can be argued that reintegrative shaming is potentially nothing more than a net-widening process of social control, without reducing the number of people subject to punitive sanctions of the state. The practices of reintegrative shaming are also being extended beyond crime and criminality to capture acts of deviancy, as illustrated in new campaigns aimed at reintegrating smokers through shaming (or equally, the various campaigns aimed at 'cleaning up Australia' through reintegrative shaming).

If the aim of the criminal justice system is to reduce the number of people being caught up in the system, programs set up to 'reintegratively shame' people as an alternative to court may simply make the overall system larger, without any positive effect in terms of reduction of crime (Jamieson & Yates 2009). It can be argued that these practices of shaming represent an extension of power into civil society. Some would argue that there needs to be a clear distinction between a process that is based in the criminal justice system, and one that properly resides within the community. The concept of reintegrative shaming blurs this distinction.

Despite these problems, republican theory has some clear strengths. First, it provides a more integrated account of crime and crime prevention, as distinct from individualistic and 'bad apple' approaches. It attempts to provide an overall view of society, and then locate criminal justice policy within this broader framework. As such, it can be seen as a comprehensive theory that provides an integrated view of all parts of the criminal justice system.

The view of society posited by republican theory as a whole also has clear advantages in terms of individual liberty over those perspectives that rely heavily on punishment and deterrence, such as certain aspects of New Right criminology outlined in Chapter 8. Republican theory is based on ideas of a system that respects rights and limits, and thus clearly upholds individual liberty better than more punitive systems.

Finally, republican theory is politically attractive. It provides justification for building a new type of consensus in society, and has an emphasis on restorative justice that is positive. Furthermore, the method of achieving lower crime rates is relatively inexpensive, in that it is based on minimal intervention. In addition, it captures many of the political concerns of the day, such as the need to take account of the victim (Braithwaite & Pettit 1994), and the emphasis on family as the basic unit in society (Braithwaite 2004).

{conclusion}

The rise in popularity of republican theory, restorative justice, and peacekeeping criminology needs to be considered. The political directions of crime in recent years have seen a concentration on individual responsibility for one's actions, with the retributivists arguing that the individual who has committed the action must be punished. Republican theory agrees that people should be responsible for their actions, but argues that our response to those actions should be constructive.

The attraction of the theory can be explained, in part, by the economic directions of criminal justice. Fiscal crises in various jurisdictions have seen governments increasingly worried about how to best constrain expenditure in order to curb state debt. In this climate, prisons are viewed as expensive, and the legal aid crisis is seen as a problem arising out of the lengthy, and hence costly, formal court process. Hence, from a strictly economic viewpoint it makes sense to look at alternative cost-effective and efficient measures of crime control.

Another attraction of the republican theory and restorative justice approaches is that they offer a
...

perspective on conflict and conflict resolution that is intrinsically humane and socially positive. As such, they provide a refreshing change from traditional law-and-order discourses. They offer messages of hope, and redemption, in a world seemingly divided by hatred and intractable social differences. Combining powerful moral critiques and practical methods of intervention, they demonstrate that alternatives are, indeed, possible and desirable.

If conditions in the rest of society undermine the cohesiveness of that society as a whole, then this will limit and circumscribe the efficacy of the proposals put forward by republican theorists. In the next chapter we look at critical criminology, which has attempted to address some of these issues.

{further reading}

Acorn, A. (2004). *Compulsory Compassion: A Critique of Restorative Justice*, University of British Colombia Press, Vancouver.

Bazemore, G. (1997). 'The "Community" in Community Justice: Issues, Themes, and Questions for the New Neighbourhood Sanctioning Models', *Justice System Journal*, 19 (2): 193–227.

Braithwaite, J. (1989). *Crime, Shame and Reintegration*, Cambridge University Press, Cambridge.

Braithwaite, J. (1995a).
'Reintegrative Shaming,
Republicanism and Policy',
in H. Barlow (ed.), *Criminology
and Public Policy: Putting
Theory to Work*, Westview Press,
Boulder: 191–206.

Braithwaite, J. (2000).
'Republican Theory and Crime
Control', in K. Bussman &
S. Karstedt (eds), *Social
Dynamics of Crime and Control:
New Theories for a World in
Transition*, Hart Publishing,
Oxford: 85–103.

Braithwaite, J. (2002).
*Restorative Justice and
Responsive Regulation*, Oxford
University Press, New York.

Braithwaite, J. & Pettit, P.
(1990). *Not Just Deserts: A
Republican Theory of Criminal
Justice*, Clarendon Press,
Oxford.

McEvoy, K. (2003). 'Beyond the
Metaphor: Political Violence,
Human Rights and "New"
Peacemaking Criminology',
Theoretical Criminology, 7 (3):
319–46.

Muncie, J., Hughes, G. &
McLaughlin, E. (eds) (2002).
*Youth Justice: Critical
Readings*, SAGE, London.

Pepinsky, H. & Quinney, R.
(eds) (1991). *Criminology as
Peacemaking*, Indiana University
Press, Bloomington, Indiana.

Pettit, P. & Braithwaite, J. (1993). 'Not Just Deserts, Even in Sentencing', *Current Issues in Criminal Justice*, 4 (3): 225–39.

Sullivan, D. & Tifft, L. (eds) (2008). *Handbook of Restorative Justice: A Global Perspective*, Routledge, Abingdon, UK.

von Hirsch, A., Roberts, J., Bottoms, A.E., Roach, K. & Schiff, M. (eds) (2003). *Restorative Justice and Criminal Justice: Competing or Reconcilable Paradigms?*, Hart Publishing, Oxford, UK.

Zehr, H. (1990). *Changing Lenses: A New Focus for Crime and Justice*, Herald Press, Scotsdale.

critical criminology

{introduction}

The aim of this chapter is to discuss the main ideas and concepts of critical criminology. This perspective combines a wide range of concerns from across the more radical approaches, such as Marxism and feminism, and attempts to develop a type of left-wing criminology that is relevant and appropriate for contemporary society.

As with many of the perspectives in criminology, critical criminology incorporates a wide number of ideas and analytical strands. A distinguishing characteristic of critical criminology is that it is generally associated with an *oppositional* position in relation to much of the work of conventional criminology, and also to many contemporary policy developments in the field of criminal justice (see Schissel & Brooks 2002; Carrington & Hogg 2002, 2011; McLaughlin 2010).

Critical criminology nevertheless exhibits a number of elements that make it a natural intellectual and strategic partner of both the Left Realist and republican approaches. As will be demonstrated in this chapter, however, politically this perspective retains a strong socialist (rather than liberal-reformist) orientation. Its analytical focus emphasises the causal significance of capitalism in the generation of and responses to 'crime' (rather than relying on multifactorial descriptions). More recently, critical criminology has also integrated many of the radical arguments developed out of postmodern analyses, especially those that problematise the definition of crime, and the power dynamics within criminal events, and the criminal justice system more widely.

social context

As much as anything, critical criminology represents a further development of the broad radical strands within criminology. In particular, it builds upon the basic concepts and strategic concerns of the Marxist and feminist perspectives. Generally speaking, it does so from the point of view of a broadly *anti-capitalist position*, which incorporates the ideas of creating a social and natural environment that is not associated with heterosexist, racist and destructive practices of production and consumption (Friedrichs 2009; DeKeseredy 2011).

There is some confusion and debate surrounding the term 'critical' criminology. It has been used by a wide range of writers to describe a wide range of theoretical and political positions (Michalowski 1996). In some discussions, Left Realism is regarded as part of the critical criminology perspective; in others, it is not. In some instances, any critique of the existing criminal justice system from any political position other than conservative has been associated with critical criminology. This simply equates 'critical' with specific criticisms, rather than using the term to identify a particular analytical framework.

Both liberal and radical approaches may call for change to existing criminal justice practices, and they may overlap on a range of conceptual and strategic issues (for example, that unequal distribution of societal resources underpins much working-class crime). However, fundamental differences in ideology and ultimate goals remain, and these must be acknowledged, as they have significant implications for criminological theory and practice.

The difficulties and lack of clarity in the use of the term 'critical' are a result of the blurring of boundaries between liberal and radical kinds of analysis and intervention. These difficulties are also a reflection of other changes occurring in society that have had a major impact upon prevailing attitudes and ideologies. The 1980s was a period of highly volatile politics on a world scale. The demise of Stalinism in the former Soviet Union and Eastern Europe represented not only the end of the Cold War, but also part of a general rethinking of politics and ideology around the world.

The notions of *glasnost* (openness) and *perestroika* (restructuring) signalled a far-reaching process of change, reform and transformation in the non-capitalist countries. Meanwhile, the world economy was steadily and rapidly being internationalised and globalised. Production, consumption, finance, culture, employment, debt, sport: everything was subject to processes that universalised certain ways of doing things, seeing things and engaging in things. Simultaneously, people became aware of the increasing fragmentation of their lives, as previous loyalties, communities and affiliations (such as links to a sporting club, neighbourhood or job) were no longer possible, relevant or appreciated.

An age of profound uncertainty had been broached. By the late 1980s, it was clear that the world would never be the same again:

- politically, in terms of traditional capitalist versus communist ideologies;
- economically, in terms of employment and distribution of wealth;
- environmentally, in terms of ecological imbalance and degradation; or
- socially, in terms of how people relate to each other across many types of interactions.

The hallmark of this period has been *rapid change*, often associated with technological innovation (in the form of the computer microchip) and the concentration of wealth and power into fewer and fewer hands on a global scale.

The world was not only an uncertain place, but also increasingly an unequal one. In trying to understand the nature of the processes of inequality, the concept of *difference* was highlighted in social analysis and reflected in the ongoing presence of the 'new social movements'. Gay and lesbian rights groups, environmental and conservation movements, pro-choice and broad women's rights organisations, animal rights activists, Third World solidarity action groups, human rights advocates, antiracist groups, anti-globalisation movements and many others were raising the issues, and voices, of those who had not previously been heard in mainstream political or academic circles.

The world outside criminology obviously has an impact upon what occurs within the discipline. Not surprisingly, then, a number of new strands of thought began to emerge alongside the established approaches, such as those we have explored in this book so far. For example, the fascination with meaning, social difference and discourse analysis was manifest in so-called *postmodern* analysis (Hunt 1991; Friedrichs 2009; DeKeseredy 2011). This describes the use of certain analytical tools to 'deconstruct' or decode the language and meaning of law and order, and of the criminal justice system, especially 'the law' (Smart 1990b, 1992). Thus, for example, feminist jurisprudence emphasised the inbuilt biases against women in a legal system premised upon certain conceptions of the 'reasonable man' (see Naffine 1990). This type of analysis uncovers the 'hidden' text of oppression as this pertains to women, ethnic minority groups and working-class people. This type of analysis has also been essential in the development of critical race theory (Ross 2010), particularly in relation to a radical critique of foundational texts such as the First Amendment of the US constitution.

The term 'postmodernism' is used in a number of different ways, some of which appear to be contradictory. Some care, therefore, has to be taken to clarify its meaning in any particular instance. For example, it has been used in reference to:

– analysis of postmodern trends (for example, the social impact of new communication and information technology; the commodification of symbols, especially as this relates to consumption)

– the idea of a postmodern society as distinct from 'modernity' (that is, one that exhibits high degrees of social differentiation, individuation and diverse forms and constructions of subjectivity or personal identity)

– postmodern techniques (methods of analysis that centre on the nature and dynamics of language)

– postmodern theory (the universalisation of its method to consider knowledge and power relations across a broad spectrum of social life)

– postmodern epistemology (a philosophical stance on the central place of language in the relationship between the 'knower' and what is 'known', which makes problematic any assigning of 'truth' to statements about the world around us).

The postmodern approaches have also gone under different names, such as 'constitutive criminology' or a 'social constructionist' paradigm (Henry & Milovanovic 1994, 2005; Arrigo & Bernard 1997; Arrigo 2003; McLaughlin 2010).

In some cases, the method of the postmodern was elevated to the level of social theory. Thus, all meaning—every association between subject (you) and object (the world around you)—is entirely an artefact of language (signs and symbols), and language, in turn, is relative to and determined by your particular perspective (Doyle 2010). In other words, there is no 'objective' world that is not constructed 'subjectively' by the author of a particular 'text'. There can be no privileged interpretation of reality.

For some, this also means the adoption of a new neutrality that favours no particular politics (neither conservative, liberal nor radical), and that ultimately may reject the idea that there are certain dominant structures of power. Such a perspective makes it difficult to speak about and act upon oppression as a structural phenomenon (see Thompson 1992).

If some of the new types of analysis stressed 'difference' and the relative rather than absolute nature of the social world, others emphasised 'commonality' and shared experience as the basis for criminological work. The idea of *peacemaking criminology* (discussed in the previous chapter) asks that we recognise our 'oneness' with the world around us. It views crime as essentially a consequence of a general violence towards, and separation from, people through the ways in which society responds to offenders. Its main themes include 'connectedness', 'caring' and 'mindfulness' (Friedrichs 1991; Pepinsky & Quinney 1991).

The relationship of increasingly fragmented societies, and pluralised modes of government, to other more homogenising social processes is also subject to criminological attention. For example, the concept of a 'risk society' (Beck 1992) has been used to describe new forms of risk related to accelerating technological change and globalisation of economic, political and social relationships. In this framework, there are a series of threats to human life that are increasingly shared by the inhabitants of the planet, such as pollution, global warming and crime. These phenomena do not respect national borders, nor do they necessarily privilege any particular 'victim' above another. The risks, in one sense, transcend the ordinary social differences of late modernity. Another related idea is that of 'ontological insecurity' (Giddens 1990, 1991), which describes the feeling of being physically and psychologically at risk in an unstable and rapidly changing world. The direct result of the collapse of traditional social structures, and the limitations of those that are meant to provide security and predictability (such as the family, school and work), results in a process of 'individualisation' (see Beck & Beck-Gernsheim 2002). This refers both to the process whereby individuals are institutionally made more responsible for their well-being (and less reliant upon state or collective support), and to the cultural and ideological prominence given to the 'project of the self' in self-managing one's choices and action.

While not unproblematic, these conceptualisations of risk, of uncertainty, of individualisation and of risk management have nevertheless spurred considerable interest and application in the specific area of crime and crime control. From a criminological perspective, attention has been directed at the ways in which governments have attempted to manage crime-related risk, in a context in which inequalities have increased and other social ills have grown (Mythen & Walklate 2006). It is argued that many Western states have responded to this by devolving responsibility for personal security on to individuals, while simultaneously adopting more draconian methods of responding to crime (see Stenson & Sullivan 2001). The individualisation of responsibility in fact masks the social differences in capacity to deal with personal risk; it also ignores the social patterning of both victimisation and offending behaviour.

The various critical criminology perspectives reflect, in many ways, the uncertainties and the hopes of the current age. Their development has been intertwined with radically altered material circumstances, and the emergence of the new social movements as political forces in society. The ideas of these perspectives have been drawn upon to varying degrees in contemporary criminological work.

basic concepts

What distinguishes critical criminology *per se* is its concern with *structures of power*. These are seen to be institutionalised in particular ways, and to reflect social interests that oppress specific categories of people. How power is conceptualised, however, marks out one of the main differences of approach within critical criminology.

Critical criminologists more or less agree that the present operation of the criminal justice system is unfair and biased, and operates in ways that advantages certain groups or classes above others. The primary task of the critical criminologist is to expose the nature of the underlying power relations that shape how different groups are treated in, and by, the criminal justice system. In many cases, the task is also seen as trying to initiate action and develop strategies that will *transform* the present social order, including the criminal justice system (Scraton & Chadwick 1991; Young 2002; McLaughlin 2010).

The focal point of critique within this perspective is how power is mobilised within the broad sphere of criminal justice. There is a range of differing approaches within critical criminology, providing many different methods, empirical studies and theoretical insights (see DeKeseredy 2011).

For present purposes, we can identify two general trends in the critical criminological literature. The 'structuralist' approach tends to focus on power as something that is ingrained in social structures and that manifests itself in the form of the action of institutions and the activities of sectional interest groups (see Scraton & Chadwick 1991). The 'postmodern' approach, on the other hand, sees power in terms of language and the ways in which knowledge production shapes human experience while simultaneously engendering conflict over meaning (see Arrigo & Bernard 1997; Lea 1998; Arrigo 2003). The differences between these approaches are seen by some writers to be so great as to warrant treatment as distinct models of social enquiry (Arrigo & Bernard 1997; Russell 1997). Others do not necessarily share this view, or are less definitive about the 'break' between the two perspectives (Hunt 1991; Henry & Milovanovic 1994, 2005; Einstadter & Henry 1995; McLaughlin 2010; DeKeseredy 2011).

Part of the complexity, and to some extent confusion, in the area of postmodern criminology arises because this form of theorising has expanded the range of disciplines from which criminology draws theoretical insight. Disciplines, each with their own separate history, may use the same term to mean very different things. There are a number of examples of this and, not surprisingly, we must clarify our meaning of one of these 'contested terms'—namely, 'structuralism'. For some postmodernists (perhaps, more accurately, poststructuralists) the term structuralism means something quite different. In this case, structuralism generally makes some reference to Saussure's theory of 'structuralism', which argued that language was a self-referential system of meaning. In this sense, a word was given meaning not because it related to a 'thing' (such as a flower) but primarily because the giving of meaning enabled some discrimination in meaning from another word (such as 'grass') within the language system itself. Language was thus 'structured' in terms of a substantially closed, formal system of meaning (see Bourdieu 1991). The meaning and existence of words could be explained most fully by way of understanding the structure of a particular language itself, not by reference to anything outside that language. Poststructuralism, as a theoretical perspective, draws heavily from linguistics; as such it tends to build, critically, upon the Saussurean meaning of the term structuralism, as opposed to the sociological meaning of the term.

Within sociology, the term structuralism has meant a theoretical perspective that places an emphasis on the way economic, political and social structures shape individual behaviour and, in the case of criminology, the definition of crime and deviance. It is this definition of structuralism that is used here.

¬ structuralism

While there are a number of different strands to structuralist criminology, in general it can be said that crime is defined in terms of *oppression* (see chart 11.1). Some groups are particularly vulnerable to oppression, including:

- the working class (especially its more powerless sections, including the 'underclass')
- women (especially those who are poor, sole parents and socially isolated)
- ethnic minority groups (especially those from non-English-speaking backgrounds and refugees)
- Indigenous people (especially those most affected by long-term colonisation processes and institutional disadvantage).

chart 11.1 | **structuralist criminology**

definition of crime	– structural forms of oppression (class, gender, 'race')
focus of analysis	– crimes of the powerful (the state, political economy, ideology) – crimes of the less powerful (specific class, gender, ethnic, 'race' groups)
cause of crime	– marginalisation, criminalisation (for example, racialisation of crime)
nature of offender	– structurally determined context, process of homogenisation, legitimation crisis
response to crime	– social empowerment, redistribution of social resources, participatory democracy
crime prevention	– antiracist campaigns, human rights emphasis, public ownership under community control
operation of criminal justice system	– emphasis on restorative justice, self-determination at justice system community level, employment orientation, open and public accountability of state officials

These groups are most likely to suffer from the weight of oppressive power relations based upon arbitrary social divisions, which lead to discrimination (such as classism, sexism, homophobia and racism) in the definition of crime, and the institutional practices of 'law and order'.

The focus of analysis for structuralist critical criminology is both the crimes of the powerful and the crimes of the less powerful. In examining the *crimes of the powerful*, attention is directed at issues relating to ideology (especially, the nature of 'law-and-order' politics), political economy (the social impacts of privatisation), and the state (managerial rather than democratic modes of rule, and as a criminal actor itself). The structural context of crime vis-à-vis capitalist development and institutional pressures is viewed as central to any explanation of crimes of the powerful (Russell 2002).

The *crimes of the less powerful* are examined from the point of view of the specific experiences of particular sections of the population. Different forms of criminality are thus linked to specific sections of the working class, particular categories of women and men, certain ethnic minority groups and Indigenous people in a variety of rural and urban settings. As this form of critical criminology has developed it has also begun to address the structures of other, less common, forms of oppressions, including those relating to sexuality, religion and age (not just youth). There is a twofold emphasis: on the *specificity* of crime and criminal involvement (specific groups, specific kinds of activity); and on the *generalist* features that unite the disparate groups (shared economic, social and political circumstances).

Crime is seen to be associated with broad processes of political economy that affect the powerful and the less powerful in quite different ways. For the powerful, there are pressures associated with the securing and maintenance of *state power*, and *specific sectional interests* in the global context of international trade and transnational corporate monopolisation (Coleman et al. 2009). For the less powerful, the cause and experience of crime are seen to lie in the interplay between *marginalisation* (separation from mainstream institutions) and *criminalisation* (intervention by state authorities) (Scraton 2007). Of particular note is the increasing *racialisation of crime*, in which certain communities are targeted for media and police attention in the 'war against crime' or the 'war against terror' and 'public disorder' (see Poynting et al. 2004).

Offending behaviour and criminal victimisation are thus linked to a social context that is structurally determined by the general allocation of societal resources and by the specific nature of police intervention in people's lives. There is a *process of homogenisation*, in which the least powerful and most vulnerable in society—the poor, the less educated and the unemployed—are filtered through the system until they constitute a disproportionate number of repeat offenders and/or recidivist prisoners.

The growing disparities between rich and poor, and the expansion in the sheer number of the poor, constitute a *legitimation crisis* for the system as a whole. One response is the swing towards 'law-and-order' politics, which entrenches and exacerbates the homogenising process of identifying and punishing offenders (Scraton 1987, 2007). A particular area of concern is the repressive nature of the state in relation to particular layers of the working class and in regard to particular communities (Coleman et al. 2009).

For structuralist critical criminology, a response to crime must be built upon a strategy of *social empowerment*. This means involving people directly in decisions about their future through direct participatory democracy. It also requires a redistribution of social resources to communities on the basis of social need and equity. To counter crimes committed by the powerful, there must be open and *public accountability* of all state officials. Further, as part of wealth redistribution, there has to be a transfer of wealth from private hands to public ownership under community control.

As a general crime-prevention measure, and to diminish the prevalence of certain crimes, critical criminologists advocate proactive strategies such as antiracist and antisexist campaigns (including re-education and retraining of state officials such as the police). Strong emphasis is given to extending and protecting *basic human rights* (which include economic, social, cultural and political rights), and institutionalising these by means of watchdog agencies (such as the Children's Commissioner and Human Rights Commissioners) and in criminal justice agency policies.

From this perspective, the criminal justice system should be based upon a model of *restorative justice*, rather than retribution and punishment. The state should not be repressive in orientation, but coercion may be required as part of the redistribution of community resources from the advantaged sectors of the population to the less advantaged. Moreover, the criminal justice system should operate openly, publicly, and with full community accountability. As far as possible, its functions should reflect self-determination at the community level, within the boundaries of human rights.

¬ postmodernism

Importantly, as Friedrichs (2009) warns, not all postmodern criminology is critical criminology. In fact, some postmodern criminology is more easily integrated into New Right and conservative approaches to crime and criminality. However, for *critical* postmodern criminologists, the starting point is the idea that *language structures thought*. Language is seen as the crucial intervening variable between social relationships and institutions, and all methods of knowing the social world. Crime is thus defined in terms of linguistic production, and relationships of power that shape the nature of this production (Hunt 1991) (see chart 11.2). The social world is effectively limited to, and constituted by, the collective reality of language. In other words, there is no necessary logical connection between the use of language and what it purports to describe—there are no 'objective truths', only different ways of speaking about and describing social reality.

Accordingly, social constructionists tend to reject the idea of any 'grand narrative' (such as technological revolution, enlightened social progress) as providing a foundation for understanding the world. This is because the social world is viewed as inherently chaotic and based upon contingency, rather than as a coherent system that is regulated in terms of some central steering mechanism (such as class struggle, social solidarity) (Russell 1997). Society is characterised as being in *constant flux and change*, and the emphasis is on fragmentation, diversity and ambiguity. As such, reality cannot be understood, depicted or changed as a whole; there is not one 'truth' but 'many truths', and these, in turn, are constantly changing.

Postmodernist writers vary considerably in their opinions regarding the importance of historical context, given their focus on the plurality of existence; this contrasts with the primacy given to history by Marxists. While some postmodern authors accord it considerable importance—for example, Foucault (1977)—others fix only on the (multiple) 'realities' of the present. As such, these approaches tend to negate the possibility of value in anything other than the present (since that is all that is 'knowable'), and it has been argued that past atrocities and social harms can thus melt into insignificance in the postmodernist agenda (Cohen 1993).

The only real universal feature of social life is the way in which individuals seek power over others by gaining knowledge of them. The focus, therefore, is on bio-power as a ubiquitous feature of social life. The point of analysis is to explore the *'micro-processes' of power*, which operate in institutions such as police, courts and prisons, in order to reveal how power is exercised and how the exercise of power engenders resistance.

Those who *control the means of expression* (including foundational documents such as constitutions or criminal codes) are seen to hold the key to controlling and exercising power over others. Simultaneously, however, it is acknowledged that where there is power (in any social relationship) there is also *resistance* to this power. Language and meaning are contested, and there is always a dynamic tension between dominant social voices and those that are silenced or expelled by the dominant modes of expression.

The key to social transformation, therefore, lies in analysing the languages that construct social relationships in a particular way, to the advantage of some and to the disadvantage of others (DeKeseredy 2011). Exposing the *discourses* (modes of speech, knowledge and categorisation of the social world) of everyday life opens the door to other (ideally, transgressive) expressions of reality that have been submerged by the dominant or hegemonic discourse. The main method of the social constructionist is that of discourse analysis, which examines how meaning and sense are constructed in everyday language. This involves a process of *deconstruction of meaning* to reveal the hidden and suppressed meanings embodied in certain social relationships.

chart 11.2 | postmodernism

definition of crime	_ not absolute _ continues struggle over control of linguistic production
focus of analysis	_ human subject _ conflicts over 'existence' or 'reality' as expressed in and through language
cause of crime	_ hegemony of dominant discourse _ suppression of alternatives
nature of offender	_ discursively constituted through dominant discourses _ relationships of resistance/power
response to crime	_ replacement discourses
crime prevention	_ conflicts over discursive frames _ new voices and listening _ proactive transgressive identity formation
operation of criminal justice system	_ localism, plurality _ deconstruction and critique _ acknowledgment of diverse 'discursive subject positions'

An important part of this deconstruction of meaning is to examine the *discursive subject positions* that inform the way in which people speak and think. For example, in the field of criminal justice there are a number of activities and social roles or positions. These include, for instance, offending (the offender), lawyering (the lawyer), policing (the police officer) and judging (the judge or magistrate) (see, for example, Shon 2002). It is argued by postmodernists that the people (subjects) who assume these positions speak, think, feel and know through the language that is embodied in these structures (Doyle 2010). Thus, the person who assumes the discursive subject position of police officer, who engages thereby in 'policing', does so in a manner that reflects and embodies what it is to 'be a police officer' (rather than, say, a husband, mother, lover or football player). Insofar as this is the case, then these subjects can be described as being decentred, in the sense of not being entirely in control of their own thoughts. They act and think like a 'police officer' from the moment that they assume or take on the policing discursive subject position (see Conti 2006).

The big question for the social constructionist is how the dominant linguistic regime (legal jargon and categories) in the criminal justice system dismisses particular languages that express a different view and experience of the social world (such as the emotional experiences of rape victims). The 'languaging' of reality is demonstrated in the legitimacy found in the acceptance of certain discursive subject positions (the judge as rational), but not others (the victim as not rational). It is argued that: 'By dismissing these oppositional languages, certain versions of how to think, act, feel and be are indirectly de-valued' (Arrigo & Bernard 1997: 44). The task, therefore, is to expose the different ways in which criminal justice is linguistically structured, and to offer a voice to those who have been silenced by the dominant discourses of the law (Arrigo 2003).

Given the central importance of language, and the study of language, it is understandable that social constructionists tend to reject causal explanations of crime that portray crime as part of a 'grand narrative' (for example, strains, biological factors) (Ferrell 1998). Rather, attention is drawn to how those who control the means of linguistic production also control the prevailing and official definitions of crime. The key questions according to Arrigo & Bernard (1997: 48) are: Who is 'languaged', and whose 'interests are valued and de-valued in the prevailing (or alternative) definitions of crime?' From this perspective, it is clear to see the common ground shared between postmodern criminology and labelling theory.

In another sense, for postmodern criminologists the 'cause' of crime is seen to lie in linguistic domination itself. That is, the linguistic domination varyingly 'criminalises' speech, thought and behaviour that resists, delegitimises or opposes the potency of the dominant discourse. This process, labelled by Bourdieu (1991) as 'symbolic violence', is a silent form of oppression, and one that is largely 'unknowable' to those who experience it, and who, at times, are complicit in its reproduction. For some postmodern critical criminologists, the solution to this dilemma is to develop *replacement discourses* that will neutralise the power of the dominant languages that regulate and discipline the lives of alienated collectivities (especially ethnic minority people, Indigenous people, women, and gay men and lesbians) (Scraton 2009). The emphasis, therefore, is on social inclusiveness, diverse modes of communication and a pluralistic culture (Young 1996). To undercut the dominance of the hegemonic discourses, and to acknowledge the specificity of different 'voices', the main focus for action (if any) is at the local level, and through decentralised means of social control and interaction. For other writers, however, any attempt to establish a replacement discourse is itself a form of linguistic imposition (Lea 1998; Morrison 1994, Butler 1997). For these people, we can deconstruct meaning, but the construction of alternative discursive frames is simply not on the agenda (as to do so implies new conflicts revolving around knowledge, power and resistance).

historical development

Critical criminology is part of an important tradition of struggle and political conflict to win or defend social and human rights within a class-divided, sexist and racist social structure. The structuralist and postmodernist strands of critical criminology share this oppositional stance to what they see as an unjust society.

Ideologically, the structuralist perspective is most closely identified with the socialist tradition and its emphasis on power relations, social conflict and change as a result of contest over resources. The guiding rhetoric is that of social justice and the importance of empowering the less powerful. This strand of critical criminology perspective is relatively new, although as a particular theoretical model within criminology it has continuity with both the Marxist and feminist approaches.

The initial development of critical criminology as a bona fide current within the mainstream of the discipline began with the coming to prominence of labelling theory and the creation of the National Deviancy Conference in 1976. It is with labelling theory and related perspectives (for example, symbolic interactionism, ethnomethodology and phenomenology) that the postmodernist strand of criminology aligns most. Sometimes referred to as 'new deviancy theorists', writers who spoke about crime as a social process challenged the discipline's conventional conceptions of, and means of dealing with, criminal justice issues, and were the forerunners to postmodernist perspectives within criminology (McLaughlin 2010). As we saw in Chapter 5, the combination of labelling and the power to label was seen to have a dramatic impact upon the person so labelled. Importantly, this perspective focused attention upon the institutions and forces of 'social reaction', and how, through professional practices, the process of crime actually occurred.

Left-wing critics of labelling theory argued that analysis of the processes and situations within which labelling took place was not enough. It was also essential to examine the structural relations of power in society, and to view crime in the context of the social relations, state institutions and political economy of advanced capitalism (Hall et al. 1978; Melossi 1985; Scraton & Chadwick 1991). It was at this point that much work was done from a Marxist perspective to identify the causal basis of crime, and to make the link between dominant institutions and ruling-class interests (Taylor et al. 1975). However, there was a tendency at times either to romanticise crime (as acts of rebellion or resistance) or to see crime solely in economic terms (as always reducible to material necessity). Later work was to explore in more detail the specific contexts and lived experiences of people involved with the criminal justice system (Hall & Scraton 1981; Scraton & McCulloch 2009; Carrington & Hogg 2011). These views remain central to structuralist forms of critical criminology.

The issues of racism, sexism and heterosexism were by and large ignored or insufficiently explained in much of the Marxist writing. This was not simply an analytical problem; it was immediately relevant from a political point of view as well (McLauglin 2010). The diminished popularity of academic Marxism in the 1980s demanded a response that could speak to a wider range of people than a more restrictive, narrowly conceived class-based approach. Furthermore, the rise of the New Right in the West, the tearing down of Stalinist institutions in the former communist nations according to capitalist free-market criteria, and the political mobilisation of the new social movements had implications for left criminology generally.

The acknowledgment of differences (in terms of specific needs, experiences and histories) and recognition of commonalities (in relation to marginalisation and criminalisation processes) were translated into a concern with all forms of oppression within the critical criminology framework. Issues of class, gender and ethnicity were seen to be interrelated, and to reflect the general institutional processes of capitalism.

At the other end of the spectrum, there was a need to keep the focus on the actions of those in power, not only in relation to those marginalised in society, but also, more generally, in the area of what has come to be known as white-collar crime. Edwin Sutherland (1983) was the first to coin this phrase in 1939, when he led a blistering attack on the actions of the respectable in society—actions that in a different context would be labelled as criminal and dealt with accordingly. Sutherland saw a need to address the inequalities in treatment of people who engaged in harmful behaviour between those with power and those without power.

This led to a steady stream of research and writing, initially in the USA and then gradually spreading worldwide, on the topic of white-collar crime (Geis & Goff 1983). The philosophical orientation of such work was not, however, Marxist. Rather, it came from Sutherland's own theorising, that of differential association (outlined in Chapter 4). Critical criminology can be seen as continuing the focus on white-collar crime, with a clearer focus on the impact of contemporary capitalism in providing opportunities for corporate criminality, and providing the justification for the lack of enforcement in the area (Alvesalo & Tombs 2002; Tombs & Whyte 2002; Maier-Katkin et al. 2009). As such, it shares a stronger legacy with Marxism than with Sutherland and his contemporaries.

The conceptual legacy of Marxism was to establish a firm interest in examining questions relating to the nature and exercise of state power (Barak 1990; Cohen 1993; Scraton 2007; Coleman et al. 2009). In a similar vein, and reinforced by feminist studies informed by postmodernist theories on the cultural and psychological basis of oppression, research was directed at the role of ideology in shaping lived experience. Racism, sexism and individualism are all bound up with certain ways in which the world is described and categorised—the definition of who is 'dangerous' and who is not, for example. The task of critical criminology was to expose the processes whereby certain groups and categories of people are deemed to be unworthy of social inclusion, and to develop strategies that could open the door to a more humane and equal society.

A foundational figure for both structuralist and postmodernist variants of critical criminology is French intellectual Michel Foucault, whose writings were first translated into English in the 1970s. In particular, critical criminologists integrated Foucault's approach to the history of discipline and punishment, which focused on the micro-processes of authority and the exercise of power (Foucault 1977). He examined the processes of discipline—including the movement away from a focus on disciplining the body to discipline of the mind—and the evolution of the prison, not as products of enlightened thinking, but rather in the light of changes to the technologies of power (Milovanovic 2002; White & Perrone 2005; Scraton & McCulloch 2009). That is, prisons represent more than merely institutions designed to deprive liberty. They also represent a disciplinary tool: a place where useful social qualities can be instilled in a manner comparable to military units. That is, a system of living and working according to strict guidelines that reward achievement and punish nonconformity (de Giorgi 2010). In particular, Foucault highlighted the role of professionals in imposing control over their subjects (prisoners), as in the manner by which psychologists, medical staff and prison officers regulate and constantly control inmates. Constant classification, surveillance and enforced disciplinary training are designed to break the will of offenders and thereby convert them into a 'docile body' easily controlled by those in authority (Fennell 2002).

The system of disciplinary punishments operates effectively as a rational power–knowledge mechanism, which exists within wider strategies of domination and subjectification (de Giorgi 2010). In short, the prison system permits the powerful upper class to continue the subjugation of the lower classes. The mechanism by which this is achieved includes developing special languages or discourses (such as 'delinquents'), which establish the boundaries between the 'normal' and the 'deviant'. For example, to work in prisons or community corrections, one must increasingly be familiar with the language and concepts of the human sciences, in order to distinguish the different types of therapy for different types of clients (Crawley 2004). The prison regime, prison language and prison architecture shape and constrain the inmate in ways that profoundly affect how they speak, move, interact, feel and think—in short, the essence of their social being (Foucault 1977). Converted into social outcasts through a continuous cycle of segregation, supervision and labelling, offenders are rendered both politically and socially harmless. They become the scapegoats for society's crime problem, thus diverting public attention away from crime perpetrated by the powerful.

Perceptions of and causal explanations for crime are thus, from this point of view, actively constructed through the specific interventions of professionals, who evaluate, categorise and repackage the human experience in their own fashion. The significance of the power–knowledge–body analysis of Foucault extends well beyond the prison walls. Indeed, the notion of 'panopticon' (which Bentham (2001 [1789]) originally described as a prison that allowed total surveillance of inmates) is for Foucault a metaphor for the total surveillance that the broader normalising and disciplining forces of society impose on the individual in institutional spheres such as schools, factories, barracks and hospitals. Surveillance is directed at maintaining 'normality' as codified by those in positions of authority; any behaviour outside of defined 'norms' is condemned and punished. How experts construct the social world through their selective discourses has a major bearing on what and who is seen as criminal and/or delinquent.

then & now

critical criminology

It is worth remembering from Chapter 1 that new theories and ideas do not develop in a vacuum, but draw from previous work (or rediscover it anew). Critical criminology, in both its structuralist and postmodernist frames, can be understood in this light. Structuralist criminology shares insights with Marxist criminology (Chapter 6) and forms of feminist criminology (Chapter 7). Postmodernist criminology shares acknowledged links with labelling perspectives (as well as symbolic interactionism and phenomenology), yet it is also possible to see connections with the ideas of Max Weber (Chapters 5 and 6), and his analysis of the way power in society is shaped through ideology and manifest in its institutions. Postmodernist criminology often traces its own roots through philosophy and linguistics rather than sociology. Language is important to both structuralist and postmodernist wings of critical criminology, although the emphasis and type of analysis will vary considerably. Each approach to the 'doing' of critical criminology is likewise increasingly confronted with globalised social processes, institutions and conflicts. Internationalisation—of power, symbols, language, production, consumption, reproduction or risk—means that critical criminology, like all criminological theories, has to continually grapple with issues of scope as well as complexity of analysis.

contemporary examples

Contemporary critical criminology is as much a result of specific cultural and political arrangements, as it is the outcome of theoretical divisions and debates. One effect of the growth and decline of interventionist governments over the last thirty years has been a lasting impact on the 'flavour' of critical criminology in the US, the UK, Canada and Australia. However, according to McLaughlin (2010: 163–6), despite this great variability, five distinct 'theoretical co-ordinates' can be identified from the work of critical criminologists. When viewed through the lens of the 'authoritarian state' thesis (Hall et al. 1978; Poulantzas 1978), the contemporary agenda can be identified by:

1\ complex analyses of the *criminalisation* process, which seek to uncover the ways that the state constrains some behaviour (via criminalisation), while leaving others unregulated (such as state and corporate crime) (Haines 2011; Sutton & Haines 2011)

2\ expanding critiques of criminal *racialisation*, especially in light of increasing state control in relation to terrorism (Jackson et al. 2010; Ross 2010; McCulloch 2010)

3\ uncovering *ideological distortion* by the state and the media, whereby complex theoretical approaches are turned into '"commonsense" crime control ideologies' (McLaughlin 2010: 164)

4\ the use of *abolitionism* as a 'replacement discourse', which problematises the taken-for-granted assumptions about the definition, nature and response to crime, and offers an alternative discourse based on harms, problems, and conflicts (not crimes and criminality) (Scraton & McCulloch 2009)

5\ a commitment to *praxis* (the integration of theory and practice in action), and working towards practical solutions (not just theoretical analyses).

The work of critical criminologists has been instrumental in exposing and illuminating the process of *criminalisation*, especially as it relates to the wide range of issues pertaining to the less powerful groups in society. The victimisation, and empowerment, of such groups as Indigenous people, immigrant communities, refugees, gay men and lesbians and working-class young people have been the subject of probing analysis and insightful discussion (see Brown & Hogg 1992a; Carrington & Hogg 2002; Selke et al. 2002; Walklate 1992, 2009). One feature of this work has been its emphasis on explaining the specific empirical aspects of a particular phenomenon, without attempting to say that 'all crime is the same' or trying to deal with 'crime in general'. Nevertheless, the discussions of specific groups (such as Indigenous people and female prisoners) and particular institutions (especially special police tactical response units and private prisons) are usually framed within a general perspective that views the state and powerful social interests (especially the corporate sector) as problematic.

In addition to criminalisation of the powerless, critical criminology has also been concerned with the harm directly perpetrated by those in positions of power. Studies of white-collar and corporate crime have pointed to the enormity of harm perpetrated in the white-collar sphere. A consistent focus of this research has been to label such acts criminal, and to call for their inclusion as quintessentially criminal acts to be dealt with accordingly (see, for examples, Shover & Wright 2001; Friedrichs 1996; Pearce & Tombs 1990; Tombs & Whyte 2002; Friedrichs 2007). In a similar vein, recent work has attempted to provide more precise, and, from a practical point of view, more operational, concepts of state crime (Barak 1990; Cohen 1993; Tombs & Whyte 2009). Thus, Green and Ward (2000, 2004) propose that the term 'state crime' be restricted to the area of overlap between violations of human rights and state organisational deviance. By using such a definition, they wish to employ a criminological understanding of those acts or omissions that contribute to, or are complicit with, breaches of human rights (Cohen 1993). Such a concept opens the door to investigation of a wide range of social harms, corruptions and violations of rights perpetrated by agencies and officials of the state.

Researchers in the area have also pointed to the way in which the structure of capitalism itself creates opportunities for crimes of the powerful. Large corporations, most notably multinational corporations, are in a position to reap considerable gains from their activities at the expense of both the environment and the weakest in society (Ruggiero & South 2010a). The market power of these large organisations gives them the opportunity to avoid effective enforcement of laws aimed at curbing their power (Barnett 1979; Alvesalo et al. 2006; Tombs & Whyte 2009). Furthermore, it has been argued that law enforcement and criminalisation of these activities may in fact have limited value, because the state has an active interest in maintaining good relations with monopoly capitalists. Other theorists working in this area point to the nature of the dual economy, where the logic of competition pushes smaller, weaker organisations to exploit their workers and spoil the environment. While large organisations have the money to put in place extensive programs aimed at reducing harm, smaller organisations are forced to cut corners to survive (Haines 1997, 2000; Tombs 2008; Tombs & Whyte 2006). The structure of capitalism is thus directly linked to the harm that organisations perpetrate.

Yet another area of recent interest is that of *green criminology* (see White 2003, 2005, 2008b, 2011; Beirne & South 2007; Ruggiero & South 2010a, 2010b). Much of this work has been directed at exposing different instances of substantive environmental injustice and ecological injustice. It has also involved critique of the actions of nation-states and transnational capital for fostering particular types of harm, and for failing to address or regulate harmful activity. Drawing upon a wide range of ideas and empirical materials, criminology that deals with environmental harm has ventured across a range of areas of concern. For example, it has documented the existence of lawbreaking with respect to pollution, disposal of toxic waste and misuse of environmental resources (Pearce & Tombs 1998; White 2009b; Ruggiero & South 2010a). Other work has emphasised the dynamic links between distribution of environmental 'risk' (particularly as these affect poor and minority populations) and the claims of non-human nature to ecological justice (Bullard 1994). It has also considered the specific place of animals in relation to issues of 'rights' and human–non-human relationships on a shared planet (Benton 1998). In general, and given the pressing nature of many environmental issues, many criminologists are now seeing environmental crime and environmental victimisation as areas for concerted analytical and practical attention, which require much more conceptual development and empirical attention (see Williams 1996; Boyd et al. 2002; Lynch & Stretesky 2003; White 2003, 2005, 2008b, 2011).

A second key feature of critical criminology is that it is one of the few perspectives that focus specifically on issues of racism and criminal *racialisation*. New Right criminology tends to attribute 'blame' for crime, and emphasise the 'bad behaviour' of community members, and the 'choices' they make to be the way they are and to do the things they do. Mainstream perspectives—such as labelling, strain and republican theories—have a more explicit concern with issues relating to racism. Here, however, the solution is often seen simply in terms of making criminal justice processes and procedures as fair and unbiased as possible. The idea is that high rates of incarceration and contact involving certain social groups are due mainly to factors—such as 'discrimination' and improper use of discretion—easily remedied by minimalist reform (see Cook & Hudson 1993).

From a critical criminological perspective, the main issue is one of structural inequality. Very often this inequality has been institutionalised—in criminal definitions and criminal justice practices—in a racist fashion (see Cunneen & White 2007; Schissel & Brooks 2002; Ross 2010; Tapia 2011). In such circumstances, insensitive and coercive policing, for instance, cannot be reduced to 'bad attitudes' on the part of the police; it stems from the structural role of the police in regulating the most marginalised sectors of a class-divided society (Hall et al. 2009). These divisions may, in turn, be associated with particular ethnic and 'race' groupings (such as Indigenous people, immigrants and refugees) (see Collins et al. 2000; Poynting et al. 2004; Ross 2010; Asquith & Poynting 2011). Issues of under-policing and over-policing are seen as flowing from broader societal pressures and divisions, which have had a particularly negative impact on Indigenous people and those from ethnic minority communities.

Contemporary Critical criminologists can also be identified by analyses that draw attention to the *ideological distortions* created under the influence of an 'authoritarian state', and moral-panic driven media whose interests are primarily financial (Greer 2010). McLaughlin suggests that consent for an increasingly punitive criminal justice system is manufactured through a 'commonsense' about what is crime, how much crime exists, and the appropriate responses to crime. In his book, *Dude, Where's My Country?*, Michael Moore (2003 cited in DeKeseredy 2011: 67) suggests that this popular understanding of crime is tainted by the 'fear drug', which works through simple repetition that 'bad, scary people are going to kill you, so place all your trust in *us*, your corporate leaders, and we will protect you'. This racialised 'commonsense' is embedded in media representations (both factual and fictive) and is part of a feedback loop between the (corporate) state, the media and the 'public' (see Chibnall 1977; Ericson et al. 1991; Sparks 1992; Eschholz 2002; Ditton et al. 2004; Jefferson 2008; Miller & McMullan 2010; Kohm & Greenhill 2011). Contributions from postmodern critical criminologists have been instrumental in uncovering the complex discourses that combine to create the common 'vision' of crime and criminality (Ferrell et al. 2008). Equally, these theorists have offered alternative visions of what it means to be criminalised and victimised. These writers point to the way postmodernism, like labelling before it, empowers those with little voice (Einstadter & Henry 1995). In this view, reality is always constituted and reconstituted in the present, but according to very specific discourses. Many postmodern critical criminologists are concerned to give a voice to those views that are currently underplayed or ignored; for example, the views of Indigenous people, women, and lesbians and gay men. Meaning is present in everything we do, but it is the task of postmodernism to unpack the complex nature of everyday 'realities', and the discourses of these realities, including those realities concerned with crime and criminality (Young 1996; Greer 2010).

What unifies the many different approaches within the critical criminology perspective is a deep concern with issues of oppression and injustice. These are seen to stem from structural inequalities in resource allocation, decision-making power and control over discourse. Accordingly, institutional reform is not seen as an end in itself, but as part of a more profound transition towards a more equal, fairer society. *Abolitionism* as a *replacement discourse* is one of the strongest themes within critical criminology. 'New penology' is not so much interested in ameliorating the violence and harm of punishment (as is the case for Left Realists), but with offering an alternative frame of reference completely (Scraton & McCulloch 2009; de Giorgi 2010). This new approach to punishment rejects the popular belief that the criminal justice system is the most appropriate place to solve issues relating to the harm of crime (de Haan 1991). And while the abolition of penal punishment is sought, critical criminologists also recognise that this alone will not solve the problems facing contemporary societies (Sim 1994). In fact, the goal of abolitionism is only achievable when the social structure of the society has been transformed. Further, instead of focusing on crime (as a codified given), critical criminologists take the logical step beyond labelling theory, to reject the representational division between criminal harm and all other harm experienced as part of social life. As suggested by McLaughlin (2010: 164), once the nature of 'crime' is no longer taken for granted, these acts 'could be reclassified for what they really are—conflicts, troubles, problems, harms etc.'. This would lead to the replacement of legal definitions such as 'intent' and 'responsibility' with concepts drawn from social definitions such as 'negligence', 'human rights' and 'accidents'. This leads many critical criminologists to adopt a vision of punishment that has more to do with restorative justice and peacekeeping criminology than the punitive, retributive penology that continues to haunt criminology (DeKeseredy 2011).

One of the hallmarks of critical criminology is its commitment to *praxis*. According to McLaughlin (2010), critical criminologists are most commonly associated with direct interventions in various law-and-order and criminal justice debates. Indeed, more than this, one of the main contributions of this strand of criminological activity has been to raise, for public discussion, a series of important social issues. For example, the work of critical criminologists has been crucial to ongoing critiques of the prison system and in the development of 'new penology', which is particularly interested in the developments relating to the consequences and privatisation of punishment (see Moyle 1994; Mathiesen 1990; Christie 1993; Sparks 1995; Carlton 2008). Much of this type of research, scholarship and commentary has been informed by a concern to publicise existing injustices, and potential abuses, of criminal justice institutions (Schissel & Brooks 2002; Carrington & Hogg 2002). More recently, this type of criminological research has been labelled 'public criminology', for its value in contributing to a social agenda on crime and criminality (Loader & Sparks 2010a, 2010b). Often, in praxis, the work of critical criminologists moves beyond the strict confines of the criminal justice system to include a variety of social issues that are thought to be instrumental in experiences of criminalisation (such as work, housing, health and leisure) (Uggen & Inderbitzin 2010).

{from theory to practice: surveillance and social control}

Coleman, R. (2003). 'Images from a Neoliberal City: The State, Surveillance and Social Control', *Critical Criminology*, 12 (1): 21–42.

In this article, Coleman turns his attention away from the conventional task of evaluating surveillance technologies as a means to control crime, to study the ways in which social control is embedded in the adoption and use of these technologies. He additionally seeks to map out the ways in which the agents of contemporary neoliberal states are 'constructing the boundaries and possibilities of the new urban frontier', and how these practices of urban regeneration have considerable consequences for the meanings of public space and the limits of state power.

According to Coleman (2003), the neoliberal state—as represented by both the US and the UK—is distinct from its predecessors in the ways it has outsourced much of its regulatory functions, particularly in terms of the management of safety and disorder. Under the logic of neoliberalism, the state has off-set its capital expenditure and, in many cases, privatised its responsibility for core functions, in order to facilitate the 're-imaging' of the city. This re-imaging necessitates the state entering into partnerships that aim to normalise a social control logic, and to build a consensus (by force or coercion) about weeding out people and practices that risk the growth of the city. For Coleman, the neoliberal state has facilitated the concentration of power and money 'within a small locally powerful and politically inoculated network, which has shaped the urban fabric in its own image' (2003: 25). Central to this powerful network of moral and spatial entrepreneurs is a 'democratic deficit', where unaccountable partnerships between business and state agents/agencies are tasked with regenerating the city, and where the city's residents are unaware and uninvited to voice opposition. To speak out is to speak against growth, regeneration, social control.

Drawing on Sorkin (1992), Coleman argues that contemporary concerns with security, order and policing the urban frontier are driven by three components, each of which is designed to facilitate a 'new city' that is open for business to people 'of the right sort'. First, the new city begins remaking itself into a predictable and known space. Second, security and concerns with safety lead to the adoption of new ways to control and segregate city inhabitants. And third, the new city assumes 'the character of a theme park' and replaces unwanted images of urban decay with a 'spuriously appropriated past' that can be sold as a modern day utopia.

Apart from problems of taste and distinction, Coleman is concerned about this 'new city' and the ways in which the state's partnerships with business and capital have led to the development of crime prevention strategies that aim to control non-criminal behaviour (2003: 27). These techniques of social control have led to the introduction of 'quality of life' and zero tolerance policing 'that has been aimed at groups perceived to demean the urban aesthetic': the unclean, sometimes petty, violators who illegitimately inhabit a sanitized urban aesthetic' (Coleman 2003: 27–8).

The success of urban regeneration in places such as Liverpool (UK) is strongly tied to the adoption of surveillance technologies. According to

Coleman (2003: 30), the 'entrepreneurial roots of camera surveillance provide a clue to the uses of CCTV as a social ordering tool'. CCTV cameras are not directed inside into the businesses and government agencies that propagate the use of this technology; rather, it is the street and, more importantly, street people who are the subjects of this technology. The CCTV images of urban decay therefore reinforce conservative definitions of crime and security, where danger and harm derive from the actions of the powerless. For Coleman, most importantly, CCTV has assisted the neoliberal state to produce knowledge about the 'criminal' that is tendentious and facilitates 'a landscape of denial that is intensifying the criminalisation of poverty' (Coleman 2003: 38).

critique

Critical criminology, since it has much in common with Marxist criminology, shares some of the same problems. In particular, it shares the problem of the definition of crime. Structuralist criminology, like Marxist criminology, defines crime very broadly, in terms of the oppression of a particular group (such as Indigenous people or other minority groups) or class (especially working people) by those with power. In this, it shares a 'human rights' definition of crime, similar to that of some Marxist criminologists (Cohen 1993). The problem with these definitions is how to conceive of differences in the abuse of human rights. For instance, how does one compare discrimination against a person of non-English-speaking background applying for a job to the genocide that occurred in the early 1990s in the former Yugoslavia? As previously discussed, *crime* and *non-crime* are dichotomous categories; they do not lend themselves easily to discerning different gradations of harm. Nevertheless, some writers are now systematically addressing these issues. This is particularly the case with respect to definitions of state and corporate crime, and definitions of environmental harm (see Green & Ward 2000; Hillyard & Tombs 2004, 2007; White 2003, 2005; Haines 2011). It also is apparent in efforts to create more sophisticated accounts of criminal action (including acts of omission) by the state, such as in the development of a model expressing the multidimensional continuum of state crime complicity (Kauzlarich et al. 2003; Scraton 2007; Coleman et al. 2009).

Some Critical criminology, like some Marxist criminology, tends to have a simple view of the nature of power. That is, there is a notion that some people have power (the powerful) and others do not (the powerless); there is no serious attempt to analyse the nature of that power. This criticism has sometimes been directed at structuralist approaches more generally. While acknowledging the need for further analysis of, and sensitivity to, the dynamics of power at a 'micro' as well as 'macro' level, structuralist criminology nonetheless maintains that social power is best understood as being concentrated in particular directions. It is seen to have substantially different effects according to different groups' resources and capacities, and this, in turn, is related to the institutionalised nature of inequality.

Given the critique of 'capitalism' that lies at the base of structuralist criminology, it needs to be able to spell out in more precise terms the nature of this capitalism in the light of processes of internationalisation and globalisation, and how its institutions (such as transnational corporations, nation-states) have an impact on the crime debate (Ericson 2007). Again, many writers are in fact now expanding their analytical horizons with respect to issues of globalisation and social and environmental harms (see Findlay 1999; Haines 2000, 2005; White 2009a, 2009b; McCulloch 2010), and it can be expected that this will be developed further over time. Yet, it is not always clear whether critical criminology is arguing that the basis of all crime is ultimately economic, or rather that the capitalist system merely exacerbates conflict and tension that exist independently from the economic relations inherent within capitalism (Selke et al. 2002). In either case, there is a need to examine the precise way in which capitalism acts to exacerbate tension and both produce and define crime.

Postmodern criminologists do not conceptualise power in the same way as those who adopt a structuralist perspective. Their view tends to draw upon the work of Foucault (1980), who points to the decentralisation of power within modern society; that is, it is not held solely by the state or in one particular class or group of people. Rather, the argument is that power is dispersed throughout society. Furthermore, power is not necessarily seen as always negative, but as a generalised feature of social life. Thus, power, when used to oppress, creates resistance, and this in itself is a source of power. According to Foucault (1977), power can be associated with pleasure as well as repression. It can also flow in more than one direction simultaneously.

Foucault's ideas have been highly influential, but at times they have been oversimplified or distorted in some postmodernist work. For example, postmodern criminology emphasises that language always constitutes, and is constituted by, the relationship between knowledge, power and resistance, and this leads to some logical dilemmas (Russell 1997). For instance, it has been pointed out that: 'If all discourses and definitions are power effects involving repression, then power is ubiquitous. It is everywhere and therefore nowhere' (Lea 1998: 173). If power, and resistance, are always present, then by what criteria are we to discern whether or not any particular social relationship is 'oppressive' or 'liberating' (Ferrell 1998; Arrigo 2003)? Here the notion of a power differential becomes central to conceptual analysis. Major problems arise if crucial qualitative distinctions are not made regarding the relative power differences between different individuals and groups.

Additionally, it has been argued that the rejection of 'grand narratives', including those that provide a normative basis for action (such as 'justice', 'rights' and 'equality'), makes it difficult to provide a rationale or justification for specific types of academic analyses or social action on particular criminal justice issues (Arrigo & Bernard 1997; Milovanovic 2002). Although postmodern criminology can expose the power relations exhibited through the languaging of social reality, big questions remain as to what is to be done with this knowledge, given that values themselves may be seen to be subjective and partial, and thus unsuitable as guides to action (Russell 1997; Loader 1998; Milovanovic 2002).

Another difficulty with the postmodernist approach is that deconstruction as a method of analysis can lead to infinite regress (Lea 1998). That is, if there is no 'objective' world, and there really is no reality outside the dynamics of language, then all knowledge is indeterminate and relative. There is no endpoint to the deconstruction process. This can be extremely confusing as words are further defined and interrogated in terms of other words, and the language of analysis becomes ever more complex and obscure. It can also preclude the necessity or capability to actually act on the understandings we currently have, since these are always changing and are always subject to further deconstruction (Russell 1997; Ferrell 1998). Furthermore, if there is no intrinsic foundation to 'facts' about the social world (because these are socially constructed through language), then what criteria can be invoked to determine whose 'voices' should be heard and which groups to support in our work? If the key criterion is that of looking to those voices that have been 'silenced' by the dominant languages of the law, then it raises the prospect of not only enabling oppressed minorities (such as ethnic minority groups) to resist better, but also, likewise, supporting extreme right-wing nationalist or white supremacist groups (such as neo-Nazis; see Lea 1998). This can only happen, however, if there is no normative basis to the work of the postmodern criminologist. But implicit in a values framework is the idea of some kind of meta-narrative regarding what is deemed to be 'good' and 'right'.

One of the strongest contradictions within both forms of critical criminology is that of crime control. Some replacement discourses offered by critical criminologists view a world without crime control (or, at least, without prisons), and where harm (rather than crime) acts as a frame of reference for social action (not legal action) (de Haan 1991; Pratt 2002). Simultaneously, critical criminologists demand increased crime control for those crimes previously ignored by the criminal justice system (industrial manslaughter, intimate-partner violence, cyber-bullying, environmental vandals). While restorative justice measures are advocated as a technique to reduce the criminalisation of the powerless, at the same time, increased policing and sentencing are proposed for state or corporate criminals. As with feminism more generally, critical criminology is caught between the future imagined, and the present lived; between regulation and deregulation, criminalisation and decriminalisation (Haines 2011).

Despite these weaknesses, critical criminology (both structuralist and postmodernist) has allowed insight into the diversity of groups that are progressively marginalised by contemporary capitalist societies and, further, how the activities of such groups become criminalised in a way that leads to further marginalisation. In doing so, it allows for a number of new voices that have not been previously heard or listened to, such as those of gay men and lesbians, and Indigenous people, and, as such, gives rise to new fields of criminological studies (for example, hate crime).

Critical criminology forces us to confront issues of the social interests in which the state acts. It highlights the potential long-term conflict that can be produced by a state that prioritises the interests of one group of society over and above the interests of other groups. In doing so, it gives advance warning of the likely social impact of the dismantling of the welfare state, of the 'racialisation' of public order policing, and of the social exclusion of people from basic citizenship rights. The result of such trends may be personalised in the form of high suicide rates (affecting the individual), and collective in the form of riots and general social unrest (affecting whole communities, as was the case in the UK in 2011).

{conclusion}

Critical criminology reflects the concerns of many different people in contemporary societies. Generally speaking, it espouses a 'liberation' philosophy that has at its centre emancipatory concerns aimed at allowing all people to participate fully in society, regardless of 'race', ethnicity, sex, class and sexual orientation. Furthermore, it includes among its concerns issues relating to the environment and animal rights. Ultimately, critical criminology views capitalism as essentially hostile to the promotion of human rights and personal empowerment, and seeks alternative social arrangements and philosophies that can result in a more inclusive society.

In many ways, critical criminology represents the cutting edge of socially progressive criminology in the twenty-first century. It represents an amalgamation of concerns and ideas drawn essentially from socialist, radical and postmodern viewpoints, and is an attempt to analyse and develop empowering intervention strategies in a rapidly changing world. As such, it offers a critique of the dynamics of global capitalism, through a mode of investigation that holds the promise of profound social transformation across many domains of social life, including, and especially, that of criminal justice.

{further reading}

Anthony, T. & Cunneen, C. (eds)
(2008). *The Critical Criminology
Companion*, Federation Press,
Sydney.

Arrigo, B. & Bernard, T. (1997).
'Postmodern Criminology in
Relation to Radical and
Conflict Criminology', *Critical
Criminology*, 8 (2): 39-60.

Beirne, P. & South, N. (eds)
(2007). *Issues in Green
Criminology: Confronting Harms
Against Environments, Humanity
and Other Animals*, Willan,
Devon.

Carrington, K. & Hogg, R. (eds)
(2002). *Critical Criminology:
Issues, Debates, Challenges*,
Willan, Devon.

Coleman, R., Sim, J., Tombs, S.
& Whyte, D. (eds) (2009). *State
Power Crime*, SAGE, London.

Cook, D. & Hudson, B. (eds)
(1993). *Racism and Criminology*,
SAGE, London.

Dragiewicz, M. & DeKeseredy, W.S.
(eds) (2011). *Routledge Handbook
of Critical Criminology*,
Routledge, London.

Henry, S. & Milovanovic, D.
(1994). 'The Constitution of
Constitutive Criminology:
A Postmodern Approach to
Criminological Theory', in
D. Nelken (ed.), *The Futures
of Criminology*, SAGE, London.

Lea, J. (1998). 'Criminology
  and Postmodernity', in
  P. Walton & J. Young (eds),
  The New Criminology Revisited,
  Macmillan, London.

McLaughlin, E., Muncie, J.
  & Hughes, G. (eds) (2003).
  *Criminological Perspectives:
  A Reader* (2nd edition), SAGE,
  London.

Schissel, B. & Brooks, C.
  (eds) (2002). *Marginality and
  Condemnation: An Introduction to
  Critical Criminology*, Fernwood,
  Halifax.

Scraton, P. & Chadwick, K.
  (1991). 'The Theoretical and
  Political Priorities of Critical
  Criminology', in K. Stenson &
  D. Cowell (eds), *The Politics
  of Crime Control*, SAGE, London:
  161–85.

Scraton, P. & McCulloch, J.
  (eds) (2009). *The Violence of
  Incarceration*, Routledge, London.

Young, A. (1996). *Imagining
  Crime: Textual Outlaws and
  Criminal Conversations*, SAGE,
  London.

conclu sion

—

As we have seen, the way in which crime is conceived, and thus prevented and controlled, is a matter of considerable dispute. Invariably, the criminological enterprise involves issues of a theoretical, empirical and political nature. The theories and perspectives we have explored in the book focus on different and often quite specific or distinct aspects of criminal activity and behaviour. Thus, for example, some theories have concentrated attention on the individual characteristics or attributes of the offender, others on the processes whereby an action or person comes to be defined as criminal, and still others on the influence of social structure on personal and group behaviour.

The diverse explanations on offer indicate, at least in part, the interdisciplinary nature of criminology. As a field of study, criminology incorporates ideas, methodologies and theoretical contributions from disciplines such as psychology, sociology, political science, history, legal studies and forensic medicine. Different starting points and different conceptual emphases stem from the diversity of academic influences in the field. However, many of the differences within criminology also reflect broader divisions with regard to the level of analysis, and the political perspective.

This is illustrated, for instance, in the debate over whether criminal behaviour is determined or voluntary. At first glance, the debate appears to be fairly straightforward. On the one hand, there are those perspectives, such as the classical and New Right, that portray human activity as entirely voluntary—as simply a matter of individual choice. On the other hand, there are those theories that present the view that behaviour is overwhelmingly determined by factors outside the individual's control, whether these are biological, psychological or social.

—

Within and across this interpretive divide, however, there is considerable variation. For example, the nature, scope and extent of determinism and voluntarism often depend upon the level of analysis. A biological approach may stress individual pathology and the fixed features of an individual's genetic make-up as the reason behind certain behaviours. A strain theorist might look at aspects of social situation, and see behaviour as a result of the combination of opportunities available and immediate learning processes. A Left Realist approach could likewise adopt a situational analysis, but with greater emphasis on social conflict and inequality, and the role of institutions of crime control, such as the police, in fostering or dampening working-class criminality. For the critical criminologist, 'choice' is circumscribed by wider structural processes of marginalisation and criminalisation, or competitive market structures, and criminal activity among both the powerful and the less powerful is seen to reflect the ways in which existing social structures ultimately narrow the scope for the full exercise of human agency.

The complex ways in which the relationship between voluntarism ('free will') and determinism ('fate') is constructed in the criminological field demonstrates the existence of a series of cross-cutting analytical and political differences that transcend strict discipline boundaries. These differences can be further highlighted by considering the underlying assumptions of criminological theory, as indicated in broad political orientation, and 'popular' conceptions of criminality and the criminal justice system. Chart 12.1 outlines how the diverse propensities (or likelihoods), motivations (or drives) and circumstances (or opportunities) underpinning criminality might be conceived according to varying political and analytical focus. The chart provides a rough guide to the different outlooks of the conservative, liberal and radical commentator, and also shows the possible divisions or emphases within each broad political persuasion.

Our presentation of 'needs', 'deeds' and 'greeds' merely indicates general tendencies and, as such, is intended to provide only a schematic conceptual map of the underlying assumptions. Nevertheless, it is useful as an analytical backdrop upon which can be placed most of the theories and perspectives discussed in this book. It is clear, however, that particular theories can encompass more than one frame of reference and are used to develop policies with diverse political starting points. The relevance of studying criminological theory lies precisely in the way it informs and assists us in understanding the actual source of and underlying rationale underpinning specific arguments and the ideas of contemporary debates over crime.

chart 12.1 | underlying assumptions of criminological theory

different reform agendas

needs	deeds	greeds
conservative political perspective		
focus on the individual's pathology and need to conform with socially accepted norms and mores. Emphasis on the need to counsel or treat the individual, which may require indeterminate sentencing.	law and order. Focus on what the individual has done. The extent of harm to the status quo dictates the extent of punishment. Key issues are retribution, punishment and deterrence.	motivation to offend, steal or rob is greed. Focus is on the greed of the 'street criminal', who shirks responsibility to get work and earn money respectably. A focus on 'moral training' and reaffirmation of conservative values.
liberal political perspective		
focus on the needs of both the victim and the offender. Needs tempered by an understanding of social conditions that influence behaviour. Emphasis on restorative justice.	civil libertarian. Focus on individual rights, determinate sentencing and due process. Notion of equality and proportionality. All should have access to equal justice, and the like offences should be treated in like manner.	greed is more likely to be associated with those who take 'more than their fair share' from a democratic society. Discussion of white-collar crime relevant here, with a focus on regulation and moral persuasion.
radical political perspective		
focus on the distortion of needs due to the capitalist system. This system places a priority on competition and the 'market'. The result is an emphasis on private profit, rather than social need, which dictates the priorities of the state.	focus on the deeds of the system, in terms of systematic bias against certain classes or ethnic groups. The degree of harm perpetrated by white-collar crime is juxtaposed against the harm perpetrated by street crime.	greed is associated with structural competitive pressures, and the widening gap between rich and poor within society. A focus on redistribution of societal resources and radical democracy.

We began the book by stating that the relationship between crime and criminology is always reflected in, and reflective of, particular conceptions of society. Each theory or perspective embodies particular values regarding 'what is' the nature of present society, and 'what ought to be' the best way to deal with social issues such as crime.

In the twenty-first century, the debates over crime and criminality look set to intensify as rapid social change continues to transform traditional social, economic and political relationships. Around the world, great upheavals are taking place, and more often than not these are associated with increasing social polarisation. As part of this change, and in this context, 'law-and-order' debates are now constantly at the centre of electoral politics and are standard fare for infotainment and 'serious media' alike.

In the light of current public perceptions about the 'crime threat'— and general unease about the future of jobs, the environment, peace and respect for human rights—it is more essential than ever to think critically about the nature of crime, how it occurs, who it affects, and what can be done to prevent or control it.

It is our hope that this book will reinforce the fact that there are indeed alternative ways to conceptualise these issues, just as there are various options we can take to deal with them at a practical level. The doing of criminological theory, research and practical intervention is always at one and the same time a statement about the kind of world each of us would like to see, and a response to the world of which we are an integral part.

The key questions that we feel are important for criminologists are:

– *What kind of 'work' should we be doing, and why?* This refers to the means and ends of intellectual production, and raises issues concerning the social implications of our practice, including the practice of 'public criminology'.

– *What kind of society do we want, and why?* This implies that, in doing what we do, there is, or ought to be, a vision of a good society towards which we can direct our efforts.

– *How do we distinguish between 'good' and 'bad' (or 'right' and 'wrong'), and why?* This is basically a question of the normative or value basis of our work.

In an era where research income strongly influences universities' business models and academics are required to work collaboratively with criminal justice partners, contemporary criminologists must also balance the incongruities that may arise between their independent research and the research undertaken for 'clients' or 'linkage' partners (White 2002c; Walters 2009). Writing for the research audience—whether this is a community organisation whose objectives complement the researcher's or a criminal justice agency that requires policy-driven outputs—shapes and influences the selection of theoretical and methodological approaches adopted. It is our belief that attempting to answer these kinds of questions is what makes the criminological endeavour meaningful, both from a personal perspective and from a societal point of view.

The uncertainties of the world we presently inhabit are mirrored in the limitations and uncertainties of contemporary criminological theory. In the end, each theory only fully makes sense when set within an appropriate societal context and values framework. The crucial challenge for the reader, therefore, is to critically question and evaluate the ethical and explanatory basis of each theory or perspective. In so doing, it is our hope that we will be better able to clarify where we stand in relation to the great issues of the day, and to determine what our specific responsibilities and interests are in building a safer, more secure and healthier future, one in which social harms such as crime are minimised.

{references}

Acorn, A. (2004). *Compulsory Compassion: A Critique of Restorative Justice*, University of British Colombia Press, Vancouver.

Agnew, R. (1992). 'Foundation for a General Strain Theory of Crime and Delinquency', *Criminology*, 30: 47–87.

Agnew, R. (2002). 'Experienced, Vicarious, and Anticipated Strain: An Exploratory Study Focussing on Physical Victimisation and Delinquency', *Justice Quarterly*, 19: 603–32.

Agnew, R. (2005). *Juvenile Delinquency: Causes and Control*, Roxbury, Los Angeles, CA.

Agnew, R. (2006a). 'General Strain Theory: Current Status and Directions for Further Research', in F.T. Cullen, J.P. Wright & K.R. Blevins (eds), *Taking Stock: The Status of Criminological Theory, Advances in Criminological Theory* (Vol. 15), Transaction Publishers, New Brunswick, NJ: 101–23.

Agnew, R. (2006b). *Pressured into Crime: An Overview of General Strain Theory*, Roxbury, Los Angeles, CA.

Agnew, R. (2010). 'A General Strain Theory of Terrorism', *Theoretical Criminology*, 14 (2): 131–53.

Agnew, R. (2011). 'Crime and Time: The Patterning of Causal Variables', *Theoretical Criminology*, 15 (2): 115–39.

Agnew, R. & Brezina, T. (2010). 'Strain Theories', in E. McLaughlin & T. Newburn (eds), *The SAGE Handbook of Criminological Theory*, SAGE, London: 96–113.

Akers, R.L. (1990). 'Rational Choice, Deterrence, and Social Learning Theory: The Path Not Taken', *Journal of Criminal Law and Criminology*. 81 (3): 653–76.

Akers, R.L. (1991). 'Self-control as a General Theory of Crime', *Journal of Quantitative Criminology*, 7 (2): 201–11.

Akers, R.L. (1997). *Criminological Theories: Introduction and Evaluation*, Roxbury Publishing, Los Angeles, CA.

Alder, C. (1985). 'Theories of Female Delinquency', in A. Borowski & J. Murray (eds), *Juvenile Delinquency in Australia*, Methuen, North Ryde.

Alder, C. (1991). 'Explaining Violence: Socioeconomics and Masculinity', in D. Chappell, P. Grabosky & H. Strang (eds), *Australian Violence: Contemporary Perspectives*, Australian Institute of Criminology, Canberra.

Alder, C. (1994). 'Women and the Criminal Justice System', in D. Chappell & P. Wilson (eds), *The Australian Criminal Justice System: The Mid-1990s*, Butterworth, Sydney.

Alder, C. & Wundersitz, J. (eds) (1994). *Family Conferencing and Juvenile Justice*, Australian Institute of Criminology, Canberra.

Alexander, J. & Smith, P. (2005). 'Introduction', in J. Alexander & P. Smith (eds), *The Cambridge Companion to Durkheim*, Cambridge University Press, Cambridge.

Allen, H. (1987). 'Rendering Them Harmless: The Professional Portrayal of Women Charged with Violent Crimes', in P. Carlen and A. Worrall (eds), *Gender, Crime and Justice*, Open University Press, Milton Keynes: 81-94.

Allen, J. (1990). '"The Wild Ones": The Disavowal of Men in Criminology', in R. Graycar (ed.), *Dissenting Opinions*, Allen & Unwin, Sydney.

Alvesalo, A. & Tombs, S. (2002). 'Working For Criminalization Of Economic Offending: Contradictions For Critical Criminology?', *Critical Criminology*, 11 (1): 21-40.

Alvesalo, A., Tombs, S., Virta, E. & Whyte, D. (2006). 'Re-Imagining Crime Prevention: Controlling Corporate Crime?', *Crime, Law and Social Change*, 45 (1): 1-25.

Anderson, E. (1999). *Code of the Street: Decency, Violence and the Moral Life of the Inner City*, W.W. Norton, New York.

Anderson, G. (2007). *Biological Influences on Criminal Behavior*, Simon Fraser University Publications/CRC Press, Boca Raton, FL.

Anthony, T. & Cunneen, C. (eds) (2008). *The Critical Criminology Companion*, Federation Press, Sydney.

Antonaccio, O. & Tittle, C. (2007). 'A Cross-National Test of Bonger's Theory of Criminality and Economic Conditions', *Criminology*, 45 (4): 925-58.

Appignanesi, L. (2008). *Mad, Bad and Sad: A History of Women and the Mind Doctors from 1800 to the Present*, Virago, New York.

Arrigo, B. & Bernard, T. (1997). 'Postmodern Criminology in Relation to Radical and Conflict Criminology', *Critical Criminology*, 8 (2): 39-60.

Arrigo, B.A. (2003). 'Postmodern Justice and Critical Criminology', in M.D. Schwartz & S.E. Hatty (eds), *Controversies in Critical Criminology*, Anderson Publishing, Cincinnati, OH.

Arsovka, J., Valinas, M. & Vanpauwen, K. (2008). 'From Micro to Macro, From Individual to State: Restorative Justice and Multi-Level Diplomacy in Divided Societies', in I. Aertsen, J. Arsovska, H-C. Rohen, M. Valinas & K. Vanspauwen (eds), *Restoring Justice after Large-scale Violent Conflicts: Kosovo, DR Congo and the Israeli-Palestinian Case*, Willan, Cullompton: 444-60.

Ashworth, A. (2002). 'Responsibilities, Rights, and Restorative Justice', *British Journal of Criminology*, 42: 578-95.

Asquith, N.L. (2007). 'Speech Act Theory, Maledictive Force and the Adjudication of Vilification in Australia', in J. Ensor, I. Polak & P. van der Merwe (eds) *New Talents 21C: Other Contact Zones*, Network Books, Perth: 179-88.

Asquith, N.L. (2008). *The Text and Context of Malediction: A Study of Antisemitic and Heterosexist Hate Violence*, VDM Verlag, Saarbrücken.

Asquith, N.L. (2010). 'Verbal and Textual Hostility in Context', in N. Chakraborti (ed.), *Hate Crime: Concepts, Policy, Future Directions*, Willan, Cullompton: 99-123.

Asquith, N.L. & Poynting, S. (2011). 'Anti-Cosmopolitanism and "Ethnic Cleansing" at Cronulla', in K. Jacobs & J. Malpas (eds), *Between the Outback and the Sea: Cosmopolitanism and Anti-Cosmopolitanism in Contemporary Australia*. Perth: UWA Press, 96-122.

Baker, A.B., Tuvblad, C. & Raine, A. (2010). 'Genetics and Crime', in E. McLaughlin & T. Newburn (eds), *The SAGE Handbook of Criminological Theory*, SAGE, London.

Barak, G. (1990). 'Crime, Criminology and Human Rights: Towards an Understanding of State Criminality', *The Journal of Human Justice*, 2 (1): 11-28.

Barak, G. (2003). 'Revisionist History, Visionary Criminology, and Needs-Based Justice', Contemporary Justice Review, 6 (December): 217-25.

Barlow, H. (1993). *Introduction to Criminology*, Harper Collins, New York.

Barnett, H. (1979). 'Wealth, Crime and Capital Accumulation', *Contemporary Crises*, 3: 173-86.

Bartels, L. (2010). *Indigenous Women's Offending Patterns: A Literature Review*, Australian Institute of Criminology, Canberra.

Bartol, C.R. & Bartol, A.M. (2005). *Criminal Behavior: A Psychosocial Approach* (7th edition), Pearson Prentice Hall, USR, NJ.

Bauman, Z. (2005). 'Durkheim's Society Revisited', in J. Alexander & P. Smith (eds), *The Cambridge Companion to Durkheim*, Cambridge University Press, Cambridge: 360-82.

Bazemore, G. (1991). 'Beyond Punishment, Surveillance and Traditional Treatment: Themes for a New Mission in US Juvenile Justice', in J. Hackler (ed.), *Official Responses to Problem Juveniles: Some International Reflections*, International Institute for the Sociology of Law, Onati.

Bazemore, G. (1997). 'The "Community" in Community Justice: Issues, Themes, and Questions for the New Neighbourhood Sanctioning Models', *The Justice System Journal*, 19 (2): 193-227.

Bazemore, G. (1998). 'Restorative Justice and Earned Redemption', *American Behavioral Scientist*, 41 (6): 768-813.

Bazemore, G. & Walgrave, L. (eds) (1999). *Restorative Juvenile Justice: Repairing the Harm of Youth Crime*, Criminal Justice Press, Monsey, NY.

Beccaria, C. (2009 [1767]). *An Essay On Crimes and Punishments* (5th edition) (trans. P. Marongui, C. Beccaria & G.R. Newman), Transaction Publishers, New Brunswick, NJ.

Beck, U. (1992). *Risk Society: Toward a New Modernity*, SAGE, London.

Beck, U. & Beck-Gernsheim, E. (2002). *Individualization: Institutionalized Individualism and its Social and Political Consequences*, SAGE, London.

Becker, H. (1963). *Outsiders: Studies in the Sociology of Deviance*, Free Press, New York.

Becker, S. & McCorkel, J.A. (2011). 'The Gender of Criminal Opportunity: The Impact of Male Co-offenders on Women's Crime', *Feminist Criminology*, 6 (2): 79–110.

Beirne, P. (1993). *Criminology: Essays on the Rise of 'Homo Criminalis'*, State University of New York Press, Albany, NY.

Beirne, P. & South, N. (eds) (2007). *Issues in Green Criminology: Confronting Harms against Environments, Humanity and Other Animals*, Willan, Devon.

Benhabib, S., Butler, J., Cornell, D. & Fraser, N. (eds) (1995). *Feminist Contentions—A Philosophical Exchange*, Routledge, New York and London.

Bennett, C. (2006). 'Taking the Sincerity Out of Saying Sorry: Restorative Justice as Ritual', *Journal of Applied Philosophy*, 23 (2): 127–43.

Bentham, J. (2001 [1789]). *Selected Writings on Utilitarianism: An Introduction to the Principles of Morals and Legislation*, Wordsworth Editions Ltd, Hertfordshire, UK.

Benton, T. (1998). 'Rights and Justice on a Shared Planet: More Rights or New Relations?', *Theoretical Criminology*, 2 (2): 149–75.

Berard, T. J. (2003). 'Ethnomethodology as Radical Sociology: An Expansive Appreciation of Melvin Pollner's "Constitutive and Mundane Versions of Labeling Theory"', *Human Studies*, 26 (4): 431–48.

Berger, P. & Luckmann, T. (1971). *The Social Construction of Reality*, Allen Lane, London.

Bichler, G., Christie-Merrall, J. & Sechrest, D. (2011). 'Examining Juvenile Delinquency within Activity Space: Building a Context for Offender Travel Patterns', *Journal of Research in Crime & Delinquency*, 40: 472–506.

Bilchick, S. (1998). *Guide for Implementing the Balanced and Restorative Justice Model*, Office of Juvenile Justice and Delinquency Prevention, Washington, DC.

Bonger, W. (1916). *Criminality and Economic Conditions*, Little, Brown, Boston.

Bottomley, S., Gunningham, N. & Parker, S. (1991). *Law in Context*, Federation Press, Sydney.

Bottoms, A. & Wiles, P. (1997). 'Environmental Criminology', in M. Maguire, R. Morgan & R. Reiner (eds), *The Oxford Handbook of Criminology* (2nd edition), Clarendon Press, Oxford.

Bottoms, A.E. (2007). 'Place, Space, Crime and Disorder', in M. Maguire, R. Morgan & R. Reiner (eds), *The Oxford Handbook of Criminology*, Oxford University Press, Oxford, UK: 528-74.

Bouffard, J., Exum, M.L. & Paternoster, R. (2000). 'Whither the Beast? The Role of Emotions in Rational Choice Theory of Crime', in S. Simpson & R. Agnew (eds), *Of Crime and Criminality: The Use of Theory in Everyday Life*, Pine Forge Press, Thousand Oaks, CA: 159-78.

Bourdieu, P. (1991) *Language and Symbolic Power* (trans. G. Raymond & M. Adamson), Cambridge, Polity Press.

Bowie, V. (2002). *Workplace Violence*, Workcover, Sydney.

Boyd, S., Chunn, D. & Menzies, R. (eds) (2002). *Toxic Criminology: Environment, Law and the State in Canada*, Fernwood, Halifax.

Braithwaite, J. (1989). *Crime, Shame and Reintegration*, Cambridge University Press, Cambridge.

Braithwaite, J. (1991). 'Poverty, Power, White-Collar Crime and the Paradoxes of Criminological Theory', *Australian and New Zealand Journal of Criminology*, 24 (1): 40-58.

Braithwaite, J. (1992). 'Reducing the Crime Problem: A Not So Dismal Criminology: The John Barry Memorial Lecture', *Australian and New Zealand Journal of Criminology*, 25 (1): 1-10.

Braithwaite, J. (1995a). 'Reintegrative Shaming, Republicanism and Policy', in H. Barlow (ed.), *Criminology and Public Policy: Putting Theory to Work*, Westview Press, Boulder.

Braithwaite, J. (1995b). 'Corporate Crime and Republican Criminological Praxis', in F. Pearce & L. Snider (eds), *Corporate Crime: Contemporary Debates*, University of Toronto Press, Toronto: 48-71.

Braithwaite, J. (2000). 'Republican Theory and Crime Control', in K. Bussman & S. Karstedt (eds), *Social Dynamics of Crime and Control: New Theories for a World in Transition*, Hart Publishing, Oxford.

Braithwaite, J. (2002). *Restorative Justice and Responsive Regulation*, Oxford University Press, New York.

Braithwaite, J. (2004). 'Families and the Republic', *Journal of Sociology and Social Welfare*, XXXI (1): 199-215.

Braithwaite, J. & Pettit, P. (1990). *Not Just Deserts: A Republican Theory of Criminal Justice*, Clarendon Press, Oxford.

Braithwaite, J. & Pettit, P. (1994). 'Republican Criminology and Victim Advocacy', *Law & Society Review*, 28 (4): 765-76.

Brake, M. (1985). *Comparative Youth Culture*, Routledge & Kegan Paul, London.

Brantingham, P.J. & Faust, F.L. (1976). 'A Conceptual Model of Crime Prevention', *Crime and Delinquency*, 22: 284-96.

Brill, H. (1982). 'Auto Theft and the Role of Big Business', *Crime and Social Justice*, 18: 62-8.

Brown, C. (1979). *Understanding Society: An Introduction to Sociological Theory*, John Murray, London.

Brown, D. (2002). 'The Politics of Law and Order', *Law Society Journal*, 40 (9): 64-72.

Brown, D. (2008). 'Giving Voice: The Prisoner and Discursive Citizenship', in T. Anthony & C. Cunneen (eds), *The Critical Criminology Companion*, Hawkins Press, Sydney: 228-39.

Brown, D. (2010). 'The Limited Benefit of Imprisonment in Controlling Crime', *Current Issues in Criminal Justice*, 22 (1): 461-72.

Brown, D. & Hogg, R. (1992a). 'Essentialism, Radical Criminology and Left Realism', *Australian and New Zealand Journal of Criminology*, 25 (3): 195-230.

Brown, D & Hogg, R. (1992b). 'Law and Order Politics', in R. Matthews & J. Young (eds), *Issues in Realist Criminology*, SAGE, London.

Brown, D. & Wilkie, M. (eds) (2002). *Prisoners as Citizens*, The Federation Press, Sydney.

Buchanan, C. & Hartley, P. (1992). *Criminal Choice: The Economic Theory of Crime and Its Implications for Crime Control*, Centre for Independent Studies, Sydney.

Budd, T. (1999). *Violence at Work: Findings from the British Crime Survey*, Home Office/Health and Safety Executive, London.

Bullard, R. (1994). *Unequal Protection: Environmental Justice and Communities of Color*, Sierra Club Books, San Francisco.

Burgess-Proctor, A. (2006). 'Intersections of Race, Class, Gender, and Crime: Future Directions for Feminist Criminology', *Feminist Criminology*, 1 (1): 27-47.

Burman, M. (2009). 'Evidencing Sexual Assault: Women in the Witness Box', *Probation Journal*, 56 (4): 379-98.

Burnett, J. (2009). 'Racism and the State: Authoritarianism and

Coercion', in R. Coleman, J. Sim, S. Tombs & D. Whyte (eds), *State Power Crime*, SAGE, London: 49–61.

Burney, E. (2005). *Making People Behave: Anti-Social Behaviour, Politics and Policy*, Willan, Devon.

Butler, J.P. (1990). *Gender Trouble: Feminism and the Subversion of Identity*, Routledge, New York.

Butler, J.P. (1997). Excitable Speech: A Politics of the Performative, Routledge, New York.

Butler, J.P. (1998). 'Merely Cultural', *New Left Review*, 227: 33–44.

Calhoun, A. and Pelech, W. (2010). 'Responding to Young People Responsible for Harm: A Comparative Study of Restorative and Conventional Approaches', *Contemporary Justice Review*, 13 (3): 287–306.

Carlen, P. (1992). 'Criminal Women, and Criminal Justice: The Limits to and Potential of, Feminist and Left Realist Perspectives', in R. Matthews & J. Young (eds), *Issues in Realist Criminology*, SAGE, London: 51–69.

Carlsmith, K.M. & Darley, J.M. (2002). 'Why Do We Punish? Deterrence and Just Deserts as Motives for Punishment', *Journal of Personality and Social Psychology*, 83 (2): 284–99.

Carlton, B. (2008). 'Isolation as Counter-Insurgency: Supermax Prisons and the War on Terror', in C. Cunneen & M. Salter (eds), *Australian & New Zealand Critical Criminology Conference Proceedings*, 19–20 June, Sydney, Australia: 77–90.

Carrington, K. (1993). *Offending Girls*, Allen & Unwin, Sydney.

Carrington, K. (1994). 'Postmodernism and Feminist Criminologies: Disconnecting Discourses', *International Journal of the Sociology of Law*, 22 (3): 261–77.

Carrington, K. & Hogg, R. (eds) (2002). *Critical Criminology: Issues, Debates, Challenges*, Willan, Devon.

Carrington, K. & Hogg, R. (2011). 'History of Critical Criminology in Australia', in M. Dragiewicz & W.S. DeKeseredy (eds), *Routledge Handbook of Critical Criminology*, Routledge, London: 46–60.

Carrington, K. & Periera, M. (2009). *Offending Youth: Sex, Crime and Justice*, Federation Press, Annandale, NSW.

Carson, W. G. (Kit) (1979). 'The Conventionalization of Early Factory Crime', *International Journal of the Sociology of Law*, 7: 37–60.

Catalano, R. & Hawkins, J. (1996). 'The Social Development Model: A Theory of Antisocial Behavior', in J. Hawkins (ed.), *Delinquency and Crime: Current Theories*,

Cambridge University Press, Cambridge.

Chambliss, W.J. (1973). 'Elites and the Creation of Criminal Law', in W. Chambliss (ed.), *Sociological Readings in the Conflict Perspective*, Addison-Wesley, Reading, MA: 430–44.

Chambliss, W. (1975a). 'A Sociological Analysis of the Law of Vagrancy', in W. Carson & P. Wiles (eds), *The Sociology of Crime and Delinquency in Britain, Vol. 1*, Martin Robertson, Oxford.

Chambliss, W. (1975b). 'The Political Economy of Crime: A Comparative Study of Nigeria and USA', in I. Taylor, P. Walton & J. Young (eds), *Critical Criminology*, Routledge & Kegan Paul, London.

Chambliss, W.J. (1975c). 'Toward a Political Economy of Crime', *Theory and Society*, 2 (2): 149–70.

Chambliss, W.J. (1978). 'You Can Get Anything You Want if You've Got the Bread', in *On the Take: Petty Crooks to Presidents*, Indiana University Press, Bloomington, IN: 74–82.

Chambliss, W. & Mankoff, M. (1976). *Whose Law, What Order? A Conflict Approach to Criminology*, John Wiley & Sons, Toronto.

Chambliss, W.J. & Seidman, R. (1971). *Law, Order, and Power*, Addison-Wesley, Reading, MA.

Chan, J., Doran, S. & Marel, C. (2010). 'Doing and Undoing

Gender in Policing', *Theoretical Criminology*, 14 (4): 425–46.

Chesney-Lind, M. (1974). 'Juvenile Delinquency and the Sexualisation of Female Crime', *Psychology Today*, July: 4–7.

Chesney-Lind, M. (2006). 'Patriarchy, Crime and Justice: Feminist Criminology in an Era of Backlash', *Feminist Criminology*, 1 (1): 6–26.

Chesney-Lind, M. (2010). 'Jailing "Bad" Girls: Girls' Violence and Trends in Female Incarceration', in M. Chesney-Lind & N. Jones (eds), *Fighting for Girls: New Perspectives on Gender and Violence*, State University of New York Press, Albany, NY: 57–82.

Chesney-Lind, M. & Shelden, R. (1992). *Girls, Delinquency and Juvenile Justice*, Brooks/Cole, California.

Chibnall, S. (1977). *Law and Order News: An Analysis of Crime Reporting in the British Press*, Tavistock, London.

Christie, N. (1993). *Crime Control as Industry: Towards Gulags Western Style?*, Routledge, London.

Cicourel, A. (1976). *The Social Organisation of Juvenile Justice*, Heinemann, London.

Cladis, M.S. (2005). 'Beyond Solidarity? Durkheim and Twenty-First Century Democracy in a Global Age', in J. Alexander & P. Smith (eds), *The Cambridge*

Companion to Durkheim, Cambridge University Press, Cambridge: 383–409.

Clarke, J., Hall, S., Jefferson, T. & Roberts, B. (1976). 'Subcultures, Cultures and Class: A Theoretical Overview', in S. Hall & T. Jefferson (eds), *Resistance Through Rituals: Youth Subcultures in Post-War Britain*, Hutchinson, London.

Clarke, R.V. (1980). 'Situational Crime Prevention; Theory and Practice', *British Journal of Criminology*, 20: 136–47.

Clarke, R.V. & Felson, M. (eds) (1993). *Routine Activity and Rational Choice (Advances in Criminological Theory, Volume 5)*, Transaction Publishers, New Brunswick, NJ.

Clarkson, C. (2008). 'Drawing the Line: Justice and the Art of Reconciliation', in F. Du Bois & A. Du Bois-Pedain (eds), *Justice and Reconciliation in Post-Apartheid South Africa*, Cambridge University Press, Cambridge, UK: 267–88.

Cloward, R. & Ohlin, L. (1960). *Delinquency and Opportunity: A Theory of Delinquent Gangs*, Free Press, Chicago.

Cohen, A. (1955). *Delinquent Boys: The Culture of the Gang*, Free Press, Chicago.

Cohen, L. & Felson, R.V. (1979). 'Social Change and Crime Rate Trends: A Routine Activity Approach', *American Sociological Review*, 44 (4): 588–608.

Cohen, S. (1967). 'Mods, Rockers and the Rest: Community Reactions to Juvenile Delinquency', *The Howard Journal*, 12: 121–30.

Cohen, S. (1972). *Folk Devils and Moral Panics*, Paladin, London.

Cohen, S. (1985). *Visions of Social Control*, Polity, Cambridge.

Cohen, S. (1988). *Against Criminology*, Transaction, New Brunswick.

Cohen, S. (1993). 'Human Rights and Crimes of the State: The Culture of Denial', *Australian and New Zealand Journal of Criminology*, 26 (2): 97–115.

Cohen, S. (2002). *Folk Devils and Moral Panics* (3rd edition), Routledge, London.

Cohen, S. & Young, J. (2004). 'Comments on Simon Cottee's "Folk Devils and Moral Panics: 'Left Idealism' Reconsidered"', *Theoretical Criminology*, 8 (1): 93–7.

Coleman, R. (2003). 'Images from a Neoliberal City: The State, Surveillance and Social Control', *Critical Criminology*, 12 (1): 21–42.

Coleman, R., Sim, J., Tombs, S. & Whyte, D. (2009). 'Introduction: State, Power, Crime', in R. Coleman, J. Sim, S. Tombs & D. Whyte (eds), *State Power Crime*, SAGE, London: 1–19.

Collins, J., Noble, G., Poynting, S. & Tabar, P. (2000). *Kebabs, Kids, Cops and Crime: Youth, Ethnicity and Crime*, Pluto Press, Sydney.

Colvin, M. & Pauly, J. (1983). 'A Critique of Criminology: Toward an Integrated Structural-Marxist Theory of Delinquency', *American Journal of Sociology*, 89 (3): 513–51.

Connell, R.W. (2000). *The Men and the Boys*, Allen & Unwin, Sydney.

Connell, R.W. (2002). 'On Hegemonic Masculinity and Violence: Response to Jefferson and Hall', *Theoretical Criminology*, 6 (1): 89–99.

Connell, R.W. (2005). *Masculinities* (2nd edition), University of California Press, California.

Conti, N. (2006). 'Role Call: Preprofessional Socialization into Police Culture', *Policing and Society*, 16 (3): 221–42.

Cook, D. & Hudson, B. (eds) (1993). *Racism and Criminology*, SAGE, London.

Cordella, P. & Siegel, L. (eds) (1996). *Readings in Contemporary Criminological Theory*, Northeastern University Press, Boston.

Cornforth, M. (1987). *Historical Materialism* (vol. 2 of *Dialectical Materialism: An Introduction*), Lawrence & Wishart, London.

Cornish, D.B. (1993). 'Theories of Action in Criminology: Learning Theory and Rational Choice Approaches', in R.V.G. Clarke & M. Felson (eds), *Routine Activity and Rational Choice (Advances in Criminological Theory, Volume 5)*, Transaction Publishers, New Brunswick, NJ: 351–82.

Cornish, D.B. & Clarke, R.V.G. (eds) (1986). *The Reasoning Criminal—Rational Choice Perspectives on Offending*, Springer-Verlag, Secaucus, NJ.

Coser, L. (1977). *Masters of Sociological Thought: Ideas in Historical and Social Context*, Harcourt Brace Jovanovich, New York.

Cottee, S. (2002). 'Folk Devils and Moral Panics: "Left Idealism" Reconsidered', *Theoretical Criminology*, 6 (4): 387–410.

Crawley, E. (2004). *Doing Prison Work: The Public & Private Lives of Prison Officers*, Willan, Cullompton.

Cullen, F.T., Wright, J.P. & Blevins, K.R. (eds) (2009). *Taking Stock: The Status of Criminological Theory*, Transaction Publishers, New Brusnwick, NJ.

Cunneen, C. (2008). 'Exploring the Relationship between Reparations, the Gross Violation of Human Rights, and Restorative Justice', in D. Sullivan & L. Tifft (eds),

Handbook of Restorative Justice:
A Global Perspective, Routledge,
Abingdon, UK: 355–68.

Cunneen, C. & White, R. (1995).
Juvenile Justice: An Australian
Perspective, Oxford University
Press, Melbourne.

Cunneen, C. & White, R. (2007).
Juvenile Justice: Youth and Crime
in Australia (3rd edition), Oxford
University Press, Melbourne.

Cunneen, C. & White, R. (2011).
Juvenile Justice: Youth and Crime
in Australia (4th edition), Oxford
University Press, Melbourne.

Daly, K. (1997). 'Different Ways
of Conceptualizing Sex/Gender
in Feminist Theory and Their
Implications for Criminology',
Theoretical Criminology, 1 (1),
25–51.

Daly, K. (2003). 'Mind the Gap:
Restorative Justice in Theory and
Practice', in A. von Hirsch,
J. Roberts, A.E. Bottoms, K. Roach
& M. Schiff (eds), Restorative
Justice and Criminal Justice:
Competing or Reconcilable
Paradigms?, Hart Publishing,
Oxford, UK: 219–36.

Daly, K. (2006). 'Restorative
Justice and Sexual Assault:
An Archival Study of Court
and Conference Cases', British
Journal of Criminology, 46 (2):
334–56.

Daly, K. (2010). 'Feminist
Perspectives in Criminology:
A Review with Gen Y in Mind',
in E. McLaughlin & T. Newburn
(eds), The SAGE Handbook of

Criminological Theory, SAGE,
London: 225–46.

Daly, K. & Chesney-Lind, M. (1988).
'Feminism and Criminology',
Justice Quarterly, 5 (4):
497–538.

Daly, K. & Maher, L. (1998).
'Crossroads and Intersections:
Building from Feminist Critique',
in K. Daly & L. Maher (eds),
Criminology at the Crossroads:
Feminist Readings in Crime and
Justice, Oxford University Press,
Oxford, UK: 1–20.

Daly, M. (1978). Gyn/ecology: The
Meta-ethics of Radical Feminism,
Beacon Press, Boston.

de Beauvoir, S. (1952 [1949]). The
Second Sex (trans. H.M. Parshley),
Vintage Books, New York.

de Giorgi, A. (2006). ReThinking
the Political Economy of
Punishment: Perspectives on
Post-Fordism and Penal Politics,
Ashgate, Aldershot, UK.

de Giorgi, A. (2010). 'State
Power, Democratic Process, and
Human Rights: Countering the
Penal Imaginary', Theoretical
Criminology, 14 (4): 369–79.

de Greiff, P. (2006). 'Repairing
the Past: Compensation for Victims
of Human Rights Violations', in
P. de Greiff (ed.), The Handbook
of Reparations, Oxford University
Press, London: 1–20.

de Haan, W. (1991). 'Abolitionism
and Crime Control: A Contradiction
in Terms', in K. Stenson &
D. Cowell (eds), The Politics

of Crime Control, SAGE, London: 203–17.

de Haan, W. & Loader, I. (2002). 'On the Emotions of Crime, Punishment and Social Control', *Theoretical Criminology*, 6 (3): 243–54.

DeKeseredy, W.S. (2010). 'Moral Panics, Violence, and the Policing of Girls: Reasserting Patriarchal Control in the New Millennium', in M. Chesney-Lind & N. Jones (eds), *Fighting for Girls: New Perspectives on Gender and Violence*, State University of New York Press, Albany, NY: 241–53.

DeKeseredy, W.S. (2011). *Contemporary Critical Criminology*, Routledge, New York.

DeKeseredy, W.S., Alvi, S. & Schwartz, M. (1997). 'Left Realism Revisited', in W.S. DeKeseredy & B. Perry (eds), *Advancing Critical Criminology: Theory and Application*, Lexington Books, Oxford, UK: 19–41.

Ditton, J., Chadee, D., Farrall, S., Gilchrist, E. & Bannister, J. (2004). 'From Imitation to Intimidation: A Note on the Curious and Changing Relationship between the Media, Crime and Fear of Crime', *British Journal of Criminology*, 44 (4): 595–610.

Dixon, D. (1990). 'Police Powers and Suspects' Rights', *Campaign for Criminal Justice Bulletin* 5 (9).

Dixon, D. (2008). 'Authorise and Regulate: A Comparative

Perspective on the Rise and Fall of a Regulatory Strategy', in E. Cape & R. Young (eds), *Regulating Policing*, Hart, Oxford: 21–44.

Dowler, K. (2003). 'Media Consumption and Public Attitudes Toward Crime and Justice: The Relationship between Fear of Crime, Punitive Attitudes, and Perceived Police Effectiveness', *Journal of Criminal Justice and Popular Culture*, 10 (2): 109–26.

Downes, D. (1966). *The Delinquent Solution*, Routledge & Kegan Paul, London.

Downes, D. & Morgan, R. (2007). 'No Turning Back: The Politics of Law and Order into the Millennium', in M. Maguire, R. Morgan & R. Reiner (eds), *The Oxford Handbook of Criminology* (4th edition), Oxford University Press, London: 201–40.

Doyle, K. (2010). 'The Subject in Peril', in M. Lee, G. Mason & S. Milivojevic (eds), *Australian & New Zealand Critical Criminology Conference Proceedings*, 1–2 July, Sydney, Australia.

Dragiewicz, M. & DeKeseredy, W.S. (eds) (2011). *Routledge Handbook of Critical Criminology*, Routledge, London.

Durkheim, E. (1960 [1893]). *The Division of Labor in Society*, Free Press, Glencoe.

Durkehim, E. (1964 [1895]). *Rules of Sociological Method* (G.E.G. Caitlin (ed.), trans. S.A. Solovay & J.H. Mueller), Free Press, New York.

Durkheim, E. (1979 [1897]).
Suicide: A Study in Sociology,
Routledge & Kegan Paul, London.

Duster, T. (2003). *Backdoor to
Eugenics* (2nd edition), Routledge,
New York.

Edwards, S. (1990). 'Violence
against Women: Feminism and the
Law', in L. Gelsthorpe & A. Morris
(eds), *Feminist Perspectives in
Criminology*, Open University
Press, Milton Keynes.

Einstadter, W. & Henry, S. (1995).
*Criminological Theory: An Analysis
of Its Underlying Assumptions*,
Harcourt Brace, New York.

Eisenstein, H. (1984). *Contemporary
Feminist Thought*, Unwin, London.

Empey, L. (1982). *American
Delinquency: Its Meaning and
Construction*, Dorsey, Chicago.

Ericson, R. (2007). *Crime in
an Insecure World*, Polity,
Cambridge, UK.

Ericson, R., Baranek, P. & Chan,
J. (1991). *Representing Order:
Crime, Law and Justice in the
News Media*, Open University
Press, Milton Keynes.

Ericson, R. & Shearing, C.D.
(1991). 'Introduction: An
Institutional Approach to
Criminology', in J. Gladstone,
R.V. Ericson & C.D. Shearing
(eds), *Criminology: A Reader's
Guide*, Centre of Criminology,
Toronto: 3–19.

Eschholz, S. (2002). 'Racial
Composition of Television
Offenders and Viewers' Fear of
Crime', *Critical Criminology*,
11 (1): 41–60.

Eurogang Research Network (2011).
'Eurogang Home Page', available
at <www.umsl.edu/~ccj/eurogang/
euroganghome.htm>, accessed
11 July 2011.

Evans, D.T. (1992). 'Left Realism
and the Spatial Study of Crime',
in D.T. Evans, N. Fyfe & D.
Herbert (eds), *Crime, Policing and
Place: Essays in Environmental
Criminology*, Routledge, London:
42–6.

Evans, D.T., Fyfe, N. & Herbert, D.
(eds) (1992). *Crime, Policing and
Place: Essays in Environmental
Criminology*, Routledge,
London.

Eysenck, H. (1984). *Crime and
Personality*, Routledge & Keagan
Paul, London.

Farrington, D. (1995). 'The
Development of Offending and
Antisocial Behavior from
Childhood: Key Findings from the
Cambridge Study of Delinquent
Development', *Journal of Child
Psychology and Psychiatry*,
36: 929–64.

Farrington, D. (1996). 'The
Explanation and Prevention
of Juvenile Offending', in
J. Hawkins (ed.), *Delinquency
and Crime: Current Theories*,
Cambridge University Press,
Cambridge.

Feeley, M. & Simon, J. (1994).
'Actuarial Justice: The Emerging
New Criminal Law', in D. Nelken

(ed.), *The Futures of Criminology*, SAGE, London.

Feeley, M. & Simon, J. (2007). 'Folk Devils and Moral Panics: An Appreciation from North America', in D. Downes, P. Rock, C. Chinkin, & C. Gearty (eds), *Crime, Social Control and Human Rights: Essays in Honour of Stanley Cohen*, Willan, Cullompton.

Feldman, P. (1993). *The Psychology of Crime*, Cambridge University Press, Cambridge.

Felson, M. (1994). *Crime and Everyday Life: Insights and Implications for Society*, Pine Forge, London.

Felson, M. & Clarke, R.V. (1998). *Opportunity Makes the Thief: Practical Theory for Crime Prevention*, Police Research Series (No. 98), Policing and Reducing Crime Unit, UK Home Office, London.

Feminist Anthology Collective (1981). *No Turning Back: Writings from the Women's Liberation Movement 1975-80*, Women's Press, London.

Fennell, P. (2002). 'Radical Risk Management, Mental Health and Criminal Justice', in N.S. Gray, J.M. Laing & L. Noaks (eds), *Criminal Justice, Mental Health and the Politics of Risk*, Cavendish, London: 70-97.

Ferrell, J. (1997). 'Youth, Crime and Cultural Space', *Social Justice*, 24 (4): 21-38.

Ferrell, J. (1998). 'Stumbling Toward a Critical Criminology (and into the Anarchy and Imagery of Postmodernism)', in J.I. Ross (ed.), *Cutting the Edge*, Praeger, Westport, CT: 63-76.

Ferrell, J., Hayward, K., Morrison, W. & Presdee, M. (eds) (2004). *Cultural Criminology Unleashed*, Glasshouse Press, London.

Ferrell, J., Hayward, K. & Young, J. (2008). *Cultural Criminology: An Invitation*, SAGE, London.

Ferrell, J. & Sanders, C. (1995). *Cultural Criminology*, Northeastern University Press, Boston.

Field, S. (1990). 'Crime & Consumption', in *Trends in Crime and Their Interpretation*, Home Office Research Study (no. 119), HMSO, London.

Fine, B. (1984). *Democracy and the Rule of Law: Liberal Ideals and Marxist Critiques*, Pluto, London.

Findlay, M. (1999). *The Globalisation of Crime*, Cambridge University Press, Cambridge.

Fishbein, D. (1990). 'Biological Perspectives in Criminology', *Criminology*, 28 (1): 27-72.

Fitzgerald, G. (1989). *Report of the Commission of Possible Illegal Activities and Associated Police Misconduct*, Queensland Government Printer, Brisbane.

Foley, T. (2008). 'Restorative Justice and Due Process Protections', *Bringing Justice and Community Together Conference*, Victoria Association of Restorative Justice, Melbourne Australia, 14 May 2008.

Forsythe, B. (1995). 'The Garland Thesis and the Origins of Modern English Prison Discipline', *The Howard Journal of Criminal Justice*, 34(3): 259–73.

Foucault, M. (1977). *Discipline and Punish: The Birth of the Prison*, Penguin, London.

Foucault, M. (1980). 'Truth and Power' in C. Gordon (ed.), *Power/Knowledge: Selected Interviews and Other Writings 1972–1977*, Pantheon, New York.

Fraser, N. (1997). 'A Rejoinder to Iris Young', *New Left Review*, 223: 126–9.

Fraser, S. (ed.) (1995). *The Bell Curve Wars: Race, Intelligence and the Future of America*, Basic Books, New York.

Freund, J. (1969). *The Sociology of Max Weber*, Vintage, New York.

Friedrichs, D. (1991). 'Introduction: Peacemaking Criminology in a World Filled with Conflict', in B. MacLean & D. Milovanovic (eds), *New Directions in Critical Criminology*, Collective Press, Vancouver.

Friedrichs, D. (1996). *Trusted Criminals: White Collar Crime in Contemporary Society*, Wadsworth, Belmont, CA.

Friedrichs, D. (2007). *Trusted Criminals: White Collar Crime in Contemporary Society* (3rd edition), Wadsworth, Belmont CA.

Friedrichs, D. (2008). 'Restorative Justice and the Criminological Enterprise', in D. Sullivan & L. Tifft (eds), *Handbook of Restorative Justice: A Global Perspective*, Routledge, Abingdon, UK: 439–51.

Friedrichs, D. (2009). 'Critical Criminology', in J.M. Miller (ed.), *21st Century Criminology: A Reference Handbook* (Vol. 1), SAGE, Thousand Oaks, CA: 210–8.

Gadd, D. & Jefferson, T. (2007). *Psychosocial Criminology*, SAGE: London.

Gadd, D., Karstedt, S. & Messner, S.F. (eds) (2011). *The SAGE Handbook of Criminological Research Methods*, SAGE, London.

Gallant, M.J. & Rhea, H.M. (2010). 'Collective Memory, International Law, and Restorative Social Processes After Conflagration: The Holocaust', *International Criminal Justice Review*, 20 (3): 265–79.

Gamble, A. (1988). *The Free Economy and the Strong State: The Politics of Thatcherism*, Macmillan, London.

Garland, D. (1988). 'British Criminology Before 1935', *British Journal of Criminology*, 28: 131–47.

Garland, D. (1990). *Punishment and Modern Society: A Study in Social Theory*, Clarendon Press, Oxford.

Garland, D. (2001). *The Culture of Control: Crime and Social Order in Contemporary Society*, University of Chicago Press, Chicago.

Garton, S. (1991). 'The Convict Origins Debate: Historians and the Problem of the "Criminal Class"', *Australian and New Zealand Journal of Criminology*, 24 (2): 66–82.

Garwood, J., Rogerson, M. & Pease, K. (2000). 'Sneaky Measurement of Crime and Disorder', in V. Jupp, P. Davies & P. Francis (eds), Doing Criminological Research, SAGE, London:157–68.

Geis, G. & Goff, C. (1983). 'Introduction', in E. Sutherland, *White-Collar Crime: The Uncut Version*, Yale University Press, New Haven.

Gelsthorpe, L. & Morris, A. (eds) (1990). *Feminist Perspectives in Criminology*, Open University Press, Milton Keynes.

Gibbons, D. (1979). *The Criminological Enterprise: Theories and Perspectives*, Prentice Hall, Englewood Cliffs, NJ.

Gibson, M. & Hahn Rafter, N. (2006). 'Editors' Introduction', in C. Lombroso, *Criminal Man* (trans. Gibson & Hahn), Duke University Press, Durham.

Giddens, A. (1990). *The Consequences of Modernity*, Polity Press, Cambridge, UK.

Giddens, A. (1991). *Modernity and Self-Identity: Self and Society in the Late Modern Age*, Polity Press, Cambridge, UK.

Gill, P. (2009). 'Intelligence, Terrorism, and the State', in R. Coleman, J. Sim, S. Tombs & D. Whyte (eds), *State Power Crime*, SAGE, London: 145–58.

Glueck, S. & Glueck, E. (1960). *Unraveling Juvenile Delinquency*, Harvard University Press, Cambridge, MA.

Goffman, I. (1959). *The Presentation of Self in Everyday Life*, Doubleday, New York.

Goodwin. V. (2008). 'The Concentration of Offending and Related Social Problems in Tasmanian Families', *TILES Briefing Paper*, No. 8, December.

Gordon, D.M. (1971). 'Class and the Economics of Crime', *Review of Radical Economics*, 3: 51–75.

Gordon, R. (1995). 'Street Gangs in Vancouver', in J. Creechan & R. Silverman (eds), *Canadian Delinquency*, Prentice Hall, Toronto.

Gordon, R. & Foley, S. (1998). *Criminal Business Organizations, Street Gangs and Related Groups in Vancouver: The Report of the Greater Vancouver Gang Study*, Ministry of Attorney-General, Vancouver.

Goring, C. (1913). *The English Convict: A Statistical Study*, His Majesty's Stationery Office, London.

Gottfredson, M. & Hirschi, T. (1990). *A General Theory of Crime*, Stanford University Press, Stanford.

Grabosky, P. & Wilson, P. (1989). *Journalism and Justice: How Crime Is Reported*, Pluto, Leichhardt, NSW.

Gray, D., Saggers, S., Atkinson, D., Sputore, B. & Bourbon, D. (2002). 'Beating the Grog: An Evaluation of the Tennant Creek Liquor Licensing Restrictions', in D. Gray & S. Saggers (eds), *Indigenous Australian Alcohol and Other Drug Issues: Research from the National Drug Research Institute*, National Drug Research Institute, Perth; 17–28.

Graycar, R. & Morgan, J. (1990). *The Hidden Gender of Law*, Federation Press, Sydney.

Green, P. & Ward, T. (2000). 'State Crime, Human Rights and the Limits of Criminology', *Social Justice*, 27 (1): 101–15.

Green, P. & Ward, T. (2004). *State Crime: Governments, Violence and Corruption*, Pluto, London.

Greenberg, D.F. (1976). 'On One-Dimensional Marxist Criminology', *Theory and Society*, 3 (4): 611–21.

Greenberg, D. (ed.) (1993). *Crime and Capitalism: Readings in Marxist Criminology*, Temple University Press, Philadelphia.

Greer, C. (2010). 'News Media Criminology', in E. McLaughlin & T. Newburn (eds), *The SAGE Handbook of Criminological Theory*, SAGE, London & New York: 490–513.

Habermas, J. (1979). *Legitimation Crisis*, Heinemann, London.

Hagan, J. (1987). *Modern Criminology: Crime, Criminal Behavior and Its Control*, McGraw-Hill, Toronto.

Haines, F. (1997). *Corporate Regulation: Beyond 'Punish or Persuade'*, Clarendon Press, Oxford.

Haines, F. (2000). 'Towards Understanding Globalisation and Control of Corporate Harm: A Preliminary Criminological Analysis', *Current Issues in Criminal Justice*, 12 (2): 166–80.

Haines, F. (2005). *Globalization and Regulatory Character: Regulatory Reform after the Kader Toy Factory Fire*, Aldershot, Ashgate.

Haines, F. (2011) *The Paradox of Regulation: What Regulation Can Achieve and What It Cannot*, Edward Elgar, Cheltenham.

Hall, N., Grieve, J. & Savage, S.P. (eds) (2009). *Policing and the Legacy of Lawrence*, Willan, Cullompton, UK.

Hall, S. (1980a). 'Popular-Democratic vs Authoritarian Populism: Two Ways of "Taking Democracy Seriously"', in A. Hunt (ed.), *Marxism and Democracy*, Lawrence & Wishart, London.

Hall, S. (1980b). 'Drifting into Law and Order Society', in J. Muncie, E. McLaughlin & M. Langan (eds) (1996), *Criminological Perspectives: A Reader* (1st edition), SAGE, London: 257–70.

Hall, S. & Jefferson, T. (eds) (1976). *Resistance Through Rituals: Youth Subcultures in Post-War Britain*, Hutchinson, London.

Hall, S., Jefferson, T., Critcher, C. & Roberts, B. (1978). *Policing the Crisis: Mugging, the State, and Law and Order*, Macmillan, London.

Hall, S. & McLennan, G. (1986). 'Custom and Law: Law and Crime as Historical Processes', in *Law and Disorder: Histories of Crime and Justice*, Open University, Milton Keynes.

Hall, S. & Scraton, P. (1981). 'Law, Class and Control', in M. Fitzgerald, G. McLennan & J. Pawson (eds), *Crime and Society: Readings in History and Theory*, Routledge & Kegan Paul and Open University Press, London.

Haller, J.S. (1971). *Outcasts from Evolution: Scientific Attitudes of Racial Inferiority*, South Illinois University Press, Carbondale & Edwardsville.

Hamilton, M. & Worthen, M.G.F. (2011). 'Sex Disparities in Arrest Outcomes for Domestic Violence', *Journal of Interpersonal Violence*, 26 (8): 1559–78.

Hancock, L. (2009). 'Crime Prevention, Community Safety and the Local State', in R. Coleman, J. Sim, S. Tombs & D, Whyte (eds), *State Power Crime*, SAGE, London: 159–73.

Haraway, D. (1991). *Simians, Cyborgs and Women: The Reinvention of Nature*, Routledge, New York.

Harris, L. & Crocker, L. (1997). 'Bad Girls: Sex Class and Feminist Agency', in L. Harris & L. Crocker (eds), *Femme: Feminists, Lesbians and Bad Girls*, Routledge, New York.

Harris, M.K. (2008). 'Transformative Justice: The Transformation of Restorative Justice', in D. Sullivan & L. Tifft (eds), *Handbook of Restorative Justice: A Global Perspective*, Routledge, Abingdon, UK: 555–66.

Harris, N. & Maruna, S. (2008). 'Shame, Sharing and Restorative Justice: A Critical Appraisal', in D. Sullivan & L. Tifft (eds), *Handbook of Restorative Justice: A Global Perspective*, Routledge, Abingdon, UK: 452–62.

Hay, C., Meldrum, R. & Mann, K. (2010). 'Traditional Bullying, Cyber Bullying and Deviance: A General Strain Theory Approach', *Journal of Contemporary Criminal Justice*, 26 (2): 130–47.

Hayward, K. (2002). 'The Vilification and Pleasures of Youthful Transgression', in J. Muncie, G. Hughes & E. McLaughlin (eds), *Youth Justice: Critical Readings*, SAGE, London.

Heitmeyer, W. (2002). 'Have Cities Ceased to Function as "Integration Machines" for Young People?', in M. Tienda & W.J. Wilson (eds), *Youth in Cities: A Cross-National Perspective*, Cambridge University Press, Cambridge.

Henry, S. & Milovanovic, D. (1994). 'The Constitution of Constitutive Criminology: A Postmodern Approach to Criminological Theory', in D. Nelken (ed.), *The Futures of Criminology*, SAGE, London.

Henry, S. & Milovanovic, D. (2005). 'Postmodernism and Constitutive Theories of Criminal Behaviour', in R.A. Wright & J.M. Miller (eds), *Encyclopedia of Criminology* (Volume 2), Routledge, New York: 1245-9.

Herrnstein, R. & Murray, C. (1994). *The Bell Curve*, Basic, New York.

Hillyard, P. & Tombs, S. (2004). 'Towards a Political Economy of Harm: States, Corporations and the Production of Inequality', in P. Hillyard, C. Pantazis, D. Gordon, S. Tombs & D. Dorling (eds), *Beyond Criminology? Taking Harm Seriously*, Pluto Press, London: 30-54.

Hillyard, P. & Tombs, S. (2007). 'From "Crime" to Social Harm?', *Crime, Law and Social Change*, 48 (1-2): 9-25.

Hirschi, T. (1969). *Causes of Delinquency*, University of California Press, Berkeley.

Hirschi, T. (1986). 'On the Compatibility of Rational Choice and Social Control Theories of Crime', in D.B. Cornish & R.V.G. Clarke (eds), *The Reasoning Criminal— Rational Choice Perspectives on Offending*, Springer-Verlag, Secaucus, NJ: 105-18.

Hogg, R. (1988). 'Taking Crime Seriously: Left Realism and Australian Criminology', in M. Findlay & R. Hogg (eds), *Understanding Crime and Criminal Justice*, Law Book Company, Sydney: 24-51.

Hogg, R. & Brown, D. (1998). *Rethinking Law and Order*, Pluto, Sydney.

Hogg R.G. (2001). 'Penality and Modes of Regulating Indigenous Peoples in Australia', *Punishment & Society*, 3 (3): 355-79.

Hogg, R.G. (2008). 'Resisting a "Law and Order" Society', in T. Anthony & C. Cunneen (eds), *The Critical Criminology Companion*, Hawkins Press, Sydney: 278-89.

Hogg, R.G. & Carrington, K. (2006). *Policing the Rural Crisis*, The Federation Press, Sydney.

Holmes, C. (1993). 'Women: Witnesses and Witches', *Past and Present*, 140: 45-78.

Homan, S. (2007). '"Why Are They All Drinking Water?" Raves, Ecstasy and the Death of Anna Wood', in S. Poynting & G. Morgan (eds), *Outrageous: Moral Panics in Australia*, ACYS, Hobart: 82-98.

Hoskin, A. (2011). 'Explaining the Link between Race and Violence with General Strain Theory', *Journal of Ethnicity in Criminal Justice*, 9 (1): 56–73.

Howe, A. (1994). *Punish and Critique: Towards a Feminist Analysis of Penality*, Routledge, London.

Howe, A. (2000). 'Postmodern Criminology and its Feminist Discontents, *Australian and New Zealand Journal of Criminology*, 33 (2): 221–36.

Huff, R. (ed.) (1996). *Gangs in America* (2nd edition), SAGE, Thousand Oaks, CA.

Hunt, A. (1991). 'Postmodernism and Critical Criminology', in T. MacLean & D. Milanovic (eds), *New Directions in Critical Criminology*, Collective Press, Vancouver: 79–95.

Hunt, A. (2004). 'Getting Marx and Foucault into Bed Together!', *Journal of Law and Society*, 31 (4): 592–609.

Hwang, S. & Akers, R.L. (2003). 'Substance Use by Korean Adolescents: A Cross-Cultural Test of Social Learning, Social Bonding, and Self-Control Theories', in R.L. Akers & G.F. Jensen (eds), *Social Leaning Theory and the Explanation of Crime*, Transaction Publishers, New Brunswick, NJ: 109–28.

Iganski, P. (2008). *'Hate Crime' and the City*, The Policy Press, Bristol, UK.

Ikpa, T.S. (2007). 'Balancing Restorative Justice Principles and Due Process Rights in Order to Reform the Criminal Justice System', *Law and Policy*, 24: 301–25.

Indermaur, D., Brown, D., Egger, S. & Hogg, R. (2002). 'Shadow Boxing with an Imaginary Enemy: A Response to "Law and Order Blues"', *Australian and New Zealand Journal of Criminology*, 35 (2): 145–58.

Inverarity, J., Lauderdale, P. & Feld, B. (1983). *Law and Society: Sociological Perspectives on Criminal Law*, Little, Brown, Boston.

Jackson, R., Murphy, E. & Poynting, S. (eds) (2010). *Contemporary State Terrorism, Theory and Practice*, Routledge, London.

Jackson-Jacobs, C. (2004). 'Taking a Beating: The Narrative Gratifications of Fighting as an Underdog', in J. Ferrell, K. Hayward, W. Morrison & M. Presdee (eds), *Cultural Criminology Unleashed*, Glasshouse Press, London.

Jaggs, D. (1986). *Neglected and Criminal: Foundations of Child Welfare Legislation in Victoria*, Phillip Institute of Technology, Melbourne.

Jamieson, J. & Yates, J. (2009). 'Young People, Youth Justice and the State', in R. Coleman, J. Sim, S. Tombs & D. Whyte (eds), *State Power Crime*, SAGE, London: 76–89.

Jefferson, T. (1997).
'Masculinities and Crimes', in
M. Maguire, R. Morgan &
R. Reiner (eds), *The Oxford
Handbook of Criminology (2nd
edition)*, Clarendon Press,
Oxford.

Jefferson, T. (2008). 'Policing
the Crisis Revisited: The State,
Masculinity, Fear of Crime and
Racism', *Crime, Media, Culture*,
4 (1): 113–21.

Jensen, V. (2001). *Why Women Kill:
Homicide and Gender Equality*.
Lynne Rienner Publishers,
Boulder, CO.

Johnston, E. (1991). *National
Report, 5 Vols, Royal Commission
into Aboriginal Deaths in Custody*,
Australian Government Publishing
Service, Canberra.

Jones, C. & Novak, T. (2009).
'Power, Politics and the Welfare
State', in R. Coleman, J. Sim,
S. Tombs & D. Whyte (eds), *State
Power Crime*, SAGE, London:
90–102.

Jones, D.W. (2008). *Understanding
Criminal Behaviour: Psychosocial
Approaches to Criminality*,
Willan, Cullompton.

Jones, T., MacLean, B. & Young, J.
(1986). *The Islington Crime
Survey*, Gower, Aldershot.

Jupp, V. (1989). *Methods of
Criminological Research*,
Routledge, London.

Kanazawa, S. (2009). 'Evolutionary
Psychology and Crime', in

A. Walsh & K. Beaver (eds),
Biosocial Criminology, Routledge,
New York: 90–110.

Karstedt, S. (2010). 'New
Institutionalism in Criminology:
Approaches, Theories and Themes',
in E. McLaughlin & T. Newburn
(eds), *The SAGE Handbook of
Criminological Theory*, SAGE,
London: 337–59.

Katz, J. (1988). *Seductions
of Crime: Moral and Sensual
Attractions in Doing Evil*, Basic
Books, New York.

Kauzlarich, D., Mullins, C. &
Matthews, R. (2003). 'A Complicity
Continuum of State Crime',
Contemporary Justice Review,
6 (3): 241–54.

Kelly, J. (1992). *A Short History
of Western Legal Theory*, Clarendon
Press, Oxford, UK.

Kinsey, R., Lea, J. & Young, J.
(1986). *Losing the Fight against
Crime*, Blackwell, Oxford.

Klein, M., Kerner, H-J., Maxson, C.
& Weitekamp, E. (eds) (2001). *The
Eurogang Paradox: Street Gangs
and Youth Groups in the US and
Europe*, Kluwer, Dordrecht.

Klein, M., Maxson, C. & Miller,
J. (eds) (1995). *The Modern Gang
Reader*, Roxbury, Los Angeles.

Kohm, S.A. & P. Greenhill (2011).
'Pedophile Crime Films as
Popular Criminology: A Problem
of Justice?', *Theoretical
Criminology*, 15 (2): 195–215.

Koonin, R. (1995). 'Breaking the Last Taboo: Child Sexual Abuse by Female Perpetrators', *Australian Social Work Journal*, 30 (2): 195–210.

Kozol, J. (1991). *Savage Inequalities: Children in America's Schools*, Crown, New York.

Kubrin, C. & Weitzer, R. (2003). 'New Directions in Social Disorganization Theory', *Journal of Research in Crime & Delinquency*, 40: 374–402.

Lacey, N. (2007). 'Legal Constructions of Crime', in M. Maguire, R. Morgan & R. Reiner (eds), *The Oxford Handbook of Criminology* (4th edition), Oxford University Press, London: 179–200.

Laslett, K. (2010). 'Crime or Social Harm? A Dialectical Perspective', *Crime, Law and Social Change*, 54 (1): 1–19.

Lea, J. (1998). 'Criminology and Postmodernity', in P. Walton & J. Young (eds), *The New Criminology Revisited*, Macmillan, London.

Lea, J. & Young, J. (1982). 'The Riots in Britain 1981: Urban Violence and Political Marginalisation', in D. Cowell, T. Jones & J. Young (eds), *Policing the Riots*, Junction, London.

Lea, J. & Young, J. (1984). *What Is to Be Done about Law and Order?*, Penguin, London.

Lees, S. (1989). 'Learning to Love', in M. Cain (ed.), *Growing Up Good*, SAGE, London.

Leighton, P. & Selman, D. (2011). 'Private Prisons, the Criminal Justice-Industrial Complex and Bodies Destined for Profitable Punishment', in M. Dragiewicz & W.S. DeKeseredy (eds), *Routledge Handbook of Critical Criminology*, Routledge, London.

Lemert, E. (1951). *Social Pathology*, McGraw-Hill, New York.

Lemert, E. (1967). *Human Deviance, Social Problems and Social Control*, Prentice Hall, Englewood Cliffs, NJ.

Lemert, E. (1969). 'Primary and Secondary Deviation', in D. Cressy & D. Ward (eds), *Delinquency, Crime and Social Process*, Harper & Row, New York.

Lemert, E. (1974). 'Beyond Mead: The Societal Reaction to Deviance', *Social Problems*, 21 (4): 457–68.

Lievore, D. (2004). 'Victim Credibility in Adult Sexual Assault Cases', *Trends and Issues in Crime and Criminal Justice* (No. 288), Australian Institute of Criminology, Canberra.

Lievore, D. (2005). *No Longer Silent: A Study of Women's Help-Seeking Decisions and Service Responses*, Australian Institute of Criminology, Canberra.

Lind, M. (1995). 'Brave New Right', in S. Fraser (ed.), *The Bell*

Curve Wars: Race, Intelligence and the Future of America, Basic, New York.

Linebaugh, P. (1976). 'Karl Marx, the Theft of Wood, and Working-Class Composition', *Crime and Social Justice*, 6 (Fall–Winter): 5–16.

Litwack, T. & Schlesinger, L. (1999). 'Dangerousness Risk Assessments: Research, Legal, and Clinical Considerations', in A. Hess & I. Weiner (eds), *The Handbook of Forensic Psychology* (2nd edition), John Wiley & Sons, New York.

Loader, I. (1998). 'Criminology and the Public Sphere: Arguments for Utopian Realism', in P. Walton & J. Young (eds), *The New Criminology Revisited*, Macmillan, London.

Loader, I. & Sparks, R. (2010a). *Public Criminology?*, Routledge, London & New York.

Loader, I. & Sparks, R. (2010b). 'What Is to Be Done with Public Criminology?', *Criminology and Public Policy*, 9 (4): 771–81.

Loeber, R. & Farrington, D. (eds) (1998). *Serious and Violent Juvenile Offenders: Risk Factors and Successful Interventions*, SAGE, Thousand Oaks, CA.

Lombroso, C. (1911). *Crime: Its Causes and Remedies*, Little, Brown, Boston.

Lowman, J. & MacLean, B. (eds) (1992). *Realist Criminology:*

Crime Control and Policing in the 1990s, University of Toronto Press, Toronto.

Lukes, S. (1973). *Emile Durkheim: His Life and Work*, Penguin, London.

Lynch, M.J. & Michalowski R. (2006). *Critical Perspective on Crime, Power and Identity* (4th edition), Criminal Justice Press, Monsey, NY.

Lynch, M.J. & Stretesky, P.B. (2003). 'The Meaning of Green: Contrasting Criminological Perspectives', *Theoretical Criminology*, 7 (2): 217–38.

Lynch, M.J. & Stretesky, P.B. (eds) (2011). *Radical and Marxist Theories of Crime*, Ashgate, Whitney, UK.

McCulloch, J. (2010). 'From Garrison State to Garrison Planet: State Terror, the War on Terror and the Rise of the Global Carceral Complex', in R. Jackson, E. Murphy & S. Poynting (eds), *Contemporary State Terrorism, Theory and Practice*, Routledge, London: 196–212.

McEvoy, K. (2003). 'Beyond the Metaphor: Political Violence, Human Rights and "New" Peacemaking Criminology', *Theoretical Criminology*, 7 (3): 319–46.

McLaughlin, E. (2010). 'Critical Criminology', in E. McLaughlin & T. Newburn (eds), *The SAGE Handbook of Criminological Theory*, SAGE, London: 153–74.

McLaughlin, E. & Muncie, J. (eds) (2005). *The SAGE Dictionary of Criminology* (2nd edition), SAGE, London.

McLaughlin, E., Muncie, J. & Hughes, G. (eds) (2003). *Criminological Perspectives: A Reader* (2nd edition), SAGE, London.

McLaughlin, E. & Newburn, T. (eds) (2010). *The SAGE Handbook of Criminological Theory*, SAGE, London.

MacLean, B. (1993). 'Left Realism, Local Crime Surveys and Policing of Racial Minorities: A Further Analysis of Data from the First Sweep of the Islington Crime Survey', *Crime, Law and Social Change*, 19: 51-86.

MacLean, B. & Milovanovic, D. (eds) (1991). *New Directions in Critical Criminology*, Collective Press, Vancouver.

McRobbie, A. & Thornton, S. (1995). 'Rethinking Moral Panic for Multi-Mediated Social Worlds', *British Journal of Sociology*, 46 (4): 559-74.

Maguire, M. (2007). 'Crime Data and Statistics', in M. Maguire, R. Morgan & R. Reiner (eds), *The Oxford Handbook of Criminology* (4th edition), Oxford University Press, London.

Maguire, M, Morgan, R. & Reiner, R. (eds) (2002). *The Oxford Handbook of Criminology* (3rd edition), Oxford University Press, London.

Maguire, M., Morgan, R. & Reiner, R. (eds) (2007). *The Oxford Handbook of Criminology* (4th edition), Oxford University Press, London.

Maier-Katkin, D., Mears, D.P. & Bernard, T.J. (2009). 'Towards a Criminology of Crimes against Humanity', *Theoretical Criminology*, 13 (2): 227-55.

Males, M. (1996). *The Scapegoat Generation: America's War on Adolescents*, Common Courage, Maine.

Marshall, T.F. (1998). *Restorative Justice: An Overview*, Restorative Justice Consortium, UK Home Office, London: 5-36.

Mason, G. (2002). *The Spectacle of Violence: Homophobia, Gender and Knowledge*, Routledge, London.

Mason, P. (2009). 'Crime, Media and the State', in R. Coleman, J. Sim, S. Tombs & D. Whyte (eds), *State Power Crime*, SAGE, London: 145-58.

Massoglia, M. & Macmillan, R. (2002). 'Deterrence, Rational Choice and Criminal Offending: A Consideration of Legal Subjectivity', in A.R. Piquero & S.G. Tibbetts (eds), *Rational Choice and Criminal Behavior: Recent Research and Future Challenges*, Routledge, New York: 323-40.

Mathiesen, T. (1990). *Prisons on Trial: A Critical Assessment*, SAGE, London.

Matthews, R. (1989). 'Alternatives to and in Prisons: A Realist Approach', in P. Carlen & D. Cook (eds), *Paying For Crime*, Open University Press, Milton Keynes.

Matthews, R. (2009). 'Beyond "So What?" Criminology: Rediscovering Realism', *Theoretical Criminology*, 13 (3): 341–62.

Matthews, R. (2010). 'Realist Criminology Revisited', in E. McLaughlin & T. Newburn (eds), *The SAGE Handbook of Criminological Theory*, SAGE, London: 193–209.

Matthews, R. & Young, J. (eds) (1992). *Issues in Realist Criminology*, SAGE, London.

Matza, D. (1964). *Delinquency and Drift*, John Wiley & Sons, New York.

Mawby, R. & Walklate, S. (1994). *Critical Victimology: International Perspectives*, SAGE, London.

Mead, G.H. (1962 [1934]). *Mind, Self, and Society*, University of Chicago Press, Chicago.

Mednick, S.A., (1985). 'Biosocial Factors and Primary Prevention of Antisocial Behaviour', in F.H. Marsh & J. Katz (eds), *Biology Crime and Ethics*, Anderson, Cincinnati.

Mednick, S.A., Gabrielli, W.F. & Hutchins, B. (1984). 'Genetic Influences in Criminal Convictions: Evidence from an Adoption Cohort', *Science*, 224: 891–93.

Mednick, S.A., Gabrielle, W.F. & Hutchings, B. (1987). *The Causes of Crime: New Biological Approaches*, Cambridge University Press, Cambridge.

Melossi, D. (1985). 'Overcoming the Crisis in Critical Criminology: Toward a Grounded Labeling Theory', *Criminology*, 23 (2): 193–208.

Merton, R. (1938). 'Social Structure and Anomie', *American Sociological Review*, 3: 672–82.

Merton, R. (1957 [1949]). *Social Theory and Social Structure*, Free Press, New York.

Messerschmidt, J. (1986). *Capitalism, Patriarchy and Crime*, Rowman & Littlefield, New Jersey.

Messerschmidt, J. (1993). *Masculinities and Crime: Critique and Reconceputalization of Theory*, Rowan and Littlefield, Lanham, MD.

Messerschmidt, J. (1997). *Crime as Structured Action: Gender, Race, Class, and Crime in the Making*, SAGE, London.

Michalowski, R.J. (1996). 'Critical Criminology and the Critique of Domination: The Story of an Intellectual Movement', *Critical Criminology*, 7(1): 11–6.

Miliband, R. (1969). *The State in Capitalist Society*, Quartet, London.

Miller, D.E. & McMullan, J.L. (2010). 'From Safety to Danger: Constructions of Crime in a

Women's Magazine', *Critical Criminology*, Online First (23 October): 27–47.

Miller, W. (1958). 'Lower Class Culture as a Generating Milieu of Gang Delinquency', *Journal of Social Issues*, 14: 51–119.

Milovanovic, D. (2002). *Critical Criminology at the Edge: Postmodern Perspectives, Integration and Applications*, Praeger, Westport, C.T.

Moffitt, T. (1993). 'The Neuropsychology of Conduct Disorder', *Development and Psychopathology*, 5 (1–2): 135–51.

Mooney, J. (1998). 'Moral Panics and the New Right: Single Mothers and Feckless Fathers', in P. Walton & J. Young (eds), *The New Criminology Revisited*, Macmillan, London.

Mooney, J. & Young, J. (2006). 'The Decline in Crime and the Rise of Anti-Social Behaviour', *Probation Journal: The Journal of Community and Criminal Justice*, 53 (4): 397–407.

Moore, M (2003). *Dude, Where's my Country?*, Warner Books, New York.

Morash, M. & Chesney-Lind, M. (2009). 'The Context of Girls' Violence: Peer Groups, Families, Schools, and Communities', in M.A. Zahn (ed.), *The Delinquent Girl*, Temple University Press, Philadelphia, PA: 182–206.

Morgan, G. (2007). 'Curfews, Children, Class and Colonialism', in S. Poynting & G. Morgan (eds), *Outrageous: Moral Panics in Australia*, ACYS Publishing, Hobart: 11–19.

Morris, A. (2002). 'Critiquing the Critics: A Brief Response to Critics of Restorative Justice', *British Journal of Criminology*, 42 (3): 596–615.

Morrison, W. (1994). 'Criminology, Modernity and the "Truth" of the Human Condition: Reflections on the Melancholy of Postmodernism', in D. Nelken (ed.), *The Futures of Criminology*, SAGE, London.

Moyer, I. (2001). *Criminological Theories: Traditional and Nontraditional Voices and Themes*, SAGE, Thousand Oaks, CA.

Moyle, P. (ed.) (1994). *Private Prisons and Police: Recent Australian Trends*, Pluto, Sydney.

Moxon, D. (2011). 'Marxism and the Definition of Crime', *In-Spire Journal of Law, Politics and Societies*, 5 (2): 102–20.

Muller, D., Blackmann, D. & Chapman, A. (eds) (1984). *Psychology and Law*, John Wiley & Sons, New York.

Muncie, J. (2010). 'Labelling, Social Reaction and Constructionism', in E. McLaughlin & T. Newburn (eds), *The SAGE Handbook of Criminological Theory*, SAGE, London.

Muncie, J. & Fitzgerald, M. (1981). 'Humanising the Deviant: Affinity and Affiliation Theories', in M. Fitzgerald, G. McLennan & J. Pawson (eds), *Crime and Society: Readings in History and Theory*, Routledge & Kegan Paul and Open University Press, London.

Muncie, J., Hughes, G. & McLaughlin, E. (eds) (2002). *Youth Justice: Critical Readings*, SAGE, London.

Murray, C. (1990). *The Emerging British Underclass*, Institute of Economic Affairs, London.

Murray, C. (1994). *Underclass: The Crisis Deepens*, Institute of Economic Affairs, London.

Mythen, G. & Walklate, S. (eds) (2006). *Beyond the Risk Society: Critical Reflections on Risk and Human Security*, Open University Press, Maidenhead, U.K.

Naffine, N. (1987). *Female Crime: The Construction of Women in Criminology*, Allen & Unwin, Sydney.

Naffine, N. (1990). *Law and the Sexes: Explorations in Feminist Jurisprudence*, Allen & Unwin, Sydney.

Naffine, N. (1997). *Feminism and Criminology*, Allen & Unwin, Sydney.

Nava, M. (1984). 'Youth Service Provision, Social Order and the Question of Girls', in A. McRobbie & M. Nava (eds), *Gender and Generation*, Macmillan, London.

Nettler, G. (1984). *Explaining Crime*, McGraw Hill, New York.

Neyhouse, T.J. (2002). *Positivism in Criminology: A Study in the History and Use of Ideas*, LFB Scholarly Pub, El Paso, TX.

Noonan, S. (2002). 'Of Death, Desire and Knowledge: Law and Social Control of Witches in Renaissance Europe', in G.M. MacDonald (ed.), *Social Context & Social Location in the Sociology of Law*, Broadview Press, Peterborough, Ontario.

O'Connor, T. (1998). 'The Contributions of Marx, Weber and Simmel: The Common Ground is the Cutting Edge', in J.I. Ross (ed.), *Cutting the Edge: Current Perspectives in Radical/Critical Criminology and Criminal Justice*, Praeger Publishers, Westport, CT: 9–17.

O'Leary, C. & Platt, T. (2001). 'Pledging Allegiance: The Revival of Prescriptive Patriotism', *Social Justice*, 28 (3): 41–4.

O'Malley, P. (1983). *Law, Capitalism and Democracy*, Allen & Unwin, Sydney.

O'Malley, P. (2010). 'Governmental Criminology', in E. McLaughlin & T. Newburn (eds), *The SAGE Handbook of Criminological Theory*, SAGE, London: 319–36.

Park, R.E., Burgess, E.W. & McKenzie, R. D. (1967 [1925]). *The City: Suggestions for Investigation of Human Behavior in the Urban Environment*, University of Chicago Press, Chicago.

Paternoster, R. & Bachman, R. (2010). 'Control Theories', in E. McLaughlin & T. Newburn (eds), *The SAGE Handbook of Criminological Theory*, SAGE, London: 114-38.

Pavlich, G. (2007). 'Ethics, Universal Principles, and Restorative Justice', in G. Johnstone & D. Van Ness (eds), *Handbook of Restorative Justice*, Willan Publishing, Cullompton: 615-30.

Pawson, R. (2006). *Evidence Based Policy: A Realist Perspective*, SAGE, London.

Payne, A.A., Gottfredson, D.C. & Kruttschmitt, C. (2009). 'Girls, Schooling and Delinquency', in M.A. Zahn (ed.), *The Delinquent Girl*, Temple University Press, Philadelphia, PA: 1-6.

Pearce, F. (1976). *Crime of the Powerful: Marxism, Crime and Deviance*, Pluto, London.

Pearce, F. & Snider, L. (1992). 'Special Edition: Crimes of the Powerful', *The Journal of Human Justice*, 3 (2).

Pearce, F. & Tombs, S. (1990). 'Ideology, Hegemony and Empiricism: Compliance Theories of Regulation', *British Journal of Criminology*, 30(4): 423-43.

Pearce, F. & Tombs, S. (1992). 'Realism and Corporate Crime', in R. Matthews & J. Young (eds), *Issues in Realist Criminology*, SAGE, London.

Pearce, F. & Tombs, S. (1993). 'US Capital Versus the Third World: Union Carbide and Bhopal', in F. Pearce & M. Woodiwiss (eds), *Global Crime Connections*, Macmillan, London.

Pearce, F. & Tombs, S. (1998). *Toxic Capitalism: Corporate Crime and the Chemical Industry*, Dartmouth, Aldershot.

Pearson, P. (1997). *When She Was Bad: Violent Women and the Myth of Innocence*, Random, Toronto.

Pepinsky, H. (1991). 'Peacemaking in Criminology and Criminal Justice', in H. Pepinsky & R. Quinney (eds), *Criminology as Peacemaking*, Indiana University Press, Bloomington.

Pepinsky, H. & Quinney, R. (eds) (1991). *Criminology as Peacemaking*, Indiana University Press, Bloomington.

Perlmutter, D. (2000). *Policing the Media: Street Cops and Public Perceptions of Law Enforcement*, SAGE, Thousand Oaks, CA.

Pettit, P. & Braithwaite, J. (1993). 'Not Just Deserts, Even in Sentencing', *Current Issues in Criminal Justice*, 4 (3): 225-39.

Pettit, P. & Braithwaite, J. (2000). 'Republicanism and Restorative Justice: An

Explanatory and Normative
Connection', in H. Strang &
J. Braithwaite (eds),
*Restorative Justice: From
Philosophy to Practice*, Aldershot,
Dartmouth.

Pickering, S. & Lambert, C. (2001).
'Immigration Detention Centres,
Human Rights and Criminology in
Australia', *Current Issues in
Criminal Justice*, 13 (2): 219–23.

Piquero, A. & Paternoster, R.
(1998). 'An Application
of Stafford and Warr's
Reconceptualization of Deterrence
to Drinking and Driving',
*Journal of Research in Crime and
Deliquency*, 32 (1): 3–39.

Piquero, A.R. & Tibbetts, S.G.
(eds) (2002). *Rational Choice
and Criminal Behavior: Recent
Research and Future Challenges*,
Routledge, New York.

Platt, A. (1977). *The Child Savers*,
University of Chicago, Chicago.

Plummer, K. (1979).
'Misunderstanding Labelling
Perspectives', in D. Downes
& P. Rock (eds), *Deviant
Interpretations*, Martin Robertson,
Oxford.

Polk, K. (1993). 'Jobs, not Gaols:
A New Agenda for Youth', in
L. Atkinson & S.-A. Gerull
(eds), *National Conference on
Juvenile Justice: Conference
Proceedings*, Australian Institute
of Criminology, Canberra.

Polk, K. (1994a). *When Men Kill:
Scenarios of Masculine Violence*,
Cambridge University Press,
Melbourne.

Polk, K. (1994b). 'Family
Conferencing: Theoretical and
Evaluative Questions', in
C. Alder & J. Wundersitz (eds),
*Family Conferencing and Juvenile
Justice*, Australian Institute of
Criminology, Canberra.

Potter, H. (1992). 'Crime, Shame
and Reintegration: Review,
Questions and Comment', *Australian
and New Zealand Journal of
Sociology*, 28 (2): 224–32.

Poulantzas, N. (1972). 'The Problem
of the Capitalist State', in
R. Blackburn (ed.), *Ideology
and the Social Sciences*, Fontana,
London.

Poulantzas, N. (1978). *State, Power
and Socialism*, Verso, London.

Poynting, S. & Morgan, G (2007).
'Introduction', in S. Poynting
& G. Morgan (eds), *Outrageous:
Moral Panics in Australia*, ACYS,
Hobart.

Poynting, S., Noble, G. Tabar,
P. & Collins, J. (2004). *Bin Laden
in the Suburbs: Criminalising the
Arab Other*, Sydney Institute of
Criminology, Sydney.

Pratt, J. (2002). 'Critical
Criminology and the Punitive
Society: Some New "Visions of
Social Control"', in R. Hogg &
K. Carrington (eds), *Critical
Criminology: Issues, Debates,
Challenges*, Willan, Cullompton:
168–84.

Pratt, J., Brown, D., Brown,
M., Hallsworth, S. and Morrison, W.
(eds) (2005). *The New Punitiveness:
Trends, Theories, Perspectives*,
Willan Press, Cullompton.

Presdee, M. (2000). *Cultural Criminology and the Carnival of Crime*, Routledge, London.

Quinney, R. (1970). *The Social Reality of Crime*, Little, Brown, Boston.

Quinney, R. (ed.) (1974a). *Crime and Justice in America: A Critical Understanding*, Little, Brown, Boston.

Quinney, R. (1974b). *Critique of Legal Order: Crime Control in Capitalist Society*, Little, Brown and Company, Boston.

Quinney, R. (1977). *Class, State and Crime: On the Theory and Practice of Criminal Justice*, David McKay, New York.

Quinney, R. (1991). 'The Way of Peace: On Crime, Suffering and Deviance', in H. Pepinsky & R. Quinney (eds), *Criminology as Peacemaking*, Indiana University Press, Bloomington.

Quinney, R. (2000). 'Criminology as Moral Philosophy, Criminologist as Witness', in R. Quinney (ed.), *Bearing Witness to Crime and Social Justice*, State University of New York Press, Albany: 193-213.

Rafter, N. (2008). *The Criminal Brain: Understanding Biological Theories of Crime*, New York University Press, New York.

Raine, A. (2002). 'Biosocial Studies of Antisocial and Violent Behavior in Children and Adults', *Journal of Abnormal Child Psychology*, 30(4): 311-26.

Reiman, J. (1998). *The Rich Get Richer and the Poor Get Prison*, Allyn & Bacon, Boston.

Reiman, J. (1999). 'The Rich (Still) Get Richer: Understanding Ideology, Outrage and Economic Bias', *The Critical Criminologist*, 9 (2): 1, 4-5.

Reiss, A. (1986). 'Why Are Communities Important in Understanding Crime?', in A. Reiss & M. Tonry (eds), *Communities and Crime*, University of Chicago Press, Chicago: 1-34.

Reiss, A. & Tonry, M. (eds) (1986). *Communities and Crime*, University of Chicago Press, Chicago.

Roche, D. (2007). 'Retribution and Restorative Justice', in G. Johnstone & D. Van Ness (eds), *Handbook of Restorative Justice*, Willan Publishing, Cullompton: 75-90.

Rock, P. (2010). 'Approaches to Victims and Victimisation', in E. McLaughlin & T. Newburn (eds), *The SAGE Handbook of Criminological Theory*. SAGE, London: 464-89.

Rose, N. (2000). 'The Biology of Culpability: Pathological Identity and Crime Control in a Biological Culture', *Theoretical Criminology*, 4 (1): 5-34.

Rosenfeld, R. & Messner, S.F. (1995). 'Crime and the American Dream' in F. Alder & W. Laufer (eds), *The Legacy of Anomie Theory*, Transaction Publishers, New Brunswick, NJ: 159-81.

Rosenthal, R. & Jacobson, L. (1968). *Pygmalion in the Classroom*, Holt Rinehart Winston, New York.

Roshier, R. (1989). *Controlling Crime: The Classical Perspective in Criminology*, Open University Press, Milton Keynes.

Ross, D. (1985). 'A Tattoo Removal Programme in Victoria', *Medical Journal of Australia*, 142: 388.

Ross, J.I. (ed.) (1998). *Cutting the Edge: Current Perspectives in Radical/Critical Criminology and Criminal Justice*, Praeger Publishers, Westport, CT.

Ross, L.E. (2010). 'A Vision of Race, Crime and Justice through the Lens of Critical Race Theory', in E. McLaughlin & T. Newburn (eds), *The SAGE Handbook of Criminological Theory*, SAGE, London: 391–409.

Rowe, C. (2002). *Biology and Crime*, Roxbury, Los Angeles.

Rowland & Klien 1996, cited in Thompson & Ricard 2009: 264.

Ruggiero, V. & South, N. (2010a). 'Green Criminology and Dirty Collar Crime', *Critical Criminology*, 18 (4): 251–62.

Ruggiero, V. & South, N. (2010b). 'Critical Criminology and Crimes Against the Environment', *Critical Criminology*, 18 (4): 245–50.

Russell, S. (1997). 'The Failure of Postmodern Criminology', *Critical Criminologist*, 8 (2): 61–90.

Russell, S. (2002). 'The Continuing Relevance of Marxism to Critical Criminology', *Critical Criminology*, 11 (2): 113–35.

Russell, S. (2003). 'The Continuing Relevance of Marxism to Critical Criminology', *Critical Criminology*, 11 (2): 113–35.

Rutter, M., Giller, H. & Hagell, A. (1998). *Antisocial Behavior by Young People*, Cambridge University Press, Cambridge.

Salmi, J. (2004). 'Violence in Democratic Societies: Towards an Analytical Framework', in P. Hillyard, C. Pantazis, S. Tombs & D. Gordon (eds), *Beyond Criminology? Taking Harm Seriously*, Pluto Press, London.

Sampson, R.J. & Laub, J.H. (2004). 'A Life-Course Theory of Cumulative Disadvantage and the Stability of Delinquency', in T.P. Thornberry (ed.), *Developmental Theories of Crime and Delinquency*, Transaction Publishers, New Brunswick, NJ: 133–62.

Sampson, R.J., Morenoff, J.D. & Gannon-Rowley, T. (2002). 'Assessing Neighborhood Effects: Social Processes and New Directions in Research', *Annual Review of Sociology*, 28: 443–78.

Sampson, R.J., Raudenbush, S.W. & Earls, F. (1997). 'Neighborhoods and Violent Crime: A Multi-Level Study of Collective Efficacy', *Science*, 277: 918–24.

Sampson, R. & Wilson, W. (1995). 'Toward a Theory of Race, Crime and Urban Inequality', in J. Hagan & R. Peterson (eds), *Crime and Inequality*, Stanford University Press, Stanford.

Sandler, J. & Freeman, N.J. (2011). 'Female Sex Offenders and the Criminal Justice System: A Comparison of Arrests and Outcomes', *Journal of Sexual Aggression*, 17 (1): 61–76.

Sarre, R. (1994). 'Violence: Patterns of Crime', in D. Chappell & P. Wilson (eds), *The Australian Criminal Justice System: The Mid-1990s*, Butterworth, Sydney.

Schiff, M. (2003). 'Models, Challenges and the Promise of Restorative Conferencing Strategies', in A. von Hirsch, J. Roberts, A.E. Bottoms, K. Roach & M. Schiff (eds) (2003), *Restorative Justice and Criminal Justice: Competing or Reconcilable Paradigms?*, Hart Publishing, Oxford, UK: 315–38.

Schinkel, W. (2004). 'The Will to Violence', *Theoretical Criminology*, 8 (1): 5–32.

Schissel, B. & Brooks, C. (eds) (2002). *Marginality and Condemnation: An Introduction to Critical Criminology*, Fernwood, Halifax.

Schur, E. (1973). *Radical Non-Intervention: Rethinking the Delinquency Problem*, Prentice Hall, Englewood Cliffs, NJ.

Schwartz, M.D. & DeKeseredy, W.S. (1991). 'Left Realist Criminology: Strengths, Weaknesses and the Feminist Critique', *Crime, Law and Social Change*, 15 (1): 51–72.

Schwendinger, H. & Schwendinger, J. (1975). 'Defenders of Order or Guardians of Human Rights', in I. Taylor, P. Walton & J. Young (eds), *Critical Criminology*, Routledge & Kegan Paul, London.

Scraton, P. (ed.) (1987). *Law, Order and the Authoritarian State: Readings in Critical Criminology*, Open University Press, Milton Keynes.

Scraton, P. (2007). *Power, Conflict and Criminalisation*, Routledge, London & New York.

Scraton, P. (2009). '"Hearing Voices, Bearing Witness": Reflections on Critical Analysis in Criminology', in C. Powell (ed.), *Critical Voices in Criminology*, Lexington Books, Plymouth, UK: 143–84.

Scraton, P. & Chadwick, K. (1991). 'The Theoretical and Political Priorities of Critical Criminology', in K. Stenson & D. Cowell (eds), *The Politics of Crime Control*, SAGE, London: 161–85.

Scraton, P. & McCulloch, J. (eds) (2009). *The Violence of Incarceration*, Routledge, London.

Scott, J., Hogg, R.G., Barclay, E. & Donnermeyer, J.F. (2007). 'There's Crime Out There, but not as We Know It: Rural Criminology— The Last Frontier', in E. Barclay, J.F. Donnermeyer,

J. Scott & R.G. Hogg (eds), *Crime in Rural Australia*, The Federation Press, Sydney: 1-12.

Scutt, J. (1990). *Women and the Law*, Law Book Company, Sydney.

Segal, L. (1987). *Is The Future Female? Troubled Thoughts on Contemporary Feminism*, Virago, London.

Selke, W., Corsaro, N. & Selke, H. (2002). 'A Working Class Critique of Criminological Theory', *Critical Criminology*, 11 (2): 93-112.

Sellers, C.S., Cochran, J.K. & Winfree, L.T. (2003). 'Social Learning Theory and Courtship Violence: An Empirical Test', in R.L. Akers & G.F. Jensen (eds), *Social Learning Theory and the Explanation of Crime*, Transaction Publishers, New Brunswick, NJ: 109-28.

Sellin, T. (1937). *Crime in the Depression*, Social Science Research Council, New York.

Sellin, T. (1938). *Culture Conflict and Crime*, Social Science Research Council, New York.

Shaw, C. & McKay, H. (1942). *Juvenile Delinquency and Urban Areas*, Chicago University Press, Chicago.

Sheldon, W. (1940). *Varieties of Human Physique*, Harper & Row, New York.

Sherman, L.W. (2010). 'Defiance, Compliance and Consilience: A General Theory of Criminology', in E. McLaughlin & T. Newburn (eds), *The SAGE Handbook of Criminological Theory*. SAGE, London: 360-90.

Shklar, J.N. (1987). *Montesquieu: Criticism and Interpretation*, Oxford University Press, Oxford.

Shoemaker, D. (1984). *Theories of Delinquency*, Oxford University Press, New York.

Shon, P.C.H. (2002). 'Bringing the Spoken Words Back In: Conversationalizing (Postmodernizing) Police-Citizen Encounter Research', *Critical Criminology*, 11 (2): 151-72.

Shover, N. & Wright, J. (2001). *Crimes of Privilege: Readings in White-Collar Crime*, Oxford University Press, New York.

Sim, J. (1994). 'The Abolitionist Approach: A British Perspective', in A. Duff et al. (eds), *Penal Theory and Practice: Tradition and Innovation in Criminal Justice*, Manchester University Press, Manchester UK: 263-84.

Simons, R.L. & Burt, C.H. (2011). 'Learning to Be Bad: Adverse Social Conditions, Social Schemas and Crime', *Criminology*, 49 (2): 553-98.

Simpson, S.S. (2000). 'The Social Control of Corporate Criminals: Shame and Informal Sanction Threats', in S.S Simpson & R. Agnew (eds), *Of Crime and Criminality: The Use of Theory in Everyday Life*, Pine Forge Press, Thousand Oaks, CA: 141-58.

Simpson, S.S. & Agnew, R. (eds) (2000). *Of Crime and Criminality: The Use of Theory in Everyday Life*, Pine Forge Press, Thousand Oaks, CA.

Simpson, S.S. & Elis, L. (1994). 'Is Gender Subordinate to Class? An Empirical Assessment of Colvin and Pauly's Structural Marxist Theory of Delinquency', *The Journal of Criminal Law and Criminology*, 85 (2): 453–80.

Sitren, A.H. & Applegate, B.K. (2007). 'Testing the Deterrent Effects of Personal and Vicarious Experience with Punishment and Punishment Avoidance', *Deviant Behavior*, 28 (1): 29–55.

Skelton, A. & Sekhonyane, M. (2007). 'Human Rights and Restorative Justice', in G. Johnstone & D. Van Ness (eds), *Handbook of Restorative Justice*, Willan Publishing, Cullompton: 580–97.

Smart, C. (1976). *Women, Crime and Criminology: A Feminist Critique*, Routledge & Kegan Paul, London.

Smart, C. (1990a). 'Law's Power, the Sexed Body and Feminist Discourse', *Journal of Law and Society*, 17 (2): 194–210.

Smart, C. (1990b). 'Feminist Approaches to Criminology: or Postmodern Woman Meets Atavistic Man', in L. Gelsthorpe & A. Morris (eds), *Feminist Perspectives in Criminology*, Open University Press, Buckingham: 70–84.

Smart, C. (1991). 'Feminist Jurisprudence' in P. Fitzpatrick, (ed.), *Dangerous Supplements: Resistance and Renewal in Jurisprudence*, Pluto Press, London: 133–58.

Smart, C. (1992). 'The Woman of Legal Discourse', *Social and Legal Studies*, 1 (1): 29–44.

Sorkin, M. (1992). 'Introduction: Variations on a Theme Park', in M. Sorkin (ed.), *Variations on a Theme Park: The New American City*, Hill Wang, New York: xi–xv.

Sparks, R.F. (1980). 'A Critique of Marxist Criminology', *Crime and Justice*, 2: 159–210.

Sparks, R.F. (1992). 'Reason and Unreason in "Left Realism": Some Problems in the Constitution of the Fear of Crime', in R. Matthews & J. Young (eds), *Issues in Realist Criminology*, SAGE, London.

Sparks, R. (1995). 'Legitimacy and Order in Prisons', *British Journal of Sociology*, 46 (1): 56–60.

Sparks, R.F., Genn, H. & Dodd, D. (1977). *Surveying Victims: A Study of the Measurement of Criminal Victimisation*, Wiley, Chichester.

Spencer, D. (2011). 'Cultural Criminology: An Invitation ... to What?', *Critical Criminology*, Online First (15 September).

Spitzer, S. (1975). 'Toward a Marxian Theory of Deviance', *Social Problems*, 22: 638–51.

Stafford, M.C. & Warr, M. (1993). 'A Reconceptualization of General and Specific Deterrence', *Journal of Research in Crime and Delinquency*, 30 (2): 123-35.

Steadman, H. (1973). 'Follow-up on Baxtrom Patients Returned to Hospitals for the Criminally Insane', *American Journal of Psychology*, 3: 317-19.

Steinart, H. (1985). 'The Amazing New Left Law and Order Campaign', *Contemporary Crises*, 9: 327-33.

Stenson, K. & Sullivan, R. (eds) (2001). *Crime, Risk and Justice: The Politics of Crime Control in Liberal Democracies*, Willan, Devon.

Strang, H. & Braithwaite, J. (eds) (2002). *Restorative Justice and Family Violence*, Cambridge University Press, Cambridge, UK.

Sullivan, C.J. & Hirschfield, P. (2011). 'Problem Behavior in the Middle School Years: An Assessment of the Social Development Model', *Journal of Research in Crime and Delinquency*, Online First (12 May).

Sullivan, D. & Tifft, L. (eds) (2008). *Handbook of Restorative Justice: A Global Perspective*, Routledge, Abingdon, UK.

Summers, A. (2002). *Damned Whores and God's Police: The Colonization of Women in Australia* (3rd edition), Penguin Books, Sydney.

Surette, R. (2010). *Media, Crime and Criminal Justice: Images,* Realities and Policies, Wadsworth CENGAGE Learning, Belmont California.

Sutherland, E. (1983). *White-Collar Crime: The Uncut Version*, Yale University Press, New Haven.

Sutherland, E. & Cressy, D. (1974). *Criminology*, Lippincott, New York.

Sutton, A., Cherney, A. & White, R. (2008). *Australian Crime Prevention: Principles, Perspectives and Practices*, Cambridge University Press, Melbourne.

Sutton, A. & Haines, F. (2011). 'Corporate and White Collar Crime', in M. Marmo, W. de Lint & D. Palmer (eds), *Criminology: An Australian Textbook* (4th edition), Thomson Reuters, Sydney.

Sykes, G. & Matza, D. (1957). 'Techniques of Neutralization: A Theory of Delinquency', *American Sociological Review*, 22: 664-70.

Tame, C. (1991). 'Freedom, Responsibility and Justice: The Criminology of the "New Right"', in K. Stenson & D. Cowell (eds), *The Politics of Crime Control*, SAGE, London.

Taniguchi, T.A., Ratcliffe, J.H. & and Taylor, R.B. (2011). 'Gang Set Space, Drug Markets, and Crime around Drug Corners in Camden', *Journal of Research in Crime and Delinquency*, 48: 327-63.

Tannenbaum, F. (1938). *Crime and the Community*, Columbia University Press, New York.

Tapia, M. (2011). 'Gang Membership and Race as Risk Factors for Juvenile Arrest', *Journal of Research in Crime and Delinquency*, 48: 364–95.

Taylor, I. (1981). *Law and Order: Arguments for Socialism*, Macmillan, London.

Taylor, I., Walton, P. & Young, J. (1973). *The New Criminology*, Routledge & Kegan Paul, London.

Taylor, I. Walton, P. & Young, J. (1975). *Critical Criminology*, Routledge & Kegan Paul, London.

Taylor, R. (2001). 'The Ecology of Crime, Fear, and Delinquency: Social Disorganization versus Social Efficacy', in R. Paternoster & R. Bachman (eds), *Explaining Criminals and Crime*, Roxbury, Los Angeles, CA: 124–39.

Thompson, A. (1992). 'Foreword: Critical Approaches to Law: Who Needs Legal Theory?', in I. Grigg-Spall & P. Ireland (eds), *The Critical Lawyers' Handbook*, Pluto, London.

Thompson, J. & Ricard, S. (2009). 'Women's Role in Serial Killing Teams: Reconstructing a Radical Feminist Perspective', *Critical Criminology*, 17: 261–75.

Tibbetts, S.G. & Gibson, C.L. (2002). 'Individual Propensity and Rational Decision Making: Recent Findings and Promising Approaches', in A.R. Piquero & S.G. Tibbetts (eds), *Rational Choice and Criminal Behavior: Recent Research and Future*

Challenges, Routledge, New York: 3–24.

Tibbetts, S.G. & Hemmens, C. (eds) (2010). *Criminological Theory: A Text/Reader*, SAGE, Thousand Oaks, CA.

Tiryakian, E.A. (2005). 'Durkheim, Solidarity and September 1', in J. Alexander & P. Smith (eds), *The Cambridge Companion to Durkheim*, Cambridge University Press, Cambridge: 305–21.

Tombs, S. (2006). '"Violence", Safety Crimes and Criminology', *British Journal of Criminology*, 47 (4): 531–50.

Tombs, S., (2008). 'Corporations and Health and Safety', in J. Minkes & L. Minkes (eds), *Corporate and White-Collar Crime*, SAGE, London: 18–38.

Tombs, S. & Whyte, D. (2002). 'Unmasking the Crimes of the Powerful', *Critical Criminology*, 11 (3): 217–36.

Tombs, S. & Whyte, D. (2006). 'Work and Risk', in S. Walklate & G. Mythen (eds), *Beyond the Risk Society: Critical Reflections on Risk and Human Security*, Open University Press, Buckingham: 169–93.

Tombs, S. & Whyte, D. (2008). *A Crisis of Enforcement: The Decriminalisation of Death and Injury at Work*, Centre for Crime and Justice Studies, London.

Tombs, S. & Whyte, D. (2009). 'The State and Corporate Crime', in R. Coleman, J. Sim, S. Tombs & D. Whyte (eds), *State Power Crime*, SAGE, London: 103-115.

Tomsen, S. (2002). *Hatred, Murder and Male Honour: Anti-Homosexual Homicides in New South Wales, 1980-2000*, Australian Institute of Criminology Research and Public Policy Series, No. 43, Canberra.

Tong, R. (1989). *Feminist Thought: A Comprehensive Introduction*, Unwin Hyman, London.

Trasler, G. (1993). 'Conscience, Opportunity, Rationality and Crime', in R.V.G. Clarke & M. Felson (eds), *Routine Activity and Rational Choice (Advances in Criminological Theory, Volume 5)*, Transaction Publishers, New Brunswick, NJ: 305-22.

Uggen, C. & Inderbitzin, M. (2010). 'Public Criminologies', *Criminology & Public Policy*, 9 (4): 725-49.

van Ness, D. (2003). 'Proposed Basic Principles on the Use of Restorative Justice: Recognising the Aims and Limits of Restorative Justice', in A. von Hirsch, J. Roberts, A.E. Bottoms, K. Roach & M. Schiff (eds), *Restorative Justice and Criminal Justice: Competing or Reconcilable Paradigms?*, Hart Publishing, Oxford, UK: 157-76.

von Hirsch, A. (1976). 'Giving Criminals Their Just Deserts', *Civil Liberties Review*, 3: 23-35.

von Hirsch, A. & Ashworth, A. (1992). 'Not Not Just Deserts: A Response to Braithwaite and Pettitt', *Oxford Journal of Legal Studies*, 12 (1): 83-98.

von Hirsch, A., Roberts, J., Bottoms, A.E., Roach, K. & Schiff, M. (eds) (2003). *Restorative Justice and Criminal Justice: Competing or Reconcilable Paradigms?*, Hart Publishing, Oxford, UK.

von Hofer, H. (2000). 'Crime Statistics as Constructs: The Case of Swedish Rape Statistics', *European Journal on Criminal Policy and Research*, 8: 77-89.

Walgrave, L. (2007). 'Integrating Criminal Justice and Restorative Justice', in G. Johnstone & D. Van Ness (eds), *Handbook of Restorative Justice*, Willan, Cullompton: 559-79.

Walklate, S. (1992). 'Researching Victims of Crime: Critical Victimology', in J. Lowman & B. MacLean (eds), *Realist Criminology: Crime Control and Policing in the 1990s*, University of Toronto Press, Toronto.

Walklate, S. (2003). '"I Can't Name Any Names but What's-His-Face up the Road Will Sort It Out": Communities and Conflict Resolution', in K. McEvoy & T. Newburn (eds), *Criminology, Conflict Resolution and Restorative Justice*, Palgrave Macmillan, Basingstoke, UK: 208-22.

Walklate, S. (2004). *Gender, Crime and Criminal Justice* (2nd edition), Willan, Cullompton.

Walklate, S. (2007). *Understanding Criminology: Current Theoretical*

Debates (3rd edition), Open
University Press, Maidenhead.

Walklate, S. (2008). 'Changing
Boundaries of the "Victim" in
Restorative Justice: So Who Is
the Victim Now?', in D. Sullivan
& L. Tifft (eds), *Handbook of
Restorative Justice: A Global
Perspective*, Routledge, Abingdon,
UK: 273–85.

Walklate, S. (2009). 'Victims and
the State', in R. Coleman, J.
Sim, S. Tombs & D, Whyte (eds),
State Power Crime, SAGE, London:
145–58.

Walters, M.A. (2010). 'A General
Theories of Hate Crime?
Strain, Doing Difference and Self-
Control', *Critical Criminology*,
Online First (6 December).

Walters, R. (2003). 'New Modes of
Governance and the Commodification
of Criminological Knowledge',
Social and Legal Studies, 12
(1): 5–26.

Walters, R. (2009). 'The State,
Knowledge Production and
Criminology', in R. Coleman,
J. Sim, S. Tombs & D. Whyte
(eds), *State Power Crime*, SAGE,
London: 200–13.

Weatherburn, D. (2002). 'Law and
Order Blues', *Australian and New
Zealand Journal of Criminology*,
35 (2): 127–44.

Weatherburn, D. & Lind, B. (2001).
Delinquent-Prone Communities,
Cambridge University Press,
Cambridge.

Webber, C. (2010). *Psychology and
Crime*, SAGE, London.

Weber, L. (2002). 'The Detention
of Asylum Seekers: 20 Reasons
Why Criminologists Should Care',
*Current Issues in Criminal
Justice*, 14 (1): 9–30.

Weber, M. (1949). *The Methodology
of the Social Sciences* (trans.
E.A. Shils & H.A. Finch), The
Free Press, New York.

White, R.D. (1994). 'Shame and
Reintegration Strategies:
Individuals, State Power and
Social Interests', in C. Alder
& J. Wundersitz (eds), *Family
Conferencing and Juvenile
Justice: The Way Forward or
Misplaced Optimism?*, Australian
Institute of Criminology,
Canberra.

White, R.D. (2002a). 'Environmental
Harm and the Political Economy
of Consumption', *Social Justice*,
29 (1–2): 82–102.

White, R. (2002b). 'Understanding
Youth Gangs', *Trends and Issues
in Criminal Justice*,
No. 237, Australian Institute
of Criminology, Canberra.

White, R.D. (2002c). 'Criminology
for Sale: Institutional Change
and Intellectual Field', *Current
Issues in Criminal Justice*,
13 (2): 127–42.

White, R. (2003). 'Environmental
Issues and the Criminological
Imagination', *Theoretical
Criminology*, 7 (4): 483–506.

White, R. (2005). 'Environmental
Harm in Global Context: Exploring
the Theoretical and Empirical
Complexities', *Current Issues in
Criminal Justice*, 16 (3): 271–85.

White, R. (2008a). 'Class Analysis and the Crime Problem', in T. Anthony & C. Cunneen (eds), *The Critical Criminology Companion*, Federation Press, Sydney.

White, R.D. (2008b). *Crimes against Nature: Environmental Criminology and Ecological Justice*, Willan, Cullompton.

White, R.D. (2009a). 'Environmental Victims and Resistance to State Crime through Transnational Activism', *Social Justice*, 36 (3): 46–60.

White, R.D. (2009b). 'Toxic Cities—Globalizing the Problem of Waste', *Social Justice*, 35 (3): 107–19.

White, R.D. (2011). *Transnational Environmental Crime: Toward an Eco-Global Criminology*, Routledge, London & New York.

White, R.D. (in press). *Provocations and Punch-Ups: Youth Gangs, Violence and Social Respect*, Institute of Criminology, University of Sydney, Sydney.

White, R. & Mason, R. (2006). 'Youth Gangs and Youth Violence: Charting the Key Dimensions', *Australian and New Zealand Journal of Criminology*, 39 (1): 54–70.

White, R. & Perrone, S. (2005). *Crime and Social Control* (2nd edition), Oxford University Press, Melbourne.

White, R. & Perrone, S. (2010). *Crime and Social Control* (3rd edition), Oxford University Press, Melbourne.

White, R. & van der Velden, J. (1995). 'Class and Criminality', *Social Justice*, 22 (1): 51–74.

White, R. & Wyn, J. (2008). *Youth and Society: Exploring the Social Dynamics of Youth Experience*, Oxford University Press, Melbourne.

Williams, C. (1996). 'An Environmental Victimology', *Social Justice*, 23 (4): 16–40.

Wilson, J.Q. (1975). *Thinking About Crime*, Vintage, New York.

Wilson, J.Q. & Herrnstein, R. (1985). *Crime and Human Nature*, Simon & Schuster, New York.

Wilson, J.Q. & Kelling, G.L. (1982). 'Broken Windows: The Police and Neighbourhood Safety', *Atlantic Monthly*, March: 29–38.

Wilson, W.J. (1996). *When Work Disappears*, Knopf, New York.

Winter, R. (2006). 'Researching Family Violence', *TILES Briefing Paper*, 2 (June).

Wood, J. (1997). *Royal Commission into the New South Wales Police Service* <www.pic.nsw.gov.au/Reports_List.asp?type=Royal> accessed 23 August 2007.

Woolf, N. (2002). *The Beauty Myth: How Images of Beauty Are Used against Women* (2nd edition), Harper, New York.

Woolford, A. (2009) *The Politics of Restorative Justice: A Critical Introduction*, Fernwood Publishing, Halifax & Winnipeg.

Wozniak, J.F. (2008). 'Poverty and Peacemaking Criminology: Beyond Mainstream Criminology', *Critical Criminology*, 16 (2): 209-23.

Wright, M. (1991). *Justice for Victims and Offenders*, Open University Press, Milton Keynes.

Young, A. (1996). *Imagining Crime: Textual Outlaws and Criminal Conversations*, SAGE, London.

Young, I.M. (1997). 'Unruly Categories: A Critique of Nancy Fraser's Dual Systems Theory', *New Left Review*, 222: 147-60.

Young, J. (1971). 'The Role of the Police as Amplifiers of Deviancy, Negotiators of Reality and Translators of Fantasy: Some Consequences of Our Present System of Drug Control as Seen in Notting Hill', in S. Cohen (ed.), *Images of Deviance*, Penguin, London.

Young, J. (1981). 'Thinking Seriously about Crime: Some Models of Criminology', in M. Fitzgerald, G. McLennon & J. Pawson (eds), *Crime and Society: Readings in History and Theory*, Routledge & Kegan Paul, London.

Young, J. (1986). 'The Failure of Criminology: The Need for a Radical Realism', in R. Matthews & J. Young (eds), *Confronting Crime*, SAGE, London: 9-30.

Young, J. (1988). 'Risk of Crime and Fear of Crime: A Realist Critique of Survey Based Assumptions', in M. Maguire & J. Pointing (eds), *Victims of Crime: A New Deal*, Open University Press, Milton Keynes.

Young, J. (1991). 'Left Realism and the Priorities of Crime Control', in K. Stenson & D. Cowell (eds), *The Politics of Crime Control*, SAGE, London.

Young, J. (1992). 'Realist Research as a Basis for Local Criminal Justice Policy', in J. Lowman & B. MacLean (eds), *Realist Criminology: Crime Control and Policing in the 1990s*, University of Toronto Press, Toronto.

Young, A. (1996). *Imagining Crime: Textual Outlaws and Criminal Conversations*, SAGE, London.

Young, J. (1999). *The Exclusive Society: Social Exclusion, Crime and Difference in Late Modernity*, SAGE, London.

Young, J. (2002). 'Critical Criminology in the 21st Century: Critique, Irony and the Always Unfinished', in R. Hogg & K. Carrington (eds), *Critical Criminology: Issues, Debates, Challenges*, Willan, Cullompton: 251-71.

Young, J. (2003). 'Merton with Energy, Katz with Structure: The Sociology of Vindictiveness and Criminology of Transgression', *Theoretical Criminology*, 7 (3): 389-414.

Young, J. (2007). *The Vertigo of Late Modernity*, SAGE, London.

Young, J. (2011). *The Criminological Imagination*, Polity Press, Cambridge, UK.

Zahn, M.A., Agnew, R. & Browne, A. (2009). 'Introduction' in M.A. Zahn (ed.), *The Delinquent Girl*, Temple University Press, Philadelphia, PA: 1-6.

Zahn, M.A. & Browne, A. (2009). 'Gender Differences in Neighborhood Effects and Delinquency' in M.A. Zahn (ed.), *The Delinquent Girl*, Temple University Press, Philadelphia, PA: 164-81.

Zehr, H. (1990). Changing Lenses: A New Focus for Crime and Justice, Herald Press, Scotsdale.

Zehr, H. & Mika, H. (1998). 'Fundamental Concepts of Restorative Justice', Contemporary Justice Review, 1 (1): 47-56.